TOURIST *and* MOTORING ATLAS

ATLAS ROUTIER *et* TOURISTIQUE

STRASSEN- *und* REISEATLAS

TOERISTISCHE WEGENATLAS

ATLANTE STRADALE *e* TURISTICO

ATLAS DE CARRETERAS *y* TURÍSTICO

Great Britain & Ireland

Contents

Inside front cover
Key to map pages

IV	**Route planning** - 1/1 000 000
XX	**Unitary Authorities**
XXI	**Shipping Services**
XXII	**Distances**

1	**Key to maps**
2	**Great Britain**- 1/300 000
76	**Ireland** - 1/300 000
104	**Greater London** -1/200 000

106	**Key: Welsh and Irish**
107	**Key to town plan symbols**
108	**Index Great Britain** **Index Ireland**

Inside back cover
Key

Sommaire

Intérieur de couverture
Tableau d'assemblage

IV	**Grands itinéraires** - 1/1 000 000
XX	**Unitary Authorities**
XXI	**Liaisons maritimes**
XXII	**Tableau de distances**

1	**Légende**
2	**Grande-Bretagne** - 1/300 000
76	**Irlande** - 1/300 000
104	**Greater London** - 1/200 000

106	**Légende : Gallois et gaélique**
107	**Légende des plans de ville**
108	**Index Grande-Bretagne** **Index Irlande**

Intérieur de couverture
Légende complète

Inhaltsübersicht

Umschlaginnenseite
Übersicht

IV	**Reiseplanung** - 1/1 000 000
XX	**Unitary Authorities**
XXI	**Schiffsverbindungen**
XXII	**Entfernungstabelle**

1	**Zeichenerklärung**
2	**Großbritannien** - 1/300 000
76	**Irland** - 1/300 000
104	**Greater London** - 1/200 000

106	**Zeichenerklärung: walisisch und irisch**
107	**Zeichenerklärung für Stadtpläne**
108	**Register Großbritannien** **Register Irland**

Umschlaginnenseite
Zeichenerklärung

Inhoud

Binnenzijde van het omslag
Overzichtskaart

IV	**Grote verbindingswegen** - 1/1 000 000
XX	**Unitary Authorities**
XXI	**Scheepvaartverbindingen**
XXII	**Afstandstabel**

1	**Verklaring van tekens**
2	**Groot-Brittannië** - 1/300 000
76	**Ierland** - 1/300 000
104	**Greater London** - 1/200 000

106	**Verklaring van de tekens: Welsh en Iers**
107	**Verklaring van de tekens: stadsplattegronden**
108	**Register Groot-Brittannië** **Register Ierland**

Binnenzijde van het omslag
Verklaring van alle tekens

Sommario

Copertina interna
Quadro d'insieme

IV **Grandi itinerari** - 1/1 000 000
XX **Unitary Authorities**
XXI **Collegamenti marittimi**
XXII **Tabella distanze**

1 **Legenda**
2 **Gran Bretagna** - 1/300 000
76 **Irlanda** - 1/300 000
104 **Greater London** - 1/200 000

106 **Legenda: Gallese e Gaelica**
107 **Legenda piante di città**
108 **Indice Gran Bretagna**
Indice Irlanda

Copertina interna
Legenda completa

Sumario

Portada interior
Mapa índice

IV **Información general** - 1/1 000 000
XX **Unitary Authorities**
XXI **Enlaces marítimos**
XXII **Cuadro de distancias**

1 **Signos convencionales**
2 **Gran Bretaña** - 1/300 000
76 **Irlanda** - 1/300 000
104 **Greater London** - 1/200 000

106 **Signos convencionales: Galés y Gaélico**
107 **Signos convencionales de los planos de ciudades**
108 **Índice Gran Bretaña**
Índice Irlanda

Contraportada interior
Signos convencionales

Town plans   Plans de villes   Stadtpläne   Stadsplattegronden   Piante di Città   Planos de ciudades

Great Britain

108 Aberdeen
109 Bath
109 Birmingham
110 Birmingham area
111 Blackpool
111 Bournemouth
111 Bradford
112 Brighton
112 Bristol
113 Cambridge
113 Canterbury
113 Cardiff/ Caerdydd
113 Carlisle
114 Chester
114 Coventry
115 Derby

115 Dover
116 Dundee
116 Durham
116 Edinburgh area
117 Edinburgh
117 Exeter
120 Glasgow area
121 Glasgow
121 Gloucester
122 Ipswich
122 Kingston upon Hull
122 Leeds
123 Leeds area
124 London

126 Leicester
126 Lincoln
126 Liverpool area
127 Liverpool
128 Manchester area
129 Manchester
130 Newcastle upon Tyne
130 Newport
130 Norwich
131 Nottingham
131 Oxford
132 Perth
133 Plymouth
133 Portsmouth
134 Reading

134 Sheffield
135 Southampton
136 Stirling
136 Stoke on Trent area
136 Stoke on Trent
137 Stratford upon Avon
137 Sunderland
137 Swansea/ Abertawe
138 Swindon
138 Warwick
138 Winchester
139 Windsor
139 Wolverhampton
139 York

Channel Tunnel
Tunnel sous la Manche

118 Folkestone Terminal
119 Terminal de Calais (F)

Ireland

141 Belfast area
142 Belfast
143 Cork/Corcaigh
144 Dublin area
145 Dublin/ Baile Átha Cliath
146 Galway/Gaillimh
146 Killarney/Cill Airne
147 Limerick/ Luimneach
147 Londonderry

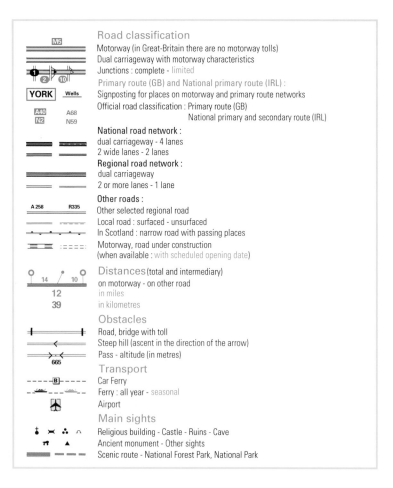

Road classification

Motorway (in Great-Britain there are no motorway tolls)
Dual carriageway with motorway characteristics
Junctions : complete - limited
Primary route (GB) and National primary route (IRL) :
Signposting for places on motorway and primary route networks
Official road classification : Primary route (GB)
National primary and secondary route (IRL)

National road network :
dual carriageway - 4 lanes
2 wide lanes - 2 lanes
Regional road network :
dual carriageway
2 or more lanes - 1 lane

Other roads :
Other selected regional road
Local road : surfaced - unsurfaced
In Scotland : narrow road with passing places
Motorway, road under construction
(when available : with scheduled opening date)

Distances (total and intermediary)
on motorway - on other road
in miles
in kilometres

Obstacles
Road, bridge with toll
Steep hill (ascent in the direction of the arrow)
Pass - altitude (in metres)

Transport
Car Ferry
Ferry : all year - seasonal
Airport

Main sights
Religious building - Castle - Ruins - Cave
Ancient monument - Other sights
Scenic route - National Forest Park, National Park

Importance des routes

Autoroute (en Grande-Bretagne, la circulation sur autoroute est gratuite)
Double chaussée de type autoroutier
Échangeurs : complet - partiels
Primary route (GB) et National primary route (IRL) :
Localités jalonnant un itinéraire autoroutier ou Primary
et figurant sur la signalisation
Numéros des routes : Primary route (GB)
National primary et secondary route (IRL)

Route de liaison nationale :
chaussées séparées - 4 voies
2 voies larges - 2 voies
Route de liaison interrégionale:
chaussées séparées
2 voies ou plus - 1voie

Autres routes :
Autre route de liaison interrégionale sélectionnée
Route locale revêtue - non revêtue
En Écosse : route très étroite avec emplacements pour croisement
(passing places)
Autoroute, route en construction
(le cas échéant : date de mise en service prévue)

Distances (totalisées et partielles)
sur autoroute - sur route
en miles
en kilomètres

Obstacles
Route, pont à péage
Forte déclivité (montée dans le sens de la flèche)
Col - altitude (en mètres)

Transport
Bac
Liaison maritime : permanente - saisonnière
Aéroport

Principales curiosités isolées
Édifice religieux - Château - Ruines - Grotte
Monument mégalithique - Autres curiosités
Itinéraire agréable - Parc forestier national, parc national

Verkehrsbedeutung der Straßen

Autobahn (Benutzung in Großbritannien kostenlos)
Schnellstraße mit getrennten Fahrbahnen
Anschlußstellen : Autobahnein- und/oder -ausfahrt
Primary route (GB) und National primary route (IRL) :
Orte, die sich an einer Autobahnstrecke oder Primary route befinden und als
Richtungshinweise angegeben sind
Straßennummern : Primary route (GB)
National primary und secondary route (IRL)

Nationale Hauptverbindungsstraße :
getrennte Fahrbahnen - 4 Fahrspuren
2 breite Fahrspuren - 2 Fahrspuren
Überregionale Verbindungsstraße :
getrennte Fahrbahnen
2 oder mehr Fahrspuren - 1 Fahrspur

Andere Straßen :
Andere überregionale Verbindungsstraße
Regionale Straße mit Belag - ohne Belag
In Schottland : sehr schmale Straße mit Ausweichstellen (passing places)
Autobahn, Straße im Bau
(ggf. voraussichtliches Datum der Verkehrsfreigabe)

Entfernungen (Gesamt- und Teilentfernung)
auf der Autobahn - auf anderen Straßen
in Meilen
in Kilometern

Verkehrsbehinderungen
Gebührenpflichtige Straße oder Brücke
Starkes Gefälle (Steigung in Pfeilrichtung)
Paß und Höhenangabe (in Metern)

Transport
Fähre
Schiffsverbindung : ganzjährig - während der Saison
Flughafen

Abgelegene, wichtige Sehenswürdigkeiten
Kirchliches Gebäude - Schloß, Burg - Ruine - Höhle
Steidenkmal - Sonstige Sehenswürdigkeiten
Reizvolle Strecke - Waldschutzgebiet, Nationalpark

Indeling der wegen

Autosnelweg (in Groot-Britannië zijn de autosnelwegen tolvrij)
Gescheiden rijbanen van het type autosnelweg
Verkeerswisselaars/knooppunten : volledig - gedeeltelijk
Primary route (GB) en National primary route (IRL) :
Plaatsen langs een autosnelweg of Primary route met bewegwijzering

Nummers van de wegen : Primary route (GB)
National primary en secondary route (IRL)

Nationale verbindingsweg :
gescheiden rijbanen - 4 rijstroken
2 brede rijstroken - 2 rijstroken
Interregionale verbindingsweg :
gescheiden rijbanen
2 of meer rijstroken - 1 rijstrook

Andere wegen :
Andere interregionale geselecteerde verbindingsweg
Lokale weg, verhard - onverhard
In Schotland : zeer smalle weg met uitwijkplaatsen (passing-places)
Autosnelweg, weg in aanleg
(indien van toepassing : vermoedelijke datum van openstelling)

Afstanden (totaal en gedeeltelijk)
op de autosnelweg - op de weg
in mijlen
in kilometers

Hindernissen
Weg of brug met tol
Steile helling (helling in de richting van de pijl)
Pas - hoogte (in meters)

Vervoer
Veerpont
Scheepvaartverbinding : permanent - alleen in het seizoen
Luchthaven

Belangrijkste afgelegen bezienswaardigheden
Kerkelijk gebouw - Kasteel - Ruïne - Grot
Megalitisch monument - Andere bezienswaardigheden
Aangenaam parcours - Natuurreservaat (bos), nationaal park

Grandi itineri   Información general

0   10   20   30   40 miles
0   10   20   30   40   50   60 km

Key to 1:1 000 000 map pages

Légende des cartes au 1:1 000 000

Zeichenerklärung der Karten 1:1 000 000

Verklaring van de tekens voor kaarten met schaal 1:1 000 000

Legenda carte scala 1:1 000 000

Signos convencionales de los mapas a escala 1:1.000.000

The primary Road network in England is currently under review. Certain roads may therefore change their status during the currency of this publication.

En Angleterre, le reseau de routes "Primary" est en cours de révision. Certaines routes peuvent changer de classement pendant la période de validité de cette publication.

Das englische Hauptstraßennetz wird z.Z. überarbeitet. Einige Straßen könnten während der Laufzeit dieser Karte umgestuft werden.

In Engeland wordt het net van de Primary Roads gewijzigd. De indeling van sommige wegen kan hierdoor worden gewijzigd.

In Inghilterra la rete stradale "Primary" è in fase di revisione. Alcune strada possone avere subito variazioni di classificazione durante il periodo di validità di questa guida.

En Inglaterra, se está revisando la red de carreteras "Primary". Algunas carreteras pueden cambiar de clasificación durante el periodo de validez de esta publicación.

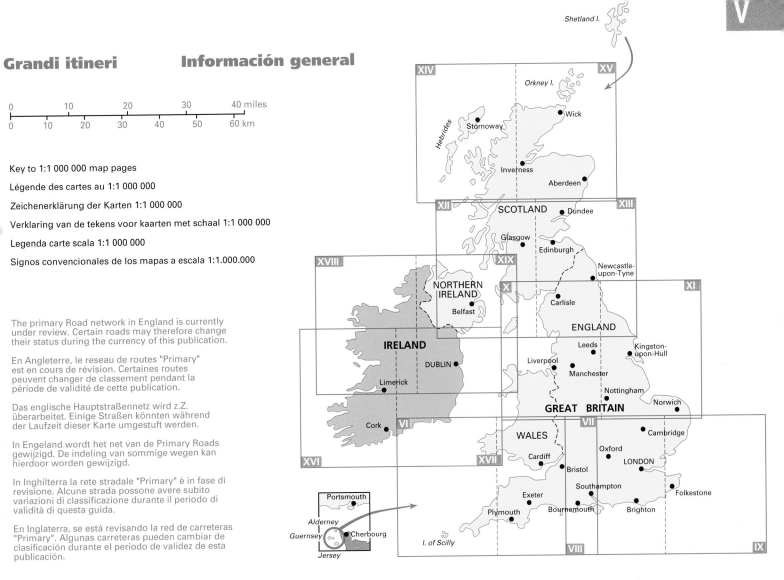

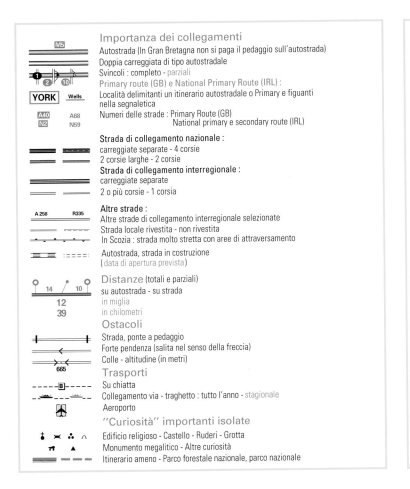

Importanza dei collegamenti

M5
Autostrada (In Gran Bretagna non si paga il pedaggio sull'autostrada)
Doppia carreggiata di tipo autostradale
Svincoli : completo - parziali
Primary route (GB) e National Primary Route (IRL) :
Località delimitanti un itinerario autostradale o Primary e figuranti nella segnaletica
Numeri delle strade : Primary Route (GB)
                      National primary e secondary route (IRL)

Strada di collegamento nazionale :
carreggiate separate - 4 corsie
2 corsie larghe - 2 corsie
Strada di collegamento interregionale :
carreggiate separate
2 o più corsie - 1 corsia

Altre strade :
Altre strade di collegamento interregionale selezionate
Strada locale rivestita - non rivestita
In Scozia : strada molto stretta con aree di attraversamento

Autostrada, strada in costruzione
(data di apertura prevista)

Distanze (totali e parziali)
su autostrada - su strada
in miglia
in chilometri

Ostacoli
Strada, ponte a pedaggio
Forte pendenza (salita nel senso della freccia)
Colle - altitudine (in metri)

Trasporti
Su chiatta
Collegamento via - traghetto : tutto l'anno - stagionale
Aeroporto

"Curiosità" importanti isolate
Edificio religioso - Castello - Ruderi - Grotta
Monumento megalitico - Altre curiosità
Itinerario ameno - Parco forestale nazionale, parco nazionale

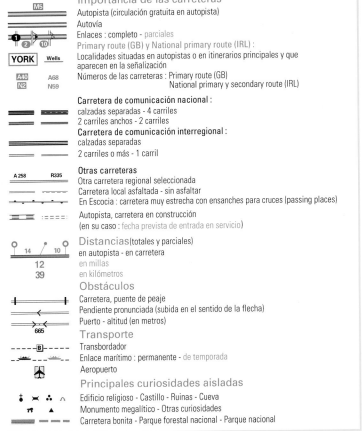

Importancia de las carreteras

M5
Autopista (circulación gratuita en autopista)
Autovía
Enlaces : completo - parciales
Primary route (GB) y National primary route (IRL) :
Localidades situadas en autopistas o en itinerarios principales y que aparecen en la señalización
Números de las carreteras : Primary route (GB)
                            National primary y secondary route (IRL)

Carretera de comunicación nacional :
calzadas separadas - 4 carriles
2 carriles anchos - 2 carriles
Carretera de comunicación interregional :
calzadas separadas
2 carriles o más - 1 carril

Otras carreteras
Otra carretera regional seleccionada
Carretera local asfaltada - sin asfaltar
En Escocia : carretera muy estrecha con ensanches para cruces (passing places)

Autopista, carretera en construcción
(en su caso : fecha prevista de entrada en servicio)

Distancias(totales y parciales)
en autopista - en carretera
en millas
en kilómetros

Obstáculos
Carretera, puente de peaje
Pendiente pronunciada (subida en el sentido de la flecha)
Puerto - altitud (en metros)

Transporte
Transbordador
Enlace marítimo : permanente - de temporada
Aeropuerto

Principales curiosidades aisladas
Edificio religioso - Castillo - Ruinas - Cueva
Monumento megalítico - Otras curiosidades
Carretera bonita - Parque forestal nacional - Parque nacional

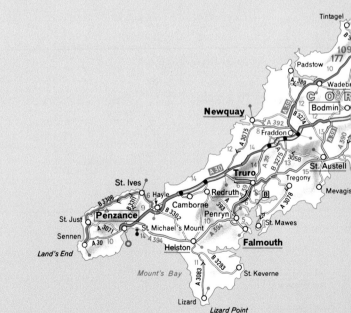

Schevening
DEN HAAG
('S-GRAVENHAGE)

Kingston upon Hull
Harwich
Hoek van Holland
Europoort
Maassl
Brielle
Vlaardin

Haringvlietdam
Goeree 42
Ouddorp
Hellevoetslu

Schouwen
Duiveland
Haamstede
Overflakkee

Zierikzee

N Beveland
Stavenisse
Tholen

Domburg
Walcheren
Veere
Goes
Berg
Zo

Walcheren
Middelburg
Z Beveland
Kruinin

Vlissingen
Hoedekenskerke

Breskens
Terneuzen

Knokke-Heist
Heist
Oostburg
IJzendijke
Sluis
Hulst

Zeebrugge
Dover
Blankenberge
De Haan
BRUGGE
(BRUGES)
Zelzate
Stekene
St-Niklaas

Oostende
Jabbeke
Oostkamp
Aalter
Eeklo
Evergem
Lokeren
Waasm

Middelkerke-Bad
Gistel
Aalter
GENT
(GAND)
Zele

Nieuwpoort
Torhout
Deinze
Wetteren
Aalst (Alost)

Koksijde-Bad
WEST
Tielt
Deinze
OOST
Aalst

De Panne
Roeselare
(Roulers)
Ingelmunster
VLAANDEREN

Bray-Dunes
VLAANDEREN
Izegem
Harelbeke
Waregem
Oudenaarde

Malo-les-Bains
Veurne
Diksmuide
Kortrijk
(Courtrai)

Dunkerque
Bergues
Ieper
(Ypres)
Menen
(Renaix)
Ronse
Geraardsbergen

Gravelines
Hondschoote
Poperinge
Wervik
Lessines
Enghien

Bourbourg
Steenvoorde
Comines
Tourcoing
Mouscron

Calais
Audruicq
Cassel
Bailleul
Roubaix
(Doornik)
Tournai

Cap Blanc Nez
Guines
Wormhout
Armentières
d'Ascq
Ath

Wissant
Ardres
Hazebrouck
LILLE
Cysoing
Leuze
Beloeil

Cap Gris Nez
Marquise
St Omer
Arques
Merville
Estaires
Hallennes
Seclin
Pont-à-Marcq

Wimereux
Lumbres
Aire
Béthune
Carvin
Orchies
St-Amand-les-Eaux
Mons
(Bergen)

Boulogne
Thérouanne
Bruay-la-Buissière
Noeux
Hénin-Beaumont
Bruay-s-l'E
Condé

le Portel
Desvres
Fauquembergues
Fruges
Lens
Liévin
Marchiennes
Quiévrain
Valenciennes
Maubeuge

Hardelot-Plage
Samer
Norrent-Fontes
la Bassée
Douai
Denain
le Quesnoy
Hautmont

Le Touquet-Paris-Plage
Étaples
Montreuil
Heuchin
Houdain
Aubigny
Arras
Aniche
Bouchain
Berlaimont
Aulnoye-Aymeries

Berck-Plage
Hesdin
St Pol-s
Beaumetz-lès-L.
Marquion
Cambrai
Caudry
Avesnes

Fort-Mahon-Plage
Campagne-les-H.
Crécy-en-P
Doullens
Pas-en-Artois
Bapaume
le Cateau
le Nouvion-en-T

le Crotoy
Rue
Auxi-le-Chau
Bernaville
Albert
Solesmes
Landrecies
la Capelle

Cayeux
St Valery
St Riquier
Acheux
Bray
Roisel
Wassigny

Ault
Mers
Abbeville
Ailly-le-H
Péronne
Bohain-en-V.
Hirson

le Tréport
Moyenneville
Domart-en-P.
Villers-Bocage
Corbie
SOMME
St Quentin
Guise

Criel
Blangy
Hallencourt
Airaines
Picquigny
Molliens-Dreuil
Oisemont
Flixecourt
Vermand

Lowestoft
Bungay
Beccles
Halesworth
Southwold
Scole
Dennington
Saxmundham
Yoxford
Leiston
Aldeburgh
Woodbridge

Felixstowe
Harwich
The Naze
Walton-on-the-Naze
Frinton-on-Sea
Clacton-on-Sea

Esbjerg
Göteborg
Hoek van Holland
Hamburg

Birchington
Margate
North Foreland
Herne Bay
Broadstairs
Ramsgate
Canterbury
Sandwich
Deal
South Foreland

Dover
Oostende
Folkestone

Tunnel
sous la Manche

Calais

PAS-DE-CALAIS

Kingston upon Hull

Kingston upon Hull
Dover

Göteborg
Amsterdam

th
Shields

ERLAND

Hartlepool

Redcar
Marske-by-the-Sea
A 1086 Saltburn-by-the-Sea
A 174 10 Brotton
Guisborough Lottus
19
dlesbrough A 174 Whitby
A 173
27 A 171
454 A 169 21 A 171
eveland Hills 21
North York Moors
National Park
25
B 1257 Scalby
Helmsley 13 Scarborough
17 A 170
Pickering 7
8 A 169 Filey
A 64 A 1039
ngwold 22 A 165
B 1257 Malton Norton 11
B 1363 Flamborough Head
65 B 1249 13 Bridlington
40 Wetwang A 614 A 165
A 166 28 Gt. Driffield
YORKSHIRE 17 Beeford
A 164 6
A 1079 Market A 614 Leven B 1244 Hornsea
14 Weighton A 1035 7
A 183 38 Beverley A 165
26 61 13
Barlby A 614 10 KINGSTON-
Howden M 62 A 164 UPON-HULL
naith 47 31 50 A 63 16 Hedon B 1242
36 Goole Humber Bridge River Withernsea
35.7 Humber A 1033
Barton-upon-Humber 11 A 1077 Patrington
Don 6 Thorne 11 N. LINCS Immingham Dock Kilnsea
5 Crowle A 160 Immingham
1 A 18 Scunthorpe N.E. Spurn Head
2 3 A 18 M 180 5 Great
Doncaster 4 A 18 Grimsby
45 A 15 418 Humberside Cleethorpes
72 Brigg A 1084
Epworth LINCS Rotterdam
Bawtry A 161 Caistor A 4613 Zeebrugge
A 614 12 A 16
A 631 A 1103 A 1031
A 638 A 620 9 A 631
Gainsborough A 631 Market Rasen Louth
East A 15 15 A 157 Mablethorpe
Retford A 1500 A 46 Wragby 50 A 157 A 1104 Sutton-on-Sea
TTS. A 57 31 31 A 1111
24 A 153 20 50 Alford A 52
eld 39 Lincoln Horncastle 15 A 1104
20 Woodhall Spa B 1183 Partney A 1028
32 A 1133 B 1188 B 1195 A 158 Skegness
Newark A 607 Spilsby
on-Trent A 15 B 1192 A 155 18
uthwell A 17 11 B 1183 39 A 52
13 A 46 Leadenham A 153 24
NGHAM 56 A 607 60 A 1121
Bingham 35 Sleaford 37
A 52 34 A 153 A 52 Boston
24 Grantham A 149 21 Sheringham
39 A 607 Hunstanton Wells-next-the-Sea Blakeney A 148 Cromer
rough 19 Sutterton B 1454 B 1335 Holt B 1159 Mundesley
A 151 Donington A 149 22 A 149 North Walsham
Melton Mowbray A 151 A 149 Fakenham B 1354 A 148 23 A 149
A 607 Bourne 45 Spalding Holbeach Sandringham B 1110 Guist A 1151 Low Street
RUTLAND A 16 28 House B 1146 Aylsham B 1150
Oakham A 15 Long Sutton 13 B 1145 A 140 A 149
EICESTER A 6003 Stamford Crowland A 1073 Wisbech A 1122 14 A 1065 East Dereham 42 A 1062
35 Uppingham Eye B 1166 Nene Swaffham 68 Bure Acle A 47 31 A 1064
56 A 6047 Guyhirn Outwell Stradsett B 1108 NORWICH Great
B 6047 Peterborough Downham Market Watton A 146 Yarmouth
Market Whittlesey March A 134 7 B 1108 Wymondham Gorleston-on-Sea
Corby GLAND

ANGUS

Brechin · A 935 · Montrose

Pitlochry · A 924 · Kirriemuir · A 926 · B 91113 · A 934

LAND · Alyth · A 926 · Glamis Castle · Glamis · A 928 · A 932 · Forfar · A 932

A 823 · Rattray · A 923 · Meigle · B 9128 · A 933 · Arbroath

Blairgowrie · Dunkeld · A 984 · Coupar Angus · Sidlaw Hills · 455 · Monifieth · Carnoustie

Perth · 31 · Dundee · Newport-on-Tay · Tayport · Buddon Ness

Auchterarder · Newburgh · A 913 · Leuchars

Auchtermuchty · Cupar · St. Andrews

FIFE · A 915 · Fife Ness

Falkland · A 912 · A 91 · Crail · Anstruther

Kinross · A 911 · Glenrothes · Leven · Methil · Pittenweem · Elie · St. Monans

Cowdenbeath · Lochgelly · Buckhaven

fermline · Kirkcaldy · Burntisland

Firth of Forth

Hopetoun House · Inverkeithing · North Berwick

Forth Bridge · S. Queensferry · Leith · Aberlady · Prestonpans

EDINBURGH · 6 · Musselburgh · Tranent · Haddington · East Linton · Dunbar

Livingston · Dalkeith · Cockburnspath · St. Abb's Head

31 · Loanhead · Lammermuir Hills · Eyemouth

Penicuik · Moorfoot Hills · SCOTTISH · Duns · Berwick-upon-Tweed

West Linton · Lauder · Greenlaw · Holy Island

Peebles · Galashiels · Earlston · Coldstream

Innerleithen · Melrose · Mellerstain · Kelso

Biggar · Newtown St. Boswells · Dryburgh

Broad Law · 840 · BORDERS · Selkirk · Belford · Bamburgh

Hawick · Jedburgh · The Cheviot 815 · Wooler

Moffat · 99 · 159 · Cheviot Hills · Northumberland · Alnwick

GALLOWAY · Carter Bar · National Park · Rothbury · Warkworth · Amble

Lockerbie · Langholm · NORTHUMBERLAND · Felton

B 7068 · The Border · Otterburn · Ashington · Newbiggin-by-the-Sea

Canonbie · Kielder Resr. · Forest · Morpeth

Longtown · Park · North Tyne · Belsay · Blyth · Bedlington

Annan · Brampton · Hadrian's Wall · Chollerford · Seaton Delaval

Bowness-on-Solway · Greenhead · NEWCASTLE-UPON-TYNE · Whitley Bay

Carlisle · Hexham · Corbridge · Prudhoe · Tynemouth · South Shields

Silloth · Abbey Town · Wigton · Thursby · Alston · Gateshead · SUNDERLAND

Aspatria · Stanley · Washington · Seaham

Bothel · CUMBRIA · Consett · Chester-le-Street · Houghton-le-Spring · Horden

Cockermouth · Lanchester · Durham · Peterlee

Keswick · Skiddaw 931 · Penrith · Wolsingham · Crook · Spennymoor · DURHAM · Hartlepool

Derwent water · Cross Fell 893 · Wear · Sedgefield

Buttermere · Ullswater · Middleton-in-Teesdale · W. Auckland · Newton Aycliffe · Billingham · Redcar

Lake District National Park · Appleby · Bishop Auckland · Stockton-on-Tees · Marske-by-the-Sea

Scafell Pikes 977 · Patterdale · Shap · Brough · Barnard Castle · Guisborough · Brotton · Loftus

Grasmere · Bowes · Darlington · Middlesbrough

Ambleside · Orton · Kirkby Stephen · Reeth · Scotch Corner · Whitby

Windermere · Tebay · Richmond · Cleveland Hills · North York Moors National Park

Coniston · Kendal · Sedbergh · Swale · Leyburn · Northallerton

Broughton-in-Furness · Whernside 736 · Hawes · Bedale · Thirsk · Scalby · Scarborough

Dalton · Sedbergh · Yorkshire Dales · Ure · Ripon · Filey

row-ness · Grange-Over-Sands · Carnforth · Ingleton · Clapham · Pateley · A 1039

Morecambe · Kirkby Lonsdale · PENNINES · NORTH YORKSHIRE · Pickering

NORTH SEA

Bergen · Stavanger · Hamburg · Göteborg · Amsterdam

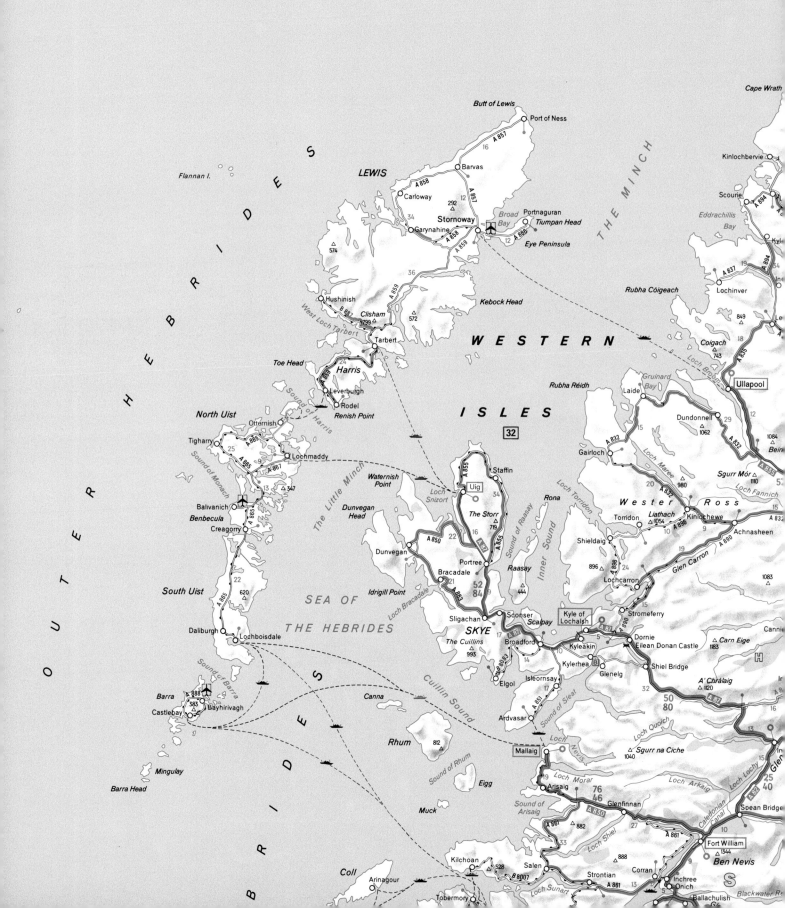

Cape Wrath

Butt of Lewis
Port of Ness
A 857
16

LEWIS
A 858
Barvas
Carloway
292
△
A 857
12
34
Stornoway
Garynahine
A 858
A 858
Broad
Bay
Portnaguran
Tiumpan Head
A 866
12
Eye Peninsula
574
△

Flannan I.

H E B R I D E S

36

Hushinish
B 887
West Loch Tarbert
A 859
Clisham
799
△
572
△
Kebock Head
Tarbert

Toe Head
24
Harris
Leverburgh
Rodel
Renish Point
Sound of Harris

W E S T E R N

Rubha Cóigeach

Kinlochbervie

Scourie
A 894
Eddrachillis
Bay
Kyl

A 837
19
Ine
Lochinver

849
△
Coigach
743
△

Ullapool
A 835
12

I S L E S
32

Rubha Réidh
Laide
Gruinard
Bay
Dundonnell
1062
△
15
1084
△
A 837
Bein

North Uist
Otternish
Tigharry
A 865
25
A 865
Lochmaddy
A 867
13
347
△
Sound of Monach
Balivanich
Benbecula
A 865
Creagorry

Waternish
Point
The Little Minch
Dunvegan
Head
Loch
Snizort
Uig
A 855
Staffin
34
Rona
The Storr
719
△
Sound of Raasay
A 850
22
A 87
A 855
16
Dunvegan
Portree
Bracadale
A 863
21
Raasay
52
84
Idrigill Point
Loch Bracadale
Sligachan
Sconser
Scalpay
SKYE
Broadford
B 8083
14
Kyleakin
10
Elgol
Isleornsay
17
Kylerhea
B
A 851
Ardvasar
Sound of Sleat

Gairloch

W e s t e r
20
A 832
980
△
1110
△
Sgurr Mór
Loch Maree
A 832
Loch Fannich

R o s s
A 832
Torridon
Liathach
1054
△
A 896
Kinlochewe
Achnasheen
A 890
10
Shieldaig
896
△
A 896
24
19
Glen Carron
Lochcarron
15
1083
△
Stromeferry
A 890
Kyle of
Lochalsh
A 87
5
Dornie
Eilean Donan Castle
Carn Eige
1183
△
Shiel Bridge
Glenelg
A 87
32
A' Chràlaig
1120
△

South Uist
A 865
620
△
22
Daliburgh
Lochboisdale
SEA OF
THE HEBRIDES
Cuillin Sound
The Cuillins
993
△

50
80
Loch Quoich
13
Sgurr na Ciche
1040
△

Barra
A 888
383
△
Castlebay
Bayhirivagh
Sound of Barra
Canna
Rhum
812
△
Sound of Rhum
Eigg

Mallaig
19
Loch Morar
Arisaig
76
46
Sound of
Arisaig
Glenfinnan
882
△
A 830
A 861
27

Mingulay

Barra Head

B R I D E S

Muck

Coll

Kilchoan
528
△
B 8007
Salen
A 861
Strontian
Loch Sunart
888
△
Corran
13

Loch Nevis
Loch
Arkaig
Loch Lochy
25
40
Glen
Spean Bridge
10
Caledonian Canal
Fort William
1344
△
Ben Nevis
Inchree
Onich
5
Ballachulish
Blackwater Re

Arinagour
Tobermory

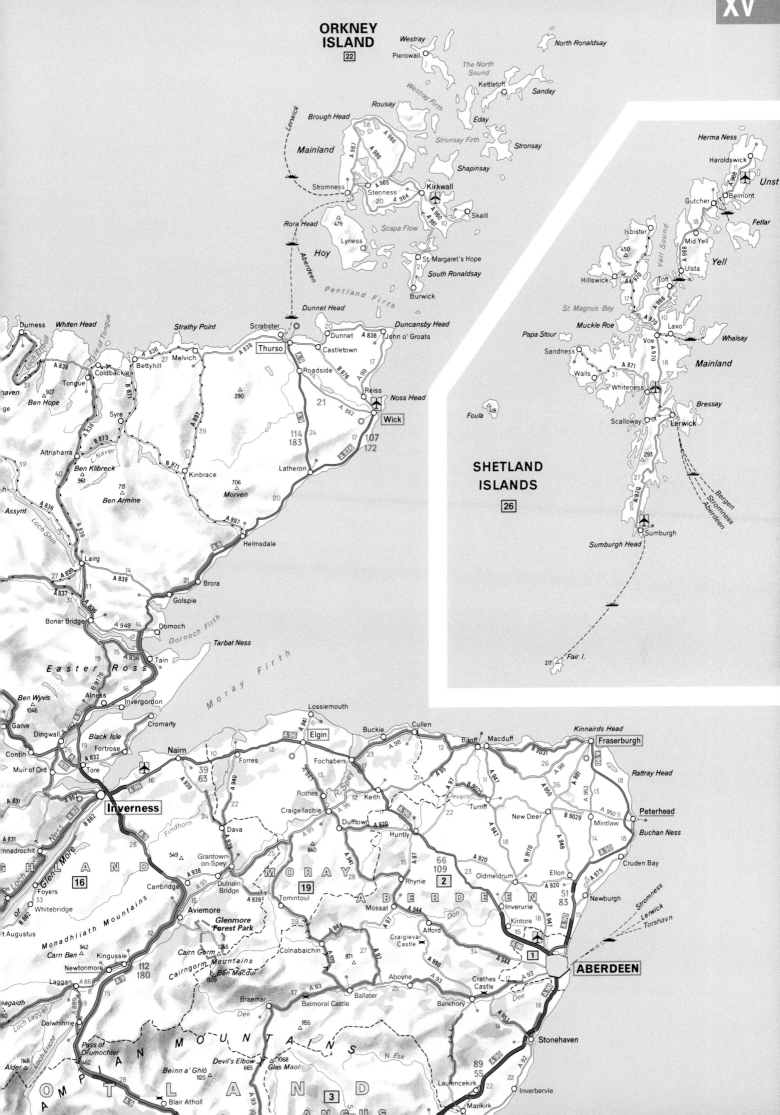

ORKNEY ISLAND
22

Westray
Pierowall
North Ronaldsay

The North Sound
Rousay
Eday
Sanday
Kettletoft
Brough Head
Westray Firth
Stronsay Firth
Stronsay
Lerwick
Mainland
A 967
A 966
38
15
Shapinsay
Rora Head
A 965
Stromness
A 964
Stenness
20
Kirkwall
Skaill
A 960
A 961
10
479
Scapa Flow
Hoy
Lyness
Aberdeen
21
St Margaret's Hope
South Ronaldsay
Burwick
Pentland Firth
Dunnet Head

Durness
Whiten Head
Strathy Point
Scrabster
Dunnet
A 836
Duncansby Head
John o' Groats
Thurso
Castletown
A 9
20
Bettyhill
Melvich
16
Roadside
B 876
A 99
17
A 836
A 836
27
Coldbackie
Reiss
Noss Head
Tongue
B 871
Syre
A 897
290
21
Wick
Ben Hope
927
31
39
A 9
114
183
24
Altnaharra
L. Naver
A 882
17
107
172
B 873
B 871
Ben Klibreck
961
Kinbrace
706
Latheron
A 838
Ben Armine
713
Morven
20
39
40
Assynt
A 897
Loch Shin
A 838
Helmsdale
A 836
Lairg
A 839
14
21
Brora
27 A 839
11
Golspie
A 837
31
Bonar Bridge
A 836
A 949
14
Dornoch
Dornoch Firth
Tarbat Ness
Tain
A 836
Easter Ross
B 9176
16
Ben Wyvis
1046
Alness
Invergordon
Moray Firth
19
15
A 836
Garve
Dingwall
Cromarty
Contin
Black Isle
Fortrose
A 832
Muir of Ord
Tore
A 831
26
A 862
A 9
16
Inverness
A 82
B 862
Findhorn
A 9
28
Foyers
16
Carrbridge
Whitebridge
B 862
Monadhliath Mountains
Carn Ban
942
Kingussie
112
180
Newtonmore
Laggan
A 86
8
15
Aviemore
Cairn Gorm
1245
Cairngorm Mountains
Ben Macdui
1309
Loch Laggan
Dalwhinnie
Pass of Drumochter
1148
Alder
462
28
Blair Atholl
A 9

Lossiemouth
Buckie
Cullen
Kinnairds Head
Fraserburgh
Elgin
A 96
A 98
Banff
Macduff
B 9031
Nairn
10
Forres
13
Fochabers
23
A 98
26
A 947
Rattray Head
A 939
39
63
A 940
Rothes
17
A 95
Deveron
A 97
B 9025
A 950
18
A 96
22
Keith
12
New Deer
B 9029
Peterhead
Craigellachie
A 95
Turriff
A 952
13
Dava
24
Dufftown
A 920
A 941
Mintlaw
A 950 9
Dulnain Bridge
840
Huntly
15
Buchan Ness
549
Grantown-on-Spey
A 938
25
66
109
23
A 947
B 9170
A 948
14
18
Tomintoul
19
Rhynie
A 97
Oldmeldrum
Ellon
A 975
Cruden Bay
A 939
MORAY
2
Mossat
A 944
Inverurie
51
83
A 920
Newburgh
Glenmore Forest Park
39
A 944
Alford
Don
Kintore
15
Colnabaichin
871
A 980
A 97
27
Craigievar Castle
A 944
1
A 90
ABERDEEN
A 93
Aboyne
34
Stromness
Lerwick
Torshavn
Braemar
17
A 93
Ballater
25
Crathes Castle
A 93
Banchory
A 957
Balmoral Castle
Dee
18
Dee
1155
Devil's Elbow
665
Glas Maol
1068
N. Esk
Stonehaven
89
55
A 90
A 92
22
Beinn a' Ghlò
1120
Laurencekirk
3
Marikirk
Inverbervie

SHETLAND ISLANDS
26

Herma Ness
Haroldswick
11
A 968
Unst
Gutcher
Belmont
Fetlar
18
Isbister
Mid Yell
450
A 968
Yell
Hillswick
A 970
Ulsta
St Magnus Bay
Toft
Whalsay
Muckle Roe
A 970
10
Laxo
Papa Stour
Voe
A 968
Sandness
A 971
Mainland
Walls
31
18
A 970
Whiteness
Bressay
Foula
418
Scalloway
Lerwick
293
27
Bergen
Stromness
Aberdeen
A 970
Sumburgh
Sumburgh Head
217
Fair I.

Inishturk
Inishbofin
Inishshark
Rinvyle Pt.

Louisburgh R 335 14 △ 763
Croagh Patrick
Murrisk
Mweelrea Mts. △ 817
19 41

Westport / Cathair na Mart
Ballintober
Ballyhaunis
Kiltamagh
Ballaghaderreen 57
Frenchpark 50 80 R 369 Elphin
ROSCOMMON
N 84 17 R 322
N 60 R 324 21 R 83 R 368 23 R 201

Killary Harbour
Letterfrack
The Twelve Pins △ 728 △ 701
Maumturk Mts.
Partry Mountains
Leenane
△ 681
Clonbur
Cong
Headford
Ballinrobe
Kilmaine
Ballymoe
Claremorris
Castlerea
Tulsk
Strokestown
R 293
Dunmore
Roscommon / Ros Comáin
Lanesborough
R 371

Clifden / An Clochán
Connemara
Maam Cross
Oughterard
Tuam / Tuaim
Glennamaddy
Mount Bellew
Ballyforan
Athlone / Baile Átha Luain
Lough Ree

Slyne Head
Roundstone
Gortmore
Carna
R 340
Lough Corrib
Spiddal
Barna
Galway / Gaillimh
Oranmore
Athenry
Craughwell
Ballinasloe / Béal Átha na Sluaighe
Clonmacnoise
Ferbane

Lettermullan
Gorumna Island
Galway Bay
Black Head
Loughrea
Clonfert
Banagher
Cloghan
Kilcormac

Aran Islands
Inishmore
Kilronan
Inishmaan
Inisheer
Ballyvaughan
Lisdoonvarna
Kilfenora
Ardrahan
Gort
Portumna
Birr
Kinnitty

Cliffs of Moher
Lahinch
Ennistimon
Milltown Malbay
Corrofin
CLARE
Tulla
Scarriff
Lough Derg
Borrisokane
Roscrea
Slieve

Spanish Point
Ennis / Inis
Nenagh / An tAonach
Moneygall
Templemore

Creegh
Knappogue
Broadford
Killaloe
Newport
Dolla
Kilkee
Kilmurry
Killaloe

Loop Head
Kilbaha
Kilrush
Killimer
Killadysert
Labasheeda
Shannon
Newmarket on Fergus
Bunratty
TIPPERARY
Milestone
Thurles / Durlas

Mouth of the Shannon
Ballybunnion
Tarbert
Askeaton
River Shannon
LIMERICK / LUIMNEACH
Holy Cross

Kerry Head
Ballyduff
Listowel
Adare
Croom
Rock of Cashel
Killenaule

Ballyheige
Newcastle West
Rathkeale
Hospital
Tipperary / Tiobraid Arann
Cashel / Caiseal
Fethard

Brandon Head
△ 951
Brandon Mountain
Tralee / Trá Lí
Tralee Bay
LIMERICK
Kilmallock
Galty Mountains
Slievenar
Caher
Clonmel / Cluain Meala
Comeragh Mts.

Sybil Head
△ 825 △ 850
Dromcolliher
Rath Luirc (Charleville)
Clogheen
Knockmealdown Mts.

Clogher Head
Dingle
Anascaul
Slieve Mish Mts.
Castleisland
Newmarket
Buttevant
Kildorrery
Mitchelstown
Lismore
Cappoquin

Great Blasket I.
Slea Head
Castlemaine
Killorglin
Boherbue
Kanturk
Mallow / Mala
Fermoy
Tallow
Dungarvan / Dún Garbhán

Dingle Bay
KERRY
Killarney / Cill Airne
Rathmore
Millstreet
Blarney
CORK / CORCAIGH

Doulus Head
Knight's Town
Valencia Island
Cahersiveen
Ring of Kerry
Carrantuohill △ 1038
Macgillycuddy's Reeks
Muckross House
L. Leane
L. Caragh
Glenbeigh
Derrynasaggart Mts.
Macroom
Coachford
Midleton
Youghal / Eochaill
Ardmore

St. Finan's Bay
Waterville
L. Currane
Mangerton Mountain △ 838
Kilgarvan
Ring of Kerry
Sneem
Kenmare
Blackwater

Bolus Head
Skellig
Lauragh
Beara
Caha Mts.
Glengarriff
Pass of Keimaneigh
Lee
Dunmanway
Bandon
Kinsale

Dursey Island
Castletownbere
Bere I.
Bantry / Beanntraí
Bantry Bay
Bandon
Clonakilty
Cobh / An Cóbh
Crosshaven
Ballycotton

Sheep's Head
Dunmanus Bay
Skull
Mizen Head
Roaringwater Bay
Skibbereen
Rosscarbery
Timoleague
Ringaskiddy
Old Head of Kinsale

Clear Island
Toe Head
Galley Head
Youghal Bay
Helvick

Swansea
Roscoff

Local government areas in England
have been subject to revision since April 1996.

En Angleterre, les limites administratives sont
en cours de modification depuis Avril 1996.

Seit April 1996 werden die englischen
Verwaltungsgrenzen neu geordnet.

Sinds april 1996 worden de administratieve grensen
in Engeland gewijzigd.

Dall'aprile 1996 in Inghilterra i confini amministrativi
sono in fase di cambiamento.

En Inglaterra, se están modificando los límites
administrativos desde Abril de 1996.

UNITARY AUTHORITIES

WALES

1. Anglesey/Sir Fôn
2. Blaenau Gwent
3. Bridgend/
   Pen-y-bont ar Ogwr
4. Caerphilly/Caerffili
5. Cardiff/Caerdydd
6. Carmarthenshire/
   Sir Gaerfyrddin
7. Ceredigion
8. Conwy
9. Denbighshire/Sir Ddinbych
10. Flintshire/Sir y Fflint
11. Gwynedd
12. Merthyr Tydfil/
    Merthyr Tudful
13. Monmouthshire/Sir Fynwy
14. Neath Port Talbot/
    Castell-nedd Phort Talbot
15. Newport/Casnewydd
16. Pembrokeshire/Sir Benfro
17. Powys
18. Rhondda Cynon Taff/
    Rhondda Cynon Taf
19. Swansea/Abertawe
20. Torfaen/Tor-faen
21. Vale of Glamorgan/
    Bro Morgannwg
22. Wrexham/Wrecsam

SCOTLAND

1. Aberdeen City
2. Aberdeenshire
3. Angus
4. Argyll and Bute
5. Clackmannanshire
6. City of Edinburgh
7. City of Glasgow
8. Dumfries and Galloway
9. Dundee City
10. East Ayrshire
11. East Dunbartonshire
12. East Lothian
13. East Renfrewshire
14. Falkirk
15. Fife
16. Highland
17. Inverclyde
18. Midlothian
19. Moray
20. North Ayrshire
21. North Lanarkshire
22. Orkney Islands
23. Perthshire and Kinross
24. Renfrewshire
25. Scottish Borders
26. Shetland Islands
27. South Ayrshire
28. South Lanarkshire
29. Stirling
30. West Dunbartonshire
31. West Lothian
32. Western Isles

SHIPPING SERVICES
Car ferries

All the year round

At least 6 sailings daily ⎯⎯⎯⎯

One or more sailings daily ⎯⎯⎯

One or more sailings weekly ⎯ ⎯ ⎯ ⎯

* Infrequent service ⋯⋯⋯⋯⋯

Hovercraft service ⏻

Seasonal

One or more sailings daily ⎯⎯⎯⎯

One or more sailings weekly ⎯ ⎯ ⎯ ⎯

* Infrequent service ⋯⋯⋯⋯⋯

The service is liable to interruption during the Christmas and New Year holidays or at other periods (eg Sundays or for maintenance) □
*Full details from companies

LIAISONS MARITIMES
Transport des autos

Permanentes

Au moins 6 liaisons par jour ⎯⎯⎯⎯

Une ou plusieurs liaisons par jour ⎯⎯⎯

Une ou plusieurs liaisons par semaine ⎯ ⎯ ⎯ ⎯

* Liaison à faible fréquence ⋯⋯⋯⋯⋯

Liaison assurée par aéroglisseur ⏻

Saisonnières

Une ou plusieurs liaisons par jour ⎯⎯⎯⎯

Une ou plusieurs liaisons par semaine ⎯ ⎯ ⎯ ⎯

* Liaison à faible fréquence ⋯⋯⋯⋯⋯

Interruption possible des services lors des fêtes de Noël et de fin d' année, ou à certaines autres périodes. □
*S'adresser aux compagnies

SCHIFFSVERBINDUNGEN
Autotransport

Ganzjährig

Mindestens 6 Fahrten täglich ⎯⎯⎯⎯

Eine oder mehrere Fahrten täglich ⎯⎯⎯

Eine oder mehrere Fahrten pro Woche ⎯ ⎯ ⎯ ⎯

*Nur wenige Fahrten ⋯⋯⋯⋯⋯

Mit Luftkissenboot ⏻

Während der Saison

Eine oder mehrere Fahrten täglich ⎯⎯⎯⎯

Eine oder mehrere Fahrten pro Woche ⎯ ⎯ ⎯ ⎯

* Nur wenige Fahrten ⋯⋯⋯⋯⋯

Um Weihnachten und Neujahr sowie gelegentlich während des Jahres kann der Fährbetrieb unterbrochen sein. □
*Auskunft erteilen die jeweiligen Gesellschaften

SCHEEPVAARTVERBINDINGEN
Vervoer van auto's

Permanente diensten

Minstens 6 diensten per dag ⎯⎯⎯⎯

Eén of meer diensten per dag ⎯⎯⎯

Eén of meer diensten per week ⎯ ⎯ ⎯ ⎯

* Slechts enkele diensten ⋯⋯⋯⋯⋯

Per hovercraft ⏻

Diensten in het zomerseizoen

Eén of meer diensten per dag ⎯⎯⎯⎯

Eén of meer diensten per week ⎯ ⎯ ⎯ ⎯

* Slechts enkele diensten ⋯⋯⋯⋯⋯

De diesten worden mogelijk onderbroken op de Kerstdagen, Nieuwjaarsdag, of gedurende bepaalde andere periodes. □
*Zich wenden tot de ondernemingen

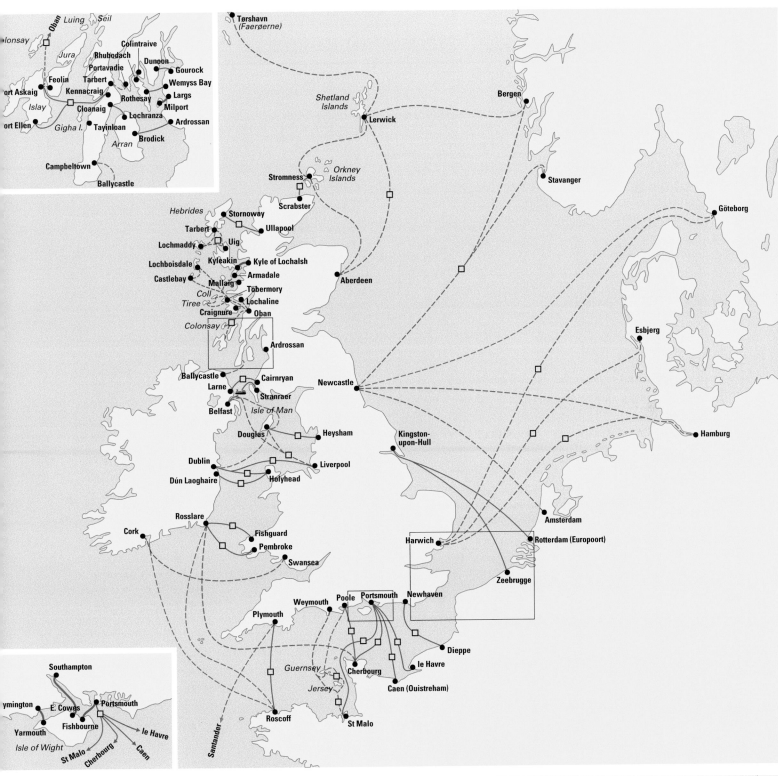
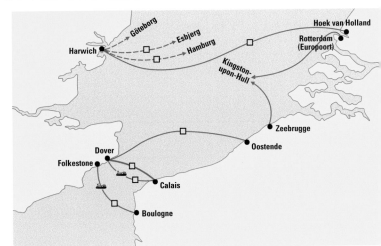

COLLEGAMENTI MARITTIMI
Trasporto di auto

ENLACES MARITIMOS
Transporte de vehiculos

Permanente — Permanentes

- Almeno 6 collegamenti quotidiani ——— Al menos 6 enlaces diarios
- Uno o più collegamenti quotidiani ——— Uno o más enlaces diarios
- Uno o più collegamenti settimanali - - - - Uno o más enlaces semanales
- * Collegamento poco frequente · · · · · · · Enlaces poco frecuentes *
- Collegamento assicurato da aliscafo 🚢 Enlace por overcraft

Stagionale — De temporada

- Uno più collegamenti quotidiani ——— Uno o varios enlaces diarios
- Uno più collegamenio settimanali - - - - Uno o varios enlaces semanales
- * Collegamento poco frequente · · · · · · · Enlaces poco frecuentes *
- □ *Possibile sospensione dei servizi in occasione delle feste natalizie, Capodanno o in particolari altri periodi* *Rivolgersi alle companie*
- □ *Posible interrupción de los servicios en Navidades y Fin de Año, o en otros periodos* *Dirigirse a las compañias*

Distances Entfernungen Afstandstabel Distanze Distancias

All distances are quoted in miles and kilometres.

miles in red

kilometres in blue

The distances quoted are not necessarily the shortest but have been based on the roads which afford the best driving conditions and are therefore the most practical.

Example:

Oxford – Killarney:

Oxford – Fishguard 214 m. or 344 km.
Rosslare – Killarney 163 m. or 261 km.
377 m. or 605 km.

Les distances sont indiquées en miles et en kilomètres

miles en rouge

kilomètres en bleu

Les distances sont comptées à partir du centre-ville et par la route la plus pratique, c'est-à-dire celle qui offre les meilleures conditions de roulage, mais qui n'est pas nécessairement la plus courte.

Exemple :

Oxford – Killarney:

Oxford – Fishguard 214 m. ou 344 km.
Rosslare – Killarney 163 m. ou 261 km.
377 m. ou 605 km.

Die Entfernungen sind in Meilen und in Kilometern angegeben.

in Rot: Meilen

in Blau: Kilometer

Die Entfernungen gelten ab Stadtmitte unter Berücksichtigung der günstigsten (nicht immer kürzesten) Strecke.

Beispiel:

Oxford – Killarney:

Oxford – Fishguard 214 m. oder 344 km.
Rosslare – Killarney 163 m. oder 261 km.
377 m. oder 605 km.

De afstanden zijn vermeld in mijl en in kilometer

mijl in het rood

kilometer in het blauw

De afstanden zijn berekend van centrum tot centrum langs de meest geschikte, maar niet noodzakelijkerwijze kortste route.

Voorbeeld:

Oxford – Killarney:

Oxford – Fishguard 214 m. of 344 km.
Rosslare – Killarney 163 m. of 261 km.
377 m. of 605 km.

Le distanze sono indicate in miglia e in chilometri.

miglia in rosso

chilometri in blu

Le distanze sono calcolate a partire dal centro delle città e seguendo la strada che, pur non essendo necessariamente la più breve, offre le migliori condizioni di viaggio.

Esempio:

Oxford – Killarney:

Oxford – Fishguard 214 m. o 344 km.
Rosslare – Killarney 163 m. o 261 km.
377 m. o 605 km.

Las distancias se indican en millas y en kilómetros.

millas en rojo

kilómetros en azul

El kilometraje está calculado desde el centro de la ciudad y por la carretera más práctica para el automovilista, que no tiene porqué ser la más corta.

Ejemplo:

Oxford – Killarney:

Oxford – Fishguard 214 m. o 344 km.
Rosslare – Killarney 163 m. o 261 km.
377 m. o 605 km.

Ireland

Kilometres

```
Belfast  422 120 167  86 314 467  36 366 116 109 311 200 227 330
  Cork       302 256 337 195  89 456  92 479 426 193 326 205 117
    Drogheda      48  35 223 348 154 246 188 135 191 204 109 210
263      Dublin        82 218 301 201 199 229 175 144 219 105 164
 75 188        Dundalk     247 382 120 281 163 110 226 171 134 245
104 159  30        Galway      215 342 104 275 250 265 144 132 228
 53 210  22  51       Killarney     501 112 476 412 261 346 227 189
195 121 139 136 154       Larne         400 122 120 345 225 261 364
291  55 216 187 238 134        Limerick      365 301 197 235 116 125
 23 284  96 125  75 213 312       Londonderry     54 373 132 258 387
228  57 153 124 175  65  70 249        Omagh           319 106 205 334
 72 298 117 142 102 171 296  76 227       Rosslare        323 164  76
 68 265  84 109  69 155 256  75 187  34       Sligo           160 295
193 120 119  90 140 165 163 215 123 232 199      Tullamore           136
124 203 127 137 106  90 215 140 146  82  66 201       Waterford
141 127  68  65  83  82 141 162  72 161 127 102  99
205  73 131 102 152 142 118 226  78 241 208  48 183  84
```

Miles

Great Britain

Kilometres

```
Aberdeen   693 964 827 751 858 368 946 108 197 949 852 238 872 741 581 176 302 523 574 879 565 440 368 776 789 635 287 804 1129 1016 938 909 378 831 361
  Birmingham   269 143 158 175 328 328 585 488 265 298 483 279 278 233 742 768 196 165 194 145 290 344  92 265  86 628 109 445 332 242 214 500 234 927
    Brighton       259 195 310 600 170 858 760 278 483 755 208 550 426 1014 1041 427 437  89 417 521 575 208 274 317 901 173 458 345  78  99 772 369 1200
431     Bristol        246  72 461 321 719 621 123 246 617 337 412 381 876 902 344 299 200 279 438 492 184 353 234 762 119 303 190 154 122 634 131 1061
600 167    Cambridge         296 426 198 643 551 370 470 581 107 428 235 812 866 247 315  91 268 330 384  87 108 144 726 133 550 437 212 214 598 356 997
514  89 161     Cardiff            493 372 751 653 182 180 648 388 365 412 908 934 376 274 251 310 469 524 235 403 265 794 170 362 249 245 216 665  65 1093
467  99 121 153    Carlisle             647 260 163 583 487 158 546 376 255 417 443 198 208 513 200 514  96 411 464 309 303 439 764 651 572 544 175 466 602
534 109 193  45 184    Dover              838 746 401 545 802 212 598 429 1006 1088 441 485 124 464 524 579 242 278 351 948 235 582 469 229 232 819 431 1192
229 204 374 287 265 307    Dundee                 89 841 744 124 764 633 473 211 284 415 466 771 458 333 260 669 681 527 190 696 1021 908 830 801 264 723 396
588 204 106 200 123 231 402    Edinburgh             743 647  73 672 536 381 258 331 323 368 639 360 241 540 589 435 199 599 924 811 732 704 213 626 443
 67 364 532 447 400 467 162 521    Exeter                 356 739 432 534 503 998 1024 466 421 295 401 560 614 316 474 356 884 251 180  73 213 179 755 241 1183
123 303 472 386 343 406 101 464  56    Fishguard           642 562 266 465 901 927 377 267 424 310 490 544 409 577 365 787 344 536 423 419 390 320 118 1086
590 165 175  76 230 113 363 250 523 462    Glasgow              702 531 410 281 289 353 363 668 355 309 247 566 619 465 149 594 919 806 727 699 139 621 466
530 186 301 153 292 112 303 339 463 402 221    Harwich              549 315 933 987 368 436 129 389 451 505 211 110 265 847 223 613 500 267 276 717 447 1118
148 300 469 383 361 403  98 499  77  46 459 399    Holyhead              354 790 817 266 156 464 200 379 433 362 490 289 676 389 714 601 523 494 186 298 975
542 174 130 210  67 242 340 132 475 418 269 349 436    Hull                 641 696  98 212 322 158 143 214 232 247 157 556 286 683 570 420 392 427 471 827
461 173 342 256 266 227 234 372 394 333 332 166 330 341    Inverness             129 584 623 928 614 501 489 825 850 696 186 853 1178 1065 987 958 421 880 188
361 145 265 237 146 256 159 267 294 237 313 289 255 196 220    Kyle of Lochalsh       639 649 954 641 575 502 852 904 750 203 879 1204 1091 1013 985 425 906 281
110 461 630 545 505 564 259 626 131 160 620 560 775 588 491 399    Leeds                  123 327  70 102 156 225 285 120 498 279 646 533 413 384 370 435 769
188 478 646 561 539 581 276 676 177 206 637 577 180 614 508 433  80    Liverpool             351  57 236 290 248 363 176 509 276 601 488 410 381 380 280 808
325 122 266 214 154 234 123 275 258 201 290 234 220 229 166  61 363 397    London                331 418 472 108 185 217 814  95 475 362 128 139 685 310 1113
357 103 271 186 196 170 130 301 290 229 262 246 271  97 132 387 404  77    Manchester             182 237 228 306 117 501 256 581 468 390 361 372 289 800
546 121  55 124  57 156 319  77 479 397 183 264 416  40 288 201 577 593 204 218    Middlesbrough          73 319 368 214 437 373 740 627 506 478 326 528 687
352  90 259 173 167 193 125 289 285 224 249 193 221 242 124  98 382 398  44  36 206    Newcastle             373 422 364 427 794 681 561 532 264 583 614
274 180 324 272 205 292  96 326 207 150 348 305 192 280 236  89 312 357  64 147 260 114    Northampton            194 115 712  72 496 383 205 177 583 294 1011
229 214 357 306 239 326  60 360 162 105 382 338 153 314 269 133 267 313  97 180 293 147  46    Norwich                195 764 240 654 541 316 318 636 462 1035
483  57 130 115  54 146 256 151 416 336 196 254 352 132 225 144 513 530 140 155  68 142 198 232    Nottingham             610 169 536 423 302 274 482 324 881
490 165 171 219  67 251 288 173 423 366 295 359 385  69 305 154 528 562 177 226 115 190 229 262 121    Oban                  739 1064 951 873 844 284 764 130
395  53 197 145  90 165 193 218 328 271 221 227 289 165 180  98 433 466  75 110  73 133 167  71 122    Oxford                431 318 137 109 612 229 1040
178 391 559 474 452 493 189 589 118 124 550 489  93 527 421 346 116 126 310 316 506 311 272 227 442 475 379    Penzance               127 394 359 936 421 1363
501  68 108  74  83 106 274 146 473 407 135 155 214 370 139 243 178 531 548 173 59 160 232 266  45 149 105 460    Plymouth              281 246 823 308 1173
702 277 285 188 342 225 475 362 635 574 112 333 571 381 444 271 732 749 407 374 295 361 460 494 308 407 333 662 268    Portsmouth            34 745 304 1173
632 207 215 118 272 155 405 291 565 504  46 263 501 311 374 354 662 679 329 332 304 295 390 423 238 336 253 591 198  79    Southampton           717 276 1145
584 151  49  96 132 152 357 142 517 453 166 326 261 614 631 257 256  80 243 315 349 128 197 188 543  85 245 175   Stranraer                 638 606
566 133  62  76 133 135 339 144 499 438 111 243 435 172 308 244 596 613 239 238  86 225 297 331 110 198 170 526  68 223 153  22    Swansea                      1065
235 311 479 394 472 419 142 509 164 133 470 199  86 447 116 266 262 264 230 237 426 231 203 164 363 395 299 177 380 582 511 463 445    Thurso
517 146 229  82 221  41 290 268 450 389 150  73 386 278 186 293 547 564 271 174 193 180 329 362 183 288 202 476 143 262 192 189 171 396
225 577 745 660 620 679 374 741 246 276 735 675 290 695 606 514 117 175 478 502 692 497 427 382 628 643 548 232 646 847 777 729 711 377 662
```

Miles

Key

A full key to symbols appears inside the front cover

Roads

Motorway - Service areas

CHIEVELEY

Junctions : complete, limited
Numbered junctions

Dual carriageway with motorway characteristics

Major road :
dual carriageway
4 lanes - 2 wide lanes
2 lanes - 2 narrow lanes
Regional road network :
dual carriageway - 2 wide lanes
2 lanes - 2 narrow lanes
Other roads : surfaced - unsurfaced

Motorway, road under construction
(with scheduled opening date)

14 10
24 39
Distances on motorway and road :
in miles - in kilometres

Transportation

Railway - Passenger station
Car ferries
(seasonal services : in red)
boat - hovercraft
ferry (maximum load : in metric tons)
Airport - Airfield

Towns

Towns having a plan in the
Michelin Guides
Red Hotel and Restaurant Guides
Green Tourist Guide

Légende

Voir la légende complète à l'intérieur de la couverture

Routes

Autoroute - Aires de service
(sur autoroute, la circulation est gratuite)

CHIEVELEY

Échangeurs : complet, partiels
Numéros d'échangeurs

Double chaussée de type autoroutier

Route de liaison principale :
à chaussées séparées
à 4 voies - à 2 voies larges
à 2 voies - à 2 voies étroites
Route de liaison régionale :
à chaussées séparées - à 2 voies larges
à 2 voies - à 2 voies étroites
Autre route : revêtue - non revêtue

Autoroute, route en construction
(le cas échéant : date de mise en service prévue)

14 10
24 39
Distances sur autoroute et route :
en miles - en kilomètres

Transports

Voie ferrée - Station voyageurs
Transport des autos
(liaisons saisonnières : signe rouge)
par bateau - par aéroglisseur
par bac (charge maximum en tonnes)
Aéroport - Aérodrome

Localités

Localités possédant un plan dans les
Guides Michelin
Rouges "Hôtels et Restaurants"
Verts "Touristiques"

Zeichenerklärung

Vollständige Zeichenerklärung siehe Umschlaginnenseite

Straßen

Autobahn-Tankstelle
(Autobahnbenutzung kostenlos)

CHIEVELEY

Anschlußstellen : Autobahnein - und/oder - ausfahrt
Nummern der Anschlußstellen

Schnellstraße mit getrennten Fahrbahnen

Hauptverbindungsstraßen :
mit getrennten Fahrbahnen
4 Fahrspuren - 2 breite Fahrspuren
2 Fahrspuren - 2 schmale Fahrspuren
Regionale Verbindungsstraßen :
mit getrennten Fahrbahnen - 2 breite Fahrspuren
2 Fahrspuren - 2 schmale Fahrspuren
Andere Straße : mit Belag - ohne Belag

Autobahn, Straße im Bau
(ggf. voraussichtliches Datum der Verkehrsfreigabe)

14 10
24 39
Entfernungsangaben
auf Autobahnen und Straßen :
in Meilen - in Kilometern

Transport

Bahnlinie - Bahnhof
Autotransport
(rotes Zeichen : saisonbedingte Verbindung)
mit dem Fährschiff - mit dem Luftkissenboot
mit der Fähre (Höchstbelastung in t)
Flughafen - Flugplatz

Ortschaften

Ort mit Stadtplan
im Michelin - Führern
Im Roten Michelin-Hotelführer
Im Grünen Michelin-Reiseführer

Verklaring van de tekens

Zie binnenkant kaft voor volledige verklaring van de tekens

Wegen

Autosnelweg - Service plaatsen
(geen tol op autosnelwegen)

CHIEVELEY

Verkeerswisselaars/Aansluitingen : volledig - gedeeltelijk
Nummers knooppunten

Gescheiden rijbanen van het type autosnelweg

Hoofdverbindingsweg :
met gescheiden rijbanen
met 4 rijstroken - met 2 brede rijstroken
met 2 rijstroken - met 2 smalle rijstroken
Secundaire verbindingswegen :
met gescheiden rijbanen - met 2 brede rijstroken
met 2 rijstroken - met 2 smalle rijstroken
Andere weg : verhard - onverhard

Autosnelweg, weg in aanleg
(indien van toepassing : vermoedelijke datum
van openstelling)

14 10
24 39
Afstanden op autosnelweg en wegen :
in mijlen - in kilometers

Vervoer

Spoorweg - Station
Vervoer van auto's
(dienst in het seizoen : rood teken)
per boot - per hovercraft
per veerpont (maximum draagvermogen in t.)
Luchthaven - Vliegveld

Plaatsen

Plaatsen met een plattegrond in de
Michelingidsen :
de Rode met Hotels en Restaurants
de Groene met toeristishe bezienswaardigheden

Legenda

Vedere la legenda completa all'interno della copertina

Strade

Autostrada - Area di servizio
(non si paga il pedaggio sull'autostrada)

CHIEVELEY

Svincoli : completo, parziali
Svincoli numerati

Doppia carreggiata di tipo autostradale

Strada principale :
a carreggiate separate
a 4 corsie - a 2 corsie larghe
a 2 corsie - a 2 corsie strette
Strada regionale :
a carreggiate separate
a 2 corsie o più - a 2 corsie strette
Altra strada : con rivestimento - senza rivestimento

Autostrada, strada in costruzione
(data di apertura prevista)

14 10
24 39
Distanze su autostrada e strada :
in miglia - in chilometri

Trasporti

Ferrovia - Stazione viaggiatori
Trasporto auto
(collegamenti stagionali : segno rosso)
per nave - per aliscafo
per chiatta (carico massimo in tonnellate)
Aeroporto - Aerodromo

Località

Località con pianta nelle
Guide Michelin
Rosse "Hotels e Ristoranti"
Verdi "Turistiche"

Signos convencionales

Para más información ver en el interior de la contraportada

Carreteras

Autopista - Áreas de servicio
(circulación gratuita en autopista)

CHIEVELEY

Accesos : completo - parciales
Números de los accesos

Autovía

Carretera general :
con calzadas separadas
con 4 carriles - con 2 carriles anchos
con 2 carriles - con 2 carriles estrechos
Carretera regional :
con calzadas separadas - con 2 carriles anchos
con 2 carriles - con 2 carriles estrechos
Otra carretera : asfaltada - sin asfaltar

Autopista, carretera en construcción
(en su caso : fecha prevista de entrada en servicio)

14 10
24 39
Distancias en autopista y en carretera :
en millas - en kilómetros

Transportes

Línea férrea - Estación de viajeros
Transporte de coches
(enlaces de temporada : signo rojo)
por barco - por overcraft
por barcaza (carga máxima en toneladas)
Aeropuerto - Aeródromo

Localidades

Localidad con plano en la Guía Michelin
Rojas "Hoteles y Restaurantes"
Verdes "Turistica"

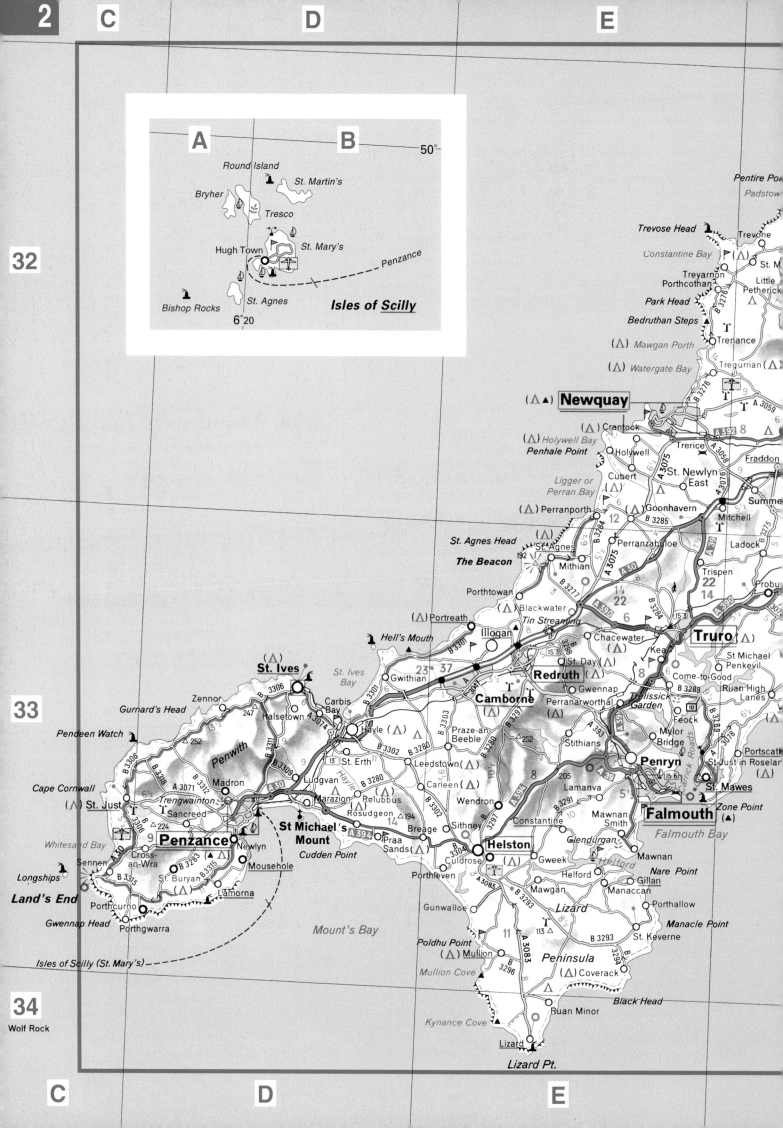

C D E

32

33

34

Isles of Scilly

A B 50°

Round Island

St. Martin's

Bryher

Tresco

Hugh Town

St. Mary's

Penzance

Bishop Rocks St. Agnes

6°20

Pentire Po

Padstow

Trevose Head Trevone

Constantine Bay St. M

Treyarnon Little
Porthcothan Petherick

Park Head B 3276 Trenance

Bedruthan Steps

(Λ) Mawgan Porth

(Λ) Watergate Bay

Tregurrian (Λ)

A 3059

(Λ ▲) **Newquay** B 3276 A 3059

(Λ) Crantock A 392 8

(Λ) Holywell Bay Trerice A 3058

Penhale Point Holywell Fraddon

A 3075 St. Newlyn

Cubert East Summe

Ligger or (Λ)

Perran Bay

(Λ) Perranporth Goonhavern Mitchell

B 3285

12 B 3284 A 39 Ladock

St. Agnes Head (Λ) Perranzabuloe Trispen

St. Agnes A 3075 22

The Beacon 192 Mithian 14 A 390 Probu

Porthtowan 3 B 3217 A 390 Truro

(Λ) Blackwater A 30 22

(Λ) Portreath B 3301 Tin Streaming 6 B 3284 15 3 A 390

Hell's Mouth Illogan B 3298 Chacewater **Truro** (Λ)

B 3301 St. Day (Λ) Kea

15 3 B 3298 St Michael

St. Ives St. Ives 23 37 A 30 **Redruth** Come-to-Good Penkevil

St. Ives Bay Gwithian (Λ) (Λ) B 3289 Ruan High

Zennor B 3306 Carbis B 3301 Gwennap Lanes

Gurnard's Head 247 Bay 1 **Camborne** Perranarworthal Trelissick Feock

Halsetown A 3074 Hayle (Λ) (Λ) Garden

Pendeen Watch Penwith 252 B 3303 A 39 Stithians Mylor

9 B 3311 13 St. Erth Praze-an- B 3280 Bridge Portscat

Madron B 3309 Beeble 252 A 393 St Just in Roselar

Cape Cornwall A 3071 Ludgvan Leedstown (Λ) B 3291 Lamanva (Λ)

(Λ) St. Just Trengwainton A 30 Marazion Carleen (Λ) 8 A 39 **Penryn**

Sancreed Relubbus Wendron A 394 St. Mawes

Penzance Rosudgeon 194 A 394 Constantine Mawnan Zone Point

9 Newlyn 14 Breage B 3291 Smith **Falmouth** (▲)

Cross- **St Michael's** B 3302 Sithney **Helston** Glendurgan Falmouth Bay

an-Wra **Mount** Praa A 394 (Λ) Mawnan

Whitesand Bay B 3293 Sands (Λ) Culdrose Gweek Helford

Mousehole Cudden Point Porthleven Gillan Nare Point

Longships Lamorna A 3083 Mawgan Manaccan

Land's End St. Buryan B 3296 Helford Porthallow

Porthcurno (Λ) Gunwalloe Lizard Manacle Point

Gwennap Head Porthgwarra Mount's Bay 11 113 B 3293 St. Keverne

Poldhu Point A 3083

Isles of Scilly (St. Mary's) (Λ) Mullion Peninsula (Λ) Coverack

Mullion Cove

Black Head

Wolf Rock Kynance Cove Ruan Minor

Lizard

Lizard Pt.

C D E

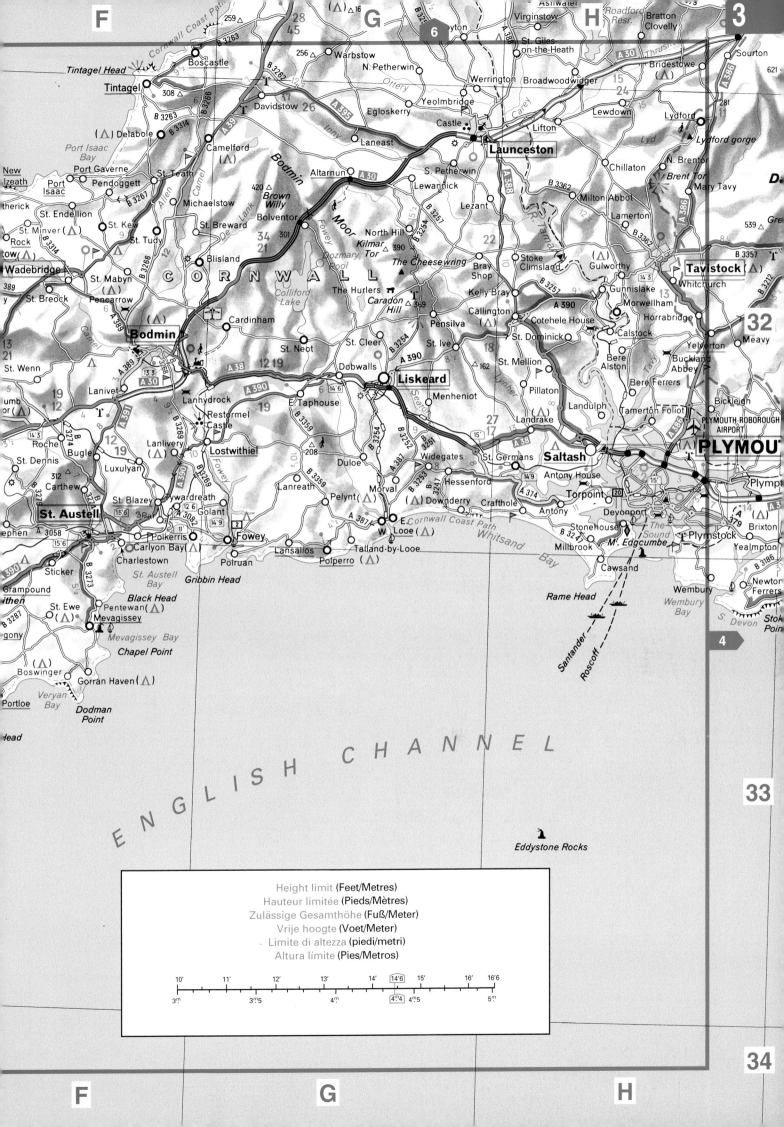

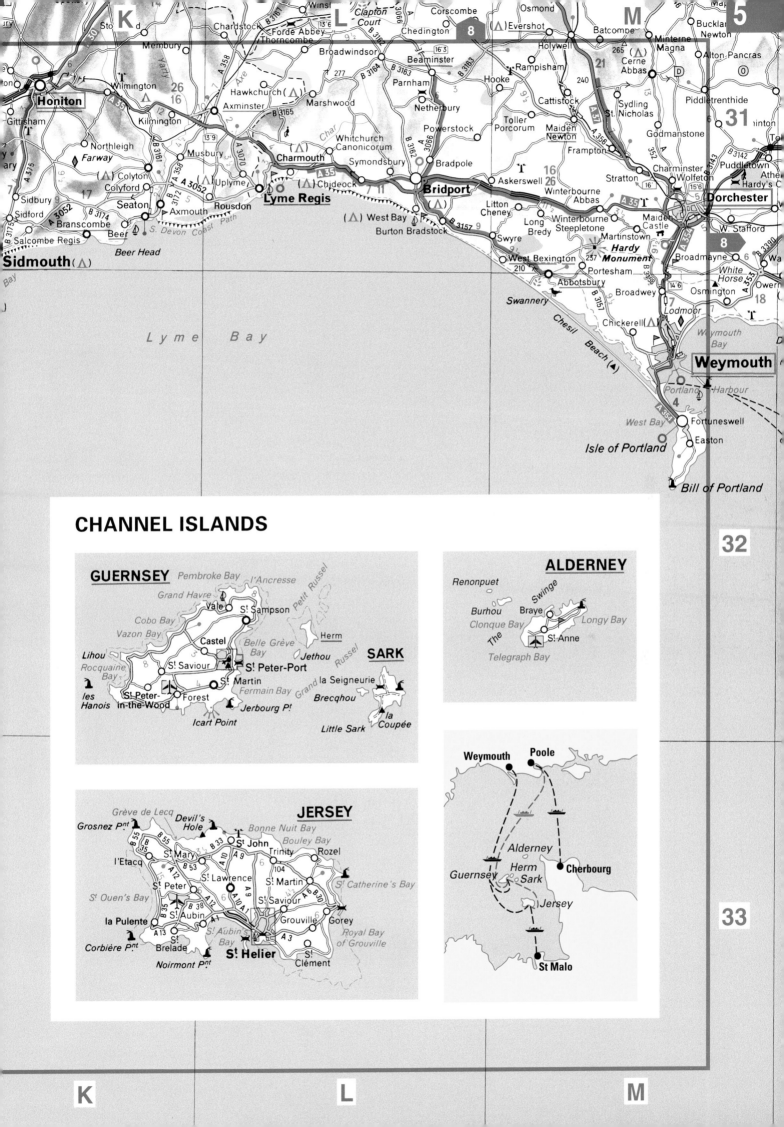

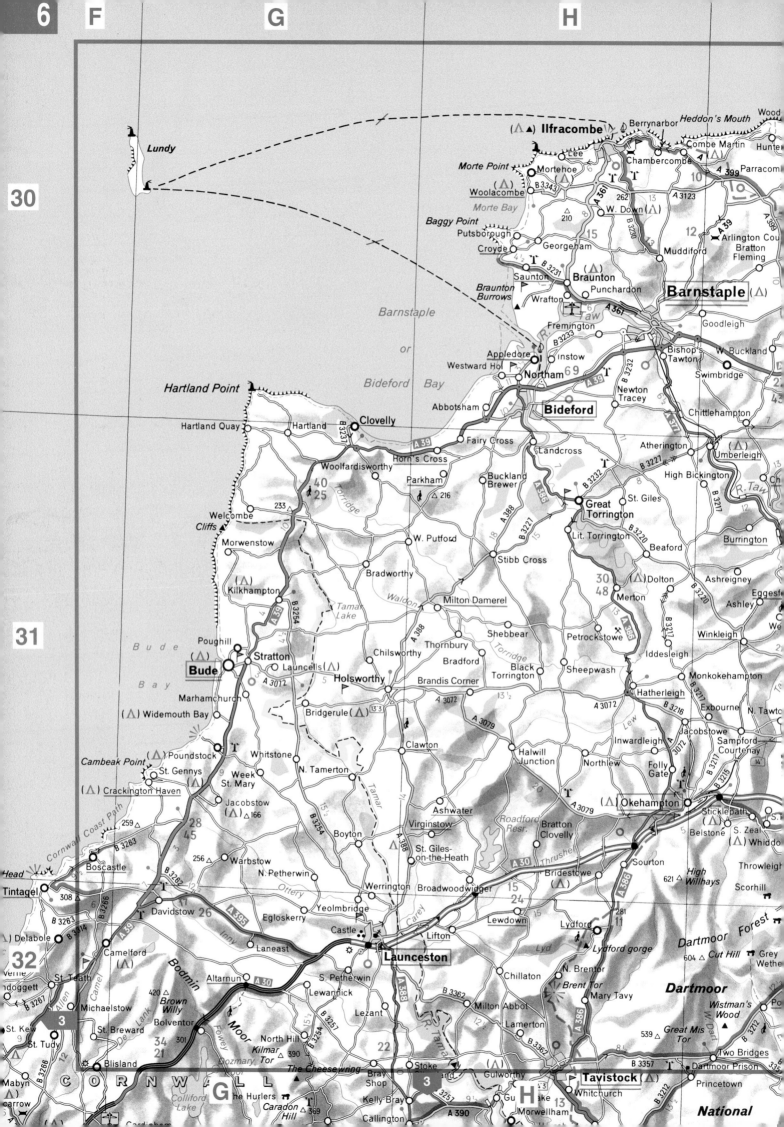

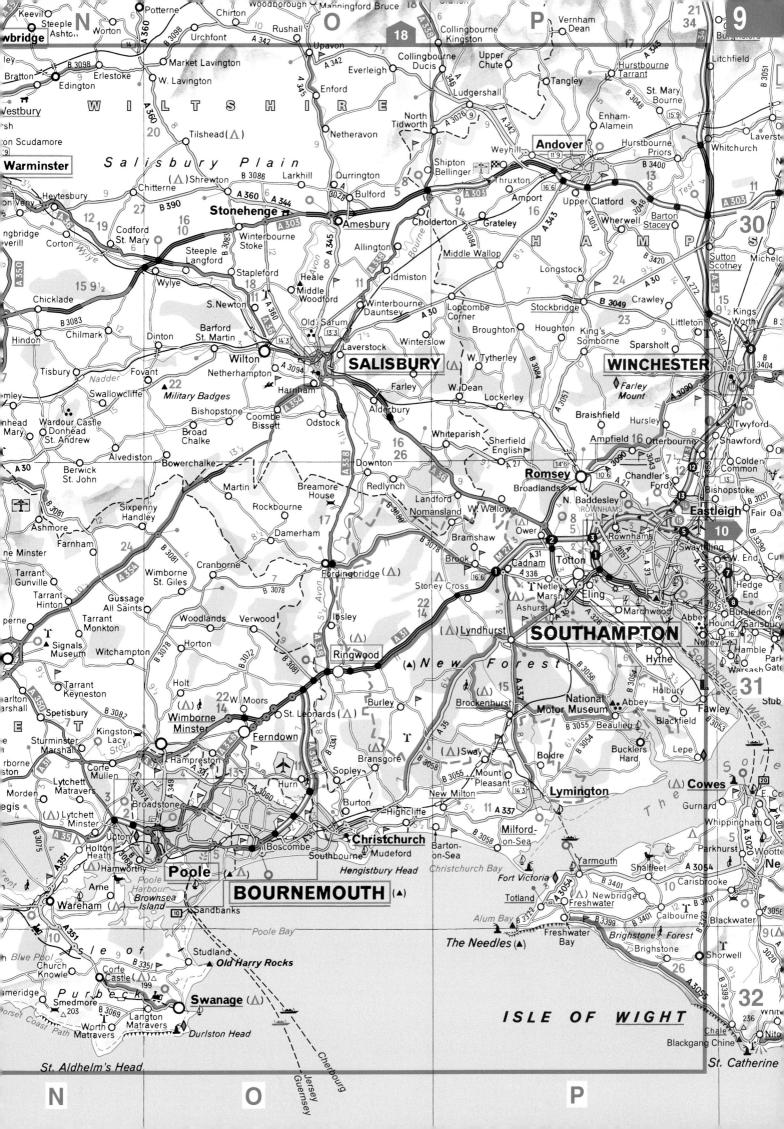

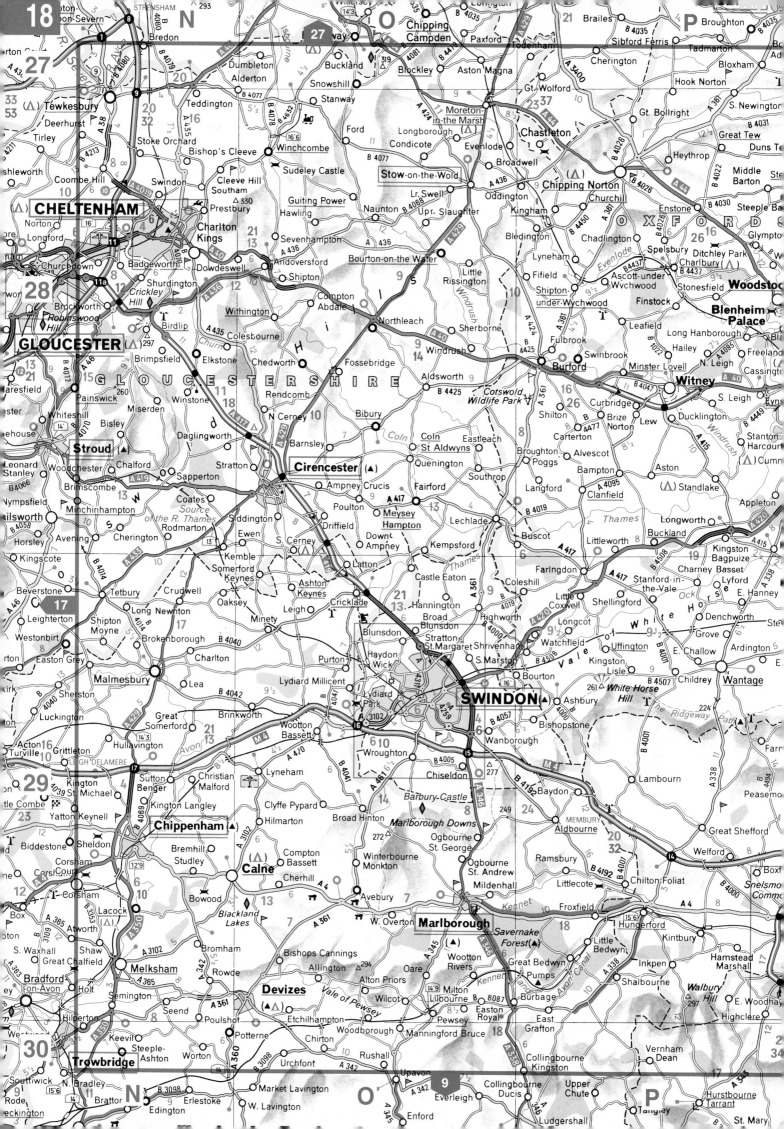

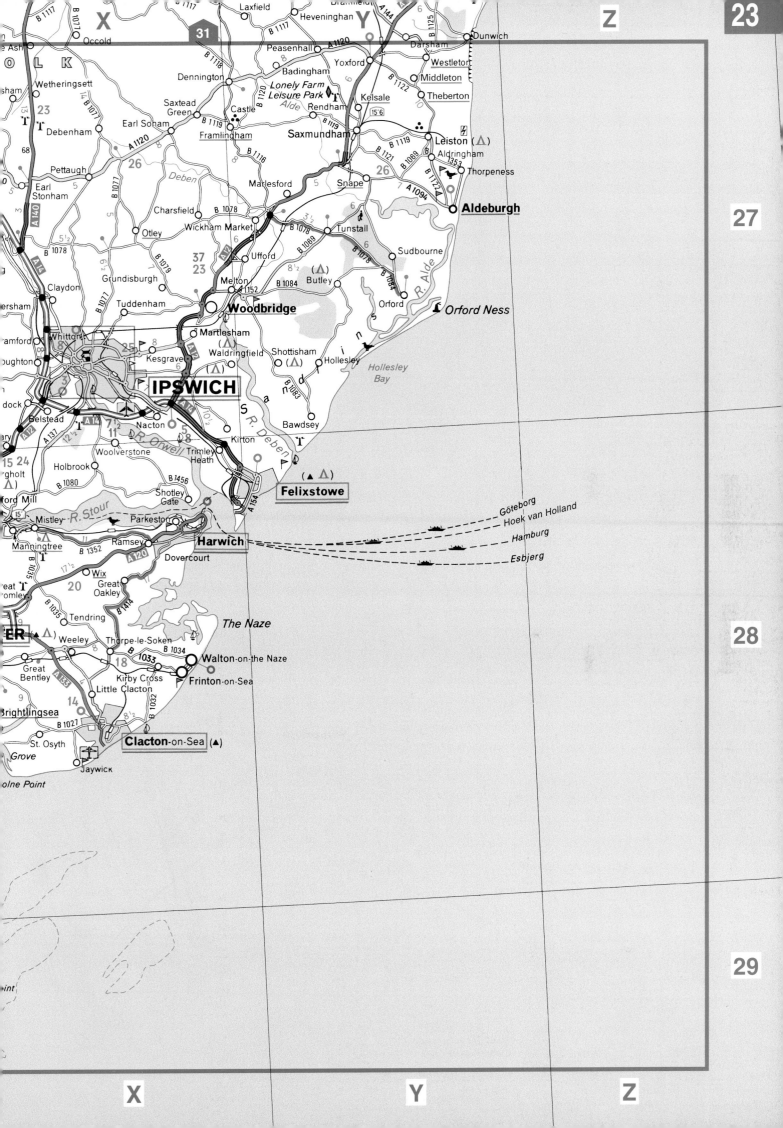

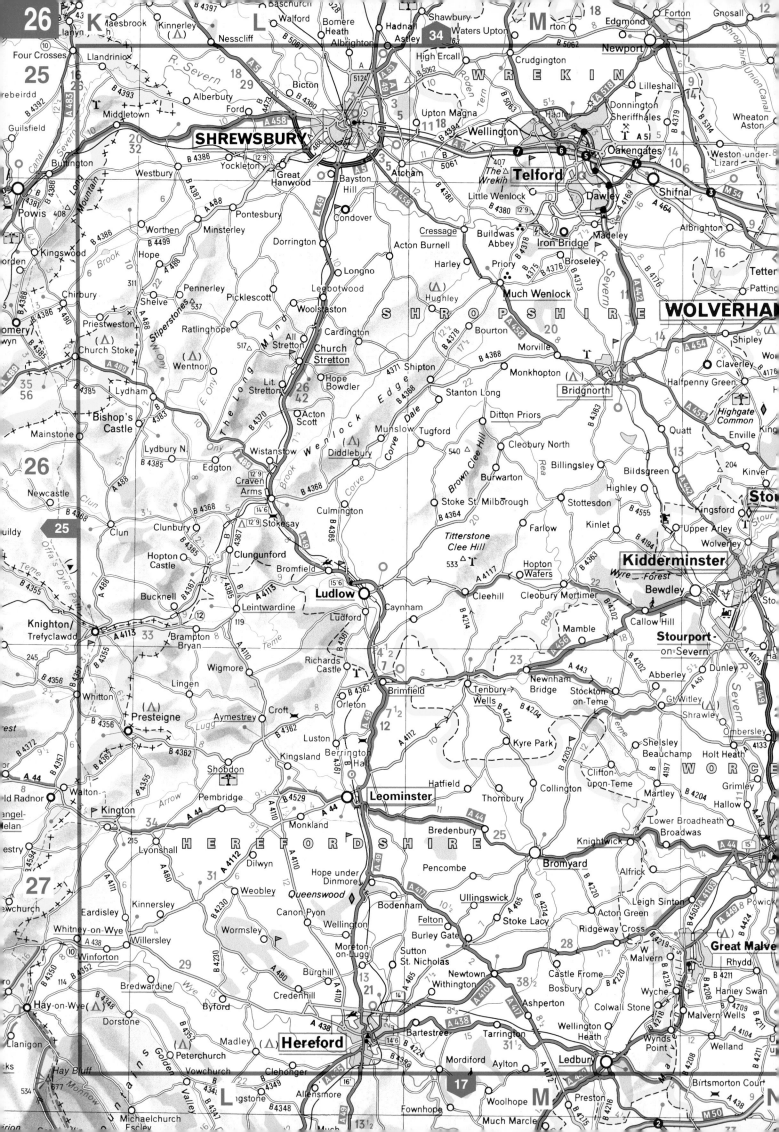

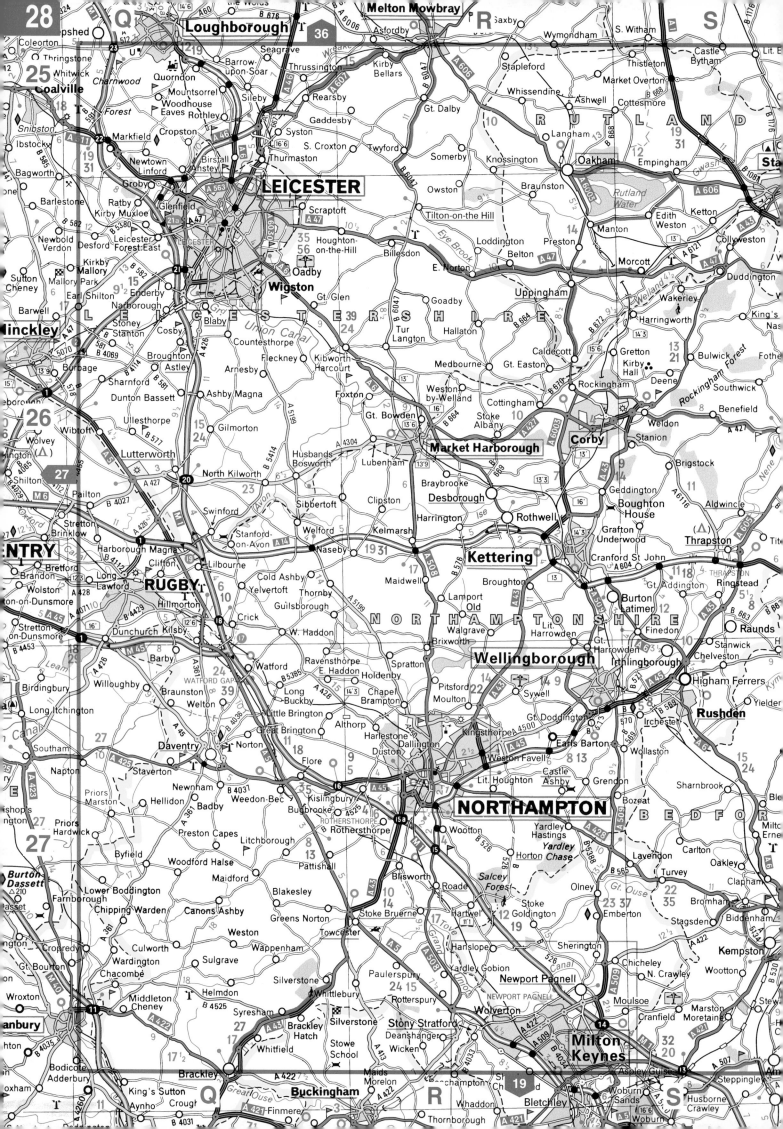

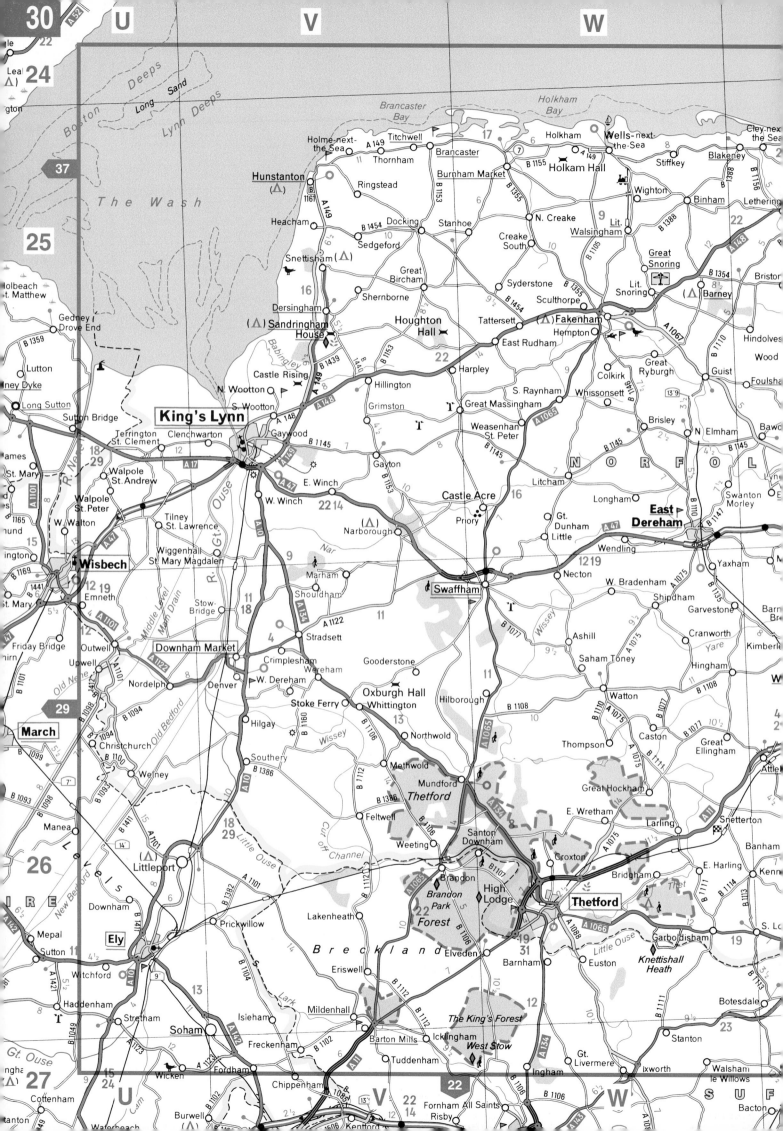

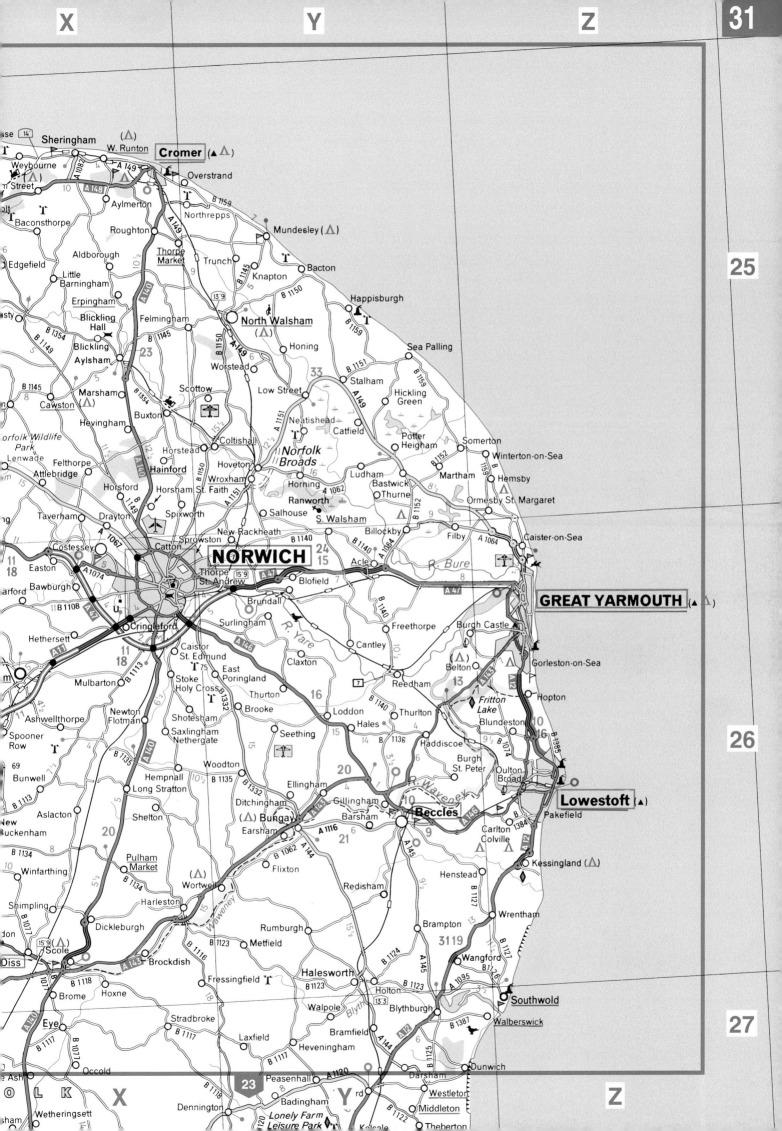

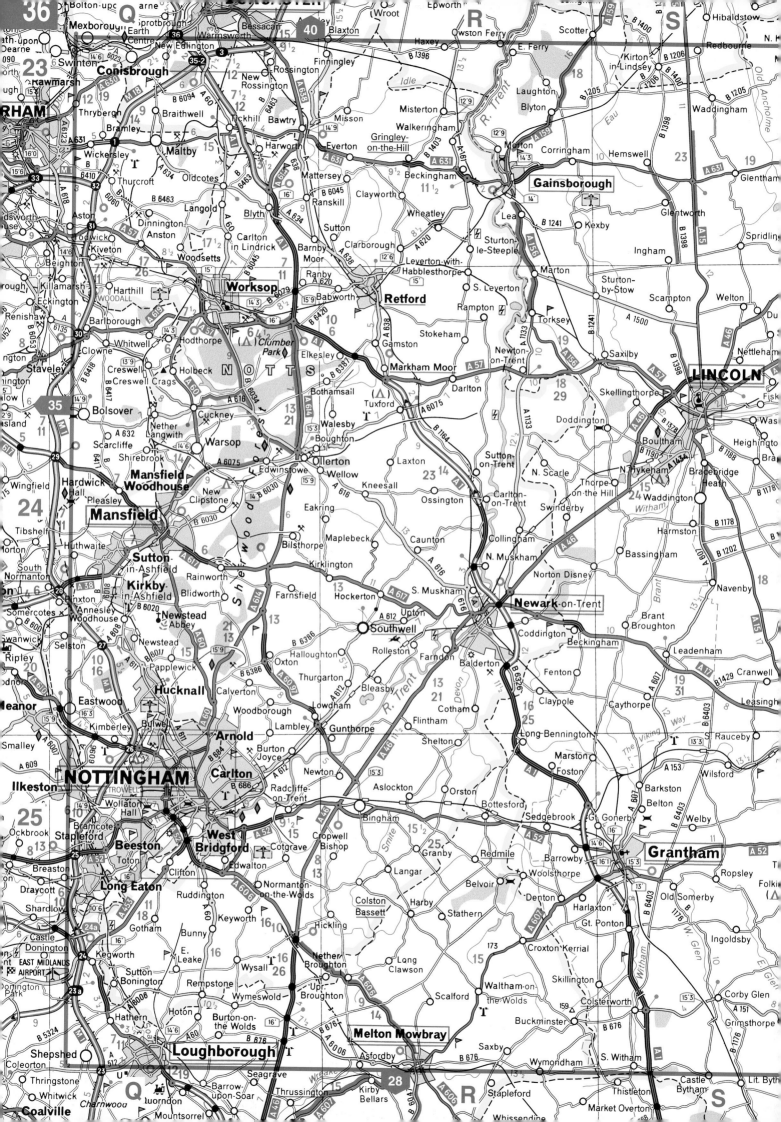

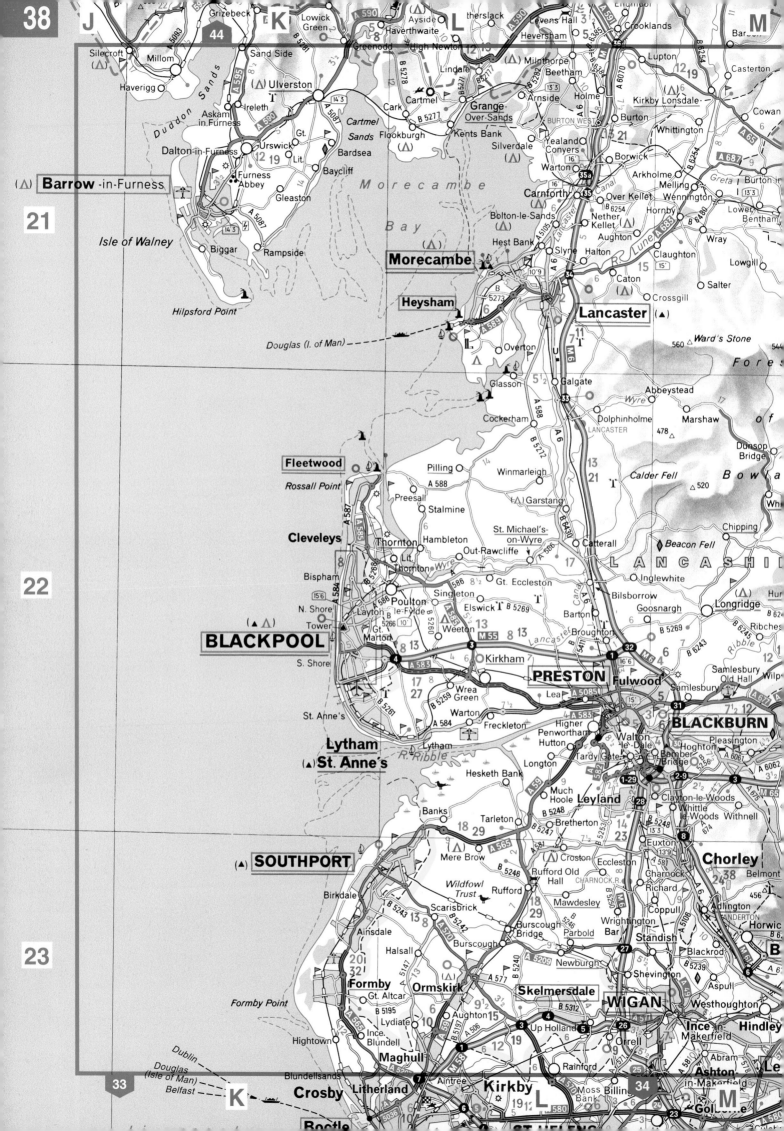

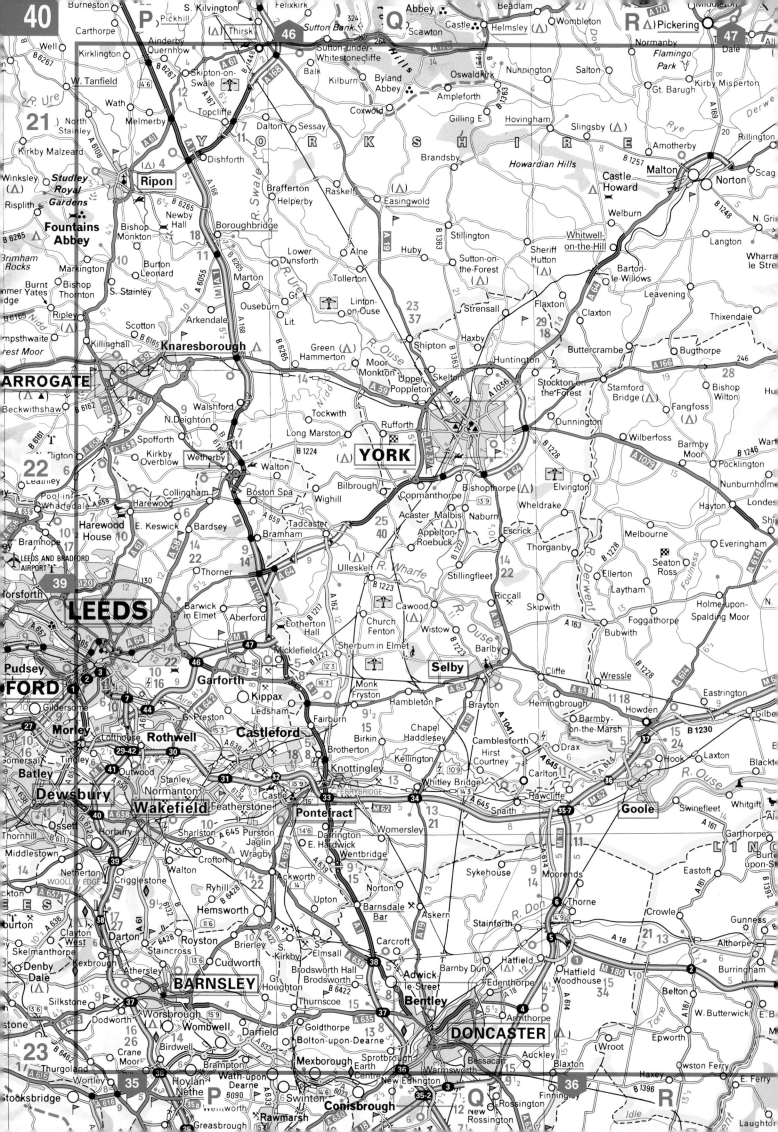

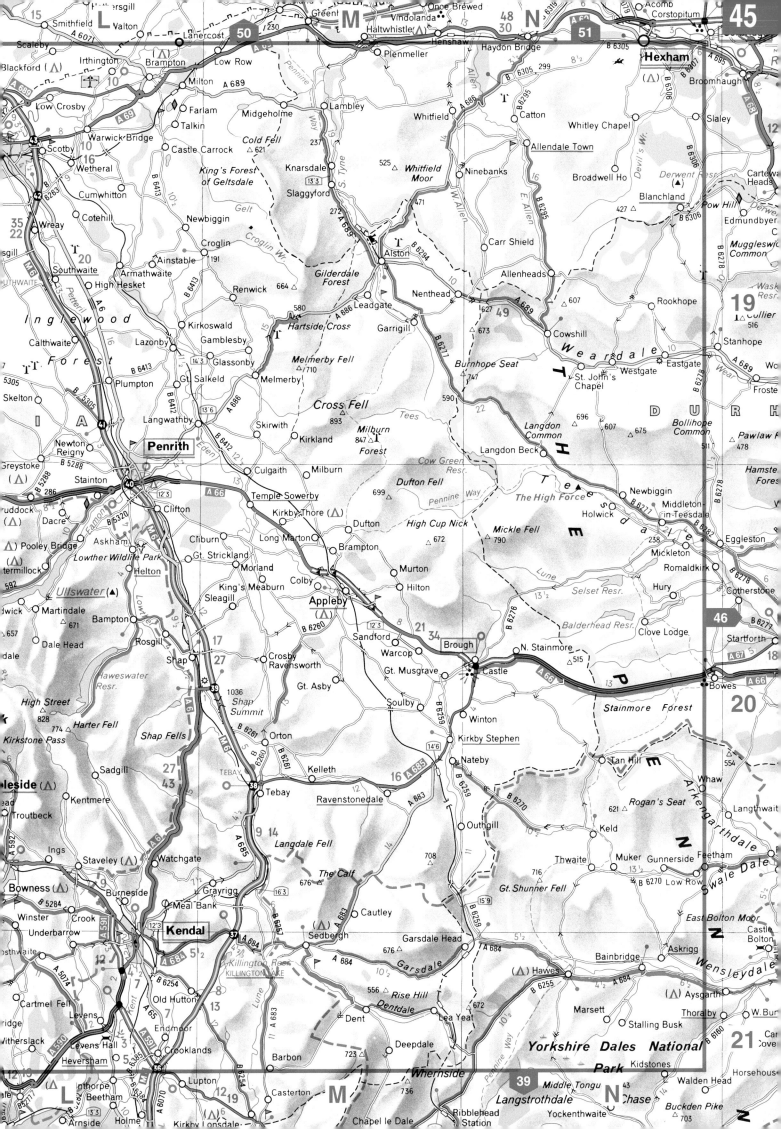

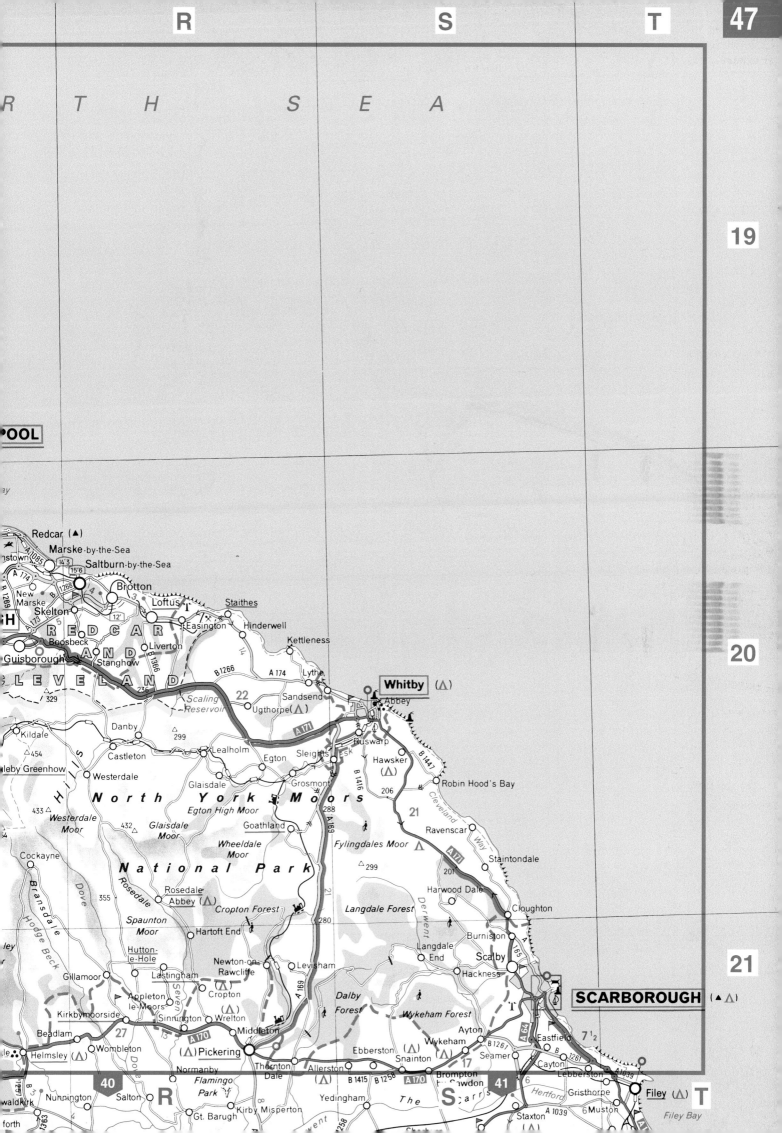

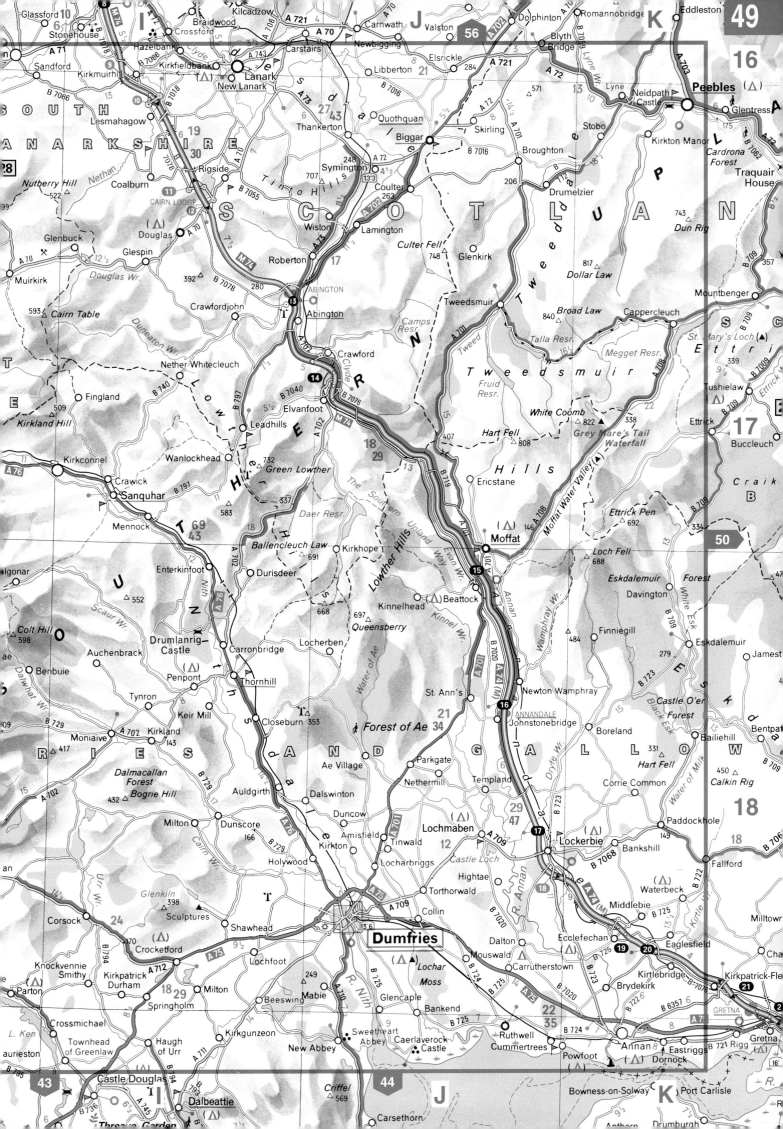

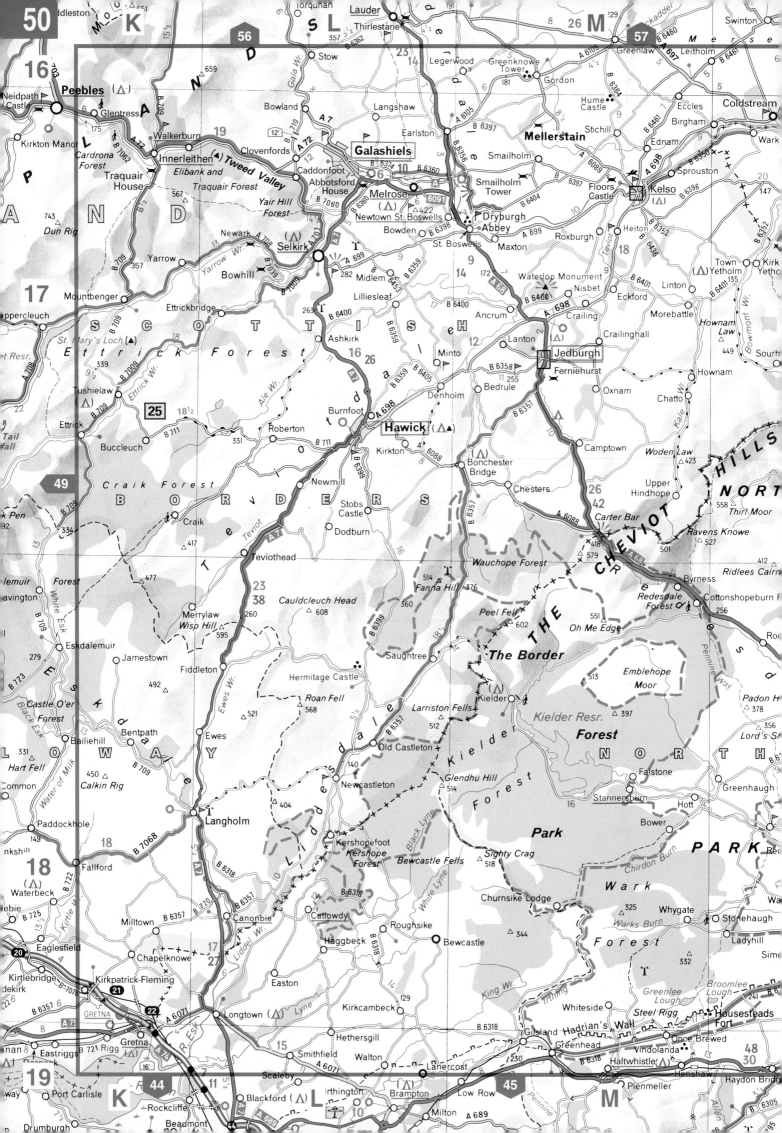

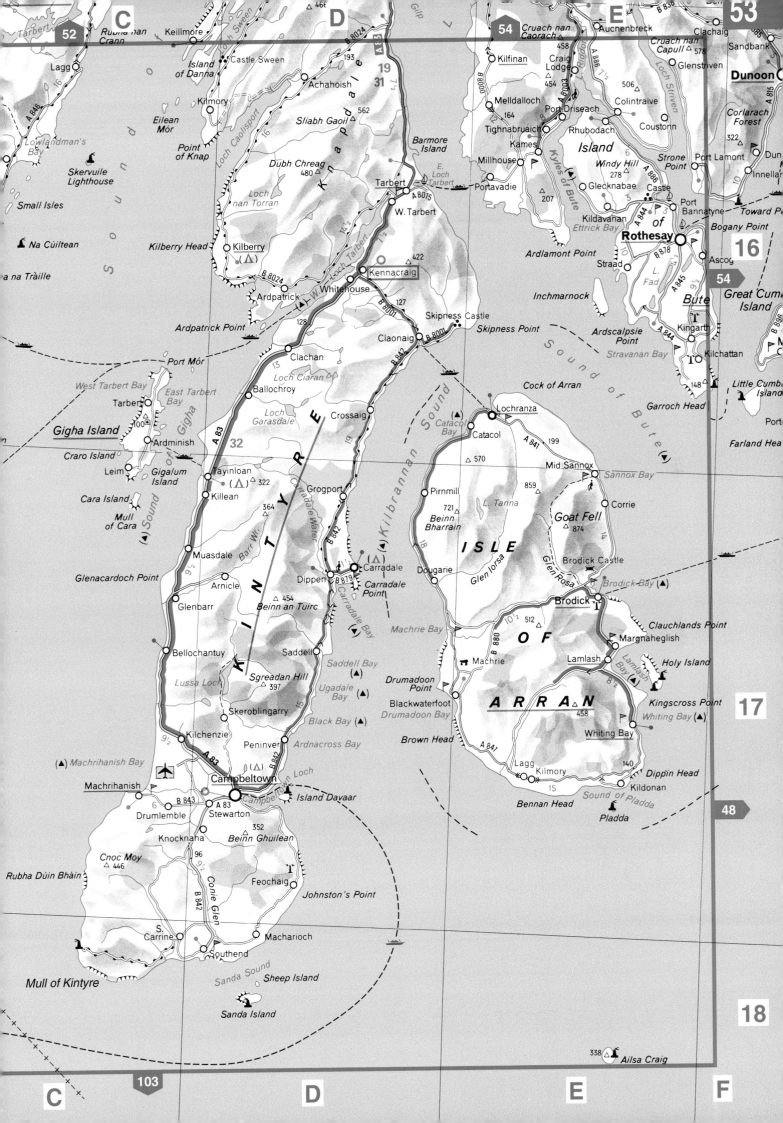

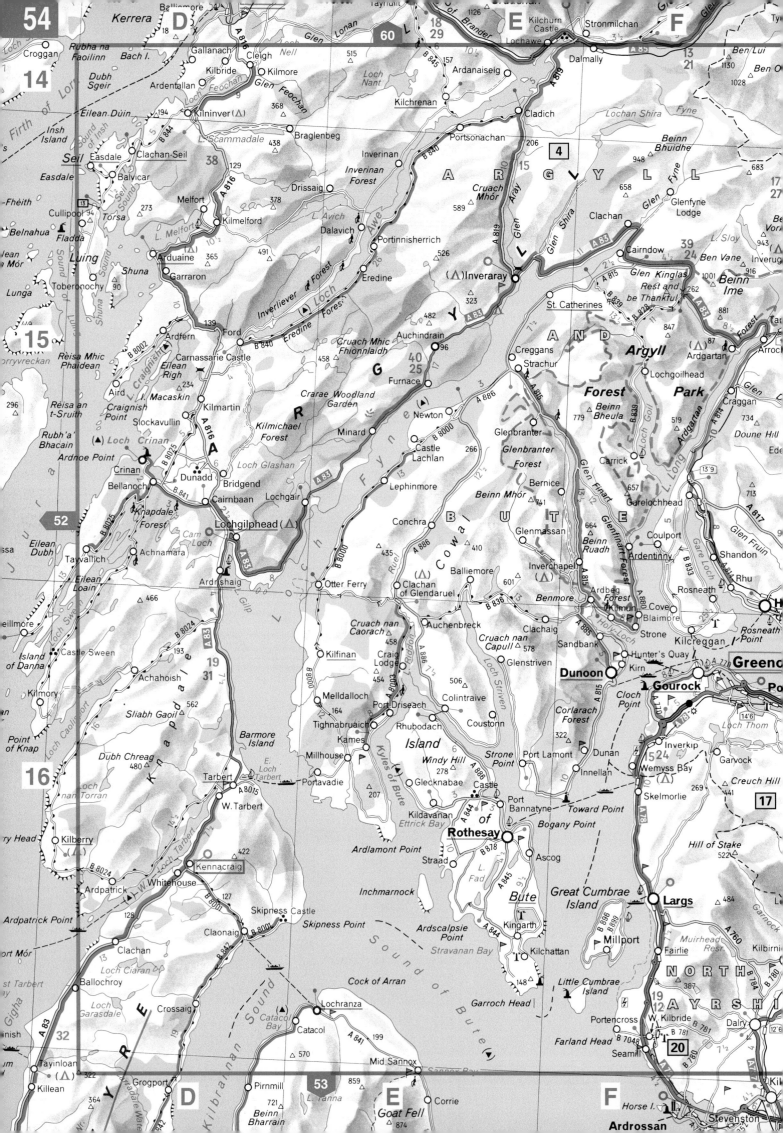

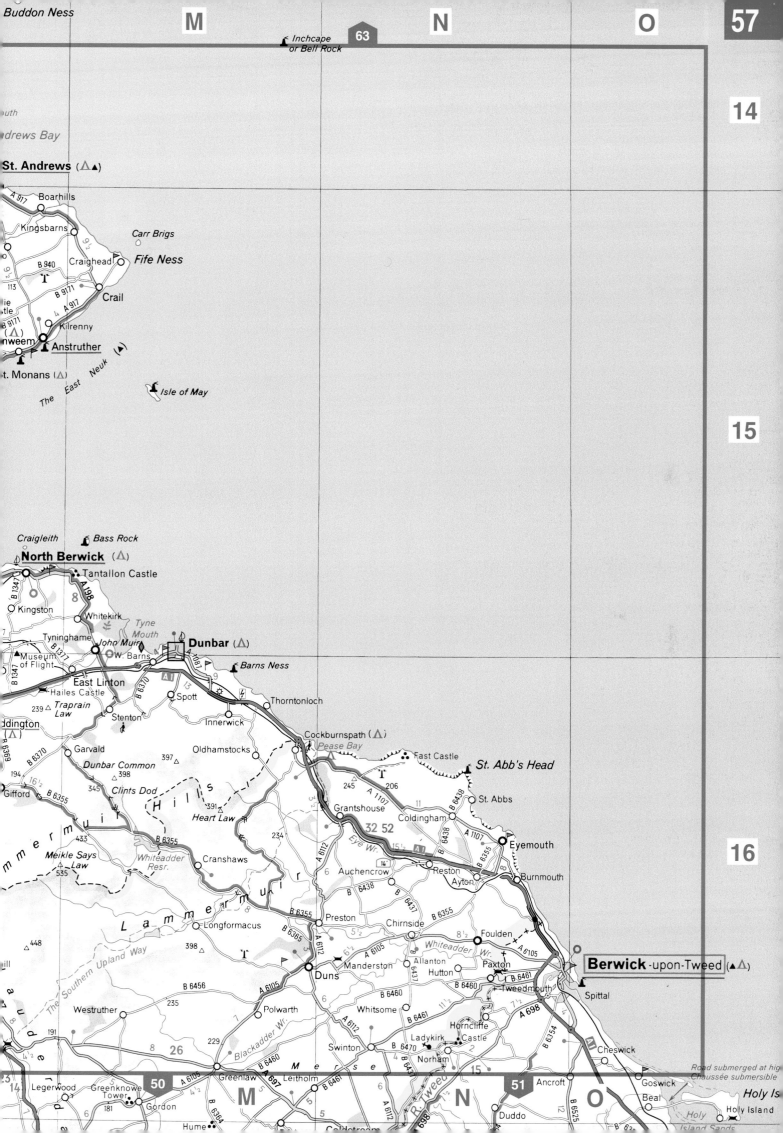

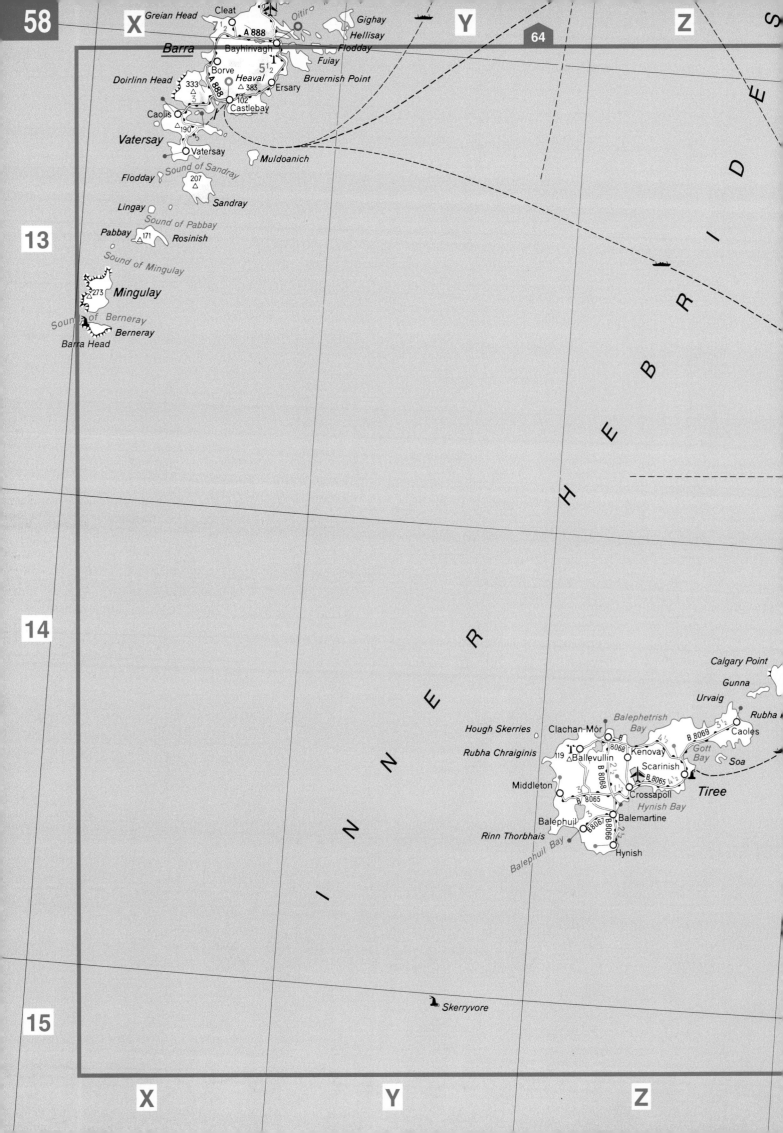

X   Y   Z

Greian Head   Cleat   *Gighay*
                                       Hellisay
Barra   A 888
        Bayhirivagh   *Flodday*
                            Fuiay
        Borve   5½
Doirlinn Head   *Heaval*   *Bruernish Point*
        333   A 888   △ 383
        3   *Ersary*
Caolis 102 Castlebay
        △ 190
Vatersay
        Vatersay
                    Muldoanich
Flodday *Sound of Sandray*
        207
        △
Lingay   *Sandray*
        Sound of Pabbay
Pabbay 171   *Rosinish*
Sound of Mingulay

△273 *Mingulay*

Sound of Berneray
        Berneray
Barra Head

64

H
E
B
B
R
I
D
E
S

I
N
N
E
R

Calgary Point
        Gunna
        Urvaig
                Rubha
        Balephetrish
        Bay
Hough Skerries Clachan-Mór   B 8069   Caoles
                B
                8068   Kenovay
Rubha Chraiginis   *Gott*
        119 Ballevullin   *Bay* Soa
        △
        B 8068
                Scarinish
Middleton   B 8065
        B 8065   Crossapoll   *Tiree*
                3   *Hynish Bay*
        B 8067   Balemartine
Balephuil B8066
Rinn Thorbhais   Hynish
        Balephuil Bay

Skerryvore

X   Y   Z

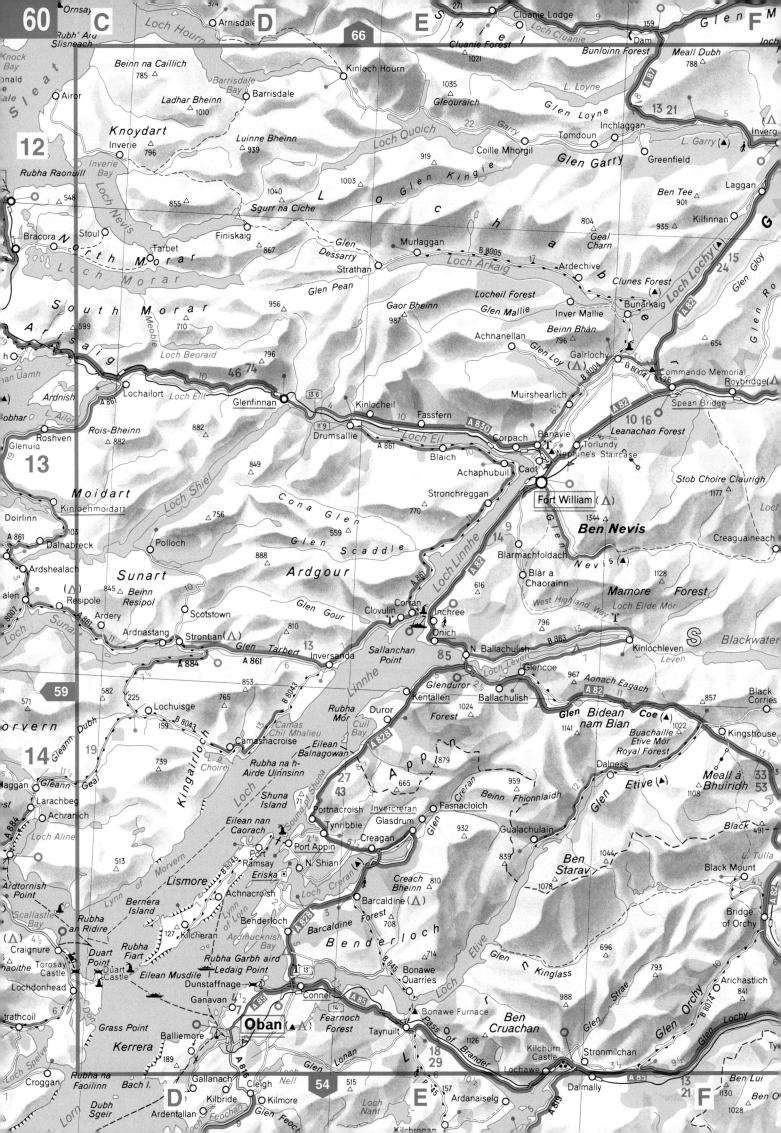

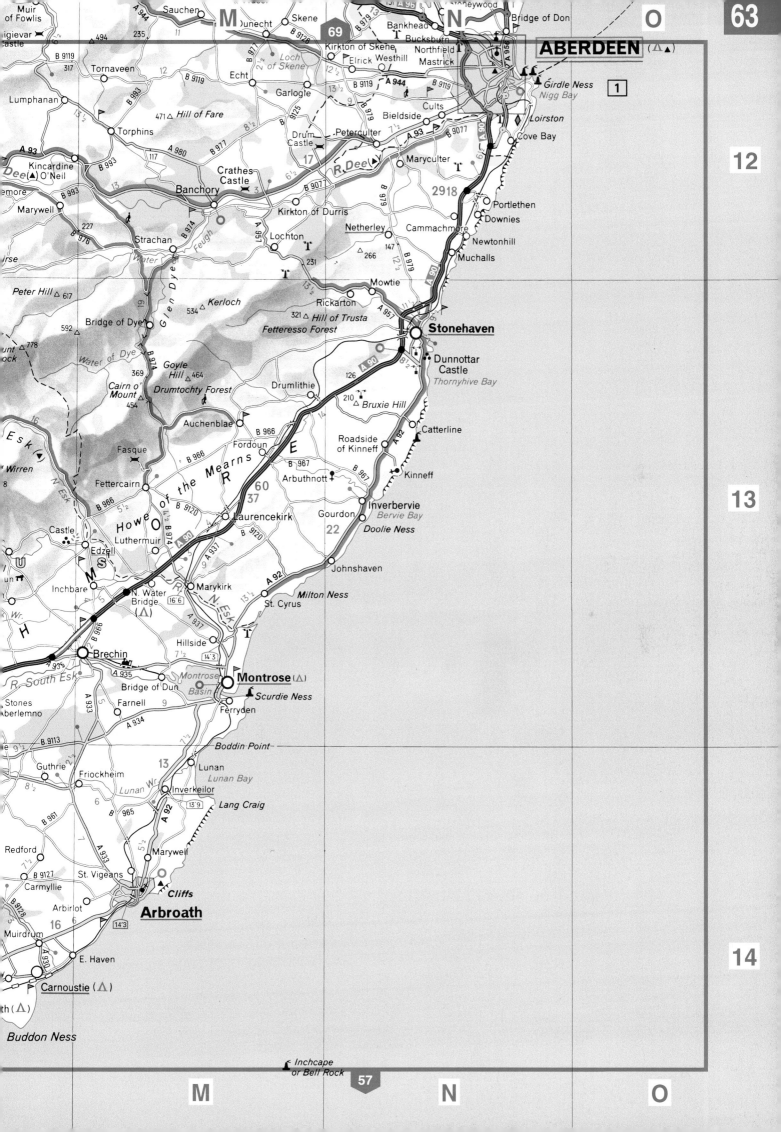

12

13

14

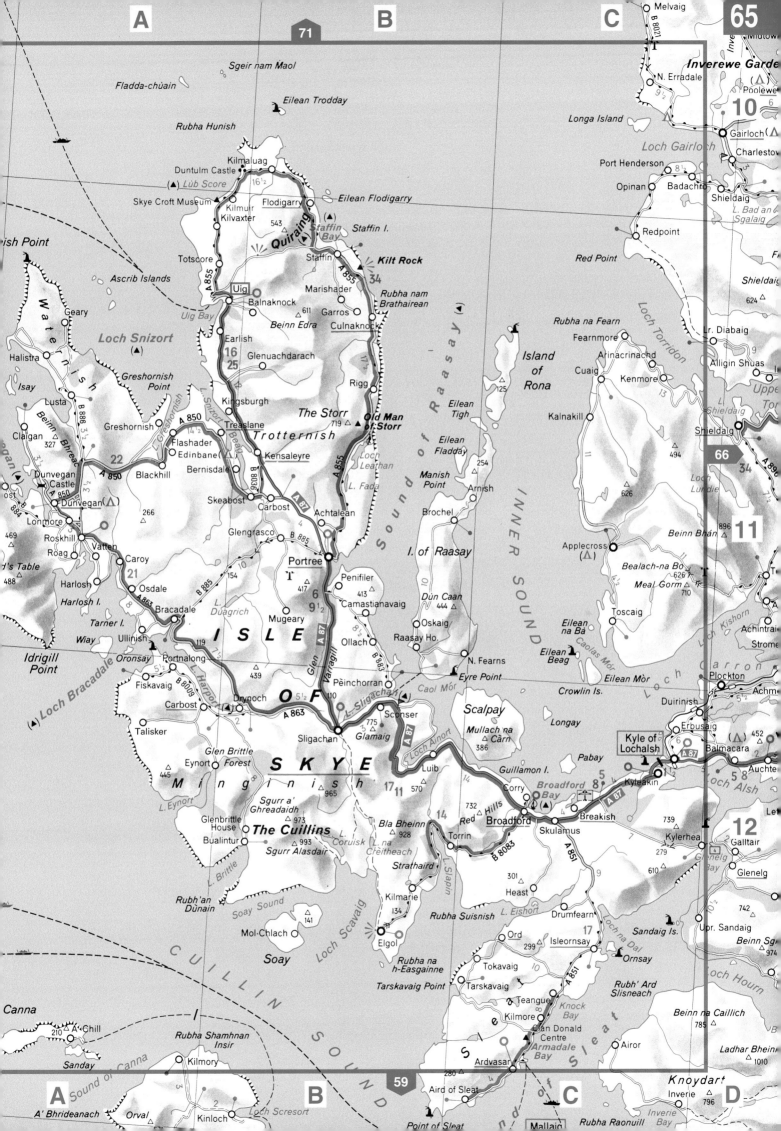

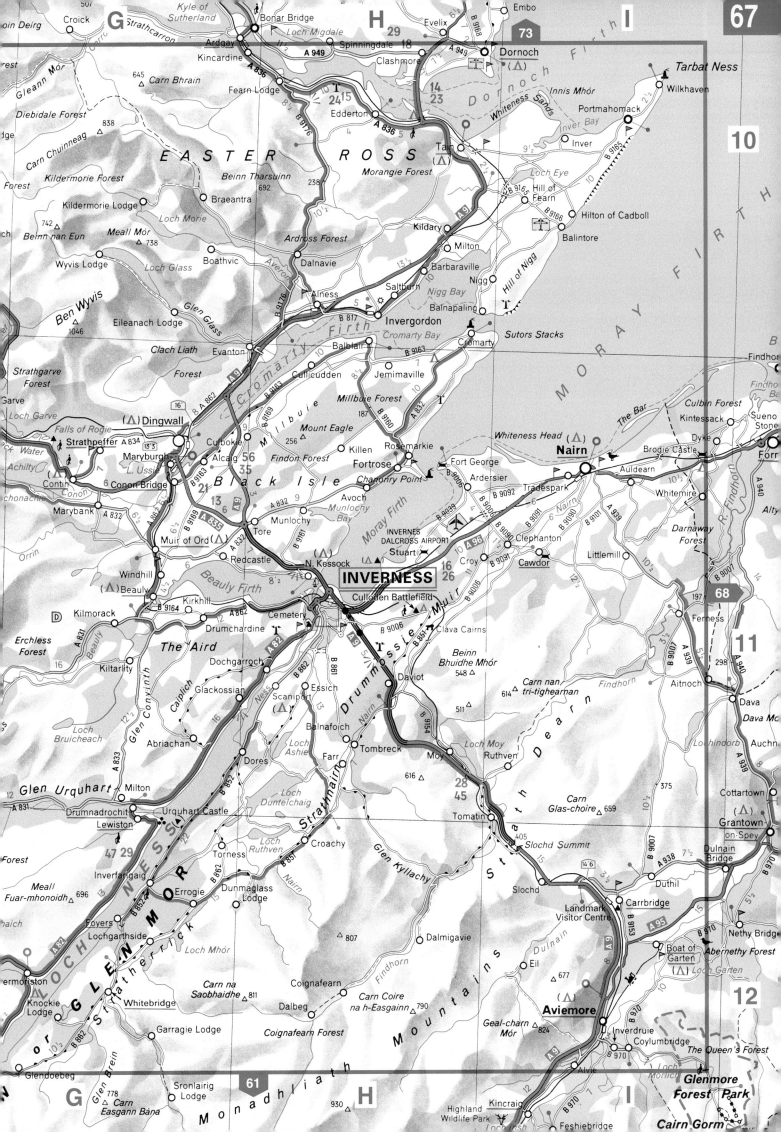

H E B R I D E S

ISLE OF LEWIS AND HARRIS

O U T E R

Arnol
Barv
Bragar
12
L. Urrahag
50
Shawbost
A 858
Loch Breivat
261
Garenin
Carloway
Dun Carloway Broch
Beinn Mholach
292
Little Bernera
Tolsta Chaolais
Tobson
Gallan Head
West Loch Roag
Pabay Mór
Breaclete
East Loch Roag
8½
L. Laxavat Ard
Aird Uig
Valtos
Breasclete
Miavaig
Vuia Mór
Great Bernera
Eilean Kearstay
Callanish
Timsgarry
Floday
Cruilivig
Standing Stones
Garynahine
St
Camas Uig
Uig
205
B 8011
13
A 858
13½
Mangersta
Loch Roag
Little Loch Roag
B 8059
Achmore
112
7
574
Enaclete
L. nam Falcag
Islivig
LEWIS
Leurbo
Aird Brenish
Suainaval
B 8011
L. Ofasay
Brenish
L. Grunavat
20
L. Trealaval
Crossbc
Loch Airigh na h-Airde
Keose
Mealasta I.
Laxay
281
Balallan
L. Erisort
Kershader
Morsgail Forest
Loch Langavat
B 8060
Kearstay
Arivruaich
L. Sgibacleit
Glenside
Scarp
308
303
A 859
36
Seaforth Head
401
Park or Pairc
Gra
Braigh Mór
Ulladale
492
572
Eishken
B 8060
Gasker
Hushinish
Tirga Mór
679
579
17½
217
Ardvourlie
Seaforth Island
Beinn Mhór
371
467
Crionaig
Hushinish Point
B 887
Forest of Harris
13
Meavaig
Clisham
799
Maaruig
Loch Seaforth
Amhuinnsuidhe
Meavaig
North Harris
Taransay Glorigs
Soay Mór
West Loch Tarbert
Ardhasaig
Rhenigidale
L. Claidh
HARRIS
Taransay
267
Isay
3
Tarbert
Lo ch Trollamarig
Eilean Mór a'Bháigh
Sound
WESTERN ISLES
506
Kyles Scalpay
334
Sound of Taransay
Luskentyre
South Harris Forest
Scotasay
Scalpay
104
[32]
Toe Head
Borve
24
16½
A 859
Drinnishadder
Scalpay
Coppay
Scarista
365
South Harris
Grosebay
Shillay
398
Manish
Northton
L. Langavat
Stockinish I.
Sound of Shillay
Brenish Point
196
Ensay
14
Pabbay
Leverburgh
Finsbay
460
Spuir
Sound of Pabbay
Killa
[64]
A 859
Rodel
Boreray
Berneray
93
Y Langay Z A
Borve
Gilsay
Renish Point
Groay
Fladda-chùain
Caola

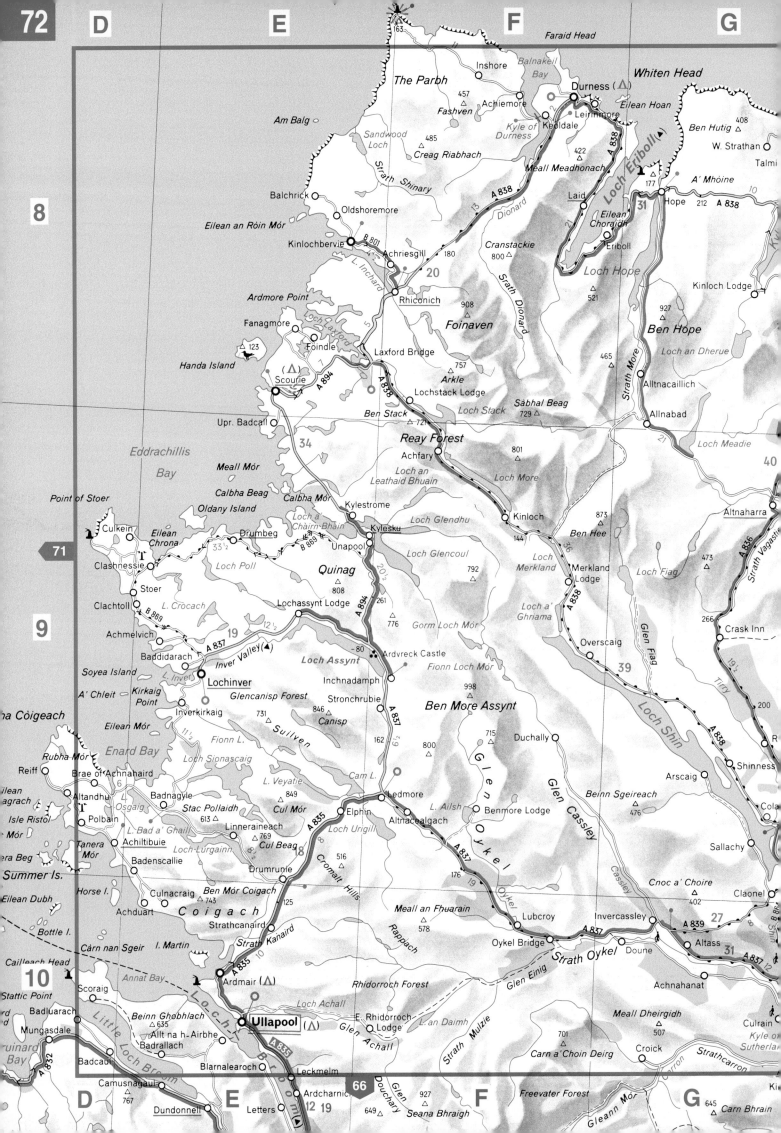

J · Stro
K · Firth
L

7

Brough Ness

Dunnet Head

Langaton Point
Island of Stroma · Nethertown
Uppertown · 51
St. John's Point
Pentland Skerries

Scarfskerry
Brough
St. John's Loch
20 · A 836 · Gills
Duncansby Head
2

Holborn Head
Mey · Canisbay
John o' Groats (△)

Brims Ness
Thurso Bay
Crosskirk · Scrabster
A 882 · A 836
Dunnet · Barrock
(△) · Castletown
Loch Heilen · 124
Skirza
Freswick · Skirza Head
Freswick Bay

Achreamie
Thurso (△)
B 874
141
B 870

Westfield
Calder Mains · Roadside
B 874
Slickly
Auckengill
A 99

Loch Calder
B 874
Bower · Lyth · Sortat
Keiss
17

hurrery
Halkirk
Myrelandhorn
Loch Shurrery
A 9
Olgrinmore · Bannskirk · L. Scarmclate
B 870
d Mor · Spittal
Loch Watten · 4 2
B 870
Reiss
Sinclair's Bay

8

Loch Caluim
Thurso
Mybster
Watten
A 882
B 874
Wick
8
Noss Head
Girnigoe and Sinclair Castles

Westerdale
B 870
21 · Haster
Staxigoe
North Head

Loch More
Badlipster
Wick
South Head

Tannach
Loch Hempriggs

44 · 71
Grey Cairns of Camster
Thrumster
Sarclet

Loch Ruard
211 · 212
Ulbster

△ 348
287
60 · 37
Hill o' Many Stanes

73
Houstry
Lybster
W. Clyth

Latheron · Forse
A 9
Janetstown

Braemore
626 · △ Scaraben
Dunbeath
20

gwell · Forest
Borgue
Berriedale

9
200

gwell
Helmsdale

Inset map

J · 4°20
Sule Skerry
5
Stack Skerry

K · 3°
L
Mull H

Bow Head
Noup Head · Pierowall
Westray · 169
Midbea · Rapness
Calfs

3°20

Westray Firth

6
Rousay · Wasbister
250 · Egilsay
B 9064 · Brinyan
Wyre
Gairsay
(▲) Brough of Birsay
Brough Head · Birsay
A 966
Kitchener Memorial
Geortth · Gurness Broch
B 9057
221
Twatt · Dounby
Stro
Skara Brae
L. of Harray
Balfour
Yesnaby
Maes Howe · Finstown
Rennibister
59° **Mainland**
Ring of Brodgar
A 965
Wideford Hill Cairn
Kirkwa
Stromness · Stenness
268 △
Graemsay
Orphir
St. Mary's
Moness
Cava
Old Man of Hoy
479
Lamb
Rora Head
Rackwick
Fara
Scapa Flow
Causeway · Burra
Lyness · Flotta
Caus
7
Hoy · St. Margar
Tor Ness
South Walls
South
Burwick
Old Hea

Pentland Firth

Dunnet Head
Stroma
58°40
Scarfskerry
Gills
Duncansby H
Scrabster · Dunnet (△) · A 8
John o' Groats (△)
Thurso
Castletown · A 9
3°

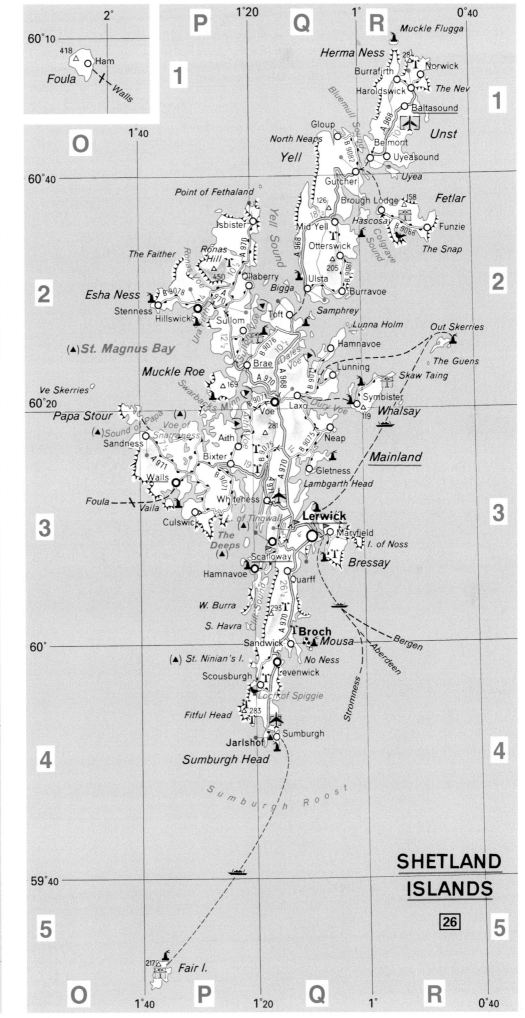

SHETLAND ISLANDS 26

ORKNEY ISLANDS 22

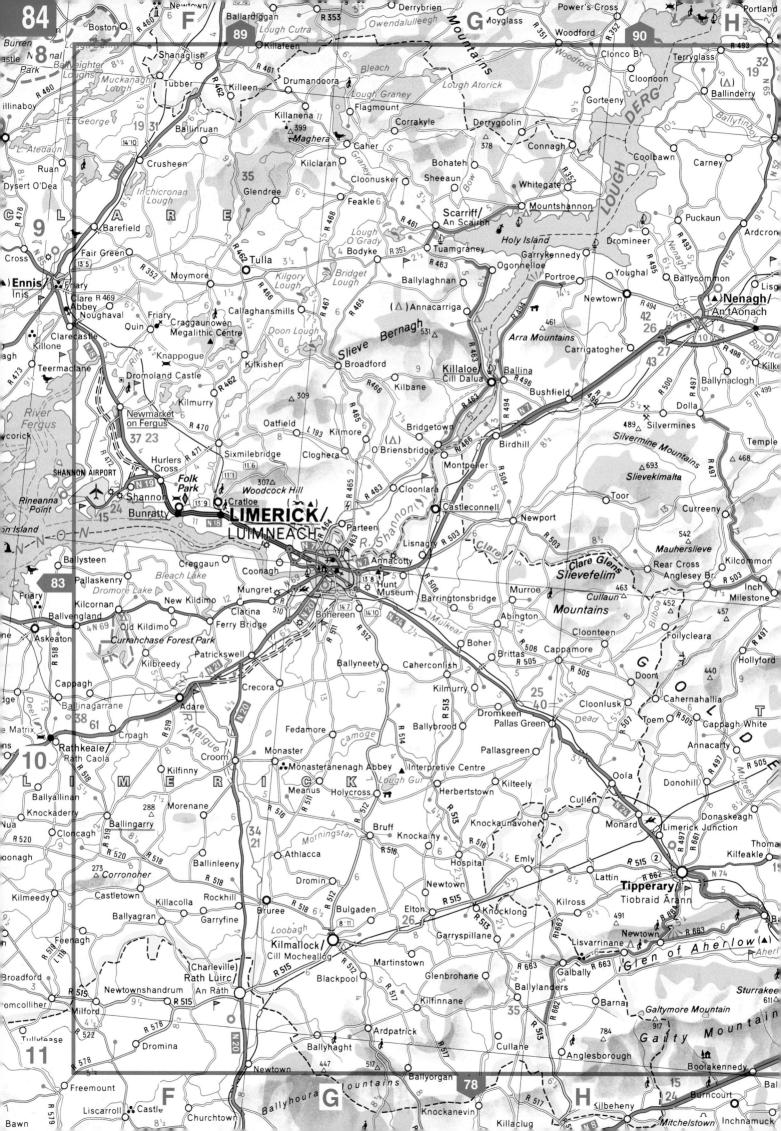

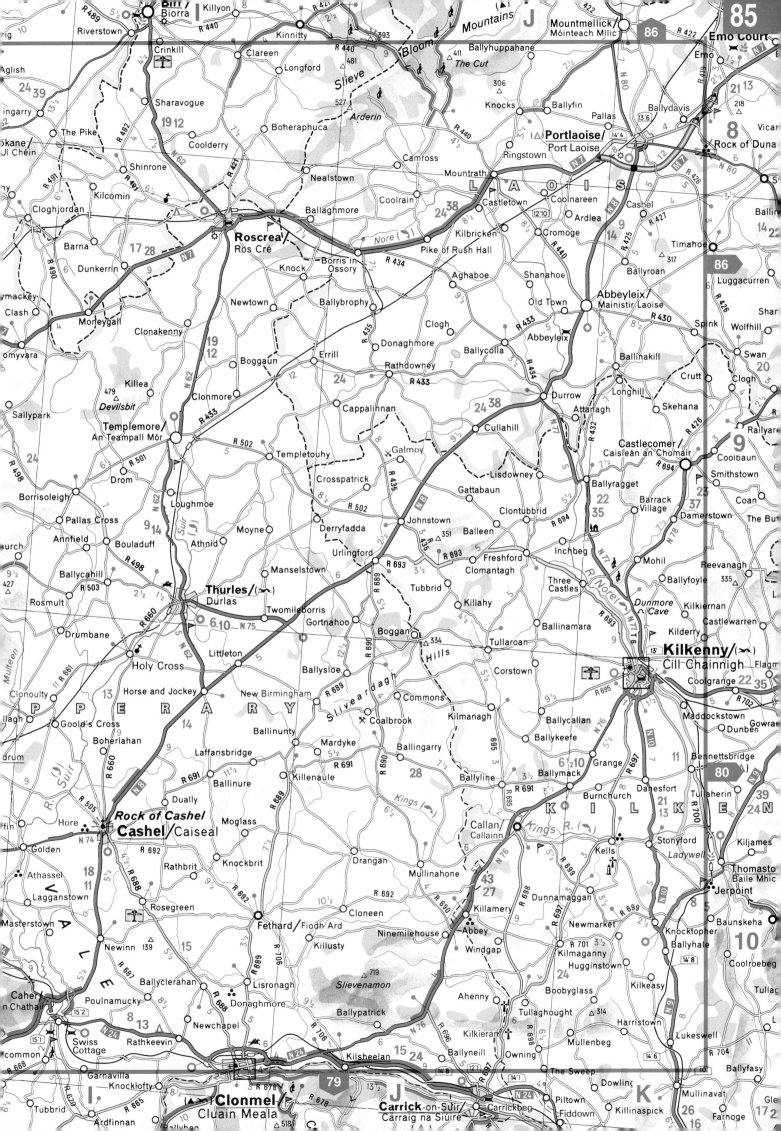

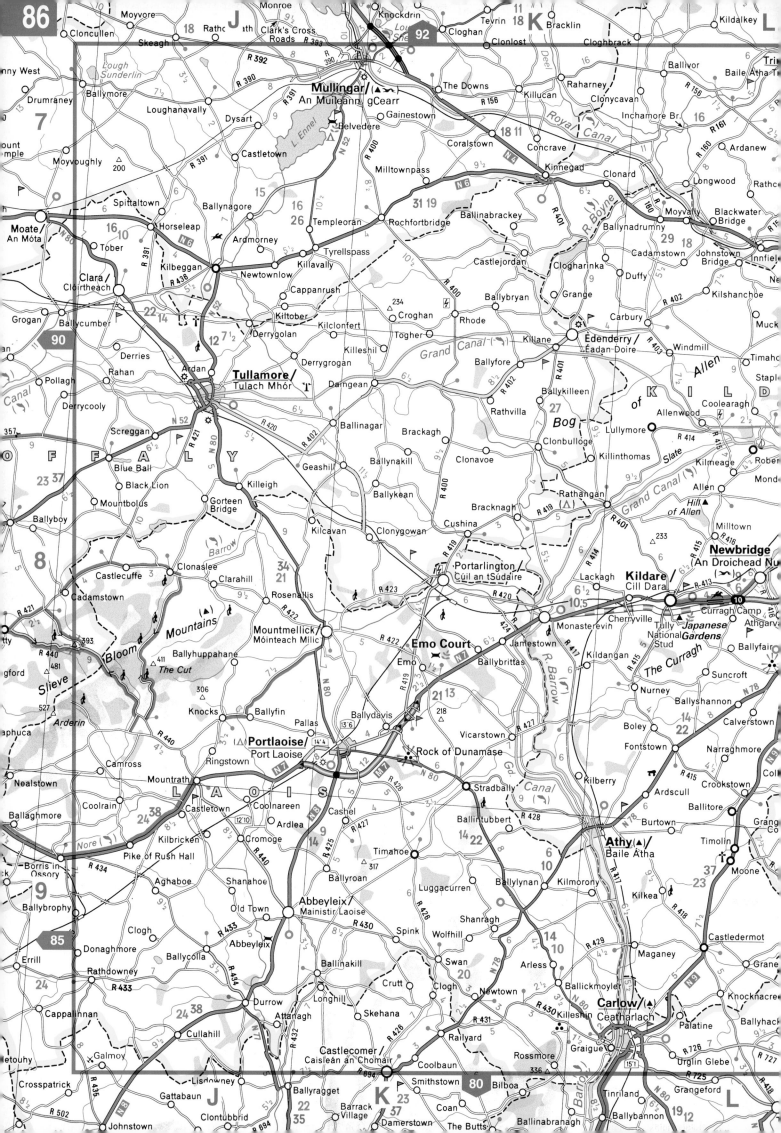

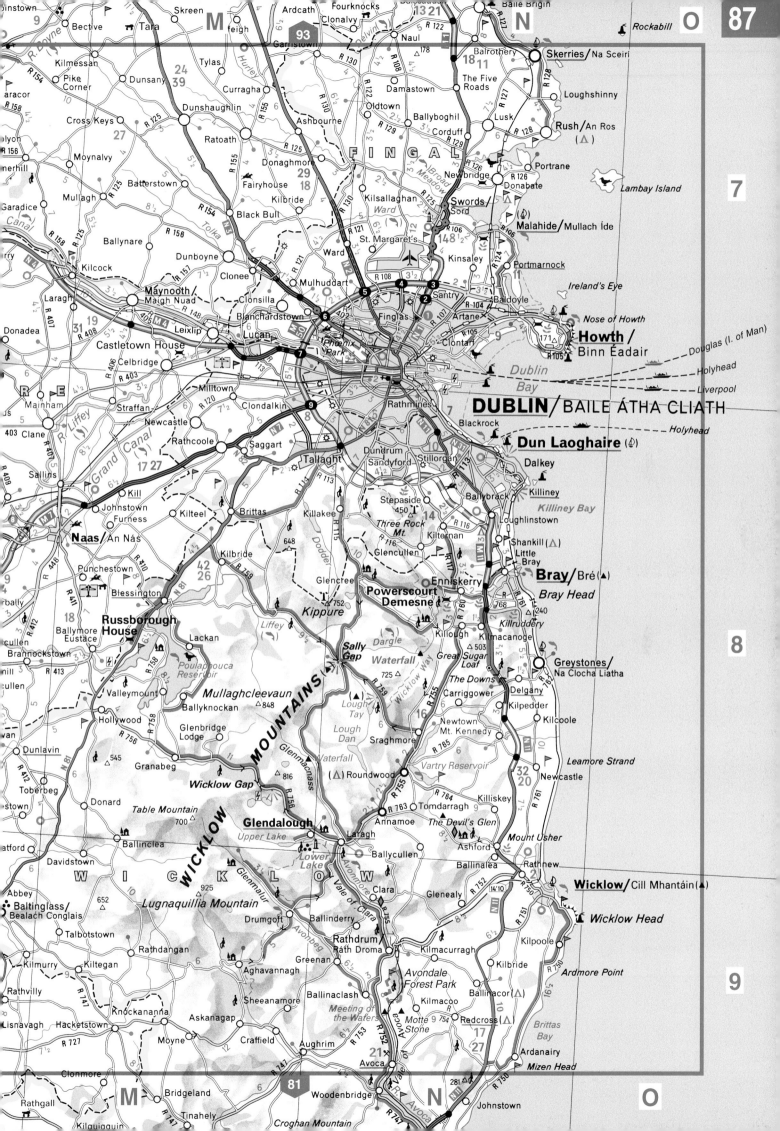

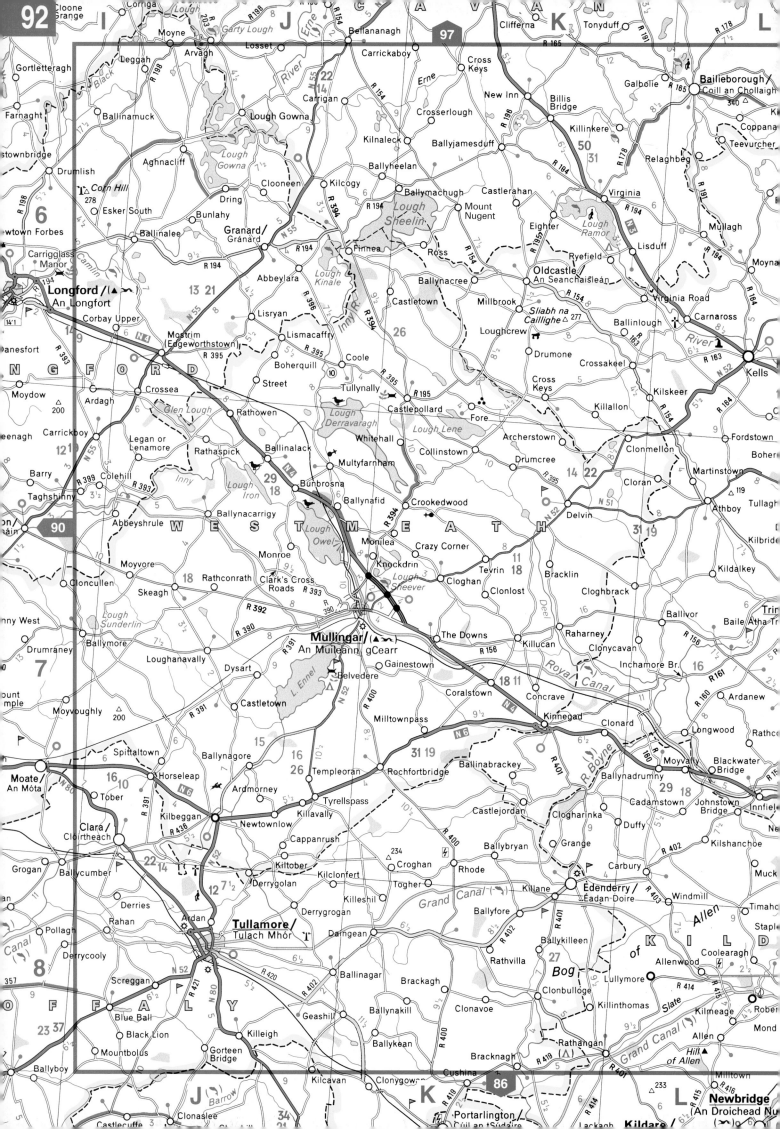

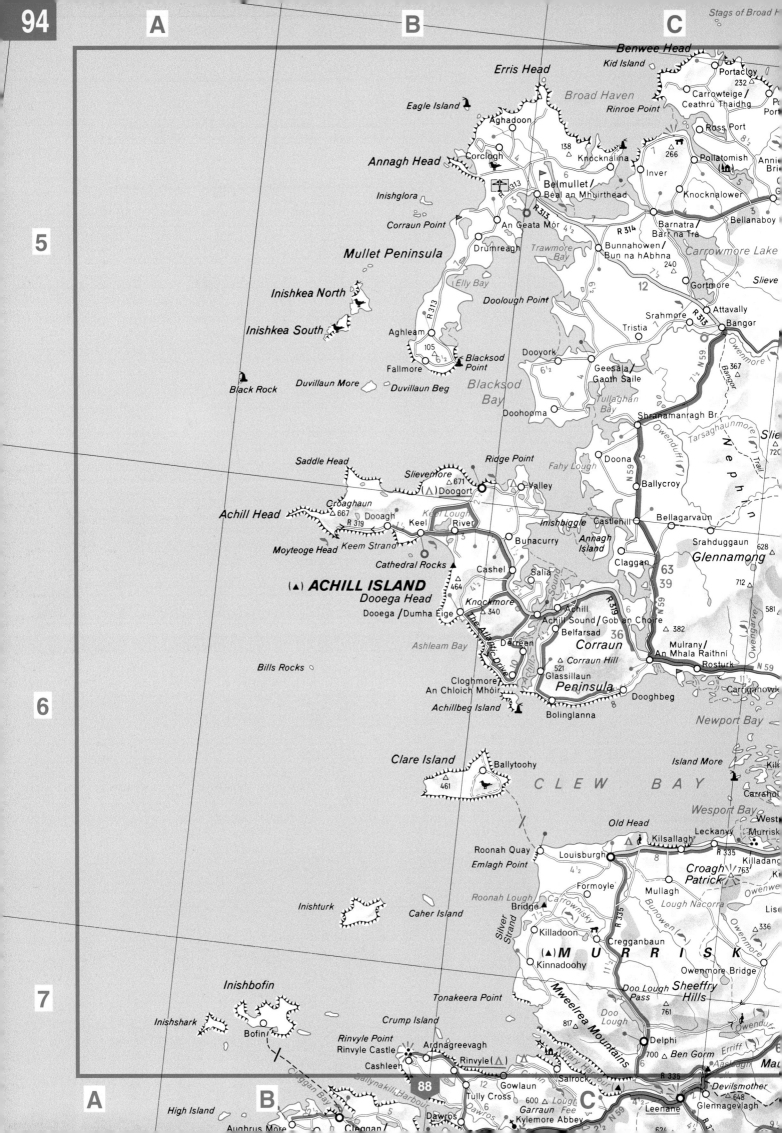

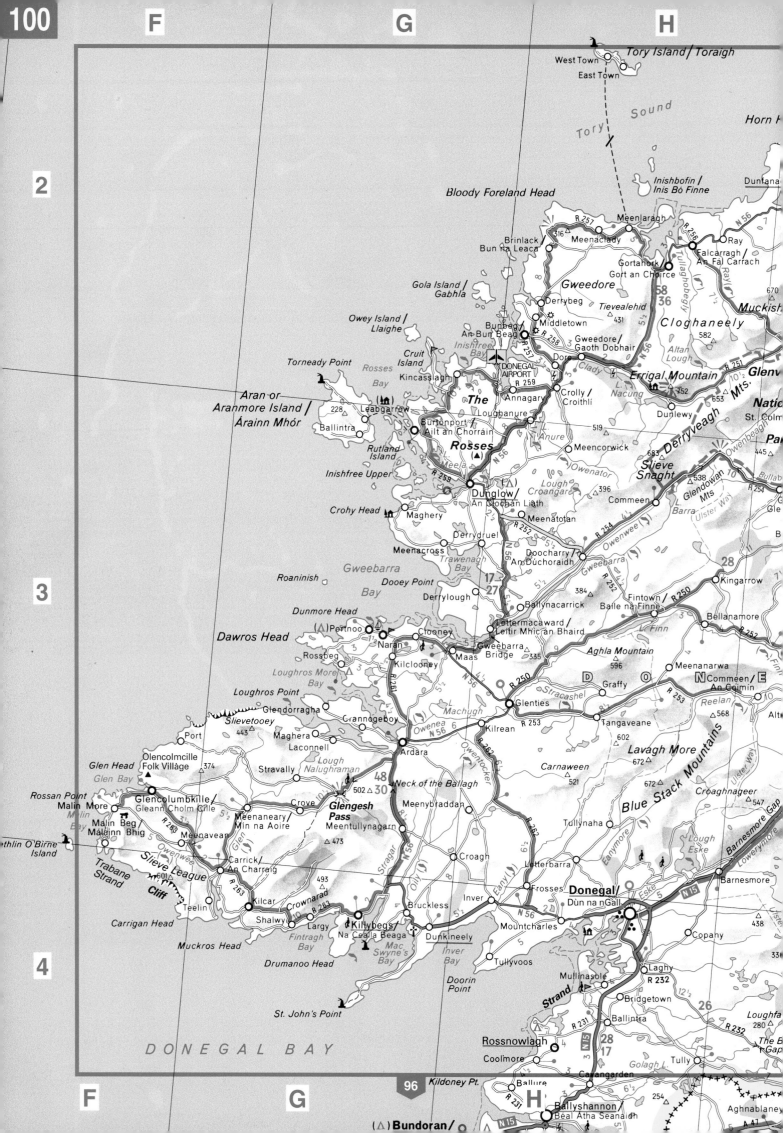

F   G   H

2

3

4

Tory Island / Toraigh
West Town
East Town
Tory Sound
Horn H
Inishbofin / Inis Bó Finne
Dunfana
Bloody Foreland Head
Meenlaragh
R 257
Brinlack
Bun na Leaca
316
Meenaclady
Ray
Falcarragh / An Fál Carrach
R 256
Gortahork
Gort an Choirce
Gweedore
670
Muckish
Gola Island / Gabhla
Derrybeg
Tievealehid
431
582
Cloghaneely
Owey Island / Llaighe
Middletown
Bunbeg
An Bun Beag
R 258
Gweedore / Gaoth Dobhair
Altan Lough
Cruit Island
Inishfree Bay
Dore
Clady
Errigal Mountain
R 251
Glenv
Torneady Point
DONEGAL AIRPORT
R 259
Crolly / Croithlí
L. Nacung
752
653
Nati
Aran or Aranmore Island / Árainn Mhór
Kincasslagh
Annagary
Dunlewy
St. Colm
228
Leabgarrow
The
Loughanure
Pa
Ballintra
Burtonport / Ailt an Chorráin
Rosses
Anure
519
Meencorwick
683
Owenbeagh
445
Slieve Snaght
Rutland Island
Meela
N 56
Owenator
396
538
R 254
Inishfree Upper
R 259
Dunglow / An Clochán Liath
Lough Croangar
Commeen
Glendowan Mts
Gle
Crohy Head
Maghery
Derrydruel
R 252
Meenatotan
Owenwee
Barra
Ulster Way
Meenacross
Doocharry / An Dúchoraidh
Gweebarra
384
R 252
Kingarrow
Roaninish
Gweebarra Bay
Trawenagh Bay
17
27
Ballynacarrick
Fintown / Baile na Finne
R 250
28
Dooey Point
Derrylough
Aghla Mountain
596
Bellanamore
Dunmore Head
Lettermacaward / Leitir Mhic an Bhaird
Meenanarwa
R 252
Dawros Head
Portnoo
Clooney
Gweebarra Bridge
335
Commeen / An Coimín
Naran
Maas
D
Graffy
O
N E
Rossbeg
Kilclooney
L. Machugh
R 250
Stracashel
R 253
Loughros More Bay
Owenea
Glenties
Tangaveane
568
Loughros Point
Grannogeboy
Kilrean
R 253
602
Glendorragha
Slievetooey
443
Maghera
Laconnell
Ardara
Owentocker
Lavagh More Mountains
672
Carnaween
521
672
Croaghnageer
547
Glencolmcille Folk Village
374
Stravally
Lough Nalughraman
48
502
30
Neck of the Ballagh
Blue Stack Mountains
Glen Head
Glen Bay
Olencolmcille
Meenybraddan
Rossan Point
Malin More
Glencolumbkille / Gleann Cholm Cille
Crove
Glengesh Pass
Meentullynagarn
473
Tullynaha
Lough Eske
Malin Bay
Meenaneary / Mín na Aoire
Lough
Malin Beg / Málainn Bhig
R 263
Meenavean
Croagh
Letterbarra
Barnesmore Gap
Lowerymore
thlin O'Birne Island
Owenwee
Carrick / An Charraig
Oily
Eanymore
Slieve League
601
493
Eany (y)
Frosses
Donegal / Dún na nGall
N 15
Barnesmore
Trabane Strand
R 263
Inver
Eske
5
Cliff
Kilcar
Crownarad
R 263
Bruckless
N 56
Stragar
438
Teelin
Shalwy
Largy
Killybegs / Na Cealla Beaga
Mountcharles
Copany
Carrigan Head
Dunkineely
Fintragh Bay
Mac Swyne's Bay
Inver Bay
Tullyvoos
Laghy
R 232
Muckros Head
Drumanoo Head
Doorin Point
Mullinasole
Strand
Bridgetown
26
St. John's Point
Ballintra
R 231
Loughfa
R 232
28
17
The B
Gap
DONEGAL BAY
Rossnowlagh
Coolmore
N 15
Tully
Golagh L.
Carangarden
Aghnablaney

Kildoney Pt.
Balliure
R 231
Ballyshannon / Béal Átha Seanaidh
R 47

F   G   H

(△) Bundoran / ○
N 15

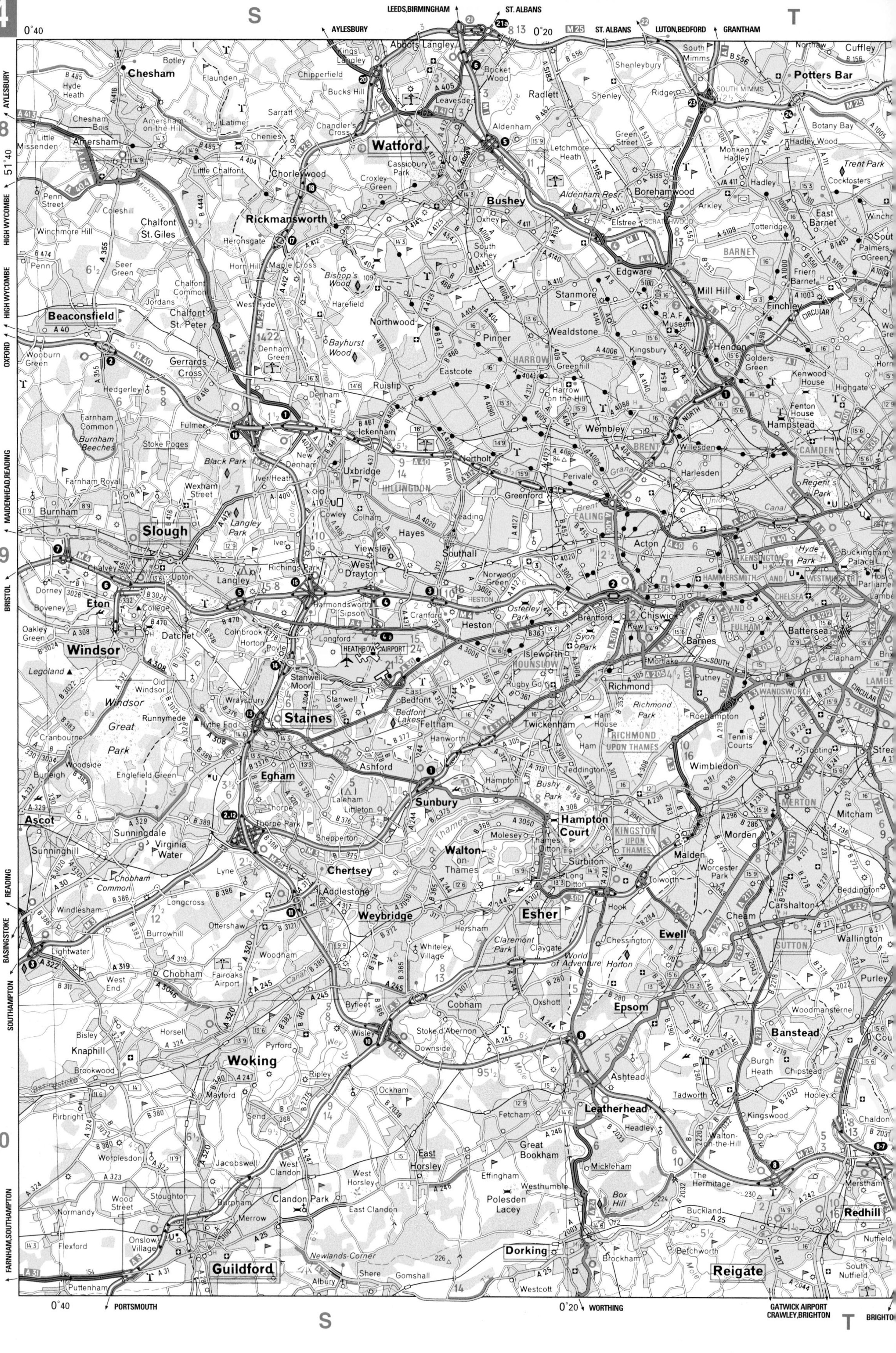

S T

LEEDS,BIRMINGHAM ST. ALBANS

AYLESBURY ST. ALBANS LUTON,BEDFORD GRANTHAM

0°40 0°20 M25

28 51°40

AYLESBURY HIGH WYCOMBE HIGH WYCOMBE OXFORD MAIDENHEAD,READING

Chesham
Botley
Flaunden
Chipperfield
Kings Langley
Abbots Langley
Bricket Wood
Shenleybury
Shenley
Radlett
South Mimms
Potters Bar
Cuffley
Northaw

Amersham
Chesham Bois
Amersham-on-the-Hill
Latimer
Chenies
Chandler's Cross
Watford
Cassiobury Park
Aldenham
Green Street
Letchmore Heath
Borehamwood
Botany Bay
Hadley Wood
Monken Hadley
Cockfosters
Trent Park

Penn Street
Coleshill
Little Chalfont
Chorleywood
Croxley Green
Bushey
Oxhey
South Oxhey
Elstree
Arkley
East Barnet
South

Winchmore Hill
Chalfont St. Giles
Rickmansworth
Heronsgate
Maple Cross
Bishop's Wood
Stanmore
Edgware
Mill Hill
Finchley
Friern Barnet

Beaconsfield
Chalfont St. Peter
Horn Hill
West Hyde
Harefield
Northwood
Wealdstone
Kingsbury
R.A.F. Museum
Hendon
Golders Green
Kenwood House
Highgate

Penn
Jordans
Chalfont Common
Denham Green
Pinner
Harrow
Greenhill
Harrow on the Hill
NORTH
Wembley
Willesden
Camden
Hampstead
Fenton House

29 BRISTOL

Wooburn Green
Gerrards Cross
Fulmer
Denham
Ickenham
Ruislip
Eastcote
Greenhill
Perivale
Harlesden
Brent
Regent's Park

Farnham Common
Burnham Beeches
Stoke Poges
Black Park
New Denham
Uxbridge
Northolt
Greenford
Ealing
Acton
Kensington

Farnham Royal
Burnham
Slough
Langley Park
Iver Heath
Cowley
Colham
Uxbridge
Yeading
Southall
Hammersmith
Hyde Park
Buckingham Palace

Eton
College
Datchet
Langley
Iver
Richings Park
West Drayton
Yiewsley
Hayes
Norwood Green
Heston
Brentford
Chiswick
Fulham
Battersea
Chelsea

Windsor
Legoland
Old Windsor
Colnbrook
Horton
Poyle
Harmondsworth
Sipson
Longford
HEATHROW AIRPORT
Cranford
Osterley Park
Isleworth
Syon Park
Kew
Barnes
Putney
Clapham

Oakley Green
Dorney
Boveney
Wraysbury
Stanwell Moor
Stanwell
East Bedfont
Bedfont Lakes
Feltham
Hounslow
Rugby Gd
Richmond
Ham House
Roehampton
Wandsworth
Tooting

Cranbourne
Windsor Great Park
Runnymede
Hythe End
Staines
Ashford
Hanworth
Twickenham
Ham
Richmond Upon Thames
Wimbledon
Tennis Courts

Woodside
Burleigh
Englefield Green
Egham
Thorpe
Laleham
Littleton
Hampton
Teddington
Bushy Park
Merton

Ascot
Sunningdale
Virginia Water
Thorpe Park
Shepperton
Sunbury
Hampton Court
Kingston Upon Thames
Malden
Mitcham

Sunninghill
Chobham Common
Lyne
Chertsey
Walton-on-Thames
Molesey
Thames Ditton
Surbiton
Long Ditton
Tolworth
Worcester Park
Morden

30 READING BASINGSTOKE SOUTHAMPTON FARNHAM,SOUTHAMPTON

Windlesham
Longcross
Burrowhill
Addlestone
Weybridge
Hersham
Esher
Claremont Park
Claygate
Chessington
Hook
Cheam
Carshalton
Beddington
Wallington

Lightwater
West End
Chobham
Woodham
Byfleet
Whiteley Village
World of Adventure
Horton
Epsom
Ewell
Purley

Bisley
Knaphill
Horsell
Pyrford
Wisley
Cobham
Stoke d'Abernon
Downside
Oxshott
Banstead
Woodmansterne
Burgh Heath
Chipstead
Hooley

Brookwood
Woking
Mayford
Ripley
Ockham
Leatherhead
Fetcham
Ashtead
Tadworth
Kingswood

Pirbright
Send
Ockham
East Horsley
Great Bookham
Mickleham
Headley
Box Hill
Walton-on-the-Hill
Chaldon

Worplesdon
Jacobswell
West Clandon
West Horsley
Effingham
Westhumble
The Hermitage
Buckland
Merstham

Wood Street
Normandy
Stoughton
Burpham
Merrow
Clandon Park
East Clandon
Polesden Lacey
Box Hill
Redhill

Flexford
Onslow Village
Newlands Corner
Shere
Gomshall
Dorking
Brockham
Reigate
Nutfield

Puttenham
Guildford
Albury
Westcott
Reigate

PORTSMOUTH WORTHING GATWICK AIRPORT CRAWLEY,BRIGHTON BRIGHTON

S T

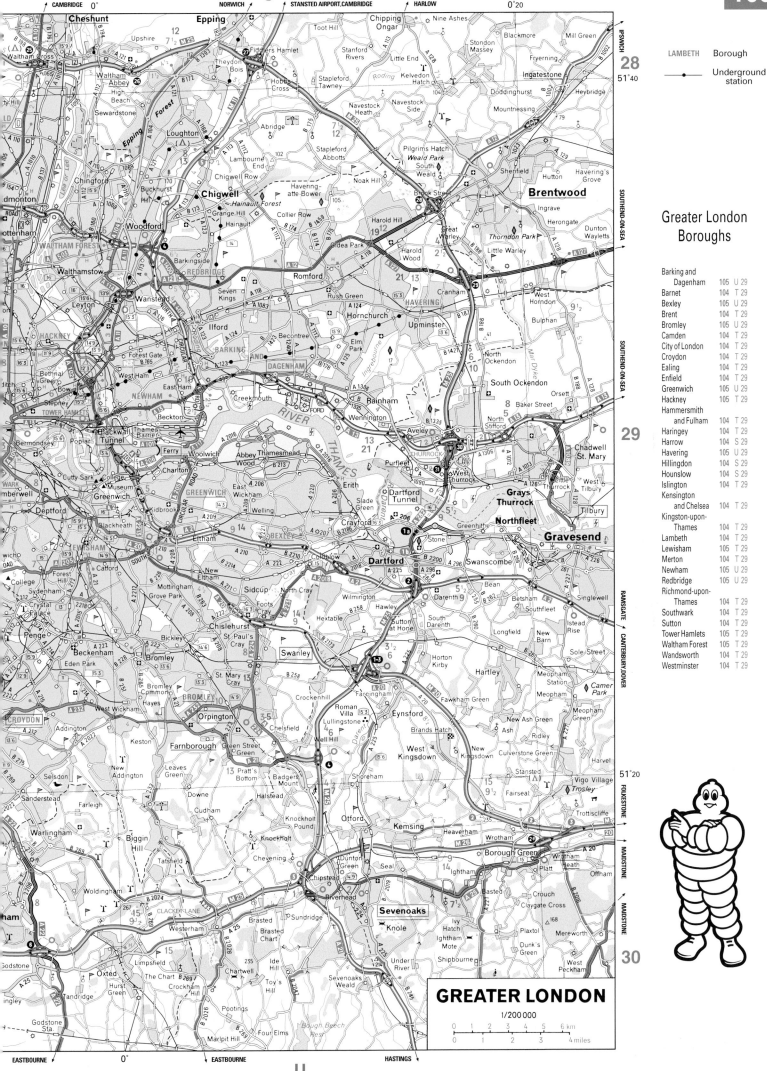

LAMBETH Borough
━━●━━ Underground station

Greater London Boroughs

GREATER LONDON

1/200 000

0	1	2	3	4	5	6 km
0		1		2		3	4 miles

Eochair   Allwedd

Bóithre		Ffyrdd
Mótarbhealach agus ionaid seirbhíse	KEELE	Traffordd a mannau gwasanaethu
Acomhail mótarbhealaigh : iomlán -teoranta		Cyfnewidfeyd : wedi'i chwblhau - cyfyngedig
Vimhreacha ceangail		Rhifau'r cyffyrdd
Carrbhealach dúbailte le saintréithe mótarbhealaigh		Ffordd ddeuol â nodweddion traffordd
Mórbhóthar :		Prif ffordd gysyltu :
carrshlí dhéach		ffordd ddeuol
4 lána - 2 leathanlána		4 lôn - 2 lôn lydan
2 lána - 2 chunglána		2 lôn - 2 lôn gul
Líonra réigiúnach bóithre :		Rhydwaith ffyrdd rhanbarthol :
carrshlí dhéach - 2 leathanlána		ffordd ddeuol - 2 lôn lydan
2 lána - 2 chunglána		2 lôn - 2 lôn gul
Bóithre eile : réidh - gan réitiú		Ffyrdd eraill - â wyneb - heb wyneb
Mótarbhealach, bóthar á dhéanamh		Traffordd, ffordd yn cael ei hadeiladu
(an dáta oscailte sceidealta, mas eol)		(Os cyfodi yr achos: dyddiad agor disgwyliedig)
Cosán - Cosán fadsli		Llwybr troed - Llwybr hir neu lwybr ceffyl
Timpeall - Bearnas is a airde (i méadair)	96	Cylchfan - Bwlch a'i uchder (mewn metrau)
Faid ar mhótarshlíte, ar bóithre :	14 10	Pellter ar ffyrdd a thraffyrdd
i mílte - i méadair	24 39	mewn miltiroedd - mewn kilometrau

Aicmiú oifigiúil bóithre		Dosbarthiad ffyrdd swyddogol
Mótarshlí	M 5	Trafford
GB: Priomhbhealach	A 38	GB: Prif ffordd
IRL: Priomhbóithre agus fobhóithre náisiúnta	N 5 N 59	IRL: Prif ffordd genedlaethol a ffordd eilradd
Bóithre eile	A 190 B 629 R561	Ffyrdd eraill
Ceann scríbe ar ghréasán bóithre priomha	YORK	Cyrchfan ar rwydwaith y prif ffrydd

Constaicí		Rhwystrau
Bóthar cúng le hionaid phasála (in Albain)		Yn yr Alban : ffordd gul â mannau pasio
Bóthar : toirmeasctha - faoi theorannú		Ffordd : gwaharddedig - cyfyngiadau arni
Bacainn dola - Bóthar aonslí		Rhwystr Toll - Unffordd
IRL: Bealach deacair nó baolach		IRL: Darn anodd neu beryglus o ffordd
Ar phríomhbóithre agus ar bhóithre réigiúnacha :		Ar brif ffyrdd a ffyrdd rhanbarthol :
Teorainneacha airde (faoi 15'6" IRL, faoi 16'6" GB)	11'9	Terfyn uchder (llai na 15'6" IRL, 16'6" GB)
Teorann Mheáchain (faoi 16 t)	10	Terfyn pwysau (llai na 16t)
Grádán (suas treo an gha)	1: 7-1 :5 +1: 5 →→→ 14-20% +20%	Graddiant (esgyn gyda'r saeth)

Iompar		Cludiant
Leithead caighdeánach - Staisiún paisinéirí		Lled safonol - Gorsaf deithwyr
Larnród thraein ghaile - Ráille tionsclaíoch		Rheilffordd ager - Trac diwydiannol
Crosaire comhréidh, iarnród ag dul		Croesfan rheilffordd :
faoi bhóthar, os cionn bóthair		rheilffordd yn croesi ffordd, o dan ffordd
Cáblashlí thionsclaíoch - Cathaoir cábla		Lein gêbl ddiwydiannol - Cadair esgyn
Longsheirbhísí (seirbhísí séasúracha : dearg)		Llongau ceir (Gwasanaethau tymhorol : mewn coch)
Bád - Árthach foluaineach		llong -llong hofran
Fartha (uas-ulach : tonnaí méadracha)	15	Fferi (llwyth uchaf : mewn tunelli metrig)
Coisithe agus lucht rothar		Teithwyr ar droed neu feic yn unig
Aerfort - Aerphairc		Maes awyr - Maes glanio

Bailte - Riarachán		Trefi - Gweinyddiaeth
Áiteanna a bhfuil plean diobh in Eolaí Michelin		Tref sydd â chynllun yn y Guide Michelin
Eolaí Dearg óstaíochta		Coch - Gwestai a Thai Bwyta
Eolaí Uaine turasóirachta		Gwyrrd - I Dwristiaid
Ionaid óstáiochta roghnaithe d'Eolaí Dearg Michelin	Ambleside	Tref sydd â chyfeiriadou yn y Michelin Red Guide
Teorainn Rialtais Áitiúil		Llywodraeth Leol
Teorainn na hAlban agus teorainn na Breataine Bige	-+-+-+-+-	Ffin Cymru, ffin yr Alban
Teorainn idirnáisiúnta - Custam	++++++++++-	Ffin ryngwladol - Tollau

Comharthaí Eile		Symbolau eraill
Crann teileachumarsáide - Teach Solais		Mast telathrebu - Goleudy
Stáisiún Giniúna - Cairéal - Mianach		Gorsaf bŵer - Chwarel - Mwyngloddio
Monarcha - Scaglann		Ffatri - Purfa
Ráschúrsa - Láthair champa, láthair charbhán		Rasio Ceffylau - Leoedd i wersylla
Timpeall rásaíochta - Cuan bád aeraíochta		Rasio Cerbydau - Harbwr cychod pleser
Machaire Gailf - Páirc Fhoraoise Náisiúnta, Páirc Náisiúnta		Cwrs golff - Parc Coedwig Cenedlaethol, Parc Cenedlaethol
IRL: Iascaireacht - Brú chumann na hóige - Ráschúrsa con		IRL: Pysgota - Hostel ieuenctid - Maes rasio milgwn
Siúlóid fhoraoise - Páirc thuaithe - Aill		Llwybr coedwig - Parc gwledig - Clogwyn

Amhairc : féach Eolaithe Michelin		Golygfeydd : gweler Llyfr Michelin
Bailte nó áiteanna inspéise, baill lóistín	Rye (▲) Elgol ◇	Trefi new fannau o ddiddordeb, mannau i aros
Foirgneamh Eaglasta - Fothrach		Adeilag eglwysig - Adfeilion
Caisleán, teach stairiúil		Castell, tŷ hanesyddol
Leacht meigiliteach - Pluais		Heneb fegalithig - Ogof
IRL: Dunfort - Cros Cheilteach - Cloigtheach		IRL: Caer - Croes Geltaidd - Twr crwn
Zú - Caomhnú nádúir, tearmannéan mara		Parc saffari, sŵ - Gwarchodfa natur
Gáirdíní - Amhairc éagsúla		Gerddi, parc - Golygfeydd amrywiol
Lánléargas - Cothrom Radhairc		Panorama - Golygfan
Bealach Aoibhinn		Ffordd dygfeydd

Comnarthaí ar phleanna bailte

Bóithre

	Mótarbhealach, carrbhealach dúbailte le saintréithe mótarbhea
	Priomh-thrébhealach
	Bóthar aonslí - Sráid : coisithe
	Sráid : neamhoiriúnach do thrácht, ach í stáit speisi
Piccadilly P	Sráid siopadóireacha - Carrchlós
B △	Bád fartha feithiclí - Droichead starrmhaidí

Ionaid inspéise
(Féach Eolaí Dearg Michelin)

	Ionad inspéise agus an príomhbhealach isteach
	Ionad inspéise adhartha
B	Ionad inspéise curtha in iúl le litir thagartha

Comharthaí Éagsúla

	Ionad eolais turasóireachta - Ospidéal
	Ardeaglais - Eaglais - Reilig
9	Gairdín, páirc, coill - Staidiam
	Galfchúrsa
	Galfchúrsa (sainrialacha do chuairteoiri)
	Foirgneamh poiblí curtha in iúl le litir thagartha :
C H	Oifigí rialtais áitiúil - Halla baile
POL M	Póitíní (ceanncheathrú) - Músaem
T U	Amharclann - Ollscoil, Coláiste
✉	Príomhoifig phoist le poste restante, teileafón
⊖ ●	Stáisiún traenach faoi thalamh

Londain

BRENT SOHO	Buirg - Limistéar
	Teorainn bhuirge - Teorainn limistéir

Symbolau ar gynlluniau'r trefi

Ffyrdd

	Trafford, ffordd ddeuol
	Prif ffordd drwodd
	Unffordd - Stryd : Cerddwr
	Stryd : Anaddas i draffig, cyfyngedig
Piccadilly P	Stryd siopa - Parc ceir
B △	Fferi geir - Pont liferi

Golygfeydd
(Gweler Llyfr Coch Michelin)

	Man diddorol a'r brif fynedfa iddo
	Lle diddorol o addoliad
B	Llythyren gyfeirio sy'n dynodi golygfa

Arwyddion amrywiol

	Canolfan croeso - Ysbyty
	Eglwys Gadeiriol - Eglwys - Mynwent
9	Gardd, parc, coedwig - Stadiwm
	Cwrs golff
	Cwrs golff (â chyfyngiadau i ymwelwyr)
	Adeilad cyhoeddus a ddynodir gan lythyren :
C H	Swyddfeydd llywodraeth leol - Neuadd y Dref
POL M	Yr Heddlu (pencadlys) - Amgueddfa
T U	Theatr - Prifysgol, Coleg
✉	Prif swyddfa bost gyda poste restante, ffôn
⊖ ●	Gorsaf danddaearol

Llundain

BRENT SOHO	Bwrdeistref - Ardal
	Ffin Bwrdeistref - Ffin yr Ardal

TOWN PLANS

Roads

Motorway - Dual carriageway with motorway characteristics
Main traffic artery
One - way street
Unsuitable for traffic, access subject to restrictions
Pedestrian street
Piccadilly Shopping street - Car park
Lever bridge - Car ferry

Sights
(See Michelin Red Guide)

Place of interest and its main entrance
Interesting place of worship
B Reference letter locating a sight

Various signs

Tourist Information Centre - Hospital
Cathedral - Church - Cemetery
Garden, park, wood - Stadium
Golf course
Golf course (with restrictions for visitors)

Public buildings located by letter :

C H County Council Offices - Town Hall
M T U Museum - Theatre - University, College
POL. Police (in large towns police headquarters)
Main post office with poste restante, telephone
Underground station

London

BRENT Borough
WEMBLEY Area
Borough boundary - Area boundary

LES PLANS

Voirie

Autoroute - Route à chaussées séparées de type autoroutier
Grand axe de circulation
Sens unique
Rue impraticable, réglementée
Rue piétonne
Piccadilly Rue commerçante - Parking
Pont mobile - Bac pour autos

Curiosités
(voir le Guide Rouge Michelin)

Bâtiment intéressant et entrée principale
Édifice religieux intéressant
B Lettre identifiant une curiosité

Signes divers

Information touristique - Hôpital
Cathédrale - Église - Cimetière
Jardin, parc, bois - Stade
Golf
Golf (réservé)

Bâtiment public repéré par une lettre :

C H Bureau de l'Administration du Comté - Hôtel de ville
M T U Musée - Théâtre - Université, grande école
POL. Police (commissariat central)
Bureau principal de poste restante, téléphone
Station de métro

Londres

BRENT Nom: d'arrondissement (borough)
WEMBLEY de quartier (area)
Limite de " borough" - d'" area "

STADTPLÄNE

Straßen

Autobahn - Schnellstraße mit getrennten Fahrbahnen
Hauptverkehrsstraße
Einbahnstraße
Gesperrte Straße, mit Verkehrsbeschränkungen
Fußgängerzone
Piccadilly Einkaufsstraße - Parkplatz
Bewegliche Brücke - Autofähre

Sehenswürdigkeiten
(siehe Roter Michelin - Hotelführer)

Sehenswertes Gebäude mit Haupteingang
Sehenswerter Sakralbau
B Referenzbuchstabe für eine Sehenswürdigkeit

Sonstige Zeichen

Informationsstelle - Krankenhaus
Kathedrale - Kirche - Friedhof
Garten, Park, Wäldchen - Stadion
Golfplatz
Golfplatz (Zutritt bedingt erlaubt)

Öffentliches Gebäude, durch einen Buchstaben gekennzeichnet :

C H Sitz der Grafschaftsverwaltung - Rathaus
M T U Museum - Theater - Universität, Hochschule
POL. Polizei (in größeren Städten Polizeipräsidium)
Hauptpostamt (potlagernde Sendungen), Telefon
U-Bahnstation

London

BRENT Name: des Verwaltungsbezirks (borough)
WEMBLEY des Stadtteils (area)
Grenze des "borough" - des "area"

PLATTEGRONDEN

Wegen

Autosnelweg - Weg met gescheiden rijbanen van het type autosnelweg
Hoofdverkeersweg
Eenrichtingsverkeer
Onbegaanbare straat, beperkt toegankelijk
Voetgangersgebied
Piccadilly Winkelstraat - Parkeerplaats
Beweegbare brug - Auto-veerpont

Bezienswaardigheden
(Zie die Rode Michelingids)

Interessant gebouw met hoofdingang
Interessant kerkelijk gebouw
B Letter die een bezienswaardigheid aangeeft

Overige tekens

Informatie voor toeristen - Ziekenhuis
Kathedraal,kerk - Begraafplaats
Tuin, park, bos - Stadion
Golfterrein
Golfterrein (beperkt toegankelijk voor bezoekers)

Openbaar gebouw, aangegeven met een letter :

C H Administratiekantoor van het graafschap - Stadhuis
M T U Museum - Schouwburg - Universiteit, hogeschool
POL. Politie (in grote steden, hoofdbureau)
Hoofdkantoor voor poste-restante, Telefoon
Metrostation

Londen

BRENT Naam: van het arrondissement (borough)
WEMBLEY van de wijk (area)
Grens van de "borough" - van de "area"

LE PIANTE

Viabilità

Autostrada - Strada a carriagate separate di tipo autostradale
Asse principale di circolazione
Senso unico
Via impraticabile, a circolazione regolamentata
Via pedonale
Piccadilly Via commerciale - Parcheggio
Ponte mobile - Traghetto per auto

Curiosità
(Vedere la Guida Rossa Michelin)

Edificio interessante ed entrata principale
Costruzione religiosa interessante
B Lettera identificante una meta o luogo d'interesse

Simboli vari

Ufficio informazioni turistiche
Cattedrale - Chiesa - Cimitero
Giardino, parco, bosco - Stadio
Golf
Golf riservato

Edificio pubblico indicato con lettera :

C H Sede dell'Amministrazione di Contea - Municipio
M T U Museo - Teatro - Università, grande scuola
POL. Polizia (Questura, nelle grandi città)
Ufficio centrale di fermo posta, telefono
Stazione della Metropolitana

Londra

BRENT Nome: del distretto amministrativo (borough)
WEMBLEY del quatiere (area)
Limite del "borough" - di "area"

PLÀNOS

Vías de circulación

Autopista - Autovía
Vía importante de circulacíon
Sentido único
Calle impraticable, de uso restringido
Calle peatonal
Piccadilly Calle comercial - Aparcamiento
Puente móvil - Barcaza para coches

Curiosidades
(Ver Guía Roja Michelin)

Edificio interesante y entrada principal
Edificio religioso interesante
B Letra que identifica una curiosidad

Signos diversos

Oficina de información de Turismo - Hospital
Catedral - Iglesia - Cementerio
Jardín, parque, bosque - Estadio
Golf
Golf (sólo para socios)

Edificio público localizado con letra :

C H Oficina de Administración del Condado - Ayuntamiento
M T U Museo - Teatro - Universidad, Escuela Superior
POL. Policía (en las grandes ciudades : Jefatura)
Oficina central de lista de correos - Teléfonos
Boca de metro

Londres

BRENT Nombre: del distrito (borough)
WEMBLEY del barrio (area)
Limite del "borough" - del "area"

Great Britain

A

Abbas Combe	8	M 30
Abberley	26	M 27
Abbey	13	X 30
Abbey Dore	17	L 28
Abbey Town	44	K 19
Abbeydale	35	P 23
Abbeystead	38	L 22
Abbots Bromley	35	O 25
Abbots Langley	20	S 28
Abbotsbury	8	M 32
Abbotsford House	50	L 17
Abbotskerswell	4	J 32
Aberaeron	24	H 27
Aberaman	16	J 28
Aberangell	25	I 25
Abercarn	16	K 29
Aberchirder	69	M 11
Abercynon	16	J 29
Aberdare / Aberdâr	16	J 28
Aberdaron	32	F 25
Aberdaugleddau / Milford Haven	14	E 28
Aberdeen	69	N 12
Aberdour	56	K 15
Aberdour Bay	69	N 10
Aberdovey / Aberdyfi	24	H 26
Abereiddy	14	E 28
Aberfeldy	61	I 14
Aberffraw	32	G 24
Aberford	40	P 22
Aberfoyle	55	G 15
Abergavenny / Y-Fenni	16	K 28
Abergele	33	J 24
Abergwaun / Fishguard	14	F 28
Abergwesyn	25	I 27
Abergwyngregyn	32	H 24
Abergynolwyn	25	I 26
Aberhonddu / Brecon	16	J 28
Aberlady	56	L 15
Aberlemno	63	L 13
Aberlour	68	K 11
Abermaw / Barmouth	24	H 25
Abernethy	56	K 15
Aberpennar / Mountain Ash	16	J 28
Aberporth	24	G 27
Abersoch	32	G 25
Abersychan	16	K 28
Abertawe / Swansea	15	I 29
Aberteifi / Cardigan	24	G 27
Abertillery	16	K 28
Aberuthven	56	J 15
Aberystwyth	24	H 26
Abingdon	19	Q 28
Abinger Common	11	S 30
Abington (South Lanarkshire)	49	I 17
Abington (Cambs.)	22	U 27
Aboyne	63	L 12
Abridge	20	U 29
Accrington	39	M 22
Achalader	60	F 14
Achanalt	66	F 11
Achaphubuil	60	E 13
Acharn	61	H 14
Achiltibuie	72	D 9
Achmelvich	72	E 9
Achmore	66	D 11
Achnasheen	66	E 11
Achnashellach Forest	66	E 11
Achray (Loch)	55	G 15
Achriesgill	72	F 8
Acklington	51	P 18
Ackworth	40	P 23
Acle	31	Y 26
Acomb	51	N 19
Acrise Place	13	X 30
Acton Turville	17	N 29
Adderbury	19	Q 27
Addingham	39	O 22
Addlestone	19	S 29
Adlington	38	M 23
Adlington Hall	35	N 24
Advie	68	J 11
Adwick-le-Street	40	Q 23
Ae (Forest of)	49	J 18
Affric (Glen)	66	F 12
Afon Dyfrdwy / Dee (River)	33	K 24
Ailort (Loch)	59	C 13
Ailsa Craig	42	E 18
Ainort (Loch)	65	B 12
Ainsdale	38	K 23
Ainwick	51	O 17
Aird (The)	67	G 11
Airgh na h-Airde (Loch)	70	Z 9
Airth	55	I 15
A La Ronde	4	J 32
Albourne	11	T 31
Albrighton	26	N 26
Albyn or Mor (Glen)	61	F 12
Alcester	27	O 27
Alconbury	29	T 26
Aldbourne	18	P 29
Aldbrough	41	T 22
Aldbury	19	S 28
Alde (River)	23	Y 27
Aldeburgh	23	Y 27
Aldenham	20	S 28
Alderley Edge	34	N 24
Alderney (Channel I.)	5	
Aldershot	10	R 30
Aldridge	27	O 26
Aldringham	23	Y 27
Aldwick	10	R 31
Alexandria	55	G 16
Alfold Crossways	10	S 30
Alford (Aberdeenshire)	69	L 12
Alford (Lincs.)	37	U 24
Alfreton	35	P 24
Alfrick	26	M 27
Alfriston	11	U 31
Aline (Loch)	59	C 14
Alkborough	41	S 22
Alkham	13	X 30
Allendale Town	45	N 19
Allerston	41	S 21
Alligin Shuas	66	D 11
Alloa	55	I 15
Alloway	48	G 17
All Stretton	26	L 26
Alltan Fhèarna (Loch an)	73	H 9
Almond (Glen)	61	I 14
Almondbank	62	J 14
Almondsbury	17	M 29
Alness	67	H 10
Alnmouth	51	P 17
Alnwick	51	O 17
Alpheton	22	W 27
Alphington	7	J 31
Alpraham	34	M 24
Alrewas	27	O 25
Alsager	34	N 24
Alsh (Loch)	66	D 12
Alston	45	M 19
Alswear	7	I 31
Altarnun	3	G 32
Altnacealgach	72	F 9
Altnaharra	72	G 9
Alton (Hants.)	10	R 30
Alton (Staffs.)	35	O 25
Alton Towers	35	O 25
Altrincham	34	M 23
Alum Bay	9	P 31
Alva	55	I 15
Alvechurch	27	O 26
Alvediston	9	N 30
Alves	68	J 11
Alvie	67	I 12
Alyth	62	K 14
Amberley	10	S 31
Amble	51	P 18
Amblecote	27	N 26
Ambleside	44	L 20
Amersham	19	S 29
Amesbury	9	O 30
Amlwch	32	G 23
Ammanford / Rhydaman	15	I 28
Ampleforth	40	Q 21
Ampthill	28	S 27
Amroth	14	G 28
An Riabhachan	66	E 11
An Socach	62	J 13
An Teallach	66	E 10
Ancroft	51	O 16
Andover	9	P 30
Andoversford	18	O 28
Andreas	42	G 20
Angle	14	E 28
Anglesey (Isle of)	32	F 24
Anglesey Abbey	22	U 27
Angmering	11	S 31
Annan	49	K 19
Annan (River)	49	J 17
Annat	66	D 11
Annat Bay	72	E 10
Annbank Station	48	G 17
Anne Hathaway's Cottage	27	O 27
Annfield Plain	46	O 19
Anstey	28	Q 25
Anston	36	Q 23
Anstruther	57	L 15
Antony House	3	H 32
Appin	60	E 14
Appleby	45	M 20
Appleby Magna	27	P 25
Appledore (Devon)	6	H 30
Appledore (Kent)	12	W 30
Appleford	19	Q 29
Aran Fawddwy	33	I 25
Arber Low	35	O 24
Arberth / Narberth	14	F 28
Arbirlot	63	M 14
Arbroath	63	M 14
Arbury Hall	27	P 26
Archiestown	68	K 11
Ard (Loch)	55	G 15
Ardarroch	66	D 11
Ardcharnich	66	E 10
Ardechive	60	E 13
Ardeonaig	61	H 14
Ardersier	67	H 11
Ardfern	54	D 15
Ardgay	73	G 10
Ardgour	60	D 14
Ardingly	11	T 30
Ardivachar	64	X 11
Ardleigh	22	W 28
Ardlui	54	F 15
Ardlussa	54	D 15
Ardmore Point	65	A 11
Ardnamurchan	59	B 13
Ardnave Point	52	B 16
Ardrishaig	54	D 15
Ardrossan	48	F 17
Ardvasar	65	C 12
Ardverikie Forest	61	G 13
Argyll	54	D 15
Argyll Forest Park	54	F 15
Arienas (Loch)	59	C 14
Arinagour	59	A 14
Arisaig	59	C 13
Arivruaich	70	Z 9
Arkaig (Loch)	60	E 13
Arkengarthdale	46	O 20
Arklet (Loch)	55	G 15
Arlingham	17	M 28
Arlington Court	6	I 30
Armadale (West Lothian)	56	I 16
Armadale Bay	65	C 12
Armadale (Highland)	73	H 8
Armitage	27	O 25
Armthorpe	40	Q 23
Arncliffe	39	N 21
Arncott	19	Q 28
Arnesby	28	Q 26
Arnisdale	66	D 12
Arnol	70	A 8
Arnold	36	Q 25
Arnside	38	L 21
Aros	59	B 14
Arran (Isle of)	53	E 17
Arreton	10	Q 31
Arrochar	54	F 15
Arundel	10	S 31
Ascot	19	R 29
Ascott House	19	R 28
Ascrib Islands	65	A 11
Asfordby	36	R 25
Ash (Kent)	13	X 30
Ash (Surrey)	10	R 30
Ash Mill	7	I 31
Ashbourne	35	O 24
Ashburton	4	I 32
Ashbury	18	P 29
Ashby de la Zouch	27	P 25
Ashcott	8	L 30
Ashdown (Derbs.)	35	O 24
Ashford (Kent)	12	W 30
Ashford (Surrey)	20	S 29
Ashie (Loch)	67	H 11
Ashingdon	21	W 29
Ashington (Northumb.)	51	P 18
Ashington (West Sussex)	11	S 31
Ashover	35	P 24
Ashperton	26	M 27
Ashtead	20	T 30
Ashton-in-Makerfield	34	M 23
Ashton Keynes	18	O 29
Ashton-under-Lyne	39	N 23
Ashton-upon-Mersey	34	M 23
Ashwell	29	T 27
Askam in Furness	38	K 21
Askern	40	Q 23
Askernish	64	X 12
Askerswell	8	L 31
Askham	45	L 20
Askrigg	45	N 21
Aspatria	44	K 19
Aspley Guise	28	S 27
Assynt (Loch)	72	E 9
Aston	35	Q 23
Aston Clinton	19	R 28
Aston Rowant	19	R 28
Aston Tirrold	19	Q 29
Astwood Bank	27	O 27
Atcham	26	L 25
Athelhampton Hall	9	N 31
Athelney	8	L 30
Atherington	6	H 31
Atherstone	27	P 26
Atherton	39	M 23
Atholl (Forest of)	61	H 13
Attleborough	30	X 26
Auchenblae	63	M 13
Auchencairn	43	I 19
Auchinleck	48	H 17
Auchleven	69	M 12
Auchnagatt	69	N 11
Auchterarder	56	I 15
Auchterderran	56	K 15
Auchterhouse	62	K 14
Auchtermuchty	56	K 15
Auchtertyre	66	D 12
Auckengill	74	K 8
Audenshaw	35	N 23
Audlem	34	M 25
Audley	34	N 24
Audley End	22	U 27
Aughton (Lancs.)	38	L 23
Auldearn	67	I 11
Auldhouse	55	H 16
Aultbea	71	D 10
Aust	17	M 29
Austwick	39	M 21
Avebury	18	O 29
Aveley	20	U 29
Avening	18	N 28
Aveton Gifford	4	I 33
Aviemore	67	I 12
Avoch	67	H 11
Avon (Glen)	68	J 12
Avon (River)	9	O 31
Avon (River) (Wilts.)	9	O 31
Avon (River) (R. Severn)	28	Q 26
Avonbridge	55	I 16
Avonmouth	17	L 29
Awe (Loch)	54	E 15
Awliscombe	7	K 31
Awre	17	M 28
Axbridge	8	L 30
Axminster	8	L 31
Axmouth	7	K 31
Aylesbury	19	R 28
Aylesford	12	V 30
Aylesham	13	X 30
Aylsham	31	X 25
Aymestrey	26	L 27
Aynho	19	Q 28
Ayr	48	G 17
Aysgarth	46	O 21
Ayton	47	S 21

B

Bà (Loch)	59	C 14
Babbacombe Bay	4	J 32
Backaland	74	L 6
Backwater Reservoir	62	K 13
Baconsthorpe	31	X 25
Bacton	31	Y 25
Bacup	39	N 22
Bad a' Ghaill (Loch)	72	E 9
Bad an Sgalaig (Loch)	66	D 10
Badachro	65	C 10
Badanloch (Loch)	73	H 9
Badcaul	72	D 10
Baddidarach	72	E 9
Badenoch	61	H 13
Badluarach	72	D 10
Badminton	17	N 29
Badrallach	72	E 10
Bae Colwyn / Colwyn Bay	33	I 24
Bagh nam Faoileann	64	Y 11
Bagillt	33	K 24
Bagshot	19	R 29
Baile Mór	59	A 15
Bainbridge	45	N 21
Bainton	41	S 22
Bakewell	35	O 24
Bala	33	J 25
Balallan	70	A 9
Balbeggie	62	J 14
Balblair	67	H 10
Balcary Point	43	I 19
Balchrick	72	E 8
Balcombe	11	T 30
Balderton	36	R 24
Baldock	20	T 28
Balemartine	58	Z 14
Balephetrish Bay	58	Z 14
Balephuil Bay	58	Z 14
Baleshare	64	X 11
Balfour	74	L 6
Balfron	55	H 15
Balintore	73	I 10
Balivanich	64	X 11
Ballabeg	42	F 21
Ballachulish	60	E 13
Ballantrae	48	E 18
Ballasalla	42	G 21
Ballater	62	K 12
Ballaugh	42	G 21
Ballingry	56	K 15
Balmaha	55	G 15
Balmedie	69	N 12
Balmoral Castle	62	K 12
Balmullo	56	L 14
Balnakeil Bay	72	F 8
Balvicar	54	D 15

ABERDEEN

Bon Accord Centre	Y
Broad Street	Y 6
Castle Street	Y 7
College Street	Z 9
Craigie Loanings	Y 12
Denburn Road	Y 14
East North Street	Y 16
George Street	Y
Great Southern Road	Z 18
Guild Street	Z 19
Justice Street	Y 21
Millburn Street	Z 23
Rosemount Terrace	Y 25
Rosemount Viaduct	Y 26
St. Andrew Street	Y 28
St Nicholas Centre	Y 29
St Nicholas Street	YZ 30
School Hill	YZ 32
South Esplanade West	Z 33
South Mount Street	Y 34
Springbank Terrace	Z 35
Spring Garden	Y 36
Trinity Centre	Z
Trinity Quay	Z 37
Union Street	Z
Union Terrace	Z 39
Upperkirkgate	Y 40
Victoria Street	Z 42
Waverley Place	Z 43
Wellington Place	Z 45
Wellington Road	Z 47
Woolmanhill	Y 48

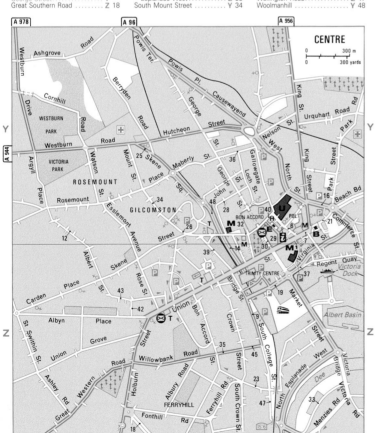

BATH
CENTRE

...mbury .... BX 2
...gyle Street .... BV 3
...ennett Street .... AV 4
...idge Street .... BVX 6
...oad Quay .... BX 7
...hapel Row .... AVX 9
...harles Street .... AX 10
...harlotte Street .... AV 12
...heap Street .... BX 13
...hurchill Bridge .... BX 14

Circus Place .... AV 16
Gay Street .... AV
Grand Parade .... BX 17
Great Stanhope Street. .... BX 18
Green Street .... BV 21
Guinea Lane .... BV 23
Henry Street .... BX 24
Lower Borough Walls .... BX 26
Milsom Street .... BV
Monmouth Place .... AVX 28
Monmouth Street .... AX 30
New Bond Street .... BV 31
New Orchard Street. .... BX 32
Nile Street .... AV 34

Northgate Street .... BVX 35
Old Bond Street .... BX 36
Orange Grove .... BX 38
Pierrepont Street .... BX 39
Quiet Street .... BV 41
Russell Street .... AV 42
Southgate Street .... BX 43
Stanley Road .... BX 45
Terrace Walk .... BX 46
Upper Borough Walls .... BX 48
Westgate Buildings .... AX 49
Westgate Street .... ABX 50
Wood Street .... AV 52
York Street .... BX 53

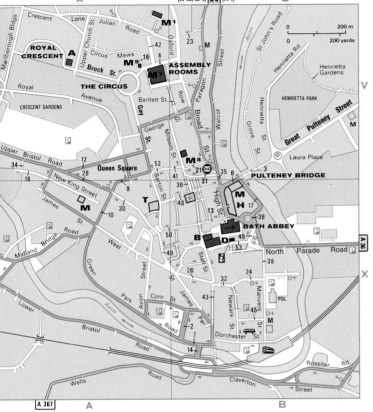

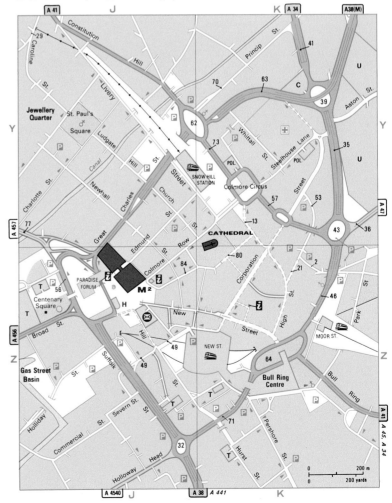

BIRMINGHAM
CENTRE

Albert St. .... KZ 2
Bull Ring Centre .... KZ
Bull St. .... KY 13
Corporation Street .... KYZ
Dale End .... KZ 21
Hall St. .... JY 29
Holloway Circus. .... JZ 32
James Watt Queensway ...... KY 35

Jennen's Rd. .... KY 36
Lancaster Circus .... KY 39
Lancaster St. .... KY 41
Masshouse Circus .... KY 43
Moor St.
  Queensway .... KZ 46
Navigation St. .... JZ 49
New St. .... JKZ
Newton St. .... KY 52
Paradise Circus .... JZ 56
Paradise Forum
  Shopping Centre .... JZ

Priory Queensway .... KY 57
St Chads Circus .... JKY 62
St Chads Ringway .... KY 63
St Martin's Circus .... KZ 64
Shadwell St. .... KY 70
Smallbrook
  Queensway .... KZ 71
Snow Hill
  Queensway .... KY 73
Summer Row .... JY 77
Temple Row .... KZ 80
Waterloo St. .... JZ 84

Bamburgh Castle	51 O 17	Barnby Moor		Bass Rock	57 M 15	Bedwas	16 K 29
Bampton (Cumbria)	45 L 20	(Notts.)	36 Q 23	Bassenthwaite	44 K 19	Bedworth	27 P 26
Bampton (Devon)	7 J 31	Barnet (London		Bassingham	36 S 24	Bee (Loch)	64 X 11
Bampton (Oxon.)	18 P 28	Borough)	20 T 29	Bath	17 M 29	Beeston	36 Q 25
Banavie	60 E 13	Barnetby-le-Wold	41 S 23	Bathgate	56 J 16	Beeswing	49 I 18
Banbury	27 P 27	Barnhill	68 J 11	Batley	39 P 22	Beinn a' Ghlò	62 I 13
Banchory	69 M 12	Barnoldswick	39 N 22	Battle	12 V 31	Beinn a'	
Banff	69 M 10	Barnsley	40 P 23	Baumber	37 T 24	Mheadhoin	
Bangor	32 H 24	Barnstaple	6 H 30	Bawdeswell	30 X 25	(Loch)	66 F 12
Bankfoot	62 J 14	Barr	48 F 18	Bawdsey	23 Y 27	Beinn Dearg	
Bankhead	69 N 12	Barra	58 X 13	Bawtry	36 Q 23	(Perthshire and	
Banks	38 L 22	Barra (Sound of)	64 X 12	Bayble	71 B 9	Kinross)	61 I 13
Bannockburn	55 I 15	Barra Head	58 X 13	Bayhead	64 X 11	Beinn Dearg	
Banstead	20 T 30	Barrhead	55 G 16	Beachy Head	11 U 31	(Highland)	66 F 10
Banwell	17 L 30	Barrhill	48 F 18	Beacon (The)	2 E 33	Beinn Heasgarnich	61 G 14
Bapchild	12 W 30	Barri / Barry	16 K 29	Beaconsfield	19 S 29	Beinn Ime	54 F 15
Bar Hill	29 U 27	Barrington Court	8 L 31	Beadnell Bay	51 P 17	Beith	55 G 16
Barbaraville	67 H 10	Barrisdale Bay	60 D 12	Beaford	6 H 31	Belbroughton	27 N 26
Barbon	45 M 21	Barrow	22 V 27	Beaminster	8 L 31	Belford	51 O 17
Barcombe Cross	11 U 31	Barrow-in-Furness	38 K 21	Beamish Hall	46 P 19	Bellingham	50 N 18
Bardney	37 T 24	Barrow-upon-		Bearsden	55 G 16	Bellshill	55 H 16
Bardsea	38 K 21	Humber	41 S 22	Bearsted	12 V 30	Belmont	75 R 1
Bardsey Island	32 F 25	Barrow-upon-Soar	28 Q 25	Beattock	49 J 18	Belnahua	52 C 15
Barfreston	13 X 30	Barrowby	36 R 25	Beauchief	35 P 24	Belper	35 P 24
Bargoed	16 K 28	Barrowford	39 N 22	Beaulieu	9 P 31	Belsay	51 O 18
Barham	13 X 30	Barry (Angus)	63 L 14	Beauly	67 G 11	Belton (North Lincs.)	40 R 23
Barking and		Barry / Barri (Vale of		Beauly Firth	67 G 11	Belton House	
Dagenham		Glamorgan)	16 K 29	Beaumaris	32 H 24	(Lincs.)	36 S 25
(London Borough)	20 U 29	Bartestree	26 M 27	Beaupré Castle	16 J 29	Belton (Norfolk)	31 Y 26
Barkston	36 S 25	Barton (Lancs.)	38 L 22	Bebington	34 L 23	Belvoir	36 R 25
Barkway	20 U 28	Barton (Staffs.)	27 O 25	Beccles	31 Y 26	Bembridge	10 Q 31
Barkwith	37 T 24	Barton in the Clay	20 S 28	Beckingham	36 R 23	Bempton	41 T 21
Barlaston	35 N 25	Barton Mills	30 V 26	Beckington	8 N 30	Ben Alder	61 G 13
Barlborough	36 Q 24	Barton-on-Sea	9 P 31	Beckton	20 U 29	Ben Armine	
Barley	29 U 27	Barton-upon-		Bedale	46 P 21	Forest	73 H 9
Barmouth /		Humber	41 S 22	Beddgelert	32 H 24	Ben Chonzie	61 I 14
Abermaw	24 H 25	Barvas	70 A 8	Beddingham	11 U 31	Ben Cruachan	60 E 14
Barmouth Bay	24 H 25	Barwell	27 P 26	Bedford	28 S 27	Ben-damph Forest	66 D 11
Barmston	41 T 21	Barwick-in-Elmet	40 P 22	Bedford Levels	29 T 26	
Barnard Castle	46 O 20	Baschurch	34 L 25	Bedfordshire		
Barnby Moor		Basildon (Berks.)	19 Q 29	(County)	28 S 27	
(East Riding of		Basildon (Essex)	21 V 29	Bedgebury		
Yorks.)	40 R 22	Basingstoke	10 Q 30	Pinetum	12 V 30	
Barnby Dun	40 Q 23	Baslow	35 P 24	Bedlington	51 P 18	

Ben Hope	72 G 8	Berry Hill	17 M 28	
Ben Klibreck	72 G 9	Berrynarbor	6 H 30	
Ben Lawers	61 H 14	Bervie Bay	63 N 13	
Ben Ledi	55 H 15	Berwick-		
Ben Lomond	55 G 15	upon-Tweed	57 O 16	
Ben Loyal	73 G 8	Berwyn	33 J 25	
Ben Macdui	62 I 12	Bethersden	12 W 30	
Ben More (Argyll		Bethesda	32 H 24	
and Bute)	59 C 14	Bettyhill	73 H 8	
Ben More (Stirling)	55 G 14	Betws-y-Coed	33 I 24	
Ben More Assynt	72 F 9	Beverley	41 S 22	
Ben Nevis	60 E 13	Bewcastle	50 L 18	
Ben Starav	60 E 14	Bewdley	26 N 26	
Ben Vorlich	55 H 14	Bexhill	12 V 31	
Ben Wyvis	67 G 10	Bexley (London		
Benbecula	64 X 11	Borough)	20 U 29	
Benderloch	60 E 14	Beyton	22 W 27	
Benenden	12 V 30	Bhaid-Luachraich		
Benfleet	21 V 29	(Loch)	71 D 10	
Benigton	37 U 25	Bhealaich (Loch a')	72 G 9	
Benllech	32 H 24	Bhraoin (Loch a')	66 E 10	
Benmore Lodge	72 F 9	Bhrollum (Loch)	70 A 10	
Benson	19 Q 29	Bibury	18 O 28	
Bentley	40 Q 23	Bicester	19 Q 28	
Benwick	29 T 26	Bickington	4 I 32	
Beoraid (Loch)	60 D 13	Bickleigh	7 J 31	
Bere Alston	3 H 32	Bicton gardens	7 K 31	
Bere Regis	8 N 31	Biddenden	12 V 30	
Berkeley	17 M 28	Biddestone	17 N 29	
Berkhamsted	19 S 28	Biddulph	35 N 24	
Berneray (near		Bidean nam Bian	60 E 14	
Barra)	58 X 13	Bideford	6 H 30	
Berneray (near		Bidford	27 O 27	
North Uist)	64 Y 10	Bieldside	69 N 12	
Bernisdale	65 B 11	Bierton	19 R 28	
Berriew	25 K 26	Bigbury	4 I 33	
Berrington Hall	26 L 27	Bigbury-on-Sea	4 I 33	
Berrow	8 K 30	Biggar	49 J 17	
Berry Head	4 J 32	Biggleswade	29 T 27	

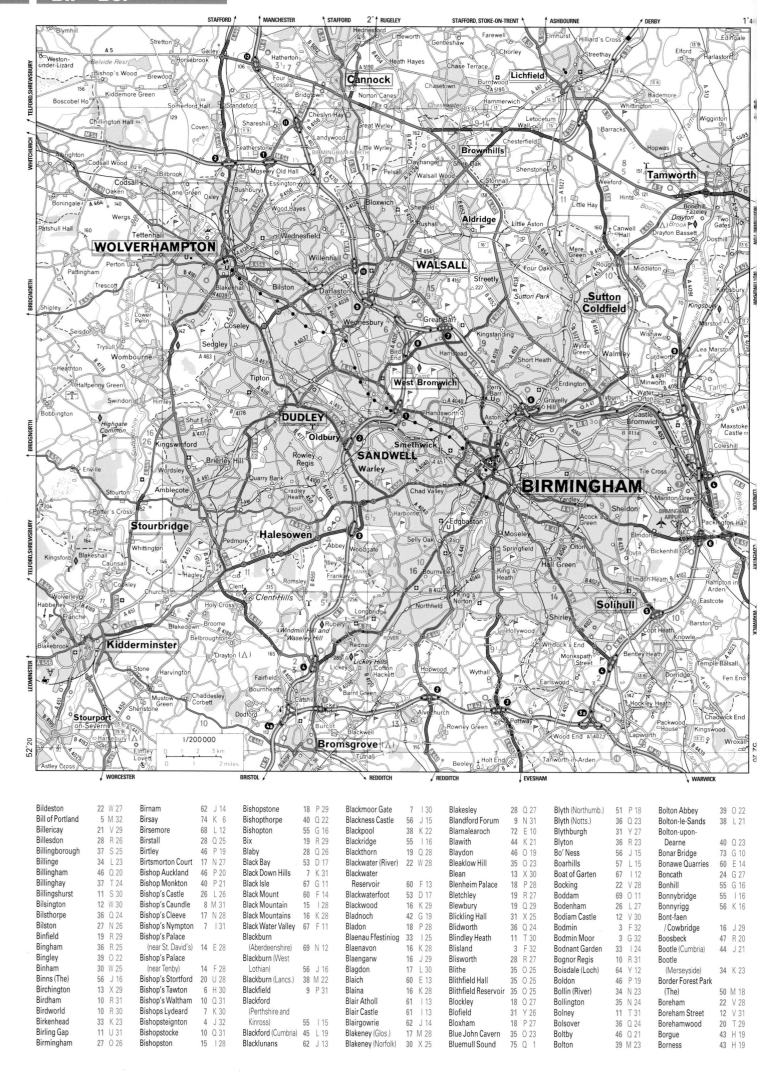

Bildeston	22 W 27	Birnam	62 J 14	Bishopstone	18 P 29	Blackmoor Gate	7 I 30	Blakesley	28 Q 27	Blyth (Northumb.)	51 P 18	Bolton Abbey	39 O 22
Bill of Portland	5 M 32	Birsay	74 K 6	Bishopthorpe	40 Q 22	Blackness Castle	56 J 15	Blandford Forum	9 N 31	Blyth (Notts.)	36 Q 23	Bolton-le-Sands	38 L 21
Billericay	21 V 29	Birsemore	68 L 12	Bishopton	55 G 16	Blackpool	38 K 22	Blarnalearoch	72 E 10	Blythburgh	31 Y 27	Bolton-upon-	
Billesdon	28 R 26	Birstall	28 Q 25	Bix	19 R 29	Blackridge	55 I 16	Blawith	44 K 21	Blyton	36 R 23	Dearne	40 Q 23
Billingborough	37 S 25	Birtley	46 P 19	Blaby	28 Q 26	Blackthorn	19 Q 28	Blaydon	46 O 19	Bo' Ness	56 J 15	Bonar Bridge	73 G 10
Billinge	34 L 23	Birtsmorton Court	17 N 27	Black Bay	53 D 17	Blackwater (River)	22 W 28	Bleaklow Hill	35 O 23	Boarhills	57 L 15	Bonawe Quarries	60 E 14
Billingham	46 Q 20	Bishop Auckland	46 P 20	Black Down Hills	7 K 31	Blackwater		Blean	13 X 30	Boat of Garten	67 I 12	Boncath	24 G 27
Billinghay	37 T 24	Bishop Monkton	40 P 21	Black Isle	67 G 11	Reservoir	60 F 13	Blenheim Palace	18 P 28	Bocking	22 V 28	Bonhill	55 G 16
Billingshurst	11 S 30	Bishop's Castle	26 L 26	Black Mount	60 F 14	Blackwaterfoot	53 D 17	Bletchley	19 R 27	Boddam	69 O 11	Bonnybridge	55 I 16
Bilsington	12 W 30	Bishop's Caundle	8 M 31	Black Mountain	15 I 28	Blackwood	16 K 29	Blewbury	19 Q 29	Bodenham	26 L 27	Bonnyrigg	56 K 16
Bilsthorpe	36 Q 24	Bishop's Cleeve	17 N 28	Black Mountains	16 K 28	Bladnoch	42 G 19	Blickling Hall	31 X 25	Bodiam Castle	12 V 30	Bont-faen	
Bilston	27 N 26	Bishop's Nympton	7 I 31	Black Water Valley	67 F 11	Bladon	18 P 28	Blidworth	36 Q 24	Bodmin	3 F 32	/ Cowbridge	16 J 29
Binfield	19 R 29	Bishop's Palace		Blackburn		Blaenau Ffestiniog	33 I 25	Blindley Heath	11 T 30	Bodmin Moor	3 G 32	Boosbeck	47 R 20
Bingham	36 R 25	(near St. David's)	14 E 28	(Aberdeenshire)	69 N 12	Blaenavon	16 K 28	Blisland	3 F 32	Bodnant Garden	33 I 24	Bootle (Cumbria)	44 J 21
Bingley	39 O 22	Bishop's Palace		Blackburn (West		Blaengarw	16 J 29	Blisworth	28 R 27	Bognor Regis	10 R 31	Bootle	
Binham	30 W 25	(near Tenby)	14 F 28	Lothian)	56 J 16	Blagdon	17 L 30	Blithe	35 O 25	Boisdale (Loch)	64 Y 12	(Merseyside)	34 K 23
Binns (The)	56 J 16	Bishop's Stortford	20 U 28	Blackburn (Lancs.)	38 M 22	Blaich	60 E 13	Blithfield Hall	35 O 25	Boldon	46 P 19	Border Forest Park	
Birchington	13 X 29	Bishop's Tawton	6 H 30	Blackfield	9 P 31	Blaina	16 K 28	Blithfield Reservoir	35 O 25	Bollin (River)	34 N 23	(The)	50 M 18
Birdham	10 R 31	Bishop's Waltham	10 Q 31	Blackford		Blair Atholl	61 I 13	Blockley	18 O 27	Bollington	35 N 24	Boreham	22 V 28
Birdworld	10 R 30	Bishops Lydeard	7 K 30	(Perthshire and		Blair Castle	61 I 13	Blofield	31 Y 26	Bolney	11 T 31	Boreham Street	12 V 31
Birkenhead	33 K 23	Bishopsteignton	4 J 32	Kinross)	55 I 15	Blairgowrie	62 J 14	Bloxham	18 P 27	Bolsover	36 Q 24	Borehamwood	20 T 29
Birling Gap	11 U 31	Bishopstocke	10 Q 31	Blackford (Cumbria)	45 L 19	Blakeney (Glos.)	17 M 28	Blue John Cavern	35 O 23	Boltby	46 Q 21	Borgue	43 H 19
Birmingham	27 O 26	Bishopston	15 I 28	Blacklunans	62 J 13	Blakeney (Norfolk)	30 X 25	Bluemull Sound	75 Q 1	Bolton	39 M 23	Borness	43 H 19

BLACKPOOL
CENTRE

Abingdon Street . . . . AY 2
Adelaide Street . . . . AY 3
Caunce Street . . . . AY 7
Church Street
Clifton Street . . . . AY 12
Cookson Street . . . . AY 14
Deansgate . . . . AY 15
George Street . . . . AY 17
Grosvenor Street . . . . AY 21
High Street . . . . AY 22
King Street . . . . AY 23
Lark Hill Street . . . . AY 24
New Bonny Street . . . . AY 25
Pleasant Street . . . . AY 27
South King St . . . . AY 35
Talbot Street . . . . AY 39
Topping Street . . . . AY 40

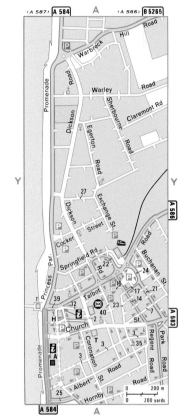

Bosbury	26	M 27	Brailes	27	P 27
Boscastle	6	F 31	Brailsford	35	P 25
Boscombe	9	O 31	Braintree	22	V 28
Bosham	10	R 31	Braishfield	9	P 30
Bosherston	14	F 29	Braithwell	36	Q 23
Boston	37	T 25	Bramcote	36	Q 25
Boston Spa	40	P 22	Bramfield	31	Y 27
Botesdale	30	W 26	Bramford	23	X 27
Bothel	44	K 19	Bramhall	35	N 23
Bothwell	55	H 16	Bramham	40	P 22
Botley	10	Q 31	Bramhope	39	P 22
Bottesford	36	R 25	Bramley (South		
Bottisham	22	U 27	Yorks.)	36	Q 23
Boughton	36	Q 24	Bramley (Surrey)	10	S 30
Boughton House	28	R 26	Brampton (Cambs.)	29	T 27
Boughton Street	12	W 30	Brampton (Cumbria)	45	L 19
Boultham	36	S 24	Brampton		
Bourne	37	S 25	(Rotherham.)	40	P 23
Bournemouth	9	O 31	Brampton (Suffolk)	31	Y 26
Bourton	8	N 30	Brancaster	30	V 25
Bourton-			Branderburgh	68	K 10
on-the-Water	18	O 28	Brandesburton	41	T 22
Bovey Tracey	4	I 32	Brandon (Durham)	46	P 19
Bovingdon	19	S 28	Brandon (Suffolk)	30	V 26
Bowerchalke	9	O 30	Branscombe	7	K 31
Bowes	46	N 20	Bransgore	9	O 31
Bowhill	50	L 17	Branston	36	S 24
Bowland			Bratton Fleming	6	I 30
(Forest of)	38	M 22	Braughing	20	U 28
Bowmore	52	B 16	Braunston	28	R 26
Bowness-on-			Braunstone	28	Q 27
Windermere	45	L 20	Braunton	6	H 30
Bowness-			Bray-on-Thames	19	R 29
on-Solway	44	K 19	Bray Shop	3	G 32
Bowood House	18	N 29	Brayton	40	Q 22
Box	17	N 29	Breadalbane	61	G 14
Box Hill	11	T 30	Bream	17	M 28
Boxford	22	W 27	Breamore House	9	O 31
Boxworth	29	T 27	Breasclete	70	Z 9
Brabourne Lees	13	W 30	Breaston	35	Q 25
Bracadale (Loch)	65	A 12	Brechin	63	M 13
Bracebridge Heath	36	S 24	Breckland	30	V 26
Brackley	28	Q 27	Brecon /		
Bracknell	19	R 29	Aberhonddu	16	J 28
Braco	55	I 15	Brecon Beacons		
Bradan Resr (Loch)	48	G 18	National Park	16	J 28
Bradfield	19	Q 29	Bredbury	35	N 23
Bradford	39	O 22	Brede	12	V 31
Bradford Abbas	8	M 31	Bredenbury	26	M 27
Bradford-on-Avon	17	N 29	Bredon	27	N 27
Brading	10	Q 31	Bredwardine	26	L 27
Bradwell	35	O 24	Brenchley	12	V 30
Bradwell-on-Sea	22	W 28	Brendon Hills	7	J 30
Bradworthy	6	G 31	Brenig Reservoir	33	J 24
Brae	75	P 2	Brent (London		
Brae Roy Lodge	61	F 13	Borough)	20	T 29
Braemar	62	J 12	Brent Knoll	8	L 30
Braeriach	62	I 12	Brent Pelham	20	U 28
Braich y Pwll	32	F 25	Brentwood	20	U 29
Bràigh Mór	70	Y 9	Brenzett	12	W 30

Borough			Borrowash	35	P 25
Green	20	U 30	Borth	24	H 26
Boroughbridge	40	P 21	Borve (Barra Isle)	58	X 13
Borrobol Forest	73	H 9	Borve (Isle of Lewis)	71	A 8

BRADFORD
CENTRE

Bank Street	AZ 4		Drewton Road	AZ 19
Broadway	BZ 8		East Parade	BZ 22
Canal Road	BZ 10		Harris Street	BZ 23
Charles Street	BZ 13		Ivegate	AZ 25
Cheapside	BZ 14		Kirkgate Centre	AZ 26
Darley Street	AZ 18		Market Street	BZ 28
			Otley Road	BZ 31
			Peckover Street	BZ 32
			Prince's Way	BZ 33
			Stott Hill	BZ 39

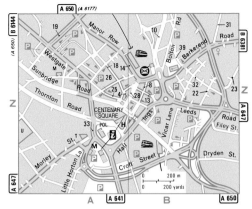

BOURNEMOUTH
CENTRE

Branksome Wood Road	CY 9	St. Michael's Road	CZ 51
Commercial Road	CY 13	St. Paul's Road	EY 52
Durley Road	CZ 17	St. Peter's Road	DY 53
Exeter Road	CDZ 20	St. Stephen's Road	CY 55
Fir Vale Road	DY 23	St. Swithuns Road South	EY 56
Gervis Place	DY 24	St. Swithins Road South	EY 56
Hinton Road	DZ 27	Square (The)	CY 63
Lansdowne (The)	DY 28	Suffolk Road	CY 64
Lansdowne Road	DY 30	Triangle (The)	CY 67
Madeira Road	DY 34	Upper Hinton Road	DZ 68
Manor Road	EY 35	West Cliff Promenade	CZ 71
Meyrick Road	EYZ 36	Westover Road	DZ 75
Old Christchurch			
Road	DY		
Post Office Road	CY 43		
Priory Road	CZ 45		
Richmond Hill	CY 47		
Russell Cotes Road	DZ 49		

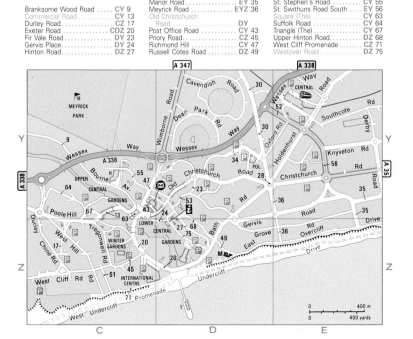

Bressay	75	Q 3	Broadwey	8	M 32	Brynbuga / Usk	17	L 28
Bretherton	38	L 22	Broadwindsor	8	L 31	Bryncethin	16	J 29
Brewlands Bridge	62	K 13	Broch of Gurness	49	J 17	Bryn-Henllan	14	F 27
Brewood	27	N 25	Brockenhurst	9	P 31	Brynmawr	16	K 28
Bride	42	G 20	Brockley	17	L 29	Bubwith	40	R 22
Bridestowe	6	H 31	Brockworth	18	N 28	Buchlyvie	55	H 15
Bridge	13	X 30	Brodick	53	E 17	Buckden (Cambs.)	29	T 27
Bridge of Allan	55	I 15	Brodick Castle	53	E 17	Buckden (North		
Bridge of Avon	68	J 11	Brodick Bay	53	E 17	Yorks.)	39	N 21
Bridge			Brodie Castle	67	I 11	Buckfast Abbey	4	I 32
of Craigisla	62	K 13	Brolass	59	B 14	Buckfastleigh	4	I 32
Bridge of Don	69	N 12	Bromborough	34	L 24	Buckhaven	56	K 15
Bridge of Earn	56	J 14	Brome	31	X 26	Buckie	68	L 10
Bridge of Gairn	68	K 12	Bromfield	26	L 26	Buckingham	28	R 27
Bridge of Orchy	60	F 14	Bromham	18	N 29	Buckinghamshire		
Bridgemary	10	Q 31	Bromley (London			(County)	19	R 28
Bridgend			Borough)	20	U 29	Buckland (Herts.)	20	T 28
/ Pen-y-bont			Brompton			Buckland (Oxon.)	18	P 28
(Bridgend)	16	J 29	(near			Buckland Abbey	3	H 32
Bridgend			Northallerton)	46	P 20	Buckland Newton	8	M 31
(Perthshire and			Brompton-by-			Buckland St. Mary	7	K 31
Kinross)	56	J 14	Sawdon	41	S 21	Bucklers Hard	9	P 31
Bridgend (Islay)	52	B 16	Brompton (Kent)	21	V 29	Buckley / Bwcle	34	K 24
Bridgend			Brompton on			Buckminster	36	R 25
of Lintrathen	62	K 13	Swale	46	O 20	Bucknell	26	L 26
Bridgnorth	26	M 26	Brompton Regis	7	J 30	Bucksburn	69	N 12
Bridgwater	8	L 30	Bromsgrove	27	N 26	Bude	6	G 31
Bridlington	41	T 21	Bromyard	26	M 27	Budleigh		
Bridport	8	L 31	Bronllys	16	K 27	Salterton	4	K 32
Brierfield	39	N 22	Brooke	31	Y 26	Bugle	3	F 32
Brierley Hill	27	N 26	Brookmans Park	20	T 28	Bugthorpe	40	R 21
Brigg	41	S 23	Broom (Loch)	72	E 10	Buildwas Abbey	26	M 26
Brighouse	39	O 22	Broomfield	7	K 30	Builth Wells /		
Brighstone	9	P 32	Broomhaugh	46	O 19	Llanfair-ym-		
Brightlingsea	21	X 28	Brora	73	H 9	Muallt	25	J 27
Brighton	11	T 31	Brotherton	40	Q 22	Bulford	9	O 30
Brightwell	19	Q 29	Brotton	47	R 20	Bulkington	27	P 26
Brigstock	28	S 26	Brough	45	N 20	Bulwell	36	Q 24
Brill	19	Q 28	Brough Head	74	J 6	Bunarkaig	60	F 13
Brimfield	26	L 27	Brough Lodge	75	R 2	Bunessan	59	B 15
Brimham Rocks	39	O 21	Brough of Birsay	74	J 6	Bungay	31	Y 26
Brimington	35	P 24	Broughton			Buntingford	20	T 28
Brinkburn Priory	51	O 18	(Cumbria)	44	J 19	Burbage (Leics.)	27	P 26
Brinklow	27	P 26	Broughton (North			Burbage (Wilts.)	18	O 29
Brinkworth	18	O 29	Lincs.)	41	S 23	Bures	22	W 28
Brinyan	74	L 6	Broughton			Burford	18	P 28
Brisley	30	W 25	(Hants.)	9	P 30	Burgess Hill	11	T 31
Bristol	17	M 29	Broughton			Burgh-by-Sands	44	K 19
Briston	30	X 25	(Lancs.)	38	L 22	Burgh-le-Marsh	37	U 24
Briton Ferry	15	I 29	Broughton			Burghead	68	J 10
Brittle (Loch)	65	B 12	(Northants.)	28	R 26	Burghley House	29	S 26
Brittwell Salome	19	Q 29	Broughton (Oxon.)	27	P 27	Burley	9	O 31
Brixham	4	J 32	Broughton-in-			Burley-in-		
Brixworth	28	R 27	Furness	44	K 21	Wharfedale	39	O 22
Brize Norton	18	P 28	Broughty Ferry	62	L 14	Burneside	45	L 20
Broad Bay	71	B 9	Brownhills	27	O 26	Burnham	19	S 29
Broad Blunsdon	18	O 29	Brownsea Island	9	O 31	Burnham Market	30	W 25
Broad Chalke	9	O 30	Broxbourne	20	T 28	Burnham-on-		
Broad Law	49	J 17	Broxburn	56	J 16	Crouch	21	W 29
Broadclyst	7	J 31	Bruichladdich	52	A 16	Burnham-on-Sea	8	L 30
Broadford	65	C 12	Brundall	31	Y 26	Burnhaven	69	O 11
Broadlands	9	P 31	Brushford	7	J 30	Burniston	47	S 21
Broadmayne	8	M 31	Bruton	8	M 30	Burnley	39	N 22
Broadstairs	13	Y 29	Brymbo	34	K 24	Burntisland	56	K 15
Broadstone	9	O 31	Brympton			Burravoe	75	Q 2
Broadwas	26	M 27	d'Evercy	8	L 31	Burray	74	L 7
Broadway	27	O 27	Brynaman	15	I 28	Burrelton	62	K 14

BRIGHTON AND HOVE

Adelaide Crescent .... AY 2
Brunswick Place .... AY 3
Brunswick Square .... AYZ 4
Chatham Place .... BX 6
Churchill Square
  Shopping Centre .... BYZ 7
Denmark Road .... BY 7
East Street .... CZ 8
Gladstone
  Terrace .... CX 12
Gloucester Place .... CY 13
Gloucester Road .... CY 14
Goldsmid Road .... BX 15
Grand Junction Road .... CZ 16
London Road CX
Market Place .... CX 20
Marlborough Place .... CY 21
Montpelier Place .... BY 22
North Street .... CZ
Old Steine .... CZ 23
Pavillon Parade .... CZ 26
Richmond Place .... CY 27
Richmond Terrace .... CX 28
St. George's Place .... CY 30
St. Peter's Place .... CX 31
Terminus Road .... BCX 32
Upper Lewes
  Road .... CX 33
Waterloo Place .... CY 39
Western Road .... ABY
York Place .... CY 42

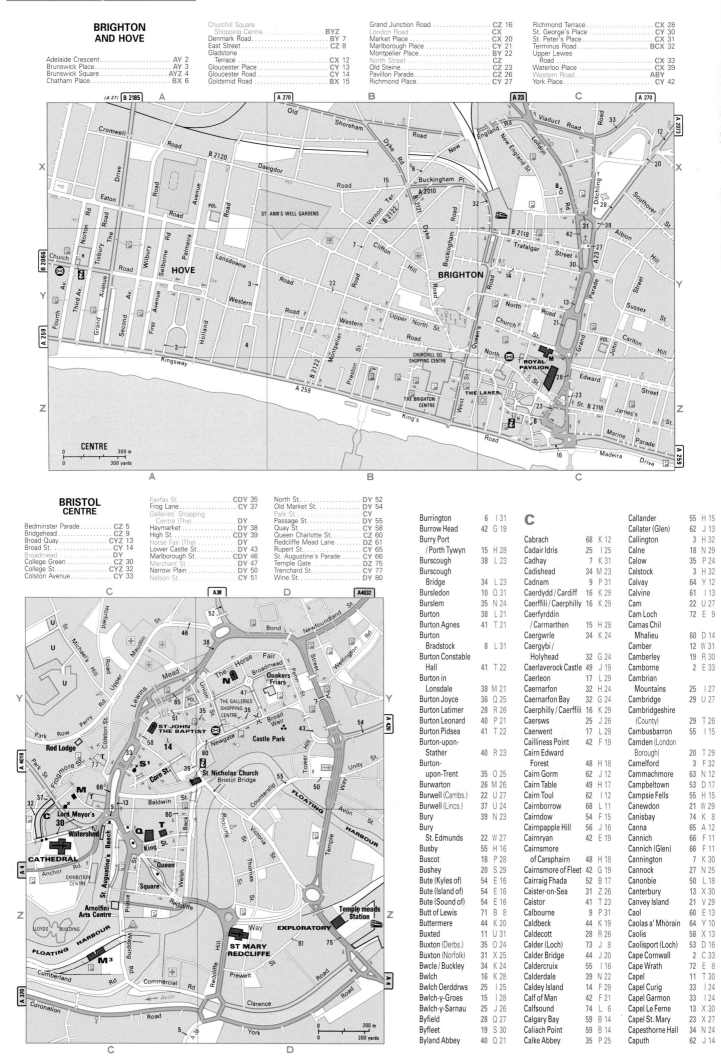

BRISTOL CENTRE

Bedminster Parade .... CZ 5
Bridgehead .... CZ 9
Broad Quay .... CYZ 13
Broad St. .... CY 14
Broadmead .... DY
College Green .... CZ 30
College St. .... CYZ 32
Colston Avenue .... CY 33
Fairfax St. .... CDY 35
Frog Lane .... CY 37
Galleries' Shopping
  Centre (The) .... DY
Haymarket .... DY 38
High St. .... CDY 39
Horse Fair (The) .... DY
Lower Castle St. .... DY 43
Marlborough St. .... CDY 46
Merchant St. .... DY 47
Narrow Plain .... DY 50
Nelson St. .... CY 51
North St. .... DY 52
Old Market St. .... DY 54
Park St. .... CY
Passage St. .... DY 55
Quay St. .... CY 58
Queen Charlotte St. .... CZ 60
Redcliffe Mead Lane .... DZ 61
Rupert St. .... CY 65
St. Augustine's Parade ..... CY 66
Temple Gate .... DZ 75
Trenchard St. .... CY 77
Wine St. .... DY 80

Burrington	6	I 31	**C**			Callander	55	H 15
Burrow Head	42	G 19				Callater (Glen)	62	J 13
Burry Port			Cabrach	68	K 12	Callington	3	H 32
/ Porth Tywyn	15	H 28	Cadair Idris	25	I 25	Calne	18	N 29
Burscough	38	L 23	Cadhay	7	K 31	Calow	35	P 24
Burscough			Cadishead	34	M 23	Calstock	3	H 32
Bridge	34	L 23	Cadnam	9	P 31	Calvay	64	Y 12
Bursledon	10	Q 31	Caerdydd / Cardiff	16	K 29	Calvine	61	I 13
Burslem	35	N 24	Caerffili / Caerphilly	16	K 29	Cam	22	U 28
Burton	38	L 21	Caerfyrddin			Cam Loch	72	E 9
Burton Agnes	41	T 21	/ Carmarthen	15	H 28	Camas Chil		
Burton			Caergwrle	34	K 24	Mhalieu	60	D 14
Bradstock	8	L 31	Caergybi /			Camber	12	W 31
Burton Constable			Holyhead	32	G 24	Camberley	19	R 30
Hall	41	T 22	Caerlaverock Castle	49	J 19	Camborne	2	E 33
Burton in			Caerleon	17	L 29	Cambrian		
Lonsdale	38	M 21	Caernarfon	32	H 24	Mountains	25	I 27
Burton Joyce	36	Q 25	Caernarfon Bay	32	G 24	Cambridge	29	U 27
Burton Latimer	28	R 26	Caerphilly / Caerffili	16	K 29	Cambridgeshire		
Burton Leonard	40	P 21	Caersws	25	J 26	(County)	29	T 26
Burton Pidsea	41	T 22	Caerwent	17	L 29	Cambusbarron	55	I 15
Burton-upon-			Cailliness Point	42	F 19	Camden (London		
Stather	40	R 23	Cairn Edward			Borough)	20	T 29
Burton-			Forest	48	H 18	Camelford	3	F 32
upon-Trent	35	O 25	Cairn Gorm	62	J 12	Cammachmore	63	N 12
Burwarton	26	M 26	Cairn Table	49	H 17	Campbeltown	53	D 17
Burwell (Cambs.)	22	U 27	Cairn Toul	62	I 12	Campsie Fells	55	H 15
Burwell (Lincs.)	37	U 24	Cairnborrow	68	L 11	Canewdon	21	W 29
Bury	39	N 23	Cairndow	54	F 15	Canisbay	74	K 8
Bury			Cairnpapple Hill	56	J 16	Canna	65	A 12
St. Edmunds	22	W 27	Cairnryan	42	E 19	Cannich	66	F 11
Busby	55	H 16	Cairnsmore			Cannich (Glen)	66	F 11
Buscot	18	P 28	of Carsphairn	48	H 18	Cannington	7	K 30
Bushey	20	S 29	Cairnsmore of Fleet	42	G 19	Cannock	27	N 25
Bute (Kyles of)	54	E 16	Cairraig Fhada	52	B 17	Canonbie	50	L 18
Bute (Island of)	54	E 16	Caister-on-Sea	31	Z 26	Canterbury	13	X 30
Bute (Sound of)	54	E 16	Caistor	41	T 23	Canvey Island	21	V 29
Butt of Lewis	71	B 8	Calbourne	9	P 31	Caol	60	E 13
Buttermere	44	K 20	Caldbeck	44	K 19	Caolas a' Mhòrain	64	Y 10
Buxted	11	U 31	Caldecott	28	R 26	Caolis	58	X 13
Buxton (Derbs.)	35	O 24	Calder (Loch)	73	J 8	Caolisport (Loch)	53	D 16
Buxton (Norfolk)	31	X 25	Calder Bridge	44	J 20	Cape Cornwall	2	C 33
Bwcle / Buckley	34	K 24	Caldercruix	55	I 16	Cape Wrath	72	E 8
Bwlch	16	K 28	Calderdale	39	N 22	Capel	11	T 30
Bwlch Oerddrws	25	I 25	Caldey Island	14	F 29	Capel Curig	33	I 24
Bwlch-y-Groes	15	I 28	Calf of Man	42	F 21	Capel Garmon	33	I 24
Bwlch-y-Sarnau	25	J 26	Calfsound	74	L 6	Capel Le Ferne	13	X 30
Byfield	28	Q 27	Calgary Bay	59	B 14	Capel St. Mary	23	X 27
Byfleet	19	S 30	Caliach Point	59	B 14	Capesthorne Hall	34	N 24
Byland Abbey	40	Q 21	Calke Abbey	35	P 25	Caputh	62	J 14

CAMBRIDGE CENTRE

ge Street	Y 2	
n Exchange Street	Z 6	
ning Street	Y 7	
e School Lane	Z 12	
fton Centre	Y	
son Street	Y 14	
g's Parade	Z 15	
dingley Rd	Y 16	
gdalene St.	Y 17	
ket Hill	Y 18	
ket Street	Y 19	
on Road	Y 20	
wmarket Road	Y 21	

Northampton Street	Y 22	
Parker Street	Z 23	
Peas Hill	Z 25	
Pembroke Street	Z 26	
Petty Cury	Y 27	
Rose Crescent	Y 28	
St. Andrew's St.	Z 30	
St John's Street	Y 31	
Short Street	Y 32	
Sidney Street	Y 34	
Trinity Street	Y 36	
Trumpington Road	Z 37	
Wheeler Street	Z 39	

COLLEGES

CHRIST'S	Y	A
CLARE	Z	B
CORPUS CHRISTI.	Z	G
DARWIN	Z	D
DOWNING	Z	E
EMMANUEL	Z	F
GONVILLE AND CAIUS	Y	G
HUGUES HALL	Z	J
JESUS	Y	K
KING'S	Z	

LUCY CAVENDISH	Y	O
MAGDALENE	Y	N
PEMBROKE	Z	N
PETERHOUSE	Z	O
QUEENS'	Z	
ST CATHARINE'S	Z	R
ST EDMUNDS HOUSE	Y	U
ST JOHN'S	Y	
SIDNEY SUSSEX	Y	P
TRINITY	Y	
TRINITY HALL	Y	V

CARDIFF/ CAERDYDD

Capitol Centre	BZ	
Castle Street	BZ 9	
Cathays Terrace	BY 10	
Central Square	BZ 12	
Church Street	BZ 14	
City Hall Road	BY 15	
College Road	BY 20	

Corbett Road	BY 21	
Customhouse Street	BZ 23	
David Street	BZ 25	
Duke Street	BZ 26	
Dumfries Place	BY 28	
Greyfriars Road	BY 29	
Guilford Street	BZ 30	
Hayes (The)	BZ 32	
High Street	BZ	
King Edward VII Avenue	BY 36	
Mary Ann Street	BZ 39	
Moira Terrace	BZ 42	

Nantes (Boulevard de)	BY 44	
Penarth Road	BZ 49	
Queen Street	BZ	
Queens Arcade Shopping Centre	BZ 54	
St. Andrews Place	BY 56	
St. David's Centre	BZ	
St. John Street	BZ 58	
St. Mary Street	BZ	
Station Terrace	BZ 61	
Stuttgarter Strasse	BY 62	
Working Street	BZ 67	

CANTERBURY

ercart Lane	YZ 2	
rough (The)	Y 4	
gate	Y	
chery Lane	Y 5	
dhall Street	Y 6	

High Street	Y 8	
Lower Bridge Street	Z 9	
Lower Chantry Lane	Z 10	
Mercery Lane	Y 12	
Palace Street	Y	
Rhodaus Town	Z 13	
Rosemary Lane	Z 14	
St. George's Place	Z 16	

St. George's Street	Z 17	
St. Margaret's Street	YZ 18	
St. Mary's Street	Z 19	
St. Peter's Street	Z 20	
St. Radigund's Street	Y 21	
Upper Bridge Street	Z 23	
Watling Street	Z 25	

CARLISLE

Annetwell Street	AY 2	
Botchergate	BZ	
Bridge Street	AY 3	
Brunswick Street	BZ 4	
Castle Street	BY 6	
Cecil Street	BZ 5	

Charlotte Street	AZ 7	
Chiswick Street	BY 8	
Church Street	AY 10	
Eden Bridge	BY 12	
English Street	BY 13	
Lonsdale Street	BY 14	
Lowther Street	BY 15	
Port Road	AY 16	
St. Marys Gate	BY 17	

Scotch Street	BY 19	
Spencer Street	BY 20	
Tait Street	BZ 21	
The Lanes Shopping Centre	BY	
Victoria Viaduct	ABZ 24	
West Tower Street	BY 26	
West Walls	ABY 27	
Wigton Road	AZ 29	

CHESTER

Boughton	2	Grosvenor Park Road	7	Northgate Street	18
Bridge Street	3	Grosvenor Street	8	Parkgate Road	20
Eastgate Street	5	Handbridge	10	Pepper Street	21
Frodsham Street	6	Little St. John Street	12	St. John Street	23
		Liverpool Road	13	St. Martins Way	24
		Lower Bridge Street	15	Vicar's Lane	25
		Nicholas Street	17	Watergate Street	

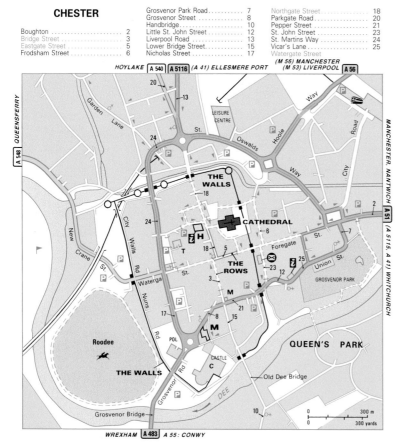

Chopwell	46 O 19	Cleckheaton	39 O 22	Coggeshall	22 W 28
Chorley	38 M 23	Cleehill	26 M 26	Coigach	72 E 10
Chorleywood	19 S 29	Cleethorpes	41 T 23	Coignafearn Forest	67 H 12
Christchurch	9 O 31	Cleeve Abbey	7 J 30	Colby	42 F 21
Chroisg (Loch a')	66 E 11	Clehonger	26 L 27	Colchester	22 W 28
Chudleigh	4 J 32	Cleigh	59 D 14	Cold Fell	45 M 19
Chulmleigh	7 I 31	Clent	27 N 26	Coldbackie	73 G 8
Church	39 M 22	Cleobury Mortimer	26 M 26	Colden Common	10 Q 31
Church Eaton	26 N 25	Cleobury North	26 M 26	Coldingham	57 N 16
Church Fenton	40 Q 22	Clephanton	67 I 11	Coldstream	50 N 17
Church Stoke	26 K 26	Clevedon	17 L 29	Coleford (Glos.)	17 M 28
Church Stretton	26 L 26	Cleveland Hills	46 Q 20	Coleford (Somerset)	8 M 30
Churchill (North		Cleveleys	38 K 22	Coleshill	27 O 26
Somerset)	17 L 29	Cley Next the Sea	30 X 25	Colgrave Sound	75 R 2
Churchill (Oxon.)	18 P 28	Cliffe	21 V 29	Coll	59 A 14
Churnet	34 N 24	Clifton Hampden	19 Q 29	Colliston	69 O 11
Churt	10 R 30	Clisham	70 Z 10	Collin	49 J 18
Cilcain	33 K 24	Clitheroe	39 M 22	Collingham (Notts.)	36 R 24
Cilgerran	24 G 27	Cliveden House	19 R 29	Collingham (West	
Cilmery	25 J 27	Clocaenog Forest	33 J 24	Yorks.)	40 P 22
Cinderford	17 M 28	Clola	69 O 11	Collyweston	28 S 26
Cirencester	18 O 28	Clophill	29 S 27	Colmonell	48 F 18
City of London		Clouds Hill	8 N 31	Coln (River)	18 O 28
(London Borough)	20 T 29	Cloughton	47 S 20	Colnabaichin	68 K 12
Clachan	53 D 16	Clova (Glen)	62 K 13	Colne	39 N 22
Clachan Mór	58 Z 14	Clovelly	6 G 31	Colne (River)	21 X 28
Clachan		Clovulin	60 E 13	Colonsay	52 B 15
of Glendaruel	54 E 15	Clowne	36 Q 24	Colpy	69 M 11
Clackavoid	62 J 13	Cluanie Loch	66 E 12	Colquhon Castle	69 N 11
Clackmannan	55 I 15	Clumber Park	36 Q 24	Colsterworth	36 S 25
Clacton-on-Sea	21 X 28	Clun	26 K 26	Coltishall	31 Y 25
Claggain Bay	52 B 16	Clunbury	26 L 26	Colwall Stone	26 M 27
Claidh (Loch)	70 A 10	Clunes Forest	60 F 13	Colwyn Bay	
Clandon Park	10 S 30	Clunie	62 J 14	/ Bae Colwyn	33 I 24
Clapham (Beds.)	28 S 27	Clutton	17 M 30	Colyton	7 K 31
Clapham (North		Clwydian Range	33 K 24	Combe Florey	7 K 30
Yorks.)	39 M 21	Clydach	15 I 28	Combe Martin	6 H 30
Clàr (Loch nan)	73 H 9	Clyde (Firth of)	48 F 17	Combwich	7 K 30
Clare	22 V 27	Clyde (River)	49 I 16	Compton (Berks.)	19 Q 29
Clashmore	67 H 10	Clydebank	55 G 16	Compton (West	
Clashnessie	72 E 9	Clydesdale	49 I 16	Sussex)	10 R 31
Clatteringshaws		Clywedog Resr.	25 J 26	Compton Castle	4 J 32
(Loch)	48 H 18	Coalville	27 P 25	Compton Wynyates	27 P 27
Clauchlands Point	53 E 17	Coatbridge	55 H 16	Comrie	55 I 14
Clavering	20 U 28	Cobham	20 S 30	Cona Glen	60 D 13
Claverley	26 N 26	Cock Bridge	68 K 12	Condover	26 L 26
Claverton Manor	17 N 29	Cockburnspath	57 M 16	Congleton	34 N 24
Clawdd-newydd	33 J 24	Cockenzie		Congresbury	17 L 29
Clawton	6 G 31	and Port Seton	56 L 16	Coningsby	37 T 24
Claxton	40 R 21	Cockermouth	44 J 20	Conisbrough	36 Q 23
Clay Cross	35 P 24	Cocking	10 R 31	Coniston	44 K 20
Claydon	23 X 27	Codford St. Mary	9 N 30	Connah's Quay	34 K 24
Claydon House	19 R 28	Codicote	20 T 28	Connel	60 D 14
Clayton	11 T 31	Codnor	35 P 24	Conon Bridge	67 G 11
Clayton-le-Moors	39 M 22	Codsall	27 N 26	Consett	46 O 19
Clayton West	39 P 23	Coe (Glen)	60 F 14	Constantine Bay	2 E 32
Cleadale	59 B 13	Coed y Brenin		Contin	67 G 11
Cleadon	46 P 19	Forest	33 I 25	Convinth (Glen)	67 G 11
Cleator Moor	44 J 20	Coedpoeth	34 K 24	Conway Falls	33 I 24

Carlton Colville	31 Z 26	Castle Kennedy	42 F 19	Chalfont		Chertsey	19 S 29			
Carlton in Lindrick	36 Q 23	Castle Lachlan	54 E 15	St. Peter	19 S 29	Cherwell (River)	19 Q 28			
Carlton-on-Trent	36 R 24	Castle Loch	42 F 19	Chalford	18 N 28	Cheselbourne	8 M 31			
Carluke	55 I 16	Castle Rising	30 V 25	Chalgrove	19 Q 29	Chesham	19 S 28			
Carmarthen		Castlebay	58 X 13	Challock	12 W 30	Chesham Bois	19 S 28			
/ Caerfyrddin	15 H 28	Castleford	40 P 22	Chambercombe		Cheshire (County)	34 M 24			
Carmel Head	32 G 23	Castlemartin	14 E 29	Manor	6 H 30	Cheshunt	20 T 28			
Carmunnock	55 H 16	Castlerigg	44 K 20	Chandler's Ford	9 P 31	Chesil Beach	8 M 32			
Carn Ban	61 H 12	Castleton (North		Channel Islands	5	Cheslyn Hay	27 N 26			
Carn Coire		Yorks.)	47 R 20	Chapel-en-le-Frith	35 O 24	Chester	34 L 24			
na h-Easgainn	67 H 12	Castleton (Derbs.)	35 O 23	Chapel St.		Chester-le-Street	46 P 19			
Carn Eige	66 E 12	Castletown	42 G 21	Leonards	37 V 24	Chesterfield	35 P 24			
Carn Glas-choire	67 I 11	Castletown	74 J 8	Chapelhall	55 I 16	Chesters Fort	51 N 18			
Carn Mairg	61 H 14	Catacol Bay	53 D 16	Chapeltown	35 P 23	Chesterton	19 Q 28			
Carnedd Llewelyn	33 I 24	Caterham	11 T 30	Chapmanslade	8 N 30	Cheviot (The)	51 N 17			
Carnforth	38 L 21	Catfield	31 Y 25	Chard	8 L 31	Cheviot Hills (The)	50 M 17			
Carnoustie	63 L 14	Catlodge	61 H 12	Chardstock	8 L 31	Chew Magna	17 M 29			
Carnwath	56 J 16	Caton	38 L 21	Charing	12 W 30	Chewton Mendip	8 M 30			
Carradale	53 D 17	Catrine	48 H 17	Charlbury	18 P 28	Chichester	10 R 31			
Carradale Bay	53 D 17	Catteral	38 L 22	Charlecote Park	27 P 27	Chickerell	8 M 32			
Carrbridge	67 I 12	Catterick	46 P 20	Charleston Manor	11 U 31	Chicklade	9 N 30			
Carrick	54 F 15	Catterick Garrison	46 O 20	Charlestown	3 F 33	Chiddingfold	10 S 30			
Carrick Roads	2 E 33	Catworth	29 S 26	Charlton Kings	18 N 28	Chiddingstone	11 U 30			
Carron (Loch)	65 C 11	Cauldcleuch Head	50 L 18	Charlton Marshall	9 N 31	Chideock	8 L 31			
Carse of Gowrie	56 K 14	Cava	74 K 7	Charlwood	11 T 30	Chigwell	20 U 29			
Carsluith	42 G 19	Cavendish	22 V 27	Charminster	8 M 31	Chilcompton	8 M 30			
Carsphairn	48 H 18	Cawdor	67 I 11	Charmouth	8 L 31	Chilham	12 W 30			
Carstairs	56 I 16	Cawood	40 Q 22	Charsfield	23 X 27	Chillingham	51 O 17			
Carterton	18 P 28	Caythorpe	36 S 24	Chartham	13 X 30	Chilmark	9 N 30			
Carterway Heads	46 O 19	Ceall (Loch nan)	59 C 13	Chartwell	11 U 30	Chiltern Hills	19 R 29			
Cartmel	38 L 21	Cefn-Coed-y-		Chastleton	18 P 28	Chilton	19 Q 29			
Cas-Gwent		cymmer	16 J 28	Chatburn	39 M 22	Chippenham	18 N 29			
/ Chepstow	17 M 29	Cefn Bryn	15 H 29	Chatham	21 V 29	Chipping	38 M 22			
Casnewydd		Cefn-mawr	34 K 25	Chatsworth House	35 P 24	Chipping Campden	27 O 27			
/ Newport	17 L 29	Ceinewydd		Chatteris	29 U 26	Chipping Norton	18 P 28			
Cassley (Glen)	72 F 9	/ New Quay	24 G 27	Chatton	51 O 17	Chipping				
Castell-Nedd /		Ceiriog (Vale of)	33 K 25	Chawleigh	7 I 31	Ongar	20 U 28			
Neath	15 I 29	Cemaes	32 G 23	Cheadle		Chipping Sodbury	17 M 29			
Castell Newydd		Cemaes Head	14 F 27	(Gtr. Mches.)	35 N 23	Chipping Warden	28 Q 27			
Emlyn / Newcast		Cemmaes	25 I 26	Cheadle (Staffs.)	35 O 25	Chirbury	25 K 26			
le Emlyn	24 G 27	Cenarth	24 G 27	Cheddar Gorge	8 L 30	Chirk	34 K 25			
Castle Acre	30 W 25	Cerne Abbas	8 M 31	Cheddington	19 S 28	Chirk Castle	33 K 25			
Castle Ashby	28 R 27	Cerrigydrudion	33 J 24	Cheddleton	35 N 24	Chirnside	57 N 16			
Castle Bolton	46 O 21	Chadderton	39 N 23	Chedington	8 L 31	Chiselbon	18 O 29			
Castle Campbell	56 I 15	Chaddesden	35 P 25	Chedworth	18 O 28	Chislet	13 X 30			
Castle Cary	8 M 30	Chadlington	18 P 28	Chelford	34 N 24	Chitterne	9 N 30			
Castle Combe	17 N 29	Chadwell		Chellaston	35 P 25	Chittlehamholt	6 I 31			
Castle Donington	35 P 25	St. Mary	20 V 29	Chelmsford	22 V 28	Chittlehampton	6 I 31			
Castle Douglas	43 I 19	Chagford	4 I 31	Cheltenham	18 N 28	Chobham	19 S 29			
Castle Drogo	4 I 31	Chàirn Bhain		Chelveston	28 S 27	Choire (Loch)	73 H 9			
Castle Fraser	69 M 12	(Loch a')	72 E 9	Chepstow		Cholesbury	19 S 28			
Castle Hedingham	22 V 28	Chalfont		/ Cas-Gwent	17 L 29	Cholsey	19 Q 29			
Castle Howard	40 R 21	St. Giles	19 S 29	Cheriton Bishop	4 I 31	Chon (Loch)	55 G 15			

COVENTRY

Bayley Lane	3	Greyfriars Lane	16	St. Nicholas (Ringway)	39
Bishop Street	5	Hales Street	17	Shopping Precincts	
Broadgate	6	High Street	22	Swanswell (Ringway)	40
Burges	7	Ironmonger Road	23	Trinity Street	41
Corporation Street		Jordan Well	26	Upper Well Street	43
Earl Street	10	Leicester Row	29	Vecquaray Street	45
Fairfax Street	12	Light Lane	30	Victoria Street	46
Far Gosford Street	13	Little Park Street	31	Warwick Road	49
Gosford Street	15	Primrose Hill		White Street	51
		Street	34	Windsor Street	52
		Queen Victoria Road	35	White Friars	
		St. Johns (Ringway)	38	(Ringway)	54

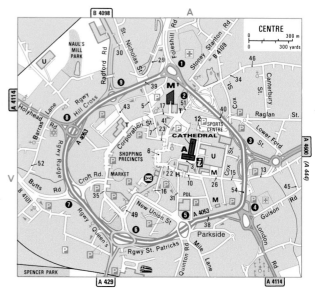

Conwy 33 I 24
Conwy (River) 33 I 24
Conwy (Vale of) 33 I 24
Cooden Beach 12 V 31
Cookham 19 R 29
Coolham 11 S 31
Coombe Bissett 9 O 30
Copdock 23 X 27
Copmanthorpe 40 Q 22
Copplestone 4 I 31
Copthorne 11 T 30
Coquet (River) 51 N 17
Corbridge 45 N 19
Corby 28 R 26
Corby Glen 36 S 25
Corfe Castle 9 N 32
Corhampton 10 Q 31
Cornhill 69 L 11
Cornhill-on-Tweed 50 N 17
Cornwall (County) 3 G 32
Cornwood 4 I 32
Corpach 60 E 13
Corpusty 31 X 25
Corran 60 E 13
Corrie 53 E 17
Corrimony 66 F 11
Corringham 21 V 29
Corryvreckan (Gulf of) 52 C 15
Corscombe 8 L 31
Corsham 18 N 29
Corsham Court 18 N 29
Corstopitum 51 N 19
Corwen 33 J 25
Cosby 28 Q 26
Cosham 10 Q 31
Costessey 31 X 26
Cotherstone 46 O 20
Cothi (River) 15 H 28
Cotswold Wildlife Park 18 O 28
Cottenham 29 U 27
Cottered 20 T 28
Cottingham (East Riding of Yorks.) 41 S 22
Cottingham (Northants.) 28 R 26
Countesthorpe 28 Q 26
Coupar Angus 62 K 14
Cove Bay 69 N 12
Coventry 27 P 26
Coverack 2 E 33
Cowal 54 E 15
Cowan Bridge 38 M 21
Cowbridge / Bont-faen 16 J 29
Cowdenbeath 56 K 15
Cowdray House 10 R 31
Cowes 10 Q 31
Cowfold 11 T 31
Cowplain 10 Q 31
Coxheath 12 V 30
Coylton 48 G 17
Crackington Haven 6 G 31
Cragside Gardens 51 O 18
Craig 66 E 11
Craig-y-nos 15 I 28
Craigellachie 68 K 11
Craighead 57 M 15
Craighouse 52 C 16
Craigievar Castle 68 L 12
Craignish (Loch) 54 D 15
Craignure 59 C 14
Craigrothie 56 L 15
Craik 50 K 17
Crail 57 M 15
Cramlington 51 P 18
Cramond 56 K 16
Cranborne 9 O 31
Cranbrook 12 V 30
Cranleigh 11 S 30
Crathes Castle 69 M 12
Crathie 62 K 12
Crathorne 46 Q 20
Craven Arms 26 L 26
Crawford 49 I 17
Crawley (Hants.) 9 P 30
Crawley (West Sussex) 11 T 30
Crawley Down 11 T 30
Creag Meagaidh 61 G 13
Creagorry 64 Y 11
Crediton 7 J 31
Creetown 42 G 19
Creran (Loch) 60 D 14

Cressage 26 M 26
Creswell 36 Q 24
Crewe 34 M 24
Crewkerne 8 L 31
Crianlarich 55 G 14
Criccieth 32 H 25
Crich 35 P 24
Crichton 56 L 16
Crick 28 Q 26
Cricket St. Thomas 8 L 31
Crickhowell 16 K 28
Cricklade 18 O 29
Crickley Hill 18 N 28
Crieff 55 I 14
Crimond 69 O 11
Crinan 54 D 15
Crinan (Loch) 54 D 15
Cringleford 31 X 26
Crocketford 49 I 18
Crockham Hill 11 U 30
Croft 26 L 27
Croft-on-Tees 46 P 20
Croggan 59 C 14
Cromalt Hills 72 E 9
Cromar 68 L 12
Cromarty 67 H 10
Cromarty Firth 67 H 11
Cromdale 68 J 12
Cromdale (Hills of) 68 J 12
Cromer 31 X 25
Cromford 35 P 24
Crondall 10 R 30
Crook 46 O 19
Crook of Devon 56 J 15
Crookham Village 10 R 30
Cropwell Bishop 36 R 25
Crosby 34 K 23
Crosby Ravensworth 45 M 20
Croscombe 8 M 30
Cross 71 B 8
Cross Fell 45 M 19
Cross Hands 15 H 28
Cross Inn 24 H 27
Crossapoll 58 Z 14
Crosshill (South Ayrshire) 48 G 18
Crosshill (Fife) 56 K 15
Crosshouse 48 G 17
Crosskeys 16 K 29
Crosskirk 73 J 8
Crossmichael 43 I 19
Crouch (River) 21 W 29
Crowborough 11 U 30
Crowcombe 7 K 30
Crow Hill 17 M 28
Crowhurst 12 V 31
Crowland 29 T 25
Crowle 40 R 23
Crowlin Island 65 C 11
Crowthorne 19 R 29
Croxley Green 20 S 29
Croy 67 H 11
Croyde 6 H 30
Croydon (London Borough) 20 T 29
Cruden Bay 69 O 11
Crudgington 26 M 25
Crudwell 18 N 29
Crug-y-bar 24 I 27
Crulivig 70 Z 9
Crymmych 14 G 28
Crynant 15 I 28
Cuckfield 11 T 30
Cuckney 36 Q 24
Cuddington 34 M 24
Cudworth 40 P 23
Cuffley 20 T 28
Cuillin Sound 65 B 12
Cuillins (The) 65 B 12
Culdrose 2 E 33
Cullen 68 L 10
Cullen Bay 68 L 10
Cullipool 54 D 15
Cullompton 7 J 31
Culmington 26 L 26
Culmstock 7 K 31
Culrain 72 G 10
Culross 56 J 15
Culter Fell 49 J 17
Cults 69 N 12
Culzean Castle 48 F 17
Cumbernauld 55 I 16
Cumbria (County) 44 K 19
Cumbrian Moutains 44 K 20

Cuminestown 69 N 11
Cummersdale 44 L 19
Cummertrees 49 J 19
Cumnock 48 H 17
Cumnor 18 P 28
Cunninghame 48 G 17
Cunninghamhead 48 G 17
Cupar 56 K 15
Curdridge 10 Q 31
Currie 56 K 16
Curry Rivel 8 L 30
Cwm 16 K 28
Cwm Bychan 32 H 25
Cwm Taf 16 J 28
Cwmbrân 17 L 29
Cwmllynfell 15 I 28
Cwmystwyth 25 I 26
Cydweli / Kidwelly 15 H 28
Cymmer 16 J 29
Cymyran Bay 32 G 24

D

Dailly 48 F 18
Daimh (Loch an) 61 G 14
Dairsie or Osnaburgh 56 L 14
Dalavich 54 E 15
Dalbeattie 43 I 19
Dalby 42 F 21
Dale 14 E 28
Daliburgh 64 X 12
Dalkeith 56 K 16
Dallas 68 J 11
Dallington 12 V 31
Dalmally 54 F 14
Dalmellington 48 G 18
Dalmeny 56 J 16
Dalnabreck 59 C 13
Dalry (North Ayrshire) 54 F 16
Dalry (Dumfries and Galloway) 48 H 18
Dalrymple 48 G 17
Dalston 44 L 19
Dalton (Dumfries and Galloway) 49 J 18
Dalton (North Yorks.) 40 P 21
Dalton in Furness 38 K 21
Damh (Loch) 66 D 11
Dan-yr-Ogof 15 I 28
Danbury 22 V 28
Dane 34 N 24
Darenth 20 U 29
Darfield 40 P 23
Darlington 46 P 20
Darowen 25 I 26
Dartford 20 U 29
Dartford Tunnel 20 U 29
Dartington 4 I 32
Dartmeet 4 I 32
Dartmoor National Park 4 I 32
Dartmouth 4 J 32
Darton 40 P 23
Darvel 48 H 17
Darwen 39 M 22
Datchet 19 S 29
Dava 68 J 11
Daventry 28 Q 27
Davidstow 3 G 32
Daviot 67 H 11
Dawley 26 M 26
Dawlish 4 J 32
Deal 13 Y 30
Dean Forest Park 17 M 28
Deanich Lodge 66 F 10
Deanston 55 H 15
Dearham 44 J 19
Deben (River) 23 X 27
Debenham 23 X 27
Dee (River) (Scotland) 69 N 12
Dee / Afon Dyfrdwy (River) (Wales) 33 K 24
Deene 28 S 26
Deeping St. Nicholas 29 T 25
Deeps (The) 75 P 3
Defford 27 N 27
Delabole 3 F 32

Delamere Forest 34 L 24
Delph 39 N 23
Denbigh / Dinbych 33 J 24
Denby Dale 39 P 23
Denham 19 S 29
Denholm 50 L 17
Denmead 10 Q 31
Dennington 23 Y 27
Denny 55 I 15
Dent 45 M 21
Denton 35 N 23
Derby 35 P 25
Derbyshire (County) 35 O 24
Dersingham 30 V 25
Dervaig 59 B 14
Derwent (River) (R. Ouse) 40 R 22
Derwent (River) (R. Trent) 35 P 24
Derwent (River) (R. Tyne) 46 O 19
Derwent Dale 35 O 23
Derwent Reservoir (Derbs.) 35 O 23
Derwent Reservoir (Northumb.) 45 N 19
Derwent Water 44 K 20
Desborough 28 R 26
Desford 28 Q 26
Detling 12 V 30
Deveron (River) 69 M 11
Devil's Beef Tub 49 J 17
Devil's Bridge / Pontarfynach 25 I 26
Devil's Elbow 62 J 13
Devil's Punch Bowl 10 R 30
Devizes 18 O 29
Devon (County) 4 J 31
Devonport 3 H 32
Dewsbury 39 P 22
Dherue (Loch an) 72 G 8
Didcot 19 Q 29
Diddlebury 26 L 26
Dilwyn 26 L 27
Dinas Dinlle 32 G 24
Dinas Head 14 F 27
Dinbych / Denbigh 33 J 24
Dinbych-y-pysgod / Tenby 14 F 28
Dingwall 67 G 11
Dinnet 68 L 12
Dinnington 36 Q 23
Dinton 9 O 30
Dirleton 57 L 15
Dishforth 40 P 21
Diss 31 X 26
Distington 44 J 20
Ditcheat 8 M 30
Ditchley Park 18 P 28
Ditchling 11 T 31
Ditton Priors 26 M 26
Doc Penfro / Pembroke Dock 14 F 28
Docherty (Glen) 66 E 11
Dochgarroch 67 H 11
Docking 30 V 25
Doddington (Cambs.) 29 U 26
Doddington (Kent) 12 W 30
Doddington (Lincs.) 36 S 24
Doddington (Northumb.) 51 O 17
Dodman Point 3 F 33
Dodworth 40 P 23
Dolfor 25 K 26
Dolgellau 25 I 25
Dolgoch Falls 24 I 26
Dollar 56 I 15
Dolton 6 H 31
Don (River) 40 Q 23
Don (River) 68 K 12
Doncaster 40 Q 23
Donington 37 T 25
Donington Park Circuit 35 P 25
Donington-on-Bain 37 T 24
Donisthorpe 27 P 25
Donnington (Berks.) 19 Q 29
Donnington (Salop) 26 M 25
Donyatt 8 L 31
Doon (Loch) 48 G 18
Dorchester (Dorset) 8 M 31

Dorchester (Oxon.) 19 Q 29
Dordon 27 P 26
Dorking 11 T 30
Dormans Land 11 U 30
Dormanstown 47 Q 20
Dornie 66 D 12
Dornoch 67 H 10
Dornoch Firth 67 H 10
Dorrington 26 L 26
Dorset (County) 8 M 31
Dorstone 26 K 27
Douchary (Glen) 66 F 10
Douglas (South Lanarkshire) 49 I 17
Douglas (Isle of Man) 42 G 21

Douglastown 62 L 14
Dounby 74 K 6
Doune 55 H 15
Dove (River) 35 O 24
Dove Cottage 44 K 20
Dovedale 35 O 24
Dover 13 X 30
Doveridge 35 O 24
Dovey / Dyfi (River) 24 I 26
Downderry 3 G 32
Downham 29 U 26
Downham Market 30 V 26
Downies 63 N 12
Downton 9 O 31
Draycott 35 P 25

Draycott-in-the-Moors 35 N 25
Drayton (Norfolk) 31 X 25
Drayton (Oxon.) 19 Q 29
Dreghorn 48 G 17
Drenewydd / Newtown 25 K 26
Dreswick Point 42 G 21
Drigg 44 J 20
Drimnin 59 C 14
Droitwich 27 N 27
Dronfield 35 P 24
Drongan 48 G 17
Druidibeg (Loch) 64 Y 12
Druim a' Chliabhain (Loch) 73 H 8

DERBY

Albert Street ... Z 2
Babington Lane ... Z 3
Bold Lane ... Y 4
Bradshaw Way ... Y 5
Cathedral Road ... Y 7
Charnwood Street ... Z 9
Corn Market ... Z 13
Corporation Street ... YZ 14
Duffield Road ... Y 17
Eagle Shopping Centre ... Z
East Street ... Z 18
Full Street ... Y 19

Iron Gate ... Y 22
Jury Street ... Y 23
King Street ... Y 25
Liversage St. ... Z 26
Market Place ... YZ 27
Midland Road ... Z 28
Mount Street ... Z 29
Normanton Road ... Z 31
Queen Street ... Z 32
St. Mary's Gate ... Y 33
St. Peter's Street ... Z 34
Sacheveral Street ... Z 36
Stafford Street ... Z 37
Victoria Street ... Z 41
Wardwick ... Z 43

DOVER

Bench Street ... 3
Biggin Street ... 4
Cannon Street ... 5
Castle Street ... 6
Charlton Green ... 7
High Street

King Street ... 13
Ladywell, Park Street ... 15
London Road ... 17
Pencester Road
Priory Road ... 18
Priory Street ... 19
Queen St. ... 20
Worthington Street ... 25

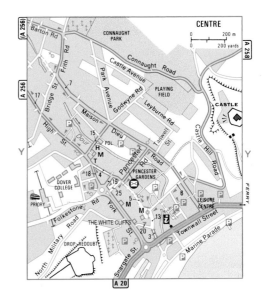

DUNDEE

Bell Street	6
City Square	7
Commercial Street	8
East Marketgait	15
High Street	17
Meadowside	23
Murraygate	25
Nethergate	26
Overgate Centre	35
Reform Street	35
St. Andrews Street	36
South Union Street	39
Trades Lane	41
Ward Road	42
Wellgate Centre	
West Bell Street	43
West Marketgait	44

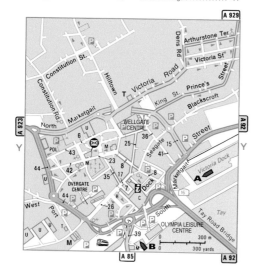

DURHAM

Alexander Crescent	A 2		Gilesgate	B 14
Castle Chare	A 3		Grove Street	A 15
Court Lane	B 5		High Street	B 16
Elvet Bridge	B 6		Market Place	A 17
Elvet Crescent	B 7		Millburngate	A 19
Flass Street	A 8		Neville Street	A 20
Framwelgate Bridge	B 10		Potters Bank	A 21
Framwelgate Waterside	B 12		Providence Row	A 21
			Saddler Street	B
			Silver Street	B 24
			Sutton Street	A 25

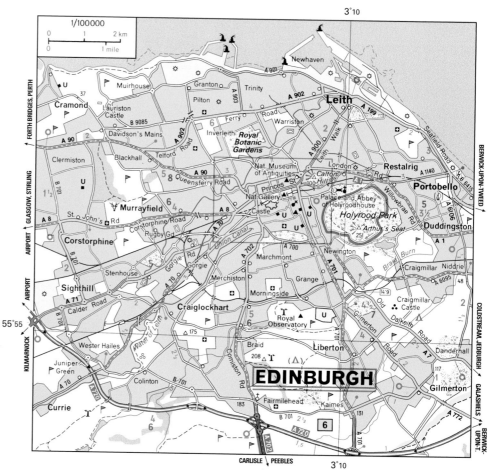

Drum Castle	69 M 12	Dunstaffnage	
Drumbeg	72 E 9	Castel	60 D 14
Drumclog	48 H 17	Dunstanburgh	
Drumlanrig Castle	49 I 18	Castle	51 P 17
Drumlithie	63 M 13	Dunster	7 J 30
Drummond Castle	55 I 14	Duntelchaig (Loch)	67 H 11
Drummore	42 F 19	Dunure	48 F 17
Drummossie Muir	67 H 11	Dunvegan	65 A 11
Drumnadrochit	67 G 11	Dunvegan (Loch)	65 A 11
Drumtochty Forest	63 M 13	Dunvegan Castle	65 A 11
Druridge Bay	51 P 18	Dunvegan Head	64 Z 11
Drybrook	17 M 28	Dunwich	31 Y 27
Dryburgh Abbey	50 M 17	Durdle Door	8 N 32
Drygarn Fawr	25 J 27	Durham	46 P 19
Drymen	55 G 15	Durham (County)	45 N 19
Ducklington	18 P 28	Durlston Head	9 O 32
Duddingston	28 S 26	Durness	72 F 8
Dudley	27 N 26	Durrington	9 O 30
Duff House	69 M 11	Dursley	17 M 28
Duffield	35 P 25	Dury Voe	75 Q 2
Dufftown	68 K 11	Duston	28 R 27
Duffus	68 J 10	Duxford	29 U 27
Duich (Loch)	66 D 12	Dyce	69 N 12
Duirinish	65 C 12	Dyfi / Dovey (River)	24 I 26
Duke's Pass	55 G 15	Dykehead	62 K 13
Dukinfield	35 N 23	Dykends	62 K 13
Dulnain Bridge	68 J 12	Dymchurch	13 W 30
Duloe	3 G 32	Dymock	17 M 28
Dulverton	7 J 30	Dyrham	17 M 29
Dumbarton	55 G 16	Dyrham Park	17 M 29
Dumfries	49 J 18	Dyserth	33 J 24
Dun Carloway			
Broch	70 Z 9	**E**	
Dunbar	57 M 15		
Dunbeath	74 J 9		
Dunblane	55 I 15	Eaglescliffe	46 P 20
Duncansby Head	74 K 8	Eaglesham	55 H 16
Dunchurch	28 Q 26	Eakring	36 R 24
Duncton	10 S 31	Ealing (London	
Dundee	62 K 14	Borough)	20 T 29
Dundonald	48 G 17	Earba (Lochan na	
Dundrennan	43 I 19	h-)	61 G 13
Dunecht	69 M 12	Earby	39 N 22
Dunfermline	56 J 15	Eardisley	26 K 27
Dungeness	13 W 31	Earl Shilton	27 Q 26
Dunholme	36 S 24	Earl Soham	23 X 27
Dunkeld	62 J 14	Earl Stonham	23 X 27
Dunkery Beacon	7 J 30	Earley Winnersh	19 R 29
Dunlop	55 G 16	Earls Barton	28 R 27
Dunnet	74 J 8	Earl's Colne	22 W 28
Dunnet Bay	74 J 8	Earls Colne	22 W 28
Dunnet Head	74 J 7	Earlsferry	56 L 15
Dunning	56 J 15	Earlston	50 L 17
Dunnottar Castle	63 N 13	Earn (Loch)	55 H 14
Dunoon	54 F 16	Earn (River)	61 H 14
Dunrobin Castle	67 I 10	Earn (River)	56 J 14
Duns	57 M 16	Easdale	54 D 15
Dunscore	49 I 18	Easebourne	10 R 31
Dunsfold	10 S 30	Easington	46 P 19
Dunsford	4 I 31	Easington Lane	46 P 19
Dunsop Bridge	38 M 22	Easingwold	40 Q 21
Dunstable	19 S 28	East Aberthaw	16 J 29
		East Barkwith	37 T 24
		East Bergholt	21 X 28
		East Brent	8 L 30
		East Budleigh	4 K 32
		East Cowes	10 Q 31
		East Dereham	30 W 25
		East Glen (River)	36 S 25
		East Grinstead	11 T 30
		East Hagbourne	19 Q 29
		East Hanney	18 P 29
		East Harling	30 W 26
		East Hendred	18 P 29
		East Hoathly	11 U 31
		East Horsley	11 S 30
		East Huntspill	8 L 30
		East Ilsley	19 Q 29
		East Kilbride	55 H 16
		East Knoyle	9 N 30
		East Lambrook	8 L 31
		East Leake	36 Q 25
		East Linton	57 M 16
		East Loch Roag	70 Z 9
		East Loch Tarbet	70 Z 10
		East Looe	3 G 32
		East Lulworth	8 N 32
		East Markham	36 R 24
		East Meon	10 Q 31
		East Midlands	
		Airport	36 Q 25
		East Moor	35 P 24
		East Rhidorroch	
		Lodge	72 F 10
		East Sussex	
		(County)	11 U 30
		East Wemyss	56 K 15
		East Wittering	10 R 31
		East Witton	46 O 21
		Eastbourne	11 U 31
		Eastbourne	11 U 31
		Eastchurch	21 W 29
		Eastdean	11 U 31
		Eastergate	10 S 31
		Easter Ross	67 G 10
		Eastergate	10 S 31
		Eastham	34 L 24
		Eastington	17 N 28
		Eastleigh	9 P 31
		Easton (Dorset)	5 M 32
		Easton (Norfolk)	31 X 26
		Easton-in-Gordano	17 L 29
		Eastriggs	49 K 19
		Eastry	13 X 30
		Eastville	37 U 24
		Eastwood	36 Q 24
		Ebbw Vale	
		/ Glyn Ebwy	16 K 28
		Ebchester	46 O 19
		Ecclefechan	49 K 18
		Eccles	34 M 23
		Eccleshall	34 N 25
		Echt	69 M 12
		Eckington (Worc.)	27 N 27
		Eckington (Derbs.)	35 P 24
		Edale	35 O 23
		Eday	74 L 6
		Edderton	67 H 10
		Eddrachillis Bay	72 E 9
		Edenbridge	11 U 30

EDINBURGH CENTRE

Bernard Terrace . . . . EZ 3
Bread Street . . . . DZ 6
Bristo Place . . . . EZ 7
Candlemaker Row . . . . EZ 9
Castle Street . . . . DY
Castlehill . . . . DZ 10
Chambers Street . . . . EZ 12
Chapel Street . . . . EZ 13
Charlotte Square . . . . CY 14
Deanhaugh Street . . . . CY 23
Douglas Gardens . . . . CY 25
Drummond Street . . . . EZ 27
Forrest Road . . . . EZ 31
Frederick Street . . . . DY
Gardner's Crescent . . . . CZ 32
George IV Bridge . . . . EZ 33
George Street . . . . DY
Grassmarket . . . . DZ 35
Hanover Street . . . . DY
High Street . . . . EYZ 37
Home Street . . . . DZ 38
Hope Street . . . . CY 39
Johnston Terrace . . . . DZ 42
King's Bridge . . . . DZ 44
King's Stables Road . . . . DZ 45
Lawnmarket . . . . EYZ 46
Leith Street . . . . EY 47
Leven Street . . . . DZ 48
Lothian Street . . . . EZ 51
Mound (The) . . . . DY 55
North Bridge . . . . EY 61
North St. Andrew
    Street . . . . EY 66
Princes Street . . . . DY
Raeburn Place . . . . CY 69
Randolph Crescent . . . . CY 71
St. Andrew Square . . . . EY 73
St. James Centre . . . . EY
St. Mary's Street . . . . EY 75
Shandwick Place . . . . CYZ 77
South Charlotte Street . . . . DY 78
South St. David Street . . . . . . DEY 79
Spittal Street . . . . DZ 83
Victoria Street . . . . EZ 84
Waterloo Place . . . . EY 87
Waverley Bridge . . . . EY 89
Waverley Market . . . . EY
West Maitland Street . . . . CZ 92

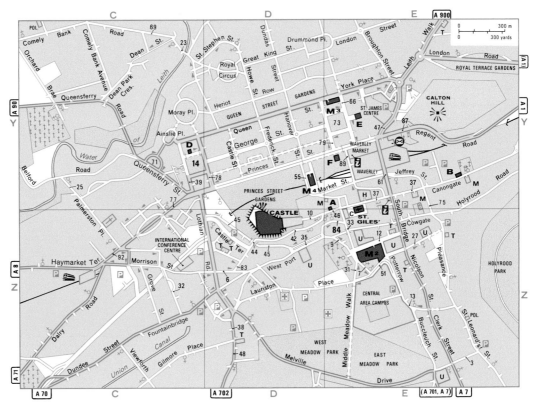

Eden (River)	44 K 19
Edgmond	34 M 25
Edinburgh	56 K 16
Edington	9 N 30
Edith Weston	28 S 26
Edlesborough	19 S 28
Edwinstowe	36 Q 24
Edzell	63 M 13
Eggerness Point	42 G 19

Eggleston	46 N 20
Egham	19 S 29
Egilsay	74 L 6
Eglingham	51 O 17
Egremont	44 J 20
Egton	47 R 20
Eigg	59 B 13
Eigheach (Loch)	61 G 13
Eight Ash Green	22 W 28

| Eil (Loch) | 60 E 13 |
| Eilde Mór (Loch) | 60 F 13 |
| Eilean
    a' Chalmain | 52 A 15 |
| Eilean Beag | 65 C 11 |
| Eilean
    Chathastail | 59 B 13 |
| Eilean Donan
    Castle | 66 D 12 |

Eilean Flodigarry	65 B 10
Eilean Mullagrach	72 D 9
Eilean nan Each	59 B 13
Eilean Troddday	65 B 10
Eilt (Loch)	60 D 13
Eishort (Loch)	65 C 12
Elan Valley	25 J 27
Elan Village	25 J 27
Elgin	68 K 11

Elgol	65 B 12
Elham	13 X 30
Elie	56 L 15
Elkesley	36 R 24
Elkstone	18 N 28
Elland	39 O 22
Ellastone	35 O 25
Ellen	69 N 11
Ellesmere	34 L 25
Ellesmere Port	34 L 24
Ellon	69 N 11
Elmdon	29 U 27
Elmswell	22 W 27
Elphin	72 E 9
Elsenham	20 U 28
Elstead	10 R 30
Elstree	20 T 29
Elswick	38 L 22
Eltisley	29 T 27
Elton	29 S 26
Elvington	40 R 22
Ely	29 U 26
Emberton	28 R 27
Embleton	51 P 17
Embo	73 I 10
Embsay	39 O 22
Emneth	29 U 26
Empingham	28 S 26
Emsworth	10 R 31
Enard Bay	72 D 9
Enderby	28 Q 26
Endon	35 N 24
Enfield (London
Borough)	20 T 29
Enford	9 O 30
Englefield
Green	19 S 29
Enham Alamein	9 P 30
Enmore	7 K 30
Ensay	59 B 14

Enstone	18 P 28
Enville	26 N 26
Eoropie	71 B 8
Eorsa	59 B 14
Eport (Loch)	64 Y 11
Epping	20 U 28
Epping Forest	20 U 29
Epsom	20 T 30
Epworth	40 R 23
Eredine Forest	54 D 15
Eriboll (Loch)	72 F 8
Ericht (Loch)	61 G 13
Eriska	60 D 14
Eriskay	64 Y 12
Erisort (Loch)	70 A 9
Ermington	4 I 32
Erpingham	31 X 25
Erraid	52 A 15
Errochty (Loch)	61 H 13
Errol	56 K 14
Ersary	58 X 13
Erskine Bridge	55 G 16
Esha Ness	75 P 2
Esher	20 S 29
Esk (Glen)	62 L 13
Esk (River)	50 K 19
Eskdale	50 K 18
Eskdalemuir	49 K 18
Essendon	20 T 28
Essex (County)	22 V 28
Essich	67 H 11
Eston	46 Q 20
Etchingham	12 V 30
Etherow (River)	35 N 23
Etherow Park	35 N 23
Etive (Glen)	60 F 14
Etive (Loch)	60 E 14
Eton	19 S 29
Ettington	27 P 27

Ettrick	50 K 17
Ettrick Forest	50 K 17
Ettrick Pen	49 K 17
Euxton	38 L 22
Evanton	67 G 11
Evercreech	8 M 30
Everleigh	9 O 30
Evershot	8 M 31
Everton	36 R 23
Evesham	27 O 27
Evesham
(Vale of)	27 O 27
Ewe (Isle of)	71 D 10
Ewell	20 T 29
Ewelme	19 Q 29
Ewhurst	11 S 30
Exbourne	4 I 31
Exe (River)	7 J 31
Exebridge	7 J 30
Exeter	7 J 31
Exford	7 J 30
Exminster	7 J 31
Exmoor National
Park	7 I 30
Exmouth	4 J 32
Exton	7 J 30
Eyam	35 O 24
Eye (Cambs.)	29 T 26
Eye (Suffolk)	31 X 27
Eye Peninsula	71 B 9
Eyemouth	57 N 16
Eynort (Loch)
(Highland)	65 A 12
Eynort (Loch)
(Western Isles)	64 Y 12
Eynsford	20 U 29
Eynsham	18 P 28
Eyre Point	65 B 12
Eythorne	13 X 30

EXETER CENTRE

Alphington Rd . . . . Z 2
Barnfield Rd . . . . Z 3
Bedford St. . . . . Y 6
Castle St. . . . . Y 7
Cathedral Close Walk . . . . YZ 13

Cowick St. . . . . Z 15
Edmund St. . . . . Z 18
Fore St. . . . . Z
Guildhall
    Shopping Centre . . . . Y
High St. . . . . Y
King St. . . . . Z 22
Mary Arches St. . . . . Z 26
Mint (The) . . . . Z 28

New Bridge St. . . . . Z 31
Palace Gate . . . . Z 36
Paul St. . . . . Y 37
Preston St. . . . . Z 40
Princesshay . . . . Y 44
Quay Hill . . . . Z 45
Queen's Terrace . . . . Y 46
St. Martin's Lane . . . . Y 49
Stepcote Hill . . . . Z 50

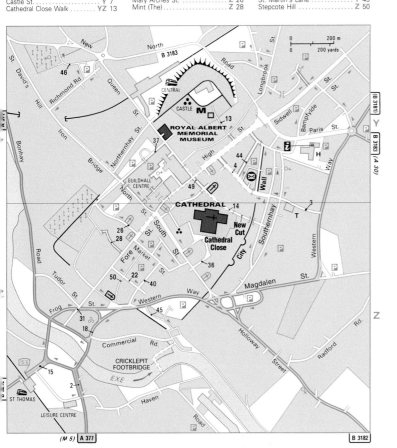

F

Fada (Loch) 64 Y 11
Fair Isle 75 P 5
Fair Oak 10 Q 31
Fairbourne 24 H 25
Fairford 18 O 28
Fairlie 54 F 16
Fairlight 12 V 31
Fakenham 30 W 25
Falfield 17 M 29
Falkirk 55 I 16
Falkland 56 K 15
Fallin 55 I 15
Falmouth 2 E 33
Fanagmore 72 E 8
Fannich (Loch) 66 E 11
Fara 74 K 7
Fareham 10 Q 31
Faringdon 18 P 29
Farleigh-
  Hungerford 17 N 30
Farley Mount 9 P 30
Farmborough 17 M 29
Farmtown 68 L 11
Farnborough
  (Hants.) 10 R 30
Farnborough
  (Warw.) 27 P 27
Farndon 36 R 24
Farne Islands 51 P 17
Farnham (Dorset) 9 N 31

Farnham (Surrey) 10 R 30
Farnham
  Royal 19 S 29
Farningham 20 U 29
Farnsfield 36 Q 24
Farnworth 39 M 23
Farrington
  Gurney 8 M 30
Farway 7 K 31
Fasnakyle Forest 66 F 11
Fasque 63 M 13
Fauldhouse 56 I 16
Faversham 12 W 30
Fawley 9 P 31
Fazeley 27 O 26
Fearnan 61 H 14
Fearnmore 65 C 11
Featherstone
  (Staffs.) 27 N 26
Featherstone
  (West Yorks.) 40 P 22
Feering 22 W 28
Felindre 25 K 26
Felinheli 32 H 24
Felixstowe 23 Y 28
Felling 46 P 19
Felpham 10 S 31
Felsted 22 V 28
Feltham 20 S 29
Felton 51 O 18
Feltwell 30 V 26
Fenstanton 29 T 27

Fenwick 51 O 17
Feochan (Loch) 54 D 14
Feolin Ferry 52 B 16
Ferndown 9 O 31
Ferness 67 I 11
Fernhurst 10 R 30
Ferryden 63 M 13
Ferryhill 46 P 19
Feshie (Glen) 61 I 12
Fetcham 11 S 30
Fetlar 75 R 2
Fetterangus 69 N 11
Fettercairn 63 M 13
Ffestiniog 33 I 25
Ffestiniog
  (Vale of) 32 H 25
Fflint / Flint 34 K 24
Fforest Fawr 16 J 28
Fiaray 64 X 12
Filey 41 T 21
Filton 17 M 29
Finchampstead 19 R 29
Finchingfield 22 V 28
Findhorn 68 J 11
Findhorn (River) 67 H 12
Findhorn Bay 68 J 11
Findochty 68 L 10
Findon 11 S 31
Finedon 28 S 26
Fingest 19 R 29
Finningley 36 R 23
Finsbay 70 Z 10

Finstock 18 P 28
Finstown 74 K 6
Fintry 55 H 15
Fionn Loch 66 D 10
Fionn Loch Mór 72 F 9
Fionnphort 59 A 15
Fishbourne 10 Q 31
Fishguard
  / Abergwaun 14 F 28
Fittleworth 10 S 31
Flackwell Heath 19 R 29
Fladbury 27 N 27
Fladda-Chùain 65 A 10
Flamborough 41 T 21
Flamborough
  Head 41 T 21
Flamingo Park 40 R 21
Flamstead 20 S 28
Flash 35 O 24
Flatford Mill 21 X 28
Fleckney 28 Q 26
Fleet 10 R 30
Fleet (Islands of) 43 H 19
Fleet (Loch) 73 H 10
Fleetwood 38 K 22
Flimby 44 J 19
Flint / Fflint 34 K 24
Flitton 20 S 27
Flitwick 19 S 27
Flodday (near
  Hellisay) 58 X 13

Flodday (near
  Sandray) 58 X 13
Flodden Field 51 N 17
Flodigarry 65 B 11
Floors Castle 50 M 17
Flotta 74 K 7
Flowerdale Forest 66 D 11
Fochabers 68 K 11
Foinaven 72 F 8
Folkestone 13 X 30
Folkingham 36 S 25
Fontmell Magna 8 N 31
Ford 54 D 15
Forde Abbey 8 L 31
Fordham 30 V 27
Fordingbridge 9 O 31
Fordoun 63 M 13
Fordyce 68 L 11
Foreland 10 Q 31
Foreland Point 7 I 30
Foremark
  Reservoir 35 P 25
Forest Row 11 U 30
Forfar 62 L 14
Formby 38 K 23
Formby Point 38 K 23
Fornham
  All Saints 22 W 27
Forres 68 J 11
Forsinard 73 I 8
Fort Augustus 66 F 12
Fort George 67 H 11

Fort Victoria 9 P 31
Fort William 60 E 13
Forter 62 K 13
Forth 56 I 16
Forth (Firth of) 56 K 15
Forth (River) 55 G 15
Forth Bridges 56 J 15
Fortingall 61 H 14
Forton 34 M 23
Fortrose 67 H 11
Fortuneswell 5 M 32
Fosdyke 37 T 25
Fotheringhay 29 S 26
Foulness Point 21 W 29
Foulridge 39 N 22
Foulsham 30 X 25
Fountains Abbey 39 P 21
Four Crosses 25 K 25
Four Elms 11 U 30
Four Marks 10 Q 30
Foveran 69 N 12
Fowey 3 G 32
Fowlmere 29 U 27
Fownhope 17 M 27
Foxdale 42 G 21
Foxholes 41 S 21
Foyers 67 G 12
Fraddon 2 F 32
Framfield 11 U 31
Framlingham 23 Y 27
Frampton-on-
  Severn 17 M 28

Framwellgate Moor 46 P 19
Frant 11 U 30
Fraserburgh 69 O 10
Fraserburgh Bay 69 O 10
Freckenham 30 V 27
Freckleton 38 L 22
Freethorpe 31 Y 26
Freevater Forest 66 F 10
Fremington 6 H 30
Frensham 10 R 30
Freshwater 9 P 31
Freshwater Bay 9 P 31
Freshwater East 14 F 29
Freshwater West 14 E 29
Fressingfield 31 X 26
Friday Bridge 29 U 26
Fridaythorpe 41 S 21
Frimley 19 R 30
Frinton-on-Sea 23 X 28
Friockheim 63 M 14
Frisa (Loch) 59 B 14
Friskney 37 U 24
Frittenden 12 V 30
Frizington 44 J 20
Frodsham 34 L 24
Froggatt 35 P 24
Frome 8 N 30
Fuday 64 X 12
Fuiay 58 X 13
Fulbourn 22 U 27
Fulwood 38 M 22

Folkestone Terminal

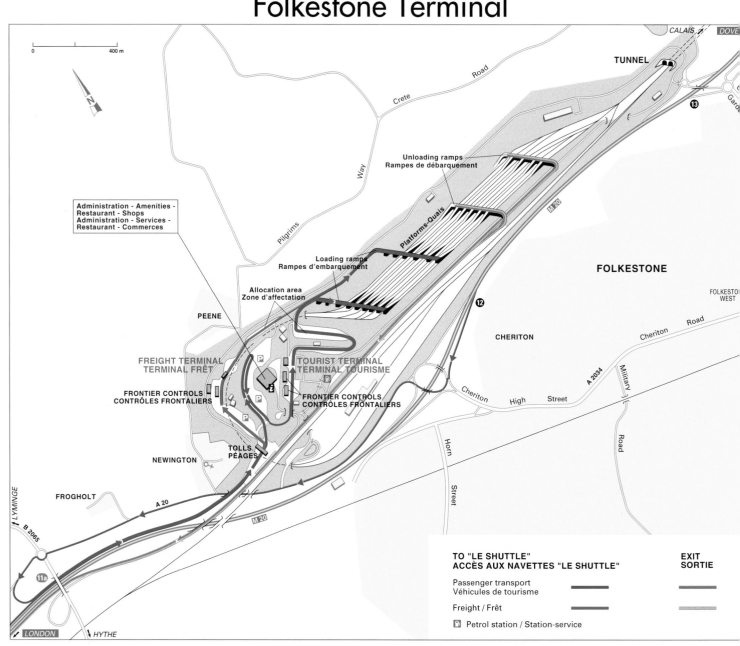

Terminal de Calais

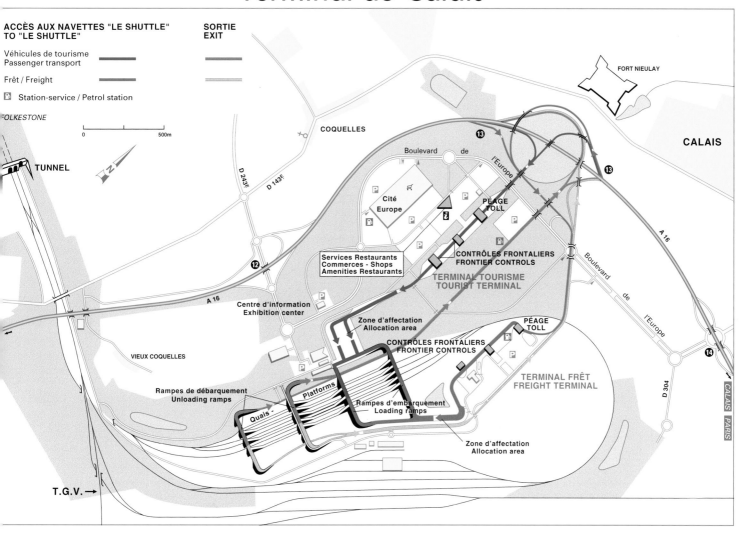

Funzie	75	R 2	Garry (Glen)			Glaisdale	47	R 20	Glentham	36	S 23	Gorseinon	15	H 29
Furness			(Perthshire and			Glamis	62	K 14	Glentress	50	K 17	Gorsleston-on-Sea	31	Z 26
Abbey	38	K 21	Kinross)	61	H 13	Glamis Castle	62	L 14	Glentworth	36	S 23	Gosberton	37	T 25
Furness Fells	44	K 20	Garry (Glen)			Glanaman	15	I 28	Glinton	29	T 26	Gosforth (Cumbria)	44	J 20
Fyfield (Essex)	20	U 28	(Highland)	60	E 12	Glas Maol	62	J 13	Glossop	35	O 23	Gosforth		
Fyvie	69	M 11	Garry (Loch)	60	F 12	Glasbury	25	K 27	Gloucester	17	N 28	(Newcastle upon		
			Garsington	19	Q 28	Glascarnoch (Loch)	66	F 10	Gloucestershire			Tyne)	51	P 18
G			Garten (Loch)	67	I 12	Glasgow	55	H 16	(County)	18	N 28	Gosport	10	Q 31
			Garth	25	J 27	Glass (Loch)	67	G 10	Glusburn	39	O 22	Gotham	36	Q 25
Gainford	46	O 20	Gartmore	55	G 15	Glasson	38	L 22	Glyn Ceiriog	33	K 25	Gott Bay	58	Z 14
Gainsborough	36	R 23	Garton-on-The-			Glastonbury	8	L 30	Glyn-Ebwy			Goudhurst	12	V 30
Gairloch	66	C 10	Wolds	41	S 21	Gleann Beag	66	F 10	/ Ebbw Vale	16	K 28	Gourdon	63	N 13
Gairlochy	60	F 13	Garve	67	F 11	Gleann Mór	67	G 10	Glyn-neath	16	J 28	Gourock	54	F 16
Gairsay	74	L 6	Garvellachs	52	C 15	Glemsford	22	V 27	Glyncorrwg	16	J 28	Gowerton	15	H 29
Galashiels	50	L 17	Garvock	54	F 16	Glen Brittle Forest	65	B 12	Glynde	11	U 31	Goxhill	41	T 22
Galgate	38	L 22	Garynahine	70	Z 9	Glen Finglas			Gnosall	34	N 25	Graemsay	74	K 7
Gallan Head	70	Y 9	Gatehouse of Fleet	43	H 19	Reservoir	55	G 15	Goat Fell	53	E 17	Grain	21	W 29
Galloway Forest			Gateshead	46	P 19	Glen More			Goathland	47	R 20	Grandtully	61	I 14
Park	48	G 18	Gateside	56	K 15	Forest Park	62	I 12	Gobowen	34	K 25	Grange-		
Galmisdale	59	B 13	Gatley	34	N 23	Glen Shee	62	J 13	Godalming	10	S 30	over-Sands	38	L 21
Galmpton	4	J 32	Gatwick Airport	11	T 30	Glenbarr	53	C 17	Godmanchester	29	T 27	Grangemouth	56	I 15
Galson	71	A 8	Gaulden Manor	7	K 30	Glenborrodale	59	C 13	Godmanstone	8	M 31	Grantham	36	S 25
Galston	48	G 17	Gayton	30	V 25	Glenbuck	49	I 17	Godshill	10	Q 32	Grantown-on-Spey	62	J 12
Galtrigill	64	Z 11	Geddington	28	R 26	Glencarse	56	K 14	Godstone	11	T 30	Grantshouse	57	N 16
Gamlingay	29	T 27	Gedney Drove End	37	U 25	Glencoe	60	E 13	Goil (Loch)	54	F 15	Grasmere	44	K 20
Gamston	36	R 24	Gedney Hill	29	T 25	Glencoul (Loch)	72	F 9	Golborne	34	M 23	Grassington	39	O 21
Ganton	41	S 21	Georgeham	6	H 30	Glendurgan			Goldthorpe	40	Q 23	Gravesend	21	V 29
Garboldisham	30	W 26	Georth	74	K 6	Garden	2	E 33	Golspie	73	I 10	Grayrigg	45	M 20
Gardenstown	69	N 10	Gerrards			Glenelg	66	D 12	Gomersal	39	O 22	Grays		
Garelochhead	54	F 15	Cross	19	S 29	Glenelg Bay	66	D 12	Gometra	59	B 14	Thurrock	20	V 29
Garenin	70	Z 9	Gifford	57	L 16	Glenfarg	56	J 15	Gomshall	11	S 30	Grayshott	10	R 30
Garforth	40	P 22	Gigha (Sound of)	53	C 17	Glenfield	28	Q 26	Goodrich	17	M 28	Grayswood	10	R 30
Gargrave	39	N 22	Gigha Island	52	C 16	Glenfinnan	60	D 13	Goodrington	4	J 32	Great Ayton	46	Q 20
Gargunnock	55	H 15	Gighay	64	Y 12	Glenforsa Airport	59	C 14	Goodwick	14	F 27	Great Baddow	22	V 28
Garioch	69	M 12	Gildersome	39	P 22	Glengorm	59	B 14	Goodwood House	10	R 31	Great Bardfield	22	V 28
Garlieston	42	G 19	Gillingham (Dorset)	8	N 30	Glengrasco	65	B 11	Goole	40	R 22	Great Barford	29	S 27
Garmouth	68	K 11	Gillingham (Kent)	21	V 29	Glenkens (The)	48	H 18	Gordon	50	M 16	Great Barr	27	O 26
Garrabost	71	B 9	Gilmerton	55	I 14	Glenlivet	68	J 11	Gorebridge	56	K 16	Great Bedwyn	18	P 29
Garrisdale			Girvan	48	F 18	Glenluce	42	F 19	Goring	19	Q 29	Great Bentley	21	X 28
Point	65	A 12	Gisburn	39	N 22	Glenmore	59	C 13	Gorm Loch Mór	72	F 9	Great Bernera	70	Z 9
			Gittisham	7	K 31	Glenrothes	56	K 15	Gorran Haven	3	F 33	Great Bircham	30	V 25

Great			Great Wakering	21	W 29
Bookham	11	S 30	Great Waltham	22	V 28
Great Bridon	46	P 20	Great Whernside	39	O 21
Great Broughton	46	Q 20	Great Witley	26	M 27
Great Chesterford	22	U 27	Great Wolford	18	P 27
Great Chishill	29	U 27	Great Wyrley	27	N 26
Great Clifton	44	J 20	Great Yarmouth	31	Z 26
Great Coates	41	T 23	Great Yeldham	22	V 27
Great Cumbrae			Greater		
Island	54	F 16	Manchester		
Great Driffield	41	S 21	(Metropolitan		
Great Dunmow	22	V 28	County)	34	N 23
Great Easton			Greatham		
(Essex)	20	U 28	(Cleveland)	46	Q 20
Great Easton			Greatham (Hants.)	10	R 30
(Leics.)	28	R 26	Greatstone-		
Great Eccleston	38	L 22	on-Sea	13	W 31
Great Ellingham	30	W 26	Greenhead	50	M 19
Great Gonerby	36	S 25	Greenholm	48	H 17
Great Grimsby	41	T 23	Greenlaw	57	M 16
Great Harwood	39	M 22	Greenock	54	F 16
Great Hockham	30	W 26	Greenodd	38	K 21
Great Horwood	19	R 28	Greens Norton	28	Q 27
Great Houghton	40	P 23	Greenwich (London		
Great Livermere	30	W 27	Borough)	20	U 29
Great Malvern	26	N 27	Grendon		
Great Massingham	30	W 25	Underwood	19	Q 28
Great Milton	19	Q 28	Gresford	34	L 24
Great Missenden	19	R 28	Greshornish (Loch)	65	A 11
Great Musgrave	45	M 20	Gretna	50	K 19
Great Oakley	21	X 28	Gretton	28	R 26
Great Ormes Head	33	I 23	Greys Court	19	R 29
Great Ouse (River)	30	V 25	Greystoke	45	L 19
Great Ouseburn	40	Q 21	Grimoldby	37	U 23
Great Ponton	36	S 25	Grimsay	64	Y 11
Great Ryburgh	30	W 25	Groby	28	Q 26
Great Sampford	22	V 28	Groombridge	11	U 30
Great Shefford	18	P 29	Grosmont	47	R 20
Great Shelford	29	U 27	Grove	18	P 29
Great Somerford	18	N 29	Gruinard Bay	71	D 10
Great Torrington	6	H 31	Gruinard Island	71	D 10

Gruinart (Loch)	52 B 16	Hagworthingham	37 U 24	Handsworth	35 P 23	Hartley	20 U 29
Grunavat (Loch)	70 Z 9	Hailsham	11 U 31	Hanley	35 N 24	Hartley Wintney	19 R 30
Grundisburgh	23 X 27	Hainton	37 T 23	Hanley Swan	26 N 27	Hartpury	17 N 28
Guardbridge	56 L 14	Halberton	7 J 31	Hanslope	28 R 27	Hartshill	27 P 26
Guernsey		Hale	34 M 23	Happisburgh	31 Y 25	Hartwell	19 R 28
(Channel I.)	5	Halesowen	27 N 26	Hapton	39 N 22	Harvington	27 O 27
Guildtown	62 J 14	Halesworth	31 Y 26	Harbertonford	4 I 32	Harwell	19 Q 29
Guildford	10 S 30	Halford	27 P 27	Harbottle	51 N 17	Harwich	23 X 28
Guisborough	47 Q 20	Halifax	39 O 22	Harbury	27 P 27	Harworth	36 Q 23
Guiseley	39 O 22	Halkirk	74 J 8	Harby	36 R 25	Hascosay	75 R 2
Guist	30 W 25	Hall	55 G 16	Hardham	10 S 31	Haselbury	
Gullane	56 L 15	Halland	11 U 31	Hardwick Hall	35 Q 24	Plucknett	8 L 31
Gunna	58 Z 14	Halling	21 V 29	Hardy Monument	8 M 31	Hasland	35 P 24
Gunnislake	3 H 32	Hallow	26 N 27	Hare Street	20 U 28	Haslemere	10 R 30
Gunthorpe	36 R 25	Halstead	22 V 28	Harewood House	40 P 22	Haslingden	39 N 22
Gurnard	10 Q 31	Haltham	37 T 24	Hargrave Green	22 V 27	Haslingfield	29 U 27
Gutcher	75 Q 1	Haltwhistle	50 M 19	Haringey (London		Hastings	12 V 31
Guyhirn	29 U 26	Halwell	4 I 32	Borough)	20 T 29	Hatch Court	8 L 31
Gwalchmai	32 G 24	Halwill Junction	6 H 31	Harlech	32 H 25	Hatfield (Herts.)	20 T 28
Gwaun-Cae-		Hambleden	19 R 29	Harleston	31 X 26	Hatfield (South	
Gurwen	15 I 28	Hambledon (Hants.)	10 Q 31	Harley	26 M 26	Yorks.)	40 Q 23
Gwbert-on-Sea	14 F 27	Hambledon (Surrey)	10 S 30	Harlington	19 S 28	Hatfield Broad Oak	20 U 28
Gweek	2 E 33	Hambleton (Lancs.)	38 L 22	Harlow	20 U 28	Hatfield Heath	20 U 28
Gwyddgrug	15 H 28	Hambleton (North		Harmston	36 S 24	Hatfield Peverel	22 V 28
Gwydir Castle	33 I 24	Yorks.)	40 Q 22	Haroldswick	75 R 1	Hatherleigh	6 H 31
		Hambleton Hills		Harpenden	20 S 28	Hathern	36 Q 25
		(The)	46 Q 21	Harpley	30 V 25	Hathersage	35 P 24
H		Hambridge	8 L 31	Harport (Loch)	65 A 12	Hatton	
Habost	71 B 8	Hamilton	55 H 16	Harray (Loch of)	74 K 6	(Aberdeenshire)	69 O 11
Hackney (London		Hammersmith and		Harringworth	28 S 26	Hatton (Derbs.)	35 O 25
Borough)	20 T 29	Fulham (London		Harris (Highland)	59 A 13	Haughton	34 N 25
Haddenham		Borough)	20 T 29	Harris (Western		Havant	10 R 31
(Bucks.)	19 R 28	Hamnavoe	75 P 3	Isles)	70 Y 10	Havenstreet	10 Q 31
Haddenham		Hampshire (County)	9 P 30	Harris (Sound of)	64 Y 10	Haverfordwest	
(Cambs.)	29 U 26	Hampstead Norris	19 Q 29	Harrogate	39 P 22	/Hwlffordd	14 F 28
Haddington	56 L 16	Hampton	27 O 26	Harrow (London		Haverhill	22 V 27
Haddiscoe	31 Y 26	Hampton		Borough)	19 S 29	Haverigg	38 K 21
Haddo House	69 N 11	Court	20 S 29	Harston	29 U 27	Havering (London	
Haddon Hall	35 P 24	Hamstead Marshall	18 P 29	Hartest	22 W 27	Borough)	20 U 29
Hadleigh (Essex)	21 V 29	Hamsterley	46 O 19	Hartfield	11 U 30	Haverthwaite	44 K 21
Hadleigh (Suffolk)	22 W 27	Hamstreet	12 W 30	Harthill	55 I 16	Hawarden	34 K 24
Hadlow	12 V 30	Hamworthy	9 N 31	Harting	10 R 31	Hawes	45 N 21
Hadnall	34 L 25	Handa Island	72 E 8	Hartington	35 O 24	Hawick	50 L 17
Hadrian's Wall	50 M 18	Handcross	11 T 30	Hartland	6 G 31	Hawkedon	22 V 27
Hagley	27 N 26	Handforth	39 N 24	Hartlebury	26 N 26	Hawkhurst	12 V 30
				Hartlepool	46 Q 19		

Hawkridge	7 J 30	Hellisay	64 X 12	Heybridge	22 W 28
Hawkshead	44 L 20	Helmdon	28 Q 27	Heysham	38 L 21
Hawkwell	21 V 29	Helmsdale	73 J 9	Heyshott	10 R 31
Hawley	19 R 30	Helmsley	47 Q 21	Heytesbury	9 N 30
Haworth	39 O 22	Helperby	40 Q 21	Heywood	39 N 23
Haxby	40 Q 21	Helpringham	37 T 25	Hibaldstow	41 S 23
Haxey	36 R 23	Helsby	34 L 24	Hidcote Manor	
Hay-on-Wye	25 K 27	Helston	2 E 33	Garden	27 O 27
Haydock	34 M 23	Helton	45 L 20	High Bentham	38 M 21
Haydon Bridge	50 N 19	Helvellyn	44 K 20	High Bickington	6 I 31
Hayfield	35 O 23	Hemel Hempstead	20 S 28	High Easter	22 V 28
Hayle	2 D 33	Hemingbrough	40 R 22	High Ercall	26 M 25
Hayling Island	10 R 31	Hempnall	31 X 26	High Force (The)	45 N 20
Haywards Heath	11 T 31	Hemsby	31 Z 25	High Halden	12 W 30
Hazelbank	49 I 16	Hemsworth	35 P 23	High Halstow	21 V 29
Hazel Grove	35 N 23	Hemyock	7 K 31	High Ham	8 L 30
Hazlemere	19 R 29	Hendy	15 H 28	High Ongar	20 U 28
Heacham	30 V 25	Henfield	11 T 31	High Peak	35 O 23
Headcorn	12 V 30	Hengoed	16 K 29	High Willhays	4 I 31
Headington	19 Q 28	Henham	20 U 28	High Wycombe	19 R 29
Headless Cross	27 O 27	Henley	27 O 27	Higham (Kent)	21 V 29
Headley	10 R 30	Henley-on-Thames	19 R 29	Higham (Lancs.)	39 N 22
Heads of Ayr	48 F 17	Henlow	29 T 27	Higham (Suffolk)	22 V 27
Heanor	35 P 24	Hennock	4 J 32	Higham Ferrers	28 S 27
Heath End	19 Q 29	Henstridge	8 M 31	Highbridge	8 L 30
Heath Hayes	27 O 25	Heptonstall	39 N 22	Highclere	18 P 29
Heathfield	11 U 31	Hereford	26 L 27	Highcliffe	9 O 31
Heathrow		Herefordshire		Higher	
Airport	20 S 29	(County)	26 M 27	Penwortham	38 L 22
Hebburn	46 P 19	Herm (Channel I.)	5	Highland Wildlife	
Hebden Bridge	39 N 22	Herma Ness	75 R 1	Park	61 I 12
Hebrides (Sea of		Hermitage	19 Q 29	Highley	26 M 26
the)	64 Z 12	Hermitage Castle	50 L 18	Highnam	17 N 28
Heckfield	19 R 29	Herne Bay	13 X 29	Hightae	49 J 18
Heckington	37 T 25	Herstmonceux	11 U 31	Hightown	38 K 23
Hednesford	27 O 25	Hertford	20 T 28	Highworth	18 O 29
Hedon	41 T 22	Hertfordshire		Hildenborough	11 U 30
Heighington		(County)	20 T 28	Hilderstone	35 N 25
(Durham)	46 P 20	Hessle	41 S 22	Hilgay	30 V 26
Heighington (Lincs.)	36 S 24	Hest Bank	38 L 21	Hill of Fearn	67 I 10
Helensburgh	54 F 15	Heswall	33 K 24	Hill of Tarvit	56 L 15
Helford	2 E 33	Hetton-le-Hole	46 P 19	Hillside	63 M 13
Hell's Mouth or		Heveningham	31 Y 27	Hillswick	75 P 2
Porth		Hever	11 U 30	Hilperton	18 N 30
Neigwl	32 G 25	Heversham	45 L 21	Hilpsford Point	38 K 21
Hellifield	39 N 22	Hevingham	31 X 25		
		Hexham	45 N 19		

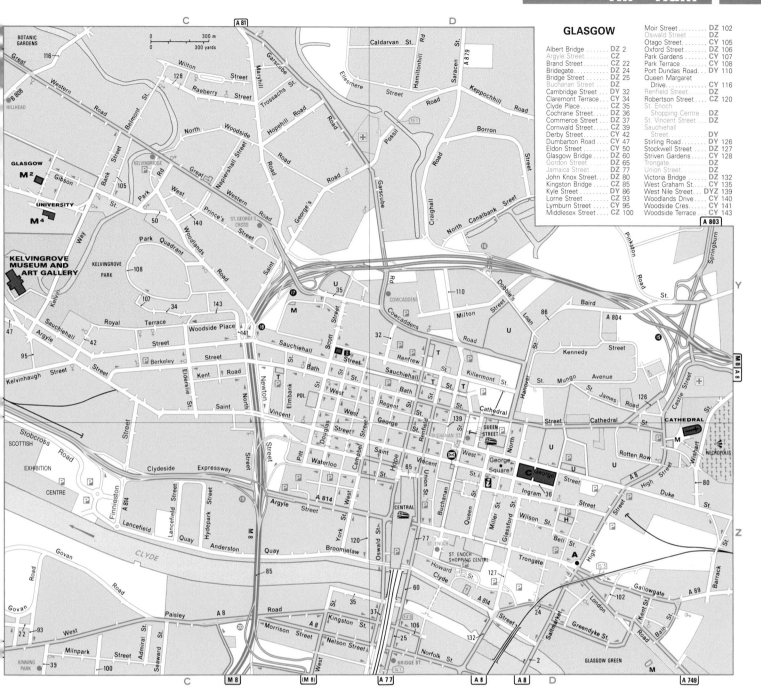

GLASGOW

Albert Bridge	DZ	2
Argyle Street	CZ	
Brand Street	CZ	22
Bridgegate	DZ	24
Bridge Street	DZ	25
Buchanan Street	DZ	
Cambridge Street	DY	32
Claremont Terrace	CY	34
Clyde Place	CZ	35
Cochrane Street	DZ	36
Commerce Street	DZ	37
Cornwald Street	DZ	39
Derby Street	CY	42
Dumbarton Road	CY	47
Eldon Street	CY	50
Glasgow Bridge	DZ	60
Gordon Street	DZ	65
Jamaica Street	DZ	77
John Knox Street	DZ	82
Kingston Bridge	CZ	85
Kyle Street	DY	86
Lorne Street	CZ	93
Lymburn Street	CY	95
Middlesex Street	CZ	100
Moir Street	DZ	102
Oswald Street	DZ	
Otago Street	CY	105
Oxford Street	CY	106
Park Gardens	CY	107
Park Terrace	CY	108
Port Dundas Road	DY	110
Queen Margaret Drive	CY	116
Renfield Street	CZ	
Robertson Street	CZ	120
St. Enoch Shopping Centre	DZ	
St. Vincent Street	DZ	
Sauchiehall Street	DY	
Stirling Road	DY	126
Stockwell Street	DZ	127
Striven Gardens	CY	128
Trongate	DZ	
Union Street	DZ	
Victoria Bridge	DZ	132
West Graham St.	DYZ	135
West Nile Street	DYZ	139
Woodlands Drive	CY	140
Woodside Cres.	CY	141
Woodside Terrace	CY	143

Hilton	35	P 25	Hollybush	48	G 17	Hooke	8	M 31	Horton Court	17	M 29	House of The			
Hinchingbrooke			Holme	38	L 21	Hook Norton	18	P 28	Horton-			Binns (The)	56	J 16
House	29	T 27	Holme upon			Hope (Flintshire)	34	K 24	in-Ribblesdale	39	N 21	Housesteads			
Hinckley	27	P 26	Spalding-Moor	40	R 22	Hope (Derbs.)	35	O 23	Horwich	38	M 23	Fort	50	N 18
Hinderwell	47	R 20	Holmes Chapel	34	M 24	Hope (Loch)	72	G 8	Houghton Hall	30	V 25	Hove	11	T 31
Hindhead	10	R 30	Holmesfield	35	P 24	Hope			Houghton House	28	S 27	Hoveton	31	Y 25
Hindley	38	M 23	Holmhead	48	H 17	under Dinmore	26	L 27	Houghton-le-			Hovingham	40	R 21
Hindon	9	N 30	Holsworthy	6	G 31	Hopeman	68	J 10	Spring	46	P 19	How Caple	17	M 28
Hingham	30	W 26	Holt (Wrexham)	34	L 24	Hopetoun House	56	J 16	Hourn (Loch)	66	D 12	Howden	40	R 22
Hinstock	34	M 25	Holt (Dorset)	9	O 31	Hopton	31	Z 26						
Hintlesham	23	X 27	Holt (Norfolk)	31	X 25	Horam	11	U 31						
Hirwaun	16	J 28	Holt (Wilts.)	18	N 29	Horbury	40	P 23						
Histon	29	U 27	Holton (Lincs.)	37	T 24	Horden	46	Q 19						
Hitcham	22	W 27	Holton (Norfolk)	31	Y 26	Horeb	24	G 27						
Hitchin	20	T 28	Holy Island			Horley	11	T 30						
Hockering	30	X 25	(Anglesey)	32	F 24	Hornby	38	M 21						
Hockley	21	V 29	Holy Island (North			Horncastle	37	T 24						
Hockley Heath	27	O 26	Ayrshire)	53	E 17	Horning	31	Y 25						
Hockliffe	19	S 28	Holy Island			Horninglow	35	P 25						
Hoddesdon	20	T 28	(Northumb.)	51	O 16	Horn's Cross	6	H 31						
Hodnet	34	M 25	Holybourne	10	R 30	Hornsea	41	T 22						
Hogsthorpe	37	U 24	Holyhead /			Horrabridge	3	H 32						
Holbeach	37	U 25	Caergybi	32	G 24	Horseheath	22	V 27						
Holbrook	21	X 28	Holystone	51	N 18	Horsell	19	S 30						
Holbury	9	P 31	Holywell /			Horsforth	39	P 22						
Holcombe	8	M 30	Treffynnon	33	K 24	Horsham	11	T 30						
Holdenby	28	R 27	Holywell Bay	2	E 32	Horsham								
Holford	7	K 30	Honiton	7	K 31	St. Faith	31	X 25						
Holkam Hall	30	W 25	Hoo			Horsmonden	12	V 30						
Hollesley Bay	23	Y 27	St. Werburgh	21	V 29	Horsted Keynes	11	T 30						
Hollingworth	35	O 23	Hook	10	R 30	Horton	9	O 31						
Howe of the			Hugh Town (I. of												
Mearns	63	M 13	Scilly)	2											
Howmore	64	X 12	Hughenden	19	R 29										
Hoxa (Sound of)	74	K 7	Huish Episcopi	8	L 30										
Hoy	74	J 7	Hull (River)	41	S 22										
Hoylake	33	K 23	Hullbridge	21	V 29										
Hoyland Nether	35	P 23	Humber (River)	41	T 23										
Hucknall	36	Q 24	Humber Bridge	41	S 22										
Huddersfield	39	O 23	Humberston	41	T 23										

GLOUCESTER
CENTRE

Black Dog Way	Y	5
Commercial Road	Y	6
Eastgate Shopping Centre	Y	
Eastgate Street	Y	10
Great Western Road	Y	12
Heathville Road	Y	13
Lower Westgate Street	Y	15
Northgate Street	Y	16
Parliament Street	Y	18
Pitt Street	Y	19
Quay Street	Y	20
Royal Oak Way	Y	21
St. Aldate Street	Y	22
St. Johns Lane	Y	23
Southgate Street	Y	
Spa Road	Y	26
Worcester Street	Y	31

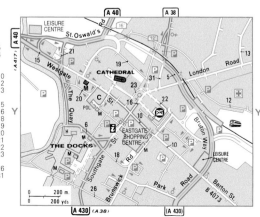

IPSWICH

Argyle Street	2	Lower Orwell Street	32
Bond Street	6	Northgate Street	33
Buttermarket Centre		Orwell Place	34
Carr Street		Queen Street	37
College Street	9	St. Helen's Street	39
	10	St. Margarets Street	40
	15	St. Nicholas Street	41
Corn Hill	16	St. Peter's Street	42
Dogs Head Street	18	Salthouse Street	43
Falcon Street	21	Silent Street	46
Franciscan Way	24	Tavern Street	
Friars Street	25	Tower Ramparts	
Grey Friars Road	26	Centre	47
Handford Road	30	Upper Orwell Street	49
Lloyds Avenue	31	Waterworks Street	51
		Westgate Street	52

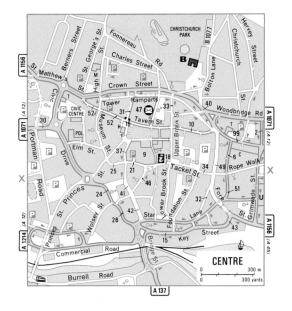

LEEDS

Aire Street	FZ 2	East Parade	FGZ 27	Park Lane	FY 64
Albion Street	GZ 3	Eastgate	GZ 31	Portland Crescent	GY 65
Bond Street	GZ 8	Hanover Way	FY 39	Queen Street	FZ 68
Bridge Street	GY 10	Headrow (The)	GY	St. John's Centre	GY
Briggate	GZ	Infirmary Street	GZ 44	St. Paul's Street	FZ 72
City Square	GZ 15	King Street	FZ 46	St. Peter's Street	GZ 73
Commercial Street	GZ 18	Kirkgate	GZ 48	Sheepscar St. South.	GY 75
Cookridge Street	GY 19	Lands Lane	GZ 49	Skinner Lane	GY 76
County Arcade	GZ 20	Marsh Lane	GZ 51	South Parade	FGZ 78
Cross Stamford St	GY 21	Meadow Lane	GZ 52	Trinity St. Shopping Centre	GZ
Crown Point Road	GZ 25	Merrion Centre	GY	Victoria Road	GZ 81
Duncan Street	GZ	Merrion Street	GY 53	Wade Lane	GY 82
		Merrion Way	GY 55	Wellington Road	FZ 83
		New Briggate	GY 57	West Street	FZ 84
		New York Road	GY 60	Westgate	FZ 85

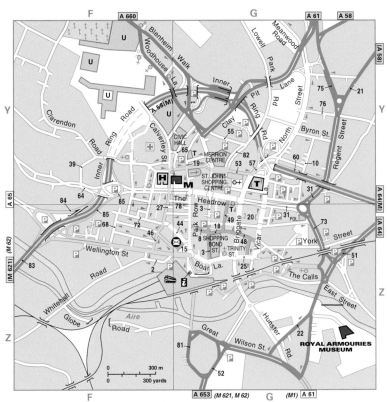

Hungerford	18 P 29	Hurlford	48 G 17	Husbands	
Hunmanby	41 T 21	Hursley	9 P 30	Bosworth	28 Q 26
Hunstanton	30 V 25	Hurst Green	12 V 30	Huthwaite	36 Q 24
Huntingdon	29 T 26	Hurstbourne Priors	9 P 30	Huttoft	37 U 24
Huntingtower		Hurstbourne		Hutton	
Castle	56 J 14	Tarrant	9 P 30	Cranswick	41 S 22
Huntly	68 L 11	Hurstpierpoint	11 T 31	Hutton Rudby	46 Q 20
Huntspill	8 L 30	Hurworth-on-Tees	46 P 20	Huyton	34 L 23

KINGSTON-UPON-HULL

		King Edward Street	Y 19
		Lowgate	Y 23
Bond Street	X 3	Market Place	Y 24
Carr Lane	Y	Paragon Street	Y 29
Commercial Road	Y 8	Prince's Dock Street	Y 32
Dock Office Row	X 10	Princes Quay Shopping Centre	Y
Dock Street	X 12	Prospect Shopping Centre	X
Ferensway	XY 14	Prospect Street	X
George Street	X	Queen Street	X 35
Grimston Street	X 15	Queen's Dock Avenue	X 36
Humber Dock Street	Y 16	Reform Street	X 37
Jameson Street	X 17	Sculcoates Bridge	X 42
Jarratt Street	X 18	Waterhouse Lane	X 47
		Whitefriargate	Y 49
		Wilberforce Drive	X 50
		Worship Street	X 52

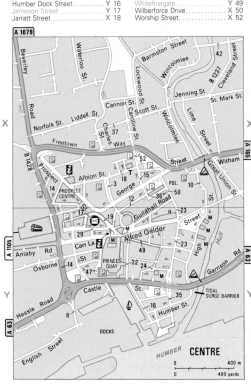

Hwlffordd		Ingliston	56 J 16	Isleornsay	65 C 12	Keir Mill	49 I 18
/ Haverfordwest	14 F 28	Ingoldmells	37 V 24	Islington (London		Keiss	74 K 8
Hyde	35 N 23	Ingoldsby	36 S 25	Borough)	20 T 29	Keith	68 L 11
Hynish Bay	58 Z 14	Ings	45 L 20	Islip	19 Q 28	Kellas	62 L 14
Hythe (Hants.)	9 P 31	Innellan	54 F 16	Ithon (River)	25 K 27	Kellie Castle	57 L 15
Hythe (Kent)	13 X 30	Inner Hebrides	58 Y 14	Iver	19 S 29	Kelly Bray	3 H 32
		Inner Sound	65 C 11	Iver Heath	19 S 29	Kelsall	34 L 24
I		Innerleithen	50 K 17	Ivinghoe	19 S 28	Kelso	50 M 17
		Insch	69 M 11	Ivybridge	4 I 32	Kelty	56 J 15
Ibstock	27 P 25	Instow	6 H 30	Ivychurch	12 W 30	Kelvedon	22 W 28
Ickleford	20 T 28	Inver (Loch)	72 E 9	Iwerne Minster	8 N 31	Kelvedon	
Icklingham	30 V 27	Inver Bay	67 I 10	Ixworth	30 W 27	Hatch	20 U 29
Ickworth House	22 V 27	Inver Valley	72 E 9			Kemble	18 N 28
Iden	12 W 31	Inverallochy	69 O 10	**J**		Kemnay	69 M 12
Iden Green	12 V 30	Inveraray	54 E 15			Kempsey	26 N 27
Idrigill Point	65 A 12	Inverbeg	55 G 15	Jacobstowe	6 H 31	Kempston	28 S 27
Ightham	20 U 30	Inverbervie	63 N 13	Janetstown	74 J 9	Kemsing	20 U 30
Ightham Mote	11 U 30	Invercreran	60 E 14	Jarrow	51 P 19	Kendal	45 L 21
Ilchester	8 L 30	Inverewe Gardens	66 C 10	Jaywick	21 X 28	Kenilworth	27 P 26
Ilderton	51 O 17	Inverey	62 J 13	Jedburgh	50 M 17	Kenmore	
Ilfracombe	6 H 30	Invergarry	60 F 12	Jedburgh Abbey	50 M 17	(Perthshire and	
Ilkeston	35 Q 25	Invergordon	67 H 10	Jersey (Channel I.)	5	Kinross)	61 I 14
Ilkley	39 O 22	Invergowrie	62 K 14	Jevington	11 U 31	Kenmore (Highland)	65 C 11
Illogan	2 E 33	Inverkeithing	56 J 15	John o' Groats	74 K 8	Kennet (River)	18 O 29
Ilmington	27 O 27	Inverkeithny	69 M 11	Johnshaven	63 N 13	Kennethmont	68 L 11
Ilminster	8 L 31	Inverkip	54 F 16	Johnston	14 F 28	Kenninghall	31 X 26
Ilsington	4 I 32	Inverkirkaig	72 E 9	Johnstone	55 G 16	Kennington (Kent)	12 W 30
Ilsley	19 Q 29	Inverliever Forest	54 D 15	Jura (Isle of)	52 B 16	Kennington (Oxon.)	19 Q 28
Immingham	41 T 23	Invermoriston	67 G 12	Jura (Sound of)	52 C 16	Kennoway	56 K 15
Immingham Dock	41 T 23	Inverness	67 H 11	Jura Forest	52 B 16	Kenovay	58 Z 14
Ince-in-Makerfield	38 M 23	Inversanda	60 D 13	Jurby West	42 G 20	Kensaleyre	65 B 11
Inch Kenneth	59 B 14	Inverurie	69 M 12			Kensington and	
Inchard (Loch)	72 E 8	Iona	59 A 15	**K**		Chelsea (London	
Inchkeith	56 K 15	Ipplepen	4 J 32			Borough)	20 T 29
Inchlaggan	60 E 12	Ipstones	35 O 24	Kames	54 E 16	Kent (County)	12 V 30
Inchmarnock	54 E 16	Ipswich	23 X 27	Katrine (Loch)	55 G 15	Kentallen	60 E 13
Inchnadamph	72 F 9	Ireby	44 K 19	Keal	37 U 24	Kentford	22 V 27
Inchture	62 K 14	Iron Acton	17 M 29	Keal (Loch na)	59 B 14	Kentisbeare	7 K 31
Indaal (Loch)	52 A 16	Iron-Bridge	26 M 26	Kearsley	39 M 23	Kenton	4 J 32
Ingatestone	22 V 28	Irthlingborough	28 S 27	Kebock Head	71 A 9	Keoldale	72 F 8
Ingham	30 W 27	Irvine	48 F 17	Kedleston Hall	35 P 25	Kerrera	60 D 14
Ingleton (Durham)	46 O 20	Isla (Glen)	62 K 13	Kegworth	36 Q 25	Kerry	25 K 26
Ingleton (North		Islay (Sound of)	52 B 16	Keighley	39 O 22	Kershader	70 A 9
Yorks.)	39 M 21	Isleham	30 V 26	Keinton Mandeville	8 M 30	Kesgrave	23 X 27
Inglewood Forest	45 L 19	Isle of Whithorn	42 G 19			Kessingland	31 Z 26

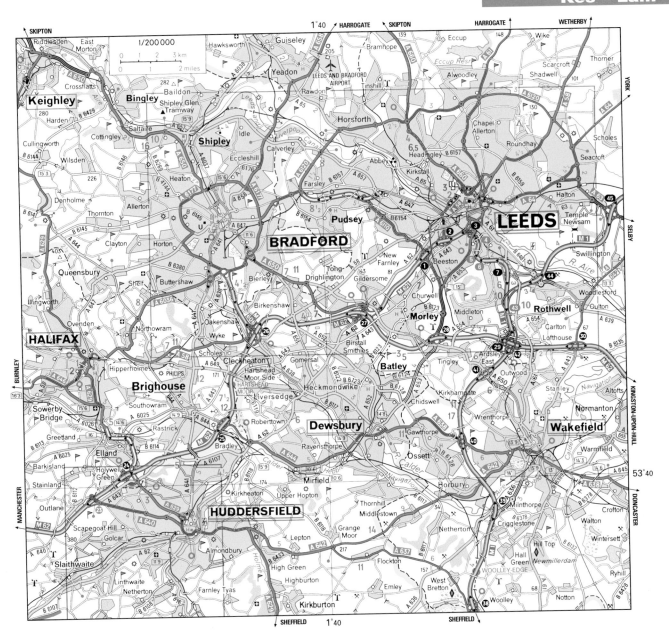

Keswick	44 K 20	Killichronan	59 C 14	Kinghorn	56 K 15	Kinlochleven	60 F 13	Kirkcudbright	43 H 19	Kirkwhelpington	51 N 18	Kyle of Tongue	72 G 8
Kettering	28 R 26	Killin	61 H 14	Kinglassie	56 K 15	Kinlochmoidart	59 C 13	Kirkcudbright		Kirriemuir	62 K 13	Kyleakin	65 C 12
Kettleshulme	35 N 24	Killinghall	40 P 21	Kings Langley	20 S 28	Kinloss	68 J 11	Bay	43 H 19	Kirtlebridge	49 K 18	Kylerhea	65 C 12
Kettletoft	74 M 6	Killingworth		Kings Worthy	10 Q 30	Kinneff	63 N 13	Kirkfieldbank	49 I 16	Kirtlington	19 Q 28	Kyles Scalpay	70 Z 10
Kettlewell	39 N 21	Kilmacolm	55 G 16	Kingsbarns	57 M 15	Kinnersley	26 L 27	Kirkham	38 L 22	Kirtomy	73 H 8	Kylestrome	72 E 9
Ketton	28 S 26	Kilmaluag	65 B 10	Kingsbridge	4 I 33	Kinross	56 J 15	Kirkhill	67 G 11	Kirton	37 T 25	Kynance Cove	2 E 34
Kew	20 T 29	Kilmany	56 L 14	Kingsclere	19 Q 30	Kintbury	18 P 29	Kirkinner	42 G 19	Kirton-		
Kexby	36 R 23	Kilmarnock	48 G 17	Kingsdown	13 Y 30	Kintore	69 M 12	Kirkintilloch	55 H 16	in-Lindsey	36 S 23	**L**
Keyingham	41 T 22	Kilmartin	54 D 15	Kingskerswell	4 J 32	Kintyre		Kirklees	39 O 23	Kishorn (Loch)	66 D 11	Laceby	41 T 23
Keymer	11 T 31	Kilmaurs	48 G 17	Kingskettle	56 K 15	(Peninsula)	53 D 17	Kirklevington	46 P 20	Kitchener		Lacey Green	19 R 28
Keynsham	17 M 29	Kilmelford	54 D 15	Kingsland	26 L 27	Kinver	26 N 26	Kirklington	36 R 24	Memorial	74 J 6	Lacock	18 N 29
Keyworth	36 Q 25	Kilmorack	67 G 11	Kingsley	35 O 24	Kippax	40 P 22	Kirkmichael		Knaresborough	40 P 21	Ladder Hills	68 K 12
Kibworth Harcourt	28 R 26	Kilmun	54 F 16	Kingsmuir	62 L 14	Kippen	55 H 15	(Perthshire and		Knarsdale	45 M 19	Ladock	2 F 33
Kidderminster	26 N 26	Kilninver	54 D 14	Kingsnorth	12 W 30	Kippford	43 I 19	Kinross)	62 J 13	Knebworth	20 T 28	Ladybank	56 K 15
Kidlington	19 Q 28	Kilnsey	39 N 21	Kingsteignton	4 J 32	Kirby Cross	21 X 28	Kirkmichael (South		Kneesworth	29 T 27	Ladybower	
Kidsgrove	34 N 24	Kiloran	52 B 15	Kingston (Moray)	68 K 10	Kirby Hall	28 S 26	Ayrshire)	48 G 17	Knighton		Reservoir	35 O 23
Kidwelly / Cydweli	15 H 28	Kilpeck	17 L 28	Kingston (Devon)	4 I 33	Kirby Muxloe	28 Q 26	Kirkmuirhill	49 I 17	/ Trefyclawdd	26 K 26	Lagg	52 C 16
Kielder	50 M 18	Kilrenny	57 L 15	Kingston Bagpuize	18 P 28	Kirdford	10 S 30	Kirknewton	56 J 16	Knightshayes		Laggan (near	
Kielder Forest	50 M 18	Kilt Rock	65 B 11	Kingston Lacy	9 N 31	Kirk Ella	41 S 22	Kirkoswald	48 F 18	Court	7 J 31	Invergarry)	60 F 12
Kielder Reservoir	50 M 18	Kilwinning	48 F 17	Kingston-upon-Hull	41 S 22	Kirk Ireton	35 P 24	Kirkpatrick		Kniveton	35 O 24	Laggan (near	
Kilbarchan	55 G 16	Kimberley	30 X 26	Kingston-upon-		Kirk Michael	42 G 21	Durham	49 I 18	Knock (Moray)	68 L 11	Newtonmore)	61 H 12
Kilbirnie	54 F 16	Kimble	19 R 28	Thames (London		Kirkbean	44 J 19	Kirkpatrick-		Knock (Western		Laggan (Loch)	61 G 13
Kilbrannan Sound	53 D 17	Kimbolton	29 S 27	Borough)	20 T 29	Kirkbride	44 K 19	Fleming	50 K 18	Isles)	71 B 9	Laggan Point	52 B 16
Kilbride	54 D 14	Kimmeridge	9 N 32	Kingstone	17 L 27	Kirkburton	39 O 23	Kirkstone Pass	45 L 20	Knockie Lodge	67 G 12	Laide	71 D 10
Kilcadzow	55 I 16	Kimpton	20 T 28	Kingswear	4 J 32	Kirkby	34 L 23	Kirkton		Knockin	34 L 25	Lair	66 E 11
Kilchattan	54 E 16	Kinbrace	73 I 9	Kingswinford	27 N 26	Kirkby Fleetham	46 P 20	of Culsalmond	69 M 11	Knole	11 U 30	Lairg	72 G 9
Kilchenzie	53 C 17	Kincardine	56 I 15	Kingswood (South		Kirkby-		Kirkton of Durris	69 M 12	Knossington	36 R 25	Lake District	
Kilchoan	59 B 13	Kincardine O' Neil	69 L 12	Glos.)	17 M 29	in-Ashfield	36 Q 24	Kirkton		Knottingley	40 Q 22	National	
Kilchrenan	54 E 14	Kinclaven	62 J 14	Kingswood (Glos.)	17 M 29	Kirkby Lonsdale	38 M 21	of Glenisla	62 K 13	Knowle	27 O 26	Park	44 K 20
Kilconquhar	56 L 15	Kincraig	61 I 12	Kington	26 K 27	Kirkby Malham	39 N 21	Kirkton		Knowsley	34 L 23	Lakenheath	30 V 26
Kilcreggan	54 F 16	Kinfauns	56 J 14	Kington Langley	18 N 29	Kirkby Malzeard	39 P 21	of Kingoldrum	62 K 13	Knoydart	60 D 12	Lamberhurst	12 V 30
Kildonan	53 E 17	King's Bromley	27 O 25	Kingussie	61 H 12	Kirkby Stephen	45 M 20	Kirkton of Largo	56 L 15	Knutsford	34 M 24	Lambeth (London	
Kildrummy	68 L 12	King's Cliffe	28 S 26	Kinloch	59 B 12	Kirkby Thore	45 M 20	Kirkton of Skene	69 N 12	Kyle Forest	48 G 17	Borough)	20 T 29
Kildrummy Castle	68 L 12	King's Lynn	30 V 25	Kinloch Rannoch	61 H 13	Kirkbymoorside	47 R 21	Kirkton		Kyle		Lambourn	18 P 29
Kilham	41 S 21	King's Somborne	9 P 30	Kinlochard	55 G 15	Kirkcaldy	56 K 15	of Strathmartine	62 K 14	of Durness	72 F 8	Lamerton	3 H 32
Kilkhampton	6 G 31	King's Sutton	28 Q 27	Kinlochbervie	72 E 8	Kirkcolm	42 E 19	Kirktown		Kyle of Lochalsh	65 C 12	Lamlash	53 E 17
Killearn	55 G 15	Kingairloch	60 D 14	Kinlocheil	60 E 13	Kirkconnel	49 I 17	of Auchterless	69 M 11	Kyle		Lamlash Bay	53 E 17
Killerton	7 J 31	Kingarth	54 E 16	Kinlochewe	66 E 11	Kirkcowan	42 G 19	Kirkwall	74 L 7	of Sutherland	72 G 10	Lammermuir Hills	56 L 16

LONDON

Abingdon Rd .... EY 2
Allsop Pl. .... HU 4
Appold Street .... PU 5
Atterbury St. .... LZ 9
Battersea Park Rd. .... JZ 19
Belvedere Rd. .... MX 23
Bernard St. .... LT 25
Bessborough St. .... KZ 30
Bethnal Green Rd. .... PT 32
Bevis Marks .... PU 34
Bishopsgate .... PU 36
Blackfriars Bridge .... NV 38
Bloomsbury St. .... LU 39
Bowling Green Lane .... NT 43
Bridgefoot .... LZ 49
Broad Sanctuary .... LY 52
Brompton Rd. .... HY
Byward St. .... PV 62
Calthorpe St. .... MT 65
Camden Passage .... NS 70
Camomile St. .... PU 71
Carriage Drive North ...... IZ 75
Chapel Market .... NS 78
Charlbert St. .... HT 79
Charterhouse Sq. .... OU 81
Charterhouse St. .... NU 83
Cornwall Rd. .... MX 108
Corporation Row .... NT 110
Cowcross St. .... NU 113
Crawford Pl. .... HU 116
Cromwell Cres. .... EZ 119
Crucifix Lane .... PX 125
Curtain Rd. .... PT 126
Dante Rd. .... NZ 129
Dufferin St. .... OT 141
Duke's Pl. .... PV 145
Durham St. .... MZ 150
Eardley Cres. .... EZ 151
Eastcheap .... PV 154
Ebury Bridge .... IZ 156
Edwardes Sq. .... EY 158
Elephant Rd. .... OZ 163
Fann St. .... OU 166
Farringdon St. .... NU 168
Fetter Lane .... NU 169
Garden Row .... NY 173
Giltspur St. .... OU 178
Goodge St. .... KU 184
Gracechurch St. .... PV 187
Great Eastern St. .... PT 192
Great George St. .... LY 193
Great Smith St. .... LY 196
Great Tower St. .... PV 197
Greycoat Pl. .... KY 200
Gunter Grove .... FZ 202
Harleyford St. .... MZ 211
Herbrand St. .... LT 218
Hercules Rd. .... MY 219
Holland Walk .... EY 225
Horseguards Av. .... LX 228
Hornton St. .... FY 229
Howland St. .... KU 232
Hunter St. .... LT 233
Hyde Rd. .... PS 235
Kensington High St. ...... EY
Kenway Rd. .... FZ 245
Knightsbridge .... HY
King's Rd. .... GHZ
King Edward St. .... OU 247
King William St. .... PV 250
Leadenhall St. .... PV 260
Little Britain. .... OU 264
Lloyd Baker St. .... MT 265
Lombard St. .... PV 268
Long Lane CITY .... OU 270
Lothbury .... PU 273
Lower Marsh .... MY 277
Lower Thames St. .... PV 278
Mansell St. .... PV 282
Middlesex St. .... PU
Miles St. .... LZ 290
Montague St. .... OU 291
Moreland St. .... OT 293
Myddelton St. .... NT 296
Nevern Place .... EZ 298
Nevern Sq. .... EZ 299
New Bridge St. .... NV 301
New Change .... OV 304
Newington Butts .... OZ 306
Newington Causeway .... OY 307
Northumberland Av. ..... LX 317
Old Bailey .... NV 318
Old Broad St. .... PU 319
Old Marylebone Rd. .... HU 324
Oxford St. .... KU
Paddington St. .... IU 333
Park Cres. .... IU 337
Parliament St. .... LY 340
Parry St. .... LZ 341
Pembroke Gdns .... EY 342
Penn St. .... PS 343
Penton Rise .... MT 344
Penton St. .... MT 345
Penywern Rd. .... FZ 347
Philbeach Gdns .... EZ 348
Piccadilly .... JX
Pilgrimage St. .... PY 349
Poole St. .... PS 350
Porchester Rd. .... FU 351
Portobello Rd. .... EV
Poultry .... OV 352
Princes St. .... PV 357
Queen's Circus .... IZ 361
Queen St. .... OV 365
Regent St. .... KV
Rossmore Rd. .... HT 369
St. Andrews St. .... NU 372
St. Bride St. .... NV 376
St. John's Wood
  High St. .... GT 378
St. John's Wood Park ... GS 379
St. Martin's-le-Grand ... OU 380
Shoreditch High St. .... PT 384
Sidmouth St. .... LT 385
Sloane St. .... HY
Snows Fields .... PX 386
Southampton Row ...... LU 387
South Pl. .... PU 391
Southwark Bridge ...... OV 395
Spencer St. .... NT 398
Spital Sq. .... PU 399
Storeys Gate .... LY 402
Tabard St. .... OY 408
Tavistock Sq. .... LT 409
Templeton Pl. .... EZ 410
Threadneedle St. ...... MX 417
Throgmorton St. .... PU 418
Tower Hill .... PV 425
Trebovir Rd. .... FZ 426
Upper Ground .... NX 428
Upper Thames St. ..... OV 431
Upper Woburn Pl. ..... LT 432
Vincent St. .... LZ 436
Warwick Av. .... FU 441
Westbourne Park Villas . FU 449

Westbourne Ter. Rd. ..... FU 452
West Smithfield. .... NU 454
Wharfdale Rd. .... LS 455
Whitechapel High St. .... PU 456
Whitehall Court. .... LX 460
Whitehall Pl. .... LX 462
Whitmore Rd. .... PS 464
Wormwood St. .... PU 472

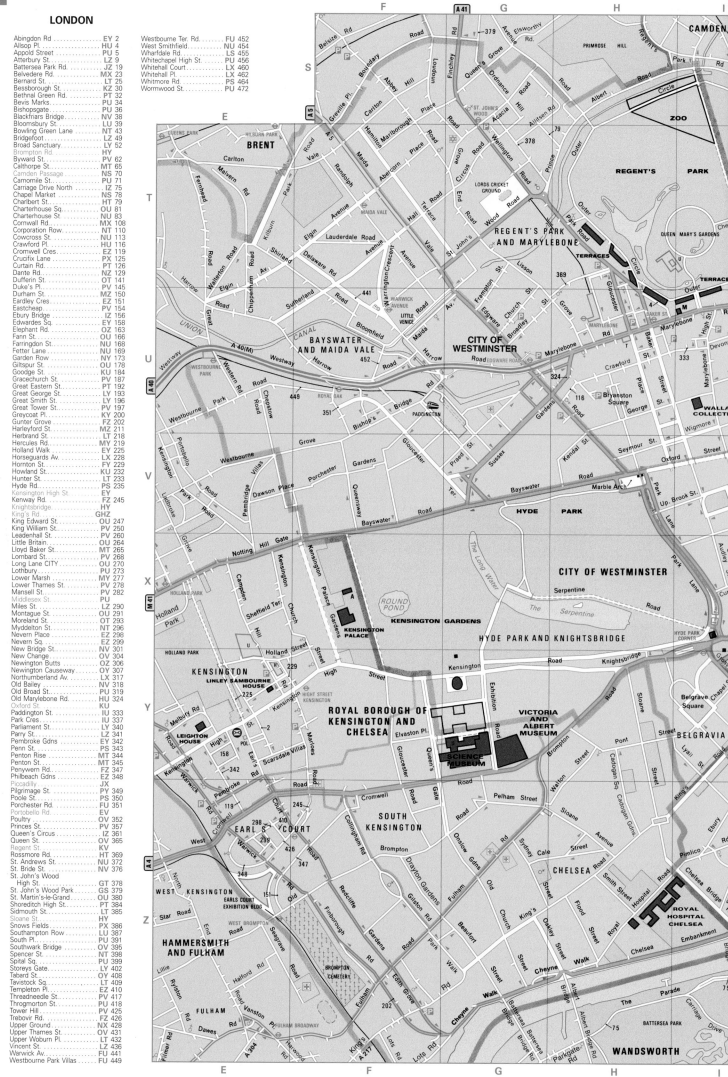

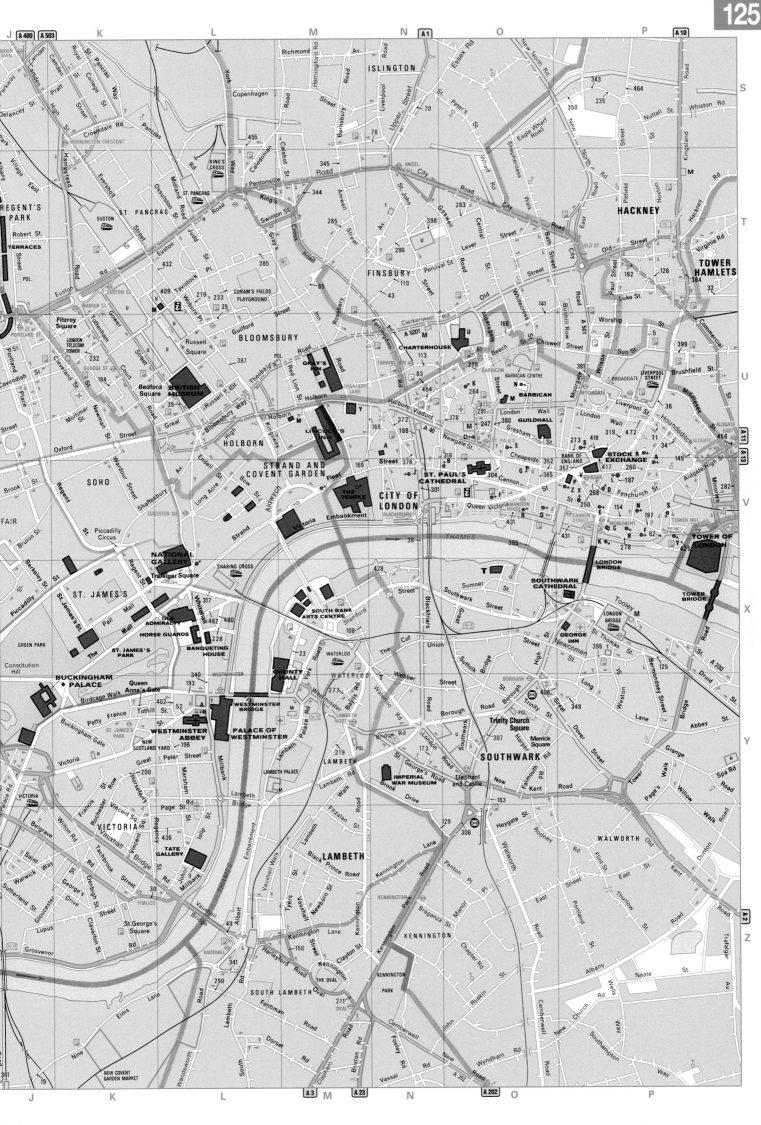

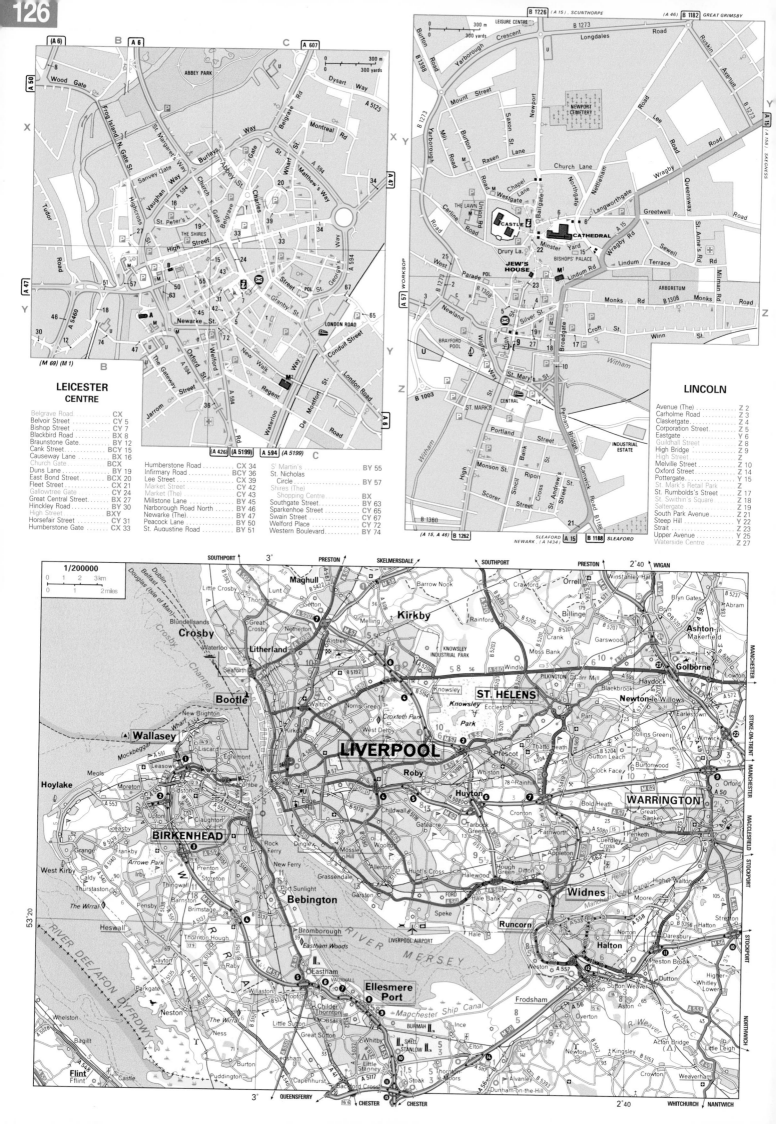

LEICESTER
CENTRE

Belgrave Road............CX
Belvoir Street ....CY 5
Bishop Street ....CY 7
Blackbird Road ....BX 8
Braunstone Gate..........BY 12
Cank Street...............BCY 15
Causeway Lane ....BX 16
Church Gate...............BCX
Duns Lane ....BY 19
East Bond Street.........BCX 20
Fleet Street ....CX 21
Gallowtree Gate ....CY 24
Great Central Street .....BX 27
Hinckley Road ....BY 30
High Street................BXY
Horsefair Street ....CY 31
Humberstone Gate ......CX 33

Humberstone Road ......CX 34
Infirmary Road ....BCY 36
Lee Street ....CX 39
Market Street ....CY 42
Market (The) ....CY 43
Millstone Lane ....BY 45
Narborough Road North ..BY 46
Newarke (The) ....BY 47
Peacock Lane ....BY 50
St. Augustine Road ......BY 51

S' Martin's ....BY 55
St. Nicholas
Circle ....BY 57
Shires (The)
Shopping Centre ......BX
Southgate Street ....BY 63
Sparkenhoe Street ......CY 65
Swain Street ....CY 67
Welford Place ....CY 72
Western Boulevard......BY 74

LINCOLN

Avenue (The) ....Z 2
Carholme Road ....Z 3
Clasketgate................Z 4
Corporation Street........Z 5
Eastgate ....Y 6
Guildhall Street ....Z 8
High Bridge ....Z 9
High Street ....Z
Melville Street ....Z 10
Oxford Street ....Z 14
Pottergate................Z 15
St. Mark's Retail Park ....Z
St. Rumbolds's Street ....Z 17
St. Swithin's Square ......Z 18
Saltergate ....Z 19
South Park Avenue......Z 21
Steep Hill ....Y 22
Strait ....Z 23
Upper Avenue ....Y 25
Waterside Centre ....Z 27

1/200000

LIVERPOOL
CENTRE

Argyle St. . . . . DZ 6
Blackburne Place . . . . EZ 11
Bold St. . . . . DZ
Brunswick Road . . . . EY 19
Canada Boulevard . . . . . . CYZ 22
Canning Place . . . . CZ 23
Church St. . . . . DY
Churchill Way . . . . DY 25
Clarence St. . . . . EYZ 26
College Lane . . . . DZ 28
Commutation Row . . . . DY 30
Cook St. . . . . CY 32
Crosshall St. . . . . DY 36
Daulby St. . . . . EY 40
Erskine St. . . . . EY 45
Fontenoy St. . . . . DY 48
Forrest St. . . . . DZ 49
George's Dock Gate . . . . . . CY 51
Grafton St. . . . . DZ 53
Great Charlotte St. . . . . DY 54
Great Howard St. . . . . CY 56
Hatton Garden . . . . DY 57
Haymarket . . . . DY 58
Hood St. . . . . DY 62
Houghton St. . . . . DY 65
Huskisson St. . . . . EZ 66
James St. . . . . CY 68
King Edward St. . . . . CY 69
Knight St. . . . . EZ 72
Leece St. . . . . EZ 73
Lime St. . . . . DY
Liver St. . . . . CZ 76
London Road . . . . DEY
Lord St. . . . . CDY
Mansfield St. . . . . DEY 80
Mathew St. . . . . CDY 81
Moss St. . . . . EY 86
Mount St. . . . . EZ 88
Myrtle St. . . . . EZ 89
Newington . . . . DZ 92
New Quay . . . . CY 93
North John St. . . . . CY 96
Norton St. . . . . EY 97
Parker St. . . . . DY 103
Prescot St. . . . . EY 105
Prince's Road . . . . EZ 107
Ranelagh St. . . . . DZ 108
Richmond St. . . . . DY 109
Roe St. . . . . DY 114
St. James Place . . . . EZ 117
St. Johns Centre . . . . DY
St. John's Lane . . . . DY 118
School Lane . . . . DYZ 122
Scotland Place . . . . DY 123
Sefton St. . . . . DZ 129
Seymour St. . . . . EY 130
Skelhorne St. . . . . DY 133
Stanley St. . . . . CDY 135
Suffolk St. . . . . DZ 137
Tarleton St. . . . . DY 139
Victoria St. . . . . DY 143
Water St. . . . . CY 150
William Brown St. . . . . DY 156
York St. . . . . DZ 157

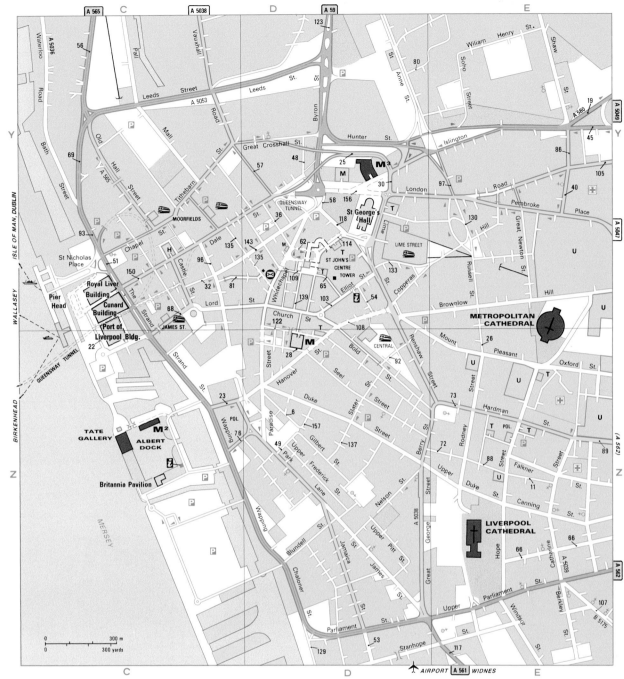

Lampeter / Llanbe		Larbert	55 I 15	Leasingham	37 S 24	Lesbury	51 P 17
dr Pont Steffan	24 H 27	Largs	54 F 16	Leathaid Bhuain		Leslie	56 K 15
Lanark	49 I 16	Larkhall	55 I 16	(Loch an)	72 F 9	Lesmahagow	49 I 17
Lancashire (County)	38 M 22	Larkhill	9 O 30	Leatherhead	20 T 30	Leswalt	42 E 19
Lancaster	38 L 21	Lasswade	56 K 16	Leathley	39 P 22	Letchworth	20 T 28
Lanchester	46 O 19	Lastingham	47 R 21	Lecale Peninsula	99 O 5	Letham (Angus)	63 L 14
Land's End	2 C 33	Latchingdon	22 W 28	Lechlade	18 O 28	Letham (Fife)	56 K 15
Landrake	3 H 32	Lauder	57 L 16	Lecht Road	68 K 12	Letheringsett	30 X 25
Lanercost	50 L 19	Lauderdale	57 L 16	Ledbury	26 M 27	Letterewe Forest	66 D 10
Langavat (Loch)		Laugharne	15 G 28	Ledmore	72 F 9	Letterston	14 F 28
(Lewis)	70 Z 9	Laughton	11 U 31	Lee	6 H 30	Leuchars	56 L 14
Langavat (Loch)		Launceston	3 G 32	Lee-on-the-Solent	10 Q 31	Leven (East Riding	
(South Harris)	70 Z 10	Laurencekirk	63 M 13	Leebotwood	26 L 26	of Yorks.)	41 T 22
Langbank	55 G 16	Lauriston Castle	63 N 13	Leeds (Kent)	12 V 30	Leven (River)	
Langdale Valley	44 K 20	Lavant	10 R 31	Leeds (West Yorks.)	40 P 22	(Highland)	60 F 13
Langenhoe	22 W 28	Lavenham	22 W 27	Leedstown	2 D 33	Leven (Fife)	56 K 15
Langford	29 T 27	Laverstoke	9 P 30	Leek	35 N 24	Leven (Loch)	60 E 13
Langholm	50 L 18	Lawford	21 X 28	Leeming Bar	46 P 21	Levens	45 L 21
Langley	19 S 29	Laxey	42 G 21	Leicester	28 Q 26	Levens Hall	45 L 21
Langold	36 Q 23	Laxey Bay	42 G 21	Leicestershire		Levenwick	75 Q 4
Langport	8 L 30	Laxfield	31 Y 27	(County)	27 P 26	Leverington	29 U 25
Langsett	35 O 23	Laxford (Loch)	72 E 8	Leigh	38 M 23	Leverton with	
Langstrothdale		Laxford Bridge	72 E 8	Leigh-on-Sea	21 V 29	Habblesthorpe	36 R 24
Chase	39 N 21	Laxo	75 Q 2	Leighton Buzzard	19 S 28	Lewdown	3 H 32
Langtoft	41 S 21	Layer-de-la-Haye	22 W 28	Leintwardine	26 L 26	Lewes	11 U 31
Langton Matravers	9 O 32	Layer Marney	22 W 28	Leiston	23 Y 27	Lewis and Harris	
Langwathby	45 L 19	Lazonby	45 L 19	Leith	56 K 16	(Isle of)	70 Z 8
Lanhydrock	3 F 32	Leaden Roding	20 U 28	Lemreway	70 A 9	Lewisham (London	
Lanivet	3 F 32	Leadenham	36 S 24	Lenham	12 W 30	Borough)	20 T 29
Lanreath	3 G 32	Leadgate	45 M 19	Lennoxtown	55 H 16	Leyburn	46 O 21
Lansallos	3 G 32	Leadhills	49 I 17	Leominster	26 L 27	Leyland	38 L 22
Lapford	7 I 31	Lealholm	47 R 20	Lerwick	75 Q 3	Leysdown-on-Sea	21 W 29

Lezant	3 G 32	Linwood	55 G 16	Littleport	29 U 26
Lhanbryde	68 K 11	Liphook	10 R 30	Littlestone-	
Liathach	66 D 11	Liskeard	3 G 32	on-Sea	13 W 31
Lichfield	27 O 25	Lismore	60 D 14	Liverpool	34 L 23
Liddesdale	50 L 18	Liss	10 R 30	Liverton	47 R 20
Lidgate	22 V 27	Litcham	30 W 25	Livet (Glen)	68 K 12
Lifton	3 H 32	Litherland	34 L 23	Livingston	56 J 16
Ligger or Perran		Little Berkhamsted	20 T 28	Lizard	2 E 34
Bay	2 E 32	Little Budworth	34 M 24	Lizard Peninsula	2 E 33
Lilleshall	26 M 25	Little Bytham	28 S 25	Llanarth	24 H 27
Limpsfield	11 U 30	Little Chalfont	19 S 28	Llanbadarn Fawr	24 H 26
Lincoln	36 S 24	Little Clacton	21 X 28	Llanbedr	32 H 25
Lincolnshire		Little Colonsay	59 B 14	Llanbedr Pont	
(County)	37 T 24	Little Cumbrae		Steffan /	
Lincolnshire Wolds	37 T 23	Island	54 F 16	Lampeter	24 H 27
Lindfield	11 T 30	Little Glenshee	62 J 14	Llanbedrog	32 G 25
Lindores	56 K 14	Little Hadham	20 U 28	Llanberis	32 H 24
Lingay (near Eriskay)	64 X 12	Little Hallingbury	20 U 28	Llanbister	25 K 26
Lingay (near Pabbay)	58 X 13	Little Loch Broom	72 D 10	Llanbrynmair	25 J 26
Lingfield	11 T 30	Little Loch Roag	70 Z 9	Llanddewi Brefi	24 I 27
Liniclate	64 X 11	Little Minch (The)	64 Z 11	Llandegla	33 K 24
Linley Head	14 E 29	Little Moreton Hall	34 M 24	Llandeilo	15 I 28
Linlithgow	56 J 16	Little Ouse (River)	30 V 26	Llandenny	17 L 28
Linn of Dee	62 J 13	Little Ouseburn	40 Q 21	Llandissilio	14 F 28
Linn of Tummel	61 I 13	Little Snoring	30 W 25	Llandovery	
Linney Head	14 E 29	Little Walsingham	30 W 25	/ Llanymddyfri	15 I 28
Linnhe (Loch)	60 D 14	Little Waltham	22 V 28	Llandrindod Wells	25 J 27
Linslade	19 R 28	Littleborough	39 N 23	Llandrinio	26 K 25
Lintmill	68 L 10	Littlebourne	13 X 30	Llandudno	33 I 24
Linton	22 U 27	Littlebury	22 U 27	Llandudno	
Linton-on-Ouse	40 Q 21	Littlecote House	18 P 29	Junction	33 I 24
Lintrathen		Littlehampton	10 S 31	Llandybie	15 H 28
(Loch of)	62 K 13				

Llandygai	32 H 24	Llanidloes	25 J 26	Llyfnant Valley	25 I 26	Lockerbie	49 J 18	Longay	65 C 12	Lower Diabaig	66 C 11	Luthrie	56 K 13
Llandysul	24 H 27	Llanilar	24 H 26	Llyn Brianne	25 I 27	Locking	17 L 30	Longbenton	51 P 18	Lowestoft	31 Z 26	Luton	20 S 28
Llanegryn	24 H 26	Llanmadoc	15 H 29	Llyn Celyn	33 I 25	Loddon	31 Y 26	Longbridge Deverill	9 N 30	Lowick	51 O 17	Luton Hoo	20 S 28
Llanelli	15 H 28	Llannefydd	33 J 24	Llyn Tegid or Bala Lake	33 J 25	Lode	22 U 27	Longburton	8 M 31	Lowick Bridge	44 K 21	Lutterworth	28 Q 26
Llanelltyd	33 I 25	Llanrhaeadr-ym-Mochnant	33 K 25	Llyswen	25 K 27	Lodsworth	10 R 31	Longfield	20 U 29	Lowther	49 I 17	Luxborough	7 J 30
Llanengan	32 G 25	Llanrhidian	15 H 29	Loanhead	56 K 16	Loftus	47 R 20	Longforgan	62 K 14	Lowther Hills	49 J 18	Lybster	74 K 9
Llanerchymedd	32 G 24	Llanrhystud	24 H 27	Lochaber	66 D 12	Logan Gardens	42 F 19	Longhope	74 K 7	Loxwood	10 S 30	Lydbury North	26 L 26
Llanfair	32 H 25	Llanrwst	33 I 24	Lochailort	60 D 13	Logie Coldstone	68 L 12	Longhorsley	51 O 18	Loyal (Loch)	73 G 8	Lydd	12 W 31
Llanfair-Caereinion	25 K 26	Llansanffraid Glan Conwy	33 I 24	Lochaline	59 C 14	Logiealmond	62 I 14	Longhoughton	51 P 17	Loyne (Loch)	60 E 12	Lydd-on-Sea	13 W 31
Llanfair-Pwllgwyngyll	32 H 24	Llansantffraid	24 H 27	Lochans	42 E 19	Lomond (Loch)	55 G 15	Longleat House	8 N 30	Lùb Score	65 A 10	Lydford	3 H 32
Llanfair-ym-Muallt / Builth	25 J 27	Llansantffraid-ym-Mechain	33 K 25	Locharbriggs	49 J 18	London	20 T 29	Longniddry	56 L 16	Lubenham	28 R 26	Lydham	26 L 26
Llanfairfechan	33 I 24	Llansawel	15 H 27	Lochawe	60 E 14	London Colney	20 T 28	Longnor	35 O 24	Lubnaig (Loch)	55 H 15	Lydiard Park	18 O 29
Llanfyllin	33 K 25	Llansilin	33 K 25	Lochay (Glen)	61 G 14	Merton (London Borough)	20 T 29	Longridge	38 M 22	Luccombe	7 J 30	Lydney	17 M 28
Llangadog	15 I 28	Llansoy	17 L 28	Lochboisdale	64 Y 12	Long Bennington	36 R 25	Longside	69 O 11	Luce Bay	42 F 19	Lyme Bay	5 L 32
Llangammarch Wells	25 J 27	Llanthony	17 K 28	Lochbuie	59 C 14	Long Buckby	28 Q 27	Longton	35 N 25	Ludgershall (Bucks.)	19 Q 28	Lyme Park	35 N 23
Llangefni	32 H 24	Llantwit Major	16 I 29	Lochcarron	66 D 11	Long Crendon	19 R 28	Longtown	50 L 18	Ludgershall (Wilts.)	9 P 30	Lyme Regis	8 L 31
Llangeinor	16 J 29	Llanuwchllyn	33 I 25	Lochearnhead	55 H 14	Long Eaton	36 Q 25	Lonmore	65 A 11	Ludgvan	2 D 33	Lyminge	13 X 30
Llangeitho	24 H 27	Llanwddyn	33 J 25	Locheport	64 Y 11	Long Hanborough	18 P 28	Looe	3 G 32	Ludham	31 Y 25	Lymington	9 P 31
Llangollen	33 K 25	Llanwenog	24 H 27	Lochgarthside	67 G 12	Long (Loch) (Angus)	62 K 14	Lorn	60 E 14	Ludlow	26 L 26	Lymm	34 M 23
Llangorse	16 K 28	Llanwrda	15 I 28	Lochgelly	56 K 15	Long (Loch) (Argyll and Bute)	54 F 15	Lorn (Firth of)	60 D 14	Lugton	55 G 16	Lympne	13 X 30
Llangrannog	24 G 27	Llanwrtyd Wells	25 J 27	Lochgilphead	54 D 15	Long Man (The)	11 U 31	Lossiemouth	68 K 10	Luichart (Loch)	66 F 11	Lympstone	4 J 32
Llangunllo	25 K 27	Llanybydder	24 H 27	Lochgoilhead	54 F 15	Long Marston	40 Q 22	Lostwithiel	3 G 32	Luing	54 D 15	Lyndhurst	9 P 31
Llangurig	25 J 26	Llanymddyfri / Llandovery	15 I 28	Lochinver	72 E 9	Long Melford	22 W 27	Loudwater	19 R 29	Lulworth Cove	8 N 32	Lyneham	18 O 29
Llangwn	17 L 28	Llanymynech	33 K 25	Lochluichart	66 F 11	Long Mountain	26 K 26	Loughborough	36 Q 25	Lumphanan	69 L 12	Lyness	74 K 7
Llangwnnadl	32 F 25	Llanystumdwy	32 H 25	Lochmaben	49 J 18	Long Mynd (The)	26 L 26	Loughor (River)	15 H 29	Lunanhead	62 L 14	Lynmouth	7 I 30
Llangwyryfon	24 H 27	Lledrod	24 I 27	Lochmaddy	64 Y 11	Long Preston	39 N 21	Loughton	20 U 29	Lundie (Loch)	66 C 11	Lynton	7 I 30
Llangybi	24 H 27	Lleyn Peninsula	32 G 25	Lochore	56 K 15	Long Stratton	31 X 26	Louth	37 U 23	Lundin Links	56 K 15	Lyon (Glen)	61 H 14
Llangynidr	16 K 28	Llwyngwril	24 H 25	Lochranza	54 E 16	Long Sutton (Lincs.)	37 U 25	Low Street	31 Y 25	Lundy	6 G 30	Lyonshall	26 L 27
Llangynog	33 J 25	Llwynmawr	33 K 25	Lochsie (Glen)	62 J 13	Long Sutton (Somerset)	8 L 30	Lowca	44 J 20	Lurgainn (Loch)	72 E 9	Lytchett Minster	9 N 31
Llanhilleth	16 K 28			Lochton	63 M 12			Lowdham	36 Q 24	Luss	55 G 15	Lytes Cary	8 L 30
				Lochwinnoch	55 G 16			Lower Bentham	38 M 21			Lytham	38 L 22
				Lochy (Loch)	60 F 13			Lower Cam	17 M 28			Lytham St. Anne's	38 K 22

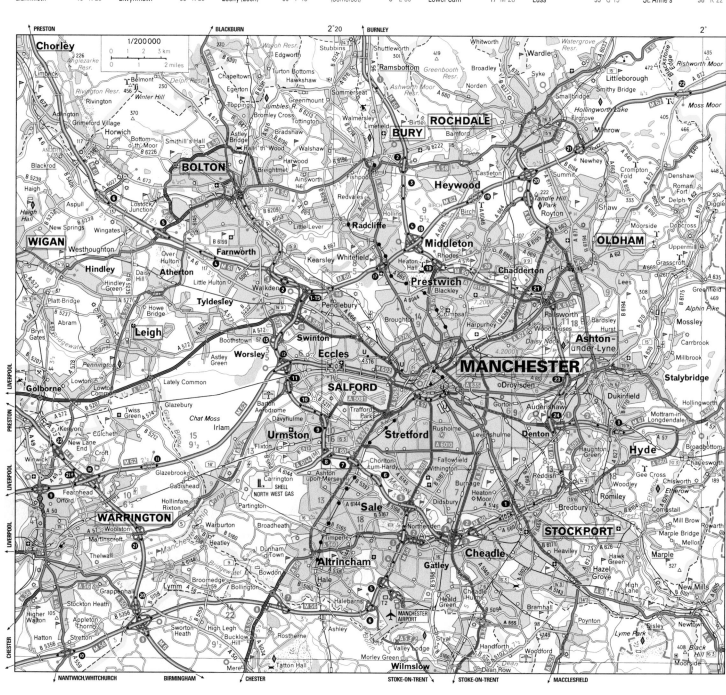

MANCHESTER
CENTRE

Addington Street .... CY 2
Albert Square .... CZ 6
Aytoun Street .... CZ 10
Blackfriars Road .... CY 15
Blackfriars Street .... CY 17
Brazennose Street .... CZ 18
Charlotte Street .... CZ 25
Cheetham Hill Road .... CY 27
Chepstow Street .... CZ 28
Chorlton Street .... CZ 29
Church Street .... CY 31
Corn Exchange .... CY 34
Dale Street .... CYZ
Deansgate
Ducie Street .... CZ 45
Fairfield Street .... CY 49
Fennel Street .... CY 50
Great Bridgewater Street .... CZ 53
Great Ducie Street .... CY 57
High Street .... CY 62
John Dalton Street .... CZ 63
King Street .... CZ 64
Liverpool Road .... CZ 68
Lloyd Street .... CZ 69
Lower Byrom St. .... CZ 70
Lower Mosley Street ...... CZ 71
Mosley Street .... CZ
Nicholas Street .... CZ 84
Parker Street .... CZ 91
Peter Street .... CZ 92
Princess Street .... CZ
St. Ann's Street .... CY 101
St. Peter's Square .... CY 104
Spring Gardens .... CZ 106
Viaduct Street .... CY 109
Whitworth Street West ...... CZ 112
Withy Grove .... CY 113
York Street .... CZ 115

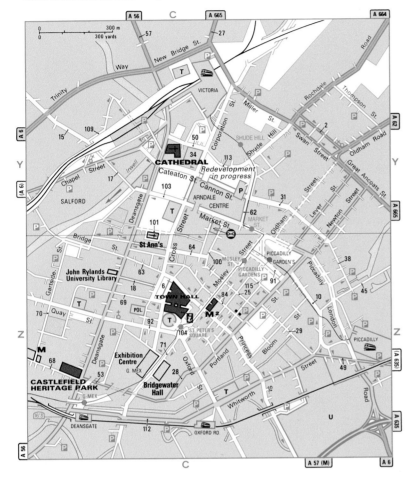

M

Maaruig	70 Z 10	Maidstone	12 V 30	Manton	28 R 26	Marsden	39 O 23
Mablethorpe	37 U 23	Mainland (Orkney		Manuden	20 U 28	Marsham	31 X 25
Mc Arthur's Head	52 B 16	Islands)	74 J 6	Mapledurham	19 Q 29	Marshchapel	37 U 23
Macaskin (Island)	54 D 15	Mainland (Shetland		Mar (Forest of)	68 J 12	Marshfield	17 N 29
Macclesfield	35 N 24	Islands)	75 R 3	Marazion	2 D 33	Marske-by-the-Sea	47 Q 20
Macduff	69 M 10	Maisemore	17 N 28	March	29 U 26	Marston Magna	8 M 31
Machars (The)	42 G 19	Malborough	4 I 33	Marcham	18 P 29	Marston	
Machir Bay	52 A 16	Malden Bradley	8 N 30	Marchwood	9 P 31	Moretaine	28 S 27
Machrihanish	53 C 17	Maldon	22 W 28	Marden	12 V 30	Martham	31 Y 25
Machrihanish Bay	53 C 17	Malham	39 N 21	Maree (Loch)	66 D 10	Martin	9 O 31
Machynlleth	25 I 26	Mallaig	59 C 12	Mareham-le-Fen	37 T 24	Martin (Isle)	72 E 10
Madderty	56 I 14	Mallory Park		Maresfield	11 U 31	Martley	26 M 27
Maddy (Loch)	64 Y 11	Circuit	27 P 26	Margam	15 I 29	Martock	8 L 31
Madeley (Salop)	26 M 26	Mallwyd	25 I 25	Margaretting	22 V 28	Marwell Zoological	
Madeley (Staffs.)	34 M 24	Malmesbury	18 N 29	Margate	13 Y 29	Park	10 Q 31
Madingley	29 U 27	Malpas	34 L 24	Margnaheglish	53 E 17	Mary Arden's	
Madron	2 D 33	Maltby	36 Q 23	Market Bosworth	27 P 26	House	27 O 27
Maenclochog	14 F 28	Maltby-le-Marsh	37 U 24	Market Deeping	37 T 25	Mary Tavy	3 H 32
Maentwrog	32 I 25	Malton	40 R 21	Market Drayton	34 M 25	Maryburgh	67 G 11
Maerdy	16 J 28	Malvern Wells	26 N 27	Market Harborough	28 R 26	Maryculter	69 N 12
Maes Howe	74 K 7	Mamble	26 M 26	Market Lavington	9 O 30	Marykirk	63 M 13
Maesteg	16 J 29	Mamore Forest	60 F 13	Market Rasen	37 T 23	Marypark	68 J 11
Maghull	38 L 23	Man (Isle of)	42 G 21	Market Weighton	41 S 22	Maryport	44 J 19
Magor	17 L 29	Manaton	4 I 32	Markfield	28 Q 25	Marywell	63 M 14
Maiden Bradley	8 N 30	Manchester	35 N 23	Markinch	56 K 15	Masham	39 P 21
Maiden Castle	8 M 31	Manea	29 U 26	Marks Tey	22 W 28	Matlock	35 P 24
Maiden Newton	8 M 31	Mangotsfield	17 M 29	Markyate	20 S 28	Matlock Bath	35 P 24
Maidenhead	19 R 29	Manningtree	21 X 28	Marlborough	18 O 29	Mattishall	30 X 26
Maidens	48 F 17	Manorbier	14 F 29	Marldon	4 J 32	Mauchline	48 G 17
Maidford	28 Q 27	Mansfield	36 Q 24	Marlow	19 R 29	Maud	69 N 11
		Mansfield		Marnhull	8 N 31	Maughold Head	42 H 21
		Woodhouse	36 Q 24	Marple	35 N 23	Mawbray	44 J 19

Maybole	48 F 17	Milborne Port	8 M 31	Mordiford	26 M 27
Mayfield (East		Milborne St.		More (Glen)	59 C 14
Sussex)	11 U 30	Andrew	8 N 31	More (Loch) (near	
Mayfield (Staffs.)	35 O 24	Mildenhall	30 V 26	Kinloch)	72 F 9
Meadie (Loch)	72 G 9	Mile End	22 W 28	More (Loch)	
Mealsgate	44 K 19	Milford	10 S 30	(near Westerdale)	73 J 8
Meare	8 L 30	Milford Haven /		Morebath	7 J 30
Measach (Falls of)	66 E 10	Aberdaugleddau	14 E 28	Morecambe	38 L 21
Measham	27 P 25	Milford-on-Sea	9 P 31	Morecambe Bay	38 L 21
Medbourne	28 R 26	Millom	38 K 21	Moreton-in-the-	
Medmenham	19 R 29	Millport	54 F 16	Marsh	18 O 28
Medway (River)	21 W 29	Milltown (Moray)	68 L 11	Moreton-in-the-	
Meidrim	15 G 28	Milltown (Highland)	66 F 11	Marsh	20 U 28
Meigle	62 K 14	Milnathort	56 J 15	Moreton-	
Melbost	71 B 9	Milngavie	55 H 16	hampstead	4 I 32
Melbourn	29 U 27	Milnrow	39 N 23	Morfa Nefyn	32 G 25
Melbourne	35 P 25	Milnthorpe	38 L 21	Moricambe Bay	44 K 19
Melfort	54 D 15	Milovaig	64 Z 11	Morie (Loch)	67 G 10
Melksham	18 N 29	Milton (Cambs.)	29 U 27	Moriston (Glen)	66 F 12
Mellerstain	50 M 17	Milton		Morley	39 P 22
Melling	38 M 21	(Dumfries and		Morlich (Loch)	67 I 12
Mellon Udrigle	71 D 10	Galloway)	42 F 19	Morpeth	51 O 18
Melmerby	45 M 19	Milton Abbas	8 N 31	Morte Bay	6 H 30
Melrose	50 L 17	Milton Abbot	3 H 32	Mortehoe	6 H 30
Meltham	39 O 23	Milton Bryan	19 S 28	Mortimer	19 Q 29
Melton Mowbray	36 R 25	Milton Ernest	28 S 27	Morton (near	
Melvaig	71 C 10	Milton Keynes	28 R 27	Bourne)	37 S 25
Melvich	73 I 8	Milton Libourne	18 O 29	Morton (near	
Menai Bridge		Milton of Campsie	55 H 16	Gainsborough)	36 R 23
/ Porthaethwy	32 H 24	Milverton	7 K 30	Morven	74 I 9
Menai Strait	32 H 24	Milwich	35 N 25	Morvern	59 C 14
Mendip Hills	17 L 30	Minard	54 E 15	Morville	26 M 26
Menston	39 O 22	Minch (The)	71 C 9	Morwelham	3 H 32
Menteith Hills	55 H 15	Minehead	7 J 30	Morwenstow	6 G 31
Mentmore	19 R 28	Minety	18 O 29	Moss Bank	34 L 23
Meonstoke	10 Q 31	Mingary	64 X 12	Mossend	55 H 16
Meopham	20 V 29	Minginish	65 B 12	Mossley	39 N 23
Mere (Cheshire)	34 M 24	Mingulay	58 X 13	Mosstodloch	68 K 11
Mere (Wilts.)	8 N 30	Minnigaff	42 G 19	Motherwell	55 I 16
Mereworth	12 V 30	Minster (near		Moulton (Lincs.)	37 T 25
Meriden	27 P 26	Ramsgate)	13 X 29	Moulton	
Merrick	48 G 18	Minster (near)	21 W 29	(Northants.)	28 R 27
Merriott	8 L 31	Minsterley	26 L 26	Moulton Chapel	29 T 25
Mersey (River)	34 M 23	Minsterworth	17 N 28	Mountain Ash	
Merseyside		Minterne Magna	8 M 31	/ Aberpennar	16 J 28
(Metropolitan		Mintlaw	69 O 11	Mount's Bay	2 D 33
County-Liverpool)	34 L 23	Minto	50 L 17	Mountsorrel	28 Q 25
Merthyr Tydfil	16 J 28	Mirfield	39 O 22	Mousa	75 Q 4
Merton (Devon)	6 H 31	Misterton (Notts.)	36 R 23	Mousehole	2 D 33
Meshaw	7 I 31	Misterton		Mouswald	49 J 18
Messingham	41 S 23	(Somerset)	8 L 31	Mow Cop	34 N 24
Metheringham	37 S 24	Mistley	21 X 28	Moy	67 H 11
Methil	56 K 15	Mitcheldean	17 M 28	Much Hoole	38 L 22
Methlick	69 N 11	Mitchell	2 E 32	Much Wenlock	26 M 26
Methven	56 J 14	Modbury	4 I 32	Muchalls	63 N 12
Methwold	30 V 26	Moelfre	32 H 23	Muck	59 B 13
Mevagissey	3 F 33	Moffat	49 J 17	Muckle Roe	75 P 2
Mexborough	40 Q 23	Moidart	60 C 13	Mudford	8 M 31
Mhór (Loch)	67 G 12	Moira	27 P 25	Muick (Loch)	62 K 13
Miavaig	70 Z 9	Mold / Yr		Muir of Fowlis	68 L 12
Michelham Priory	11 U 31	Wyddgrug	33 K 24	Muir of Ord	67 G 11
Mickleover	35 P 25	Monadhliath		Muirdrum	63 L 14
Mickleton	27 O 27	Mountains	67 H 12	Muirhead	55 H 16
Mid Ardlaw	69 N 10	Monar (Loch)	66 E 11	Muirkirk	49 H 17
Mid Calder	56 J 16	Monaughty		Muirshearlich	60 E 13
Mid Sannox	53 E 17	Forest	68 J 11	Muker	45 N 20
Mid Yell	75 Q 2	Moneydie	62 J 14	Muldoanich	58 X 13
Midbea	74 L 6	Moniaive	49 I 18	Mull (Isle of)	59 B 14
Middle Wallop	9 P 30	Monifieth	62 L 14	Mull (Sound of)	59 C 14
Middle Rasen	37 S 23	Monikie	62 L 14	Mull of Oa	52 A 17
Middleham	46 O 21	Monk Fryston	40 Q 22	Mull of Galloway	42 F 20
Middlesbrough	46 Q 20	Monkokehampton	6 H 31	Mullardoch	
Middlestown	39 P 23	Monks Eleigh	22 W 27	(Loch)	66 E 12
Middleton (Argyll		Monksilver	7 K 30	Mullion	2 E 33
and Bute)	58 Z 14	Monmouth		Mumbles (The)	15 I 29
Middleton		/ Trefynwy	17 L 28	Mundesley	31 Y 25
(Gtr. Mches.)	39 N 23	Monreith	42 G 19	Mundford	30 V 26
Middleton Cheney	28 Q 27	Montacute	8 L 31	Munlochy	67 H 11
Middleton-		Montgarrie	68 L 12	Munlochy Bay	67 H 11
in-Teesdale	45 N 20	Montgomery		Munslow	26 L 26
Middleton-on-Sea	10 S 31	/ Trefaldwyn	25 K 26	Murrayfield	56 K 16
Middleton		Montrose	63 M 13	Murton	46 P 19
St George	46 P 20	Monymusk	69 M 12	Musselburgh	56 K 16
Middletown	26 K 25	Moonen Bay	64 Z 11	Muthill	55 I 15
Middlewich	34 M 24	Moorfoot Hills	56 K 16	Mwnt	24 G 27
Midhurst	10 R 31	Moors (The)	42 F 19	Mybster	74 J 8
Midlem	50 L 17	Morar	59 C 13	Mynach Falls	25 I 26
Midsomer Norton	8 M 30	Moray Firth	67 H 11	Mynydd Eppynt	25 J 27
Migdale (Loch)	73 H 10	Morchard Bishop	7 I 31	Mynydd Preseli	14 F 28

N

Na Cùiltean	52	C 16
Nafferton	41	S 21
Nailsworth	17	N 28
Nairn	67	I 11
Nant (Loch)	54	E 14
Nant-y-Moch Reservoir	25	I 26
Nantgwynant Valley	32	H 24
Nantwich	34	M 24
Nantyglo	16	K 28
Napton	28	Q 27
Narberth / Arberth	14	F 28
Narborough	30	V 25
Nash Point	16	J 29
Nateby	45	M 20
National Exhibition Centre (N.E.C.)	27	O 26
National Motor Museum	9	P 31
Navenby	36	S 24
Naver (Loch)	72	G 9
Nayland	22	W 28
Naze (The)	23	X 28
Neath (River)	15	I 28
Neath / Castell-nedd	15	I 29
Needham Market	23	X 27
Needles (The)	9	P 32
Nefyn	32	G 25
Neidpath Castle	49	K 17
Neilston	55	G 16
Neist Point	64	Z 11
Nelson	39	N 22
Nene (River)	29	T 26
Ness	71	B 8
Ness (Loch)	67	G 12
Neston	34	K 24
Nether Broughton	36	R 25
Nether Langwith	36	Q 24
Nether Stowey	7	K 30
Netheravon	9	O 30
Netherhampton	9	O 30
Nethertown	74	K 7
Nethy Bridge	68	J 12
Netley	9	P 31
Nettlebed	19	R 29
Nettleham	36	S 24
Nevern	14	F 27
Nevis (Glen)	60	E 13
Nevis (Loch)	60	C 12
New Abbey	49	J 19
New Aberdour	69	N 11
New Alresford	10	Q 30
New Buckenham	31	X 26
New Byth	69	N 11
New Cumnock	48	H 17
New Deer	69	N 11
New Forest	9	P 31
New Forest Forest Park	9	P 31
New Galloway	48	H 18
New Holland	41	S 22
New Hythe	12	V 30
New Leeds	69	N 11
New Mills	35	O 23
New Milton	9	P 31
New Pitsligo	69	N 11
New Quay / Ceinewydd	24	G 27
New Romney	12	W 31
New Rossington	36	Q 23
New Sauchie	55	I 15
New Scone	56	J 14
New Tredegar	16	K 28
Newark-on-Trent	36	R 24
Newbiggin-by-the-Sea	51	P 18
Newbigging	62	L 14
Newbold Verdon	27	P 26
Newborough	32	G 24
Newbridge-on-Wye	25	J 27
Newburgh (Lancashire)	38	L 23
Newburgh (Aberdeenshire)	69	N 12
Newburgh (Fife)	56	K 14

NEWPORT

Allt-yr-yn Avenue	AY	2
Bellevue Lane	BX	5
Blewitt Street	AX	7
Caerau Crescent	AXY	9
Cambrian Centre	AX	
Capel Street	AY	10
Clarence Place	AX	12
Clyffard Crescent	AX	13
Clytha Park Road	AX	14
Commercial Street	AXY	15
Dewsland Park Road	AY	17
Dock Street	AX	19
Godfrey Road	AX	21
Hereford Street	AX	24
High Street	AX	26
John Frost Square	AX	27
Kensington Place	AX	30
Keynsham Avenue	AY	32
Kingsway Centre	AX	
Lower Dock Street	AXY	35
Malpas Road	AX	37
Newport Bridge	AX	39
Oakfield Road	AX	42
Queensway	AX	44
Summerhill Avenue	AX	47
Waterloo Road	AY	50

NEWCASTLE UPON TYNE

Blackett Street	CY	
Bridge Street	CZ	10
Broad Chare	CZ	12
Collingwood Street	CZ	25
Eldon Square Shopping Centre	CYZ	
Forth Street	CZ	30
George Street	CZ	32
Great North Road	CY	33
Grey Street	CZ	
Jesmond Road	CY	40
John Dobson Street	CY	41
Leazes Park Road	CY	43
Low Friar Street	CZ	46
Market Street	CZ	47
Mosley Street	CZ	50
Neville Street	CZ	52
New Bridge St. West	CY	53
Newgate Street	CZ	
Northumberland Street	CY	56
Pilgrim Street	CZ	57
Railway Street	CZ	60
St. Mary's Place	CY	65
St. Nicholas Street	CZ	66
Scotswood Road	CZ	70
Thornton Street	CZ	80
Wellington Street	CY	84
Westmorland Rd	CZ	88

NORWICH

Bank Plain	Y	2
Bethel Street	Z	4
Castle Mall Shopping Centre	Z	
Castle Meadow	Z	6
Cattle Market Street	Z	7
Chapel Field North	Z	9
Charing Cross	Y	10
Colegate	Y	14
Elm Hill	Y	
Exchange Street	YZ	15
Gentleman's Walk	Z	17
Grapes Hill	Y	19
London Street	YZ	26
Market Avenue	Z	28
Rampant Horse Street	Z	32
Red Lion Street	Z	33
St. Andrew's Street	Y	36
St. George's Street	Y	38
St. Stephen's Street	Z	
Thorn Lane	Z	42
Timber Hill	Z	43
Tombland	Y	
Upper King Street	Y	46
Wensum Street	Y	49
Westlegate	Z	50
Whitefriars	Y	51

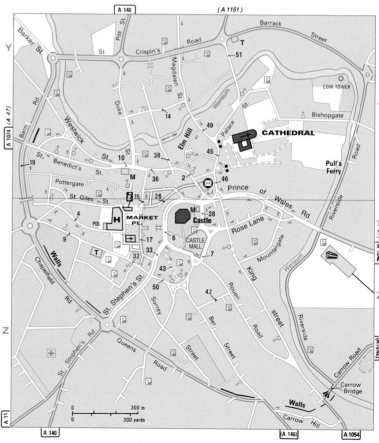

North Harris	64	Z 10	Northiam	12	V 31	Oathlaw	62	L 13
North Hinksey	19	Q 28	Northleach	18	O 28	Oban	60	D 14
North Holmwood	11	T 30	Northop	33	K 24	Ochil Hills	56	I 15
North Kelsey	41	S 23	Northton	70	Y 10	Ochiltree	48	G 17
North Kessock	67	H 11	Northumberland			Ockley	10	S 30
North Leigh	18	P 28	(County)	50	M 18	Odiham	10	R 30
North Morar	60	C 13	Northumberland			Ogbourne St.		
North Newbald	41	S 22	National Park	51	N 18	George	18	O 29
North Nibley	17	M 29	Northwich	34	M 24	Ogmore Vale	16	J 29
North Petherton	8	K 30	Northwold	30	V 26	Ogmore-by-Sea	16	J 29
North Petherwin	6	G 31	Norton	40	R 21	Oich (Loch)	61	F 12
North Ronaldsay	74	M 5	Norton Fitzwarren	7	K 30	Oidhche		
North Shields	51	P 18	Norton St. Philip	8	N 30	(Loch na h-)	66	D 11
North Somercotes	37	U 23	Norwich	31	X 26	Oigh-Sgeir	59	Z 13
North Sound (The)	74	L 6	Noss Head	74	K 8	Okeford Fitzpaine	8	N 31
North Sunderland	51	P 17	Noss (Isle of)	75	Q 3	Okehampton	6	H 31
North Thoresby	37	T 23	Nottingham	36	Q 25	Old Alresford	10	Q 30
North Tidworth	9	P 30	Nottinghamshire			Old Bolingbroke	37	U 24
North Uist	64	X 11	(County)	36	Q 24	Old Deer	69	N 11
North Walsham	31	Y 25	Nuneaton	27	P 26	Old Fletton	29	T 26
North			Nunney	8	M 30	Old Harry Rocks	9	O 32
Warnborough	10	R 30	Nunthorpe	46	Q 20	Old Head	74	L 7
North Weald			Nunton	64	X 11	Old Kilpatrick	55	G 16
Bassett	20	U 28	Nutley	11	U 30	Old Knebworth	20	T 28
North York Moors						Old Leake	37	U 24
National Park	47	R 20	**O**			Old Man of Hoy	74	J 7
Northallerton	46	P 20				Old Man of Storr	65	B 11
Northam	6	H 30	Oa (The)	52	B 17	Old Radnor	25	K 27
Northampton	28	R 27	Oadby	28	Q 26	Old Rayne	69	M 11
Northamptonshire			Oakengates	26	M 25	Old' Sarum	9	O 30
(County)	28	R 26	Oakham	36	R 25	Old Sodbury	17	M 29
Northchapel	10	S 30	Oakhill	8	M 30	Old Warden	29	S 27
Northchurch	19	S 28	Oare	12	W 30	Old Windsor	19	S 29
Northfleet	20	V 29				Oldany Island	72	E 9

NOTTINGHAM CENTRE

_ Street	DZ	2
_ r Gate	DY	4
_ Gate	DYZ	5
_rd Street	DY	6
_l Marsh Centre	DZ	
_ Street	DY	13
_n Street	CY	14
_gton Street	DZ	15
_n Street	DY	16
_ Gate	CZ	19
_ Street	DY	20
_oside (Poultry)	DY	22
_rook Street	DY	27
_er Gate	DYZ	28
_ing Street	DY	30
_ng Street	DY	31
_e Gate	DY	35
_ Street	DZ	39
_w Stone	DZ	41
_ Street	CDY	42
_ Edward Street	DY	43
_ Gate	DZ	48
_ Row	CY	49
_ Pavement	DZ	50
_ers Street	DY	52
_m Street	DY	56
_n Street	CY	57
_nes Street	CYZ	58

Smithy Row			Toll House Hill	CY	65
(Long Row)	DY	59	Upper Parliament		
South Parade	CY	60	Street	CDY	
South Sherwood Street	CY	61	Victoria Centre	DY	
Southwell Road	DY	62	Victoria Street	DY	67
Stoney Street	DYZ	63	Wheeler Gate	CYZ	69

Newburn	51	O 19	Newmilns	48	G 17	Newtown /		
Newbury	19	Q 29	Newnham (Glos.)	17	M 28	Drenewydd		
Newby Bridge	38	L 21	Newnham (Kent)	12	W 30	(Powys)	25	K 26
Newby Hall	40	P 21	Newnham Bridge	26	M 27	Newtown		
Newcastle Emlyn /			Newport /			St. Boswells	50	L 17
Castell Newydd			Casnewydd			Newtyle	62	K 14
Emlyn	24	G 27	(Newport)	17	L 29	Neyland	14	F 28
Newcastle-			Newport			Nigg Bay	67	H 10
under-Lyme	34	N 24	(Pembrokes)	14	F 27	Nine Ladies	35	P 34
Newcastle-upon-			Newport (Essex)	20	U 28	Ninfield	12	V 31
Tyne Airport	51	O 18	Newport (I.O.W.)	10	Q 31	Nith (River)	44	J 19
Newcastle-			Newport (Salop)	34	M 25	Niths	49	I 18
upon-Tyne	51	P 19	Newport-on-Tay	62	L 14	Niton	10	Q 32
Newcastleton	50	L 18	Newport Pagnell	28	R 27	Norfolk (County)	30	W 25
Newchurch	12	W 30	Newquay	2	E 32	Norfolk Broads	31	Y 25
Newdigate	11	T 30	Newstead	36	Q 24	Norham	57	N 16
Newent	17	M 28	Newstead Abbey	36	Q 24	Normandy	10	S 30
Newgale	14	E 28	Newton	39	M 22	Normanton	40	P 22
Newhall	34	M 24	Newton Abbot	4	J 32	North Ashton	34	L 23
Newham (London			Newton-Aycliffe	46	P 20	North Baddesley	9	P 31
Borough)	20	U 29	Newton Ferrers	4	H 33	North Ballachulish	60	E 13
Newhaven	11	U 31	Newton-le-Willows	34	M 23	North Berwick	57	L 15
Newick	11	U 31	Newton Longville	19	R 28	North Bovey	4	I 32
Newington	21	V 29	Newton Mearns	55	H 16	North Bradley	8	N 30
Newland	17	M 28	Newton Poppleford	7	K 31	North Cadbury	8	M 30
Newlyn	2	D 33	Newton St. Cyres	7	J 31	North Cave	41	S 22
Newmachar	69	N 12	Newton Stewart	42	G 19	North Channel	53	D 18
Newmains	55	I 16	Newton Wamphray	49	J 18	North Creake	30	W 25
Newmarket (Isle of			Newtongrange	56	K 16	North Curry	8	L 30
Lewis)	71	A 9	Newtonmore	61	H 12	North Erradale	65	C 10
Newmarket			Newtown (Cheshire)	35	N 23	North Esk (Riv.)	63	L 13
(Suffolk)	22	V 27	Newtown			North Foreland	13	Y 29
Newmill	68	L 11	(Heref.)	26	M 27	North Grimston	40	R 21

OXFORD

Blue Boar Street	BY	2	Hythe Bridge Street	BZ	12	Pembroke Street	BZ 31
Broad Street	BZ	3	Little Clarendon Street	BY	13	Queen's Lane	BZ 33
Castle Street	BZ	5	Logic Lane	BZ	14	Queen Street	BZ 34
Clarendon Shopping Centre	BZ		Magdalen Street	BYZ	16	Radcliffe Square	BZ 35
Cornmarket Street	BZ	6	Magpie Lane	BZ	17	St. Michael	
George Street	BZ	9	New Inn Hall Street	BZ	20	Street	BZ 40
High Street	BZ		Norfolk Street	BZ	21	Turl Street	BZ 41
			Old Greyfriars Street	BZ	23	Walton Crescent	BY 42
			Oriel Square	BZ	24	Westgate Shopping Centre	BZ
			Park End Street	BZ	30	Worcester Street	BZ 47

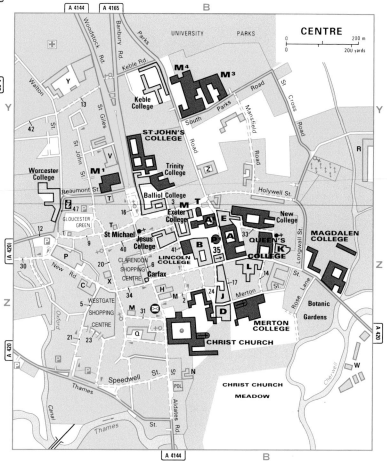

CENTRE

COLLEGES

ALL SOULS	BZ	E	LINACRE	BZ	A	ST CROSS	BY	W
BALLIOL	BY		LINCOLN	BZ		ST EDMUND'S	BZ	N
BRASENOSE	BZ	D	MAGDALEN	BZ		ST HILDA'S	BZ	Z
CHRIST CHURCH	BZ		MERTON	BZ		ST JOHN'S	BY	
CORPUS			NEW	BZ		ST PETER'S	BZ	U
CHRISTI	BZ	K	NUFFIELD	BZ	B	SOMERVILLE	BY	R
EXETER	BZ		ORIEL	BZ	J	TRINITY	BY	
HERTFORD	BZ	P	PEMBROKE	BZ	Q	UNIVERSITY	BZ	L
JESUS	BZ		QUEEN'S	BZ		WADHAM	BY	X
KEBLE	BY		ST CATHERINE'S	BY	V	WORCESTER	BY	

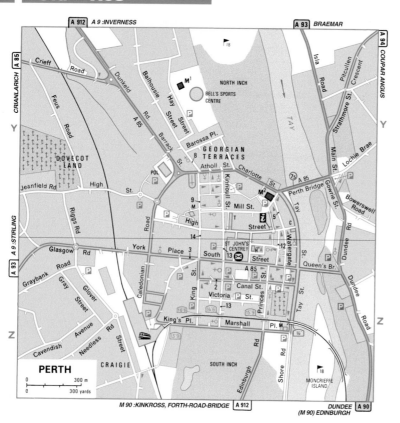

Oldbury	27 N 26	Ouse (River)		Park Gate	10 Q 31	Pendine Sands	15 G 28				
Oldcotes	36 Q 23	(English Channel)	11 T 30	Park of Pairc	70 A 9	Pendlebury	39 N 23				
Oldham	39 N 23	Ouse (River) (North		Parkeston	21 X 28	Penfro /					
Oldmeldrum	69 N 11	Sea)	40 Q 21	Parkhurst	10 Q 31	Pembroke	14 F 28				
Ollaberry	75 P 2	Out Skerries	75 R 2	Parnham House	8 L 31	Penicuik	56 K 16				
Ollay (Loch)	64 X 12	Outer Hebrides	70 W 10	Parrett (River)	8 K 30	Penifiler	65 B 11				
Ollerton	36 Q 24	Outwell	29 U 26	Partney	37 U 24	Penistone	39 P 23				
Olney	28 R 27	Overseal	27 P 25	Parton	44 J 20	Penketh	34 L 23				
Olveston	17 M 29	Overstrand	31 Y 25	Partridge Green	11 T 31	Penkridge	27 N 25				
Ombersley	26 N 27	Overton (Wrexham)	34 L 25	Pass of LLanberis	32 H 24	Penmaenmawr	33 I 24				
Onchan	42 G 21	Overton (Hants.)	10 Q 30	Patchway	17 M 29	Pennines (The)	45 N 19				
Onich	60 E 13	Overton (Lancs.)	38 L 21	Pateley Bridge	39 O 21	Pennyghael	59 B 14				
Orchy (Glen)	60 F 14	Overtown	55 I 16	Path of Condie	56 J 15	Penpont	49 I 18				
Ord	65 C 12	Ower	9 P 31	Pathhead	56 L 16	Penrhyn Bay	33 I 24				
Orford	23 Y 27	Owermoigne	8 N 32	Patna	48 G 17	Penrhyndeudraeth	32 H 25				
Orford Ness	23 Y 27	Owslebury	10 Q 30	Patrington	41 T 22	Penrith	45 L 19				
Ormesby	46 Q 20	Oxburgh Hall	30 V 26	Patrixbourne	13 X 30	Penryn	2 E 33				
Ormesby		Oxford	19 Q 28	Patterdale	45 L 20	Penshaw	46 P 19				
St. Margaret	31 Z 25	Oxfordshire		Pattingham	26 N 26	Penshurst	11 U 30				
Ormskirk	38 L 23	(County)	18 P 28	Paulerspury	28 R 27	Pentire Point	2 F 32				
Oronsay	52 B 15	Oxted	11 T 30	Paull	41 T 22	Pentland Firth	74 K 7				
Orosay		Oxwich Bay	15 H 29	Paulton	17 M 30	Pentland Hills	56 J 16				
(near Fuday)	64 X 12	Oykel (Glen)	72 F 9	Peacehaven	11 T 31	Pentland					
Orosay (near		Oykel Bridge	72 F 10	Peak District		Skerries	74 L 7				
Lochboisdale)	64 X 12	Oyne	69 M 12	National Park	35 O 23	Penwith	2 D 33				
Orphir	74 K 7			Peasedown St.		Penybont	25 K 27				
Orrin (Glen)	66 F 11	**P**		John	17 M 30	Penzance	2 D 33				
Orrin Reservoir	66 F 11			Peasenhall	23 Y 27	Perranporth	2 E 32				
Orsay	52 A 16	Pabay	65 C 12	Peasmarsh	12 W 31	Pershore	27 N 27				
Orsett	20 V 29	Pabbay (near Harris)	70 Y 10	Peat Inn	56 L 15	Perth	56 J 14				
Orton	45 M 20	Pabbay (near		Peatknowe	69 M 11	Peterborough	29 T 26				
Orwell	29 T 27	Mingulay)	58 X 13	Peebles	49 K 17	Peterculter	69 N 12				
Orwell (River)	21 X 28	Pabbay (Sound of)	70 Y 10	Peel	42 F 21	Peterhead	69 O 11				
Osborne House	10 Q 31	Padbury	19 R 28	Peel Fell	50 M 18	Peterlee	46 P 19				
Osdale	65 A 11	Paddock Wood	12 V 30	Pegwell Bay	13 Y 30	Petersfield	10 R 30				
Osgaig (Loch)	72 E 9	Padiham	39 N 22	Peldon	22 W 28	Peterstow	17 M 28				
Osmington	8 M 32	Padstow	2 F 32	Pelynt	3 G 32	Petham	13 X 30				
Ossett	39 P 22	Pagham	10 R 31	Pembridge	26 L 27	Pett	12 V 31				
Oswaldtwistle	39 M 22	Paignton	4 J 32	Pembroke Dock		Pettaugh	23 X 27				
Oswestry	34 K 25	Painscastle	25 K 27	/ Doc Penfro	14 F 28	Petworth	10 S 31				
Otford	20 U 30	Painswick	17 N 28	Pembroke / Penfro	14 F 28	Pevensey Bay	12 V 31				
Othery	8 L 30	Paisley	55 G 16	Pembrokeshire		Pewsey	18 O 29				
Otley (Suffolk)	23 X 27	Palnackie	43 I 19	Coast		Pickering	47 R 21				
Otley (West Yorks.)	39 O 22	Pangbourne	19 Q 29	National Park	14 F 29	Picton Castle	14 F 28				
Otterbourne	9 P 30	Papa Stour	75 O 3	Pembury	12 V 30	Piddletrenthide	8 M 31				
Otterburn	51 N 18	Papa Westray	74 L 5	Pen-y-bont		Piercebridge	46 O 20				
Otterswick	75 Q 2	Paps of Jura	52 B 16	/ Bridgend	16 J 29	Pierowall	74 L 6				
Otterton	4 K 32	Parbh (The)	72 F 8	Pen-y-groes	32 H 24	Pilgrims					
Ottery St. Mary	7 K 31	Parbold	38 L 23	Penalun	14 F 29	Hatch	20 U 29				
Oulton Park Circuit	34 M 24	Parc Cefn Onn	16 K 29	Penarth	16 K 29	Pilling	38 L 22				
Oulton Broad	31 Z 26	Parham House	11 S 31	Pencarrow	3 F 32	Pilning	17 M 29				
Oundle	28 S 26			Pendine	14 G 28	Pilton	8 M 30				

Pinchbeck	37 T 25	Porthaethwy	
Pinhoe	7 J 31	/ Menai Bridge	32 H 24
Pirbright	10 S 30	Porthcawl	15 I 29
Pirton	20 T 28	Porthcurno	2 D 33
Pitcaple	69 M 12	Porthgwarra	2 C 33
Pitlochry	62 I 13	Porthleven	2 E 33
Pitmedden	69 N 11	Porthmadog	32 H 25
Pittenween	57 L 15	Porthyrhyd	15 H 28
Pladda	53 E 17	Portinnisherrich	54 E 15
Plaistow	10 S 30	Portishead	17 L 29
Plas Newydd		Portknockie	68 L 10
(Anglesey)	32 H 24	Portland	
Plas Newydd		(Isle of)	5 M 32
(Denbighshire)	33 K 25	Portlethen	69 N 12
Pleasley	36 Q 24	Portmahomack	67 I 10
Plockton	66 D 11	Portnacroish	60 D 14
Pluckley	12 W 30	Portnaguran	71 B 9
Plumbland	44 K 19	Portnahaven	52 A 16
Plymouth	3 H 32	Portobello	56 K 16
Plympton	4 H 32	Portreath	2 E 33
Plymstock	3 H 32	Portree	65 B 11
Plynlimon		Portscatho	2 F 33
(Pumlumon		Portskerra	73 I 8
Fawr)	25 I 26	Portskewett	17 L 29
Pocklington	40 R 22	Portslade	11 T 31
Point of Ayr		Portsmouth	10 Q 31
(Flintshire)	33 K 23	Portsoy	69 L 10
Point Lynas	32 H 23	Portuairk	59 B 13
Point of Ayre (Isle of		Postbridge	4 I 32
Man)	42 G 20	Potter Heigham	31 Y 25
Polbain	72 D 9	Potter Street	20 U 28
Polegate	11 U 31	Potterne	18 N 30
Polesden		Potters Bar	20 T 28
Lacey	11 S 30	Potterspury	28 R 27
Polesworth	27 P 26	Potton	29 T 27
Polkerris	3 F 32	Poughill	6 G 31
Pollock House	55 H 16	Poulton-	
Polmont	56 I 16	le-Fylde	38 L 22
Polperro	3 G 33	Poundstock	6 G 31
Polruan	3 G 33	Powburn	51 O 17
Pondersbridge	29 T 26	Powerstock	8 L 31
Pontardawe	15 I 28	Powick	26 N 27
Pontarddulais	15 H 28	Powis	25 K 26
Pontarfynach		Powmill	56 J 15
/ Devil's Bridge	25 I 26	Powys (County)	25 J 26
Pontefract	40 Q 22	Poynings	11 T 31
Ponteland	51 O 18	Poynton	35 N 23
Ponterwyd	25 I 26	Praa Sands	2 D 33
Pontesbury	26 L 26	Praze-an-Beeble	2 E 33
Pontllyfni	16 K 28	Prees	34 M 25
Pontrhydygroes	25 I 26	Preesall	38 L 22
Pontrilas	17 L 28	Prescot	34 L 23
Pontsticill	16 J 28	Prestatyn	33 J 23
Pontyclun	16 J 29	Prestbury	35 N 24
Pontycymer	16 J 29	Presteigne	26 K 27
Pontypool /		Preston (East Riding	
Pontypwl	17 K 28	of Yorks.)	41 T 22
Pontypridd	16 J 29	Preston (Kent)	13 X 30
Pontypwl /		Preston (Lancs.)	38 L 22
Pontypool	17 K 28	Preston (West	
Poole	9 O 31	Sussex)	11 S 31
Poole Bay	9 O 31	Preston	
Poolewe	66 D 10	Candover	10 Q 30
Pooley Bridge	45 L 20	Prestonpans	56 L 16
Pooltiel (Loch)	64 Z 11	Prestwich	39 N 23
Porlock	7 J 30	Prestwick	48 G 17
Port Appin	60 D 14	Prestwood	19 R 28
Port Askaig	52 B 16	Priest Island	71 D 10
Port Bannatyne	54 E 16	Princes	
Port Charlotte	52 A 16	Risborough	19 R 28
Port Ellen	52 B 17	Princethorne	27 P 26
Port Erin	42 F 21	Princetown	4 I 32
Port-Eynon	15 H 29	Priors	
Port-Eynon		Marston	28 Q 27
Point	15 H 29	Probus	2 F 33
Port Glasgow	54 F 16	Prosen (Glen)	62 K 13
Port		Prudhoe	46 O 19
Henderson	65 C 10	Puckeridge	20 U 28
Port Isaac	3 F 32	Puddletown	8 M 31
Port Lamont	54 E 16	Pudsey	39 P 22
Port Logan	42 F 19	Pulborough	10 S 31
Port Mór	59 B 13	Pulham	
Port		Market	31 X 26
of Menteith	55 H 15	Purbeck	
Port of Ness	71 B 8	(Isle of)	9 N 32
Port St. Mary	42 F 21	Purbrook	10 Q 31
Port Talbot	15 I 29	Purley	19 Q 29
Port William	42 G 19	Purse Caundle	
Portchester	10 Q 31	Manor	8 M 31
Portesham	8 M 31	Purston	
Portgordon	68 K 11	Jaglin	40 P 22
Porth	16 J 29	Purton	18 O 29
Porth Neigwl		Putsborough	6 H 30
or Hell's Mouth	32 G 25	Pwllheli	32 G 25
Porth Tywyn		Pyecombe	11 T 31
/ Burry Port	15 H 28	Pyle	15 I 29

Q		
Quainton	19 R 28	
Quantock Hills	7 K 30	
Quarr	10 Q 31	
Quedgeley	17 N 28	
Queen Camel	8 M 30	
Queen Elizabeth		
Forest Park	55 G 15	
Queenborough	21 W 29	
Queensbury	39 O 22	
Queensferry	34 K 24	
Quinag	72 E 9	
Quinish Point	59 B 14	
Quiraing	65 B 11	
Quoich (Loch)	60 E 12	
Quorndon	28 Q 25	
Quothquan	49 J 17	

R		
Raasay (Island of)	65 B 11	
Raasay (Sound of)	65 B 11	
Rackwick	74 J 7	
Radcliffe	39 N 23	
Radcliffe-on-Trent	36 Q 25	
Radlett	20 T 29	
Radnor Forest	25 K 27	
Radstock	8 M 30	
Radyr	16 K 29	
Rafford	68 J 11	
Raglan	17 L 28	
Ragley Hall	27 O 27	
Rainford	38 L 23	
Rainham	21 V 29	
Rainworth	36 Q 24	
Ramsbottom	39 N 23	
Ramsbury	18 P 29	
Ramsey (Cambs.)	29 T 26	
Ramsey (Isle of		
Man)	42 G 21	
Ramsey Bay	42 G 21	
Ramsey Island	14 D 28	
Ramsey St. Mary's	29 T 26	
Ramsgate	13 Y 29	
Ramsgill	39 O 21	
Ranfurly	55 G 16	
Rannoch (Loch)	61 H 13	
Rannoch Moor	61 F 14	
Ranskill	36 Q 23	
Ranworth	31 Y 25	
Rapness	74 L 6	
Rappach	72 F 10	
Ratby	28 Q 26	
Rathen	69 O 11	
Rattray	62 K 14	
Rattray Head	69 O 11	
Raunds	28 S 26	
Ravenglass	44 J 20	
Ravenstonedale	45 M 20	
Rawcliffe	40 R 22	
Rawmarsh	35 P 23	
Rawtenstall	39 N 22	
Rayleigh	21 V 29	
Read	39 M 22	
Reading	19 R 29	
Reay	73 I 8	
Reay Forest	72 F 9	
Reculver	13 X 29	
Red Wharf Bay	32 H 24	
Redbourn	20 S 28	
Redbourne	36 S 23	
Redbridge (London		
Borough)	20 U 29	
Redcar	47 Q 20	
Redcliff Bay	17 L 29	
Redditch	27 O 27	
Redford	63 L 14	
Redhill	11 T 30	
Redpoint	65 C 11	
Redruth	2 E 33	
Redwick	17 L 29	
Reedham	31 Y 26	
Reekie Linn	62 K 13	
Reeth	46 O 20	
Reigate	11 T 30	
Reighton	41 T 21	
Reiss	74 K 8	
Rempstone	36 Q 25	
Rendham	23 Y 27	
Renfrew	55 G 16	
Renish Point	70 Z 10	
Renishaw	35 P 24	
Renton	55 G 16	
Resort (Loch)	70 Z 9	

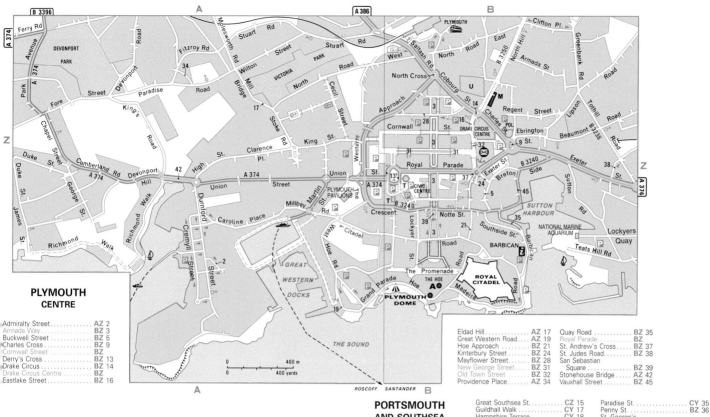

PLYMOUTH
CENTRE

0 — 400 m
0 — 400 yards

ROSCOFF SANTANDER

Admiralty Street	AZ	2
Armada Way	BZ	3
Buckwell Street	BZ	5
Charles Cross	BZ	9
Cornwall Street	BZ	
Derry's Cross	BZ	13
Drake Circus	BZ	14
Drake Circus Centre	BZ	
Eastlake Street	BZ	16
Eldad Hill	AZ	17
Great Western Road	AZ	19
Hoe Approach	BZ	21
Kinterbury Street	BZ	24
Mayflower Street	BZ	28
New George Street	BZ	31
Old Town Street	BZ	32
Providence Place	AZ	34
Quay Road	BZ	35
Royal Parade	BZ	
St. Andrew's Cross	BZ	37
St. Judes Road	BZ	38
San Sebastian Square	BZ	39
Stonehouse Bridge	AZ	42
Vauxhall Street	BZ	45

PORTSMOUTH
AND SOUTHSEA

Alec Rose Lane	CY	2
Arundel St.	CY	5
Bellevue Terrace	CZ	6
Cascade Centre	CY	
Charlotte St.	CY	7
Commercial Rd.	CY	
Eldon St.	CY	10
Great Southsea St.	CZ	15
Guildhall Walk	CY	17
Hampshire Terrace	CY	18
Hard (The)	BY	20
High St.	BYZ	21
Isambard Brunel Rd	CY	22
Landport Terrace	CY	25
Lombard St.	BYZ	29
Main Rd.	BY	31
Norfolk St.	CYZ	32
Ordnance Row	BY	34
Palmerston Rd.	CZ	
Paradise St.	CY	35
Penny St.	BZ	36
St. George's Square	BY	39
St. Michael's Rd	CY	41
Southsea Terrace	CZ	43
Spring St.	CY	45
Stanhope Rd	CY	48
Unicorn Rd.	CY	49
Warblington St.	BY	53
White Hart Rd	BYZ	57
Wiltshire St.	CY	59

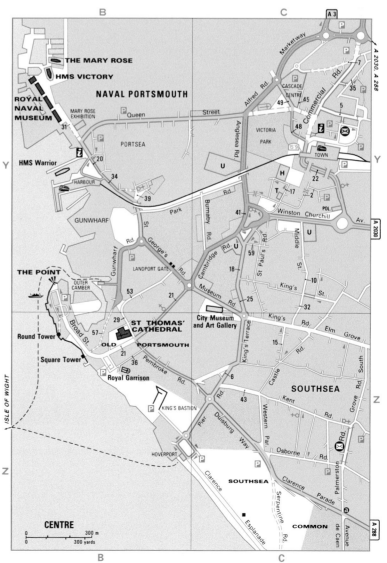

CENTRE

0 — 300 m
0 — 300 yards

Restalrig	56	K 16	Ripe	11	U 31
Restormel Castle	3	G 32	Ripley (Derbs.)	35	P 24
Retford	36	R 24	Ripley (North Yorks.)	40	P 21
Rhaeadr / Rhayader	25	J 27	Ripley (Surrey)	19	S 30
Rhaeadr Ddu	33	I 25	Ripon	40	P 21
Rhayader / Rhaeadr	25	J 27	Rippingale	37	S 25
Rheidol (Vale of)	25	I 26	Ripponden	39	O 22
Rhiconich	72	F 8	Risca	16	K 29
Rhinns of Galloway (The)	42	E 19	Rishton	39	M 22
Rhinns of Kells	48	G 18	Ristol (Isle)	72	D 9
Rhondda	16	J 29	Roag (Loch)	70	Z 9
Rhoose	16	J 29	Roberton	50	L 17
Rhoscolyn	32	G 24	Robertsbridge	12	V 31
Rhoscrowther	14	E 28	Robin Hood's Bay	47	S 20
Rhosllanerchrugog	34	K 24	Roby	34	L 23
Rhosneigr	32	G 24	Rocester	35	O 25
Rhossili	15	H 29	Roch	3	F 32
Rhu	54	F 15	Rochdale	39	N 23
Rhuddlan	33	J 24	Roche	3	F 32
Rhum	59	A 13	Rochester	21	V 29
Rhuthun / Ruthin	33	K 24	Rochford	21	W 29
Rhyd-Ddu	32	H 24	Rock	3	F 32
Rhydaman / Ammanford	15	I 28	Rockcliffe (Cumbria)	44	K 19
Rhydcymerau	24	H 27	Rockcliffe (Dumfries and Galloway)	43	I 19
Rhydd	26	N 27	Rode	8	N 30
Rhyddhywel	25	J 26	Rodel	64	Z 10
Rhydowen	24	H 27	Rogart	73	H 9
Rhyl	33	J 24	Rogerstone	16	K 29
Rhymney / Rhymmi	16	K 28	Rolleston-on-Dove (Staffs.)	35	P 25
Rhynie	68	L 12	Rolleston (Notts.)	36	R 24
Ribble (River)	39	N 22	Rolvenden	12	V 30
Ribblesdale	39	N 21	Roman Villa	10	S 31
Ribchester	38	M 22	Romiley	35	N 23
Riccall	40	Q 22	Romney Marsh	12	W 30
Riccarton	48	G 17	Romsey	9	P 31
Richborough	13	X 30	Romsley	27	N 26
Richmond	46	O 20	Rona (Island of)	65	C 11
Richmond-upon-Thames (London Borough)	20	T 29	Ronaldsway	42	G 21
			Ronas Voe	75	P 2
Rickmansworth	19	S 29	Ronay	64	Y 11
Ridgeway Path (The)	18	P 29	Roos	41	T 22
Rievaulx Abbey	46	Q 21	Rootpark	56	I 16
Rigside	49	I 17	Ropsley	36	S 25
Rillington	40	R 21	Rora Head	74	J 7
Rimsdale (Loch)	73	H 9	Rosedale Abbey	47	R 20
Ringford	43	H 19	Rosehearty	69	N 11
Ringmer	11	U 31	Rosemarket	14	F 28
Ringstead	28	S 26	Rosemarkie	67	H 11
Ringwood	9	O 31	Roshven	59	C 13
Ringwould	13	Y 30	Roslin	56	K 16
Rinnes (Glen)	68	K 11	Ross of Mull	52	B 15
Rinns of Islay	52	A 16	Ross-on-Wye	17	M 28
Rinns Point	52	A 16	Rossall Point	38	K 22
			Rossett	34	L 24
			Rothbury	51	O 18

Rothbury Forest	51	O 18
Rotherfield	11	U 30
Rotherham	35	P 23
Rothes	68	K 11
Rothesay	54	E 16
Rothienorman	69	M 11
Rothiesholm	74	M 6
Rothwell (Leeds.)	40	P 22
Rothwell (Northants.)	28	R 26
Rottingdean	11	T 31
Roughton	31	X 25
Rousay	74	K 6
Rowland's Castle	10	R 31
Rowland's Gill	46	O 19
Rownhams	9	P 31
Rowsley	35	P 24
Roxwell	22	V 28
Roy (Glen)	60	F 13
Royal Greenwich Observatory	12	V 31
Royal Leamington Spa	27	P 27
Royal Military Academy	19	R 29
Royal Tunbridge Wells	11	U 30
Roybridge	60	F 13
Roydon (Essex)	20	U 28
Roydon (Norfolk)	31	X 26
Royston (Herts.)	29	T 27
Royston (South Yorks.)	40	P 23
Royton	39	N 23
Ruabon	34	K 25
Ruan High Lanes	2	F 33
Ruan Minor	2	E 34
Ruardean	17	M 28
Rubbha na Faing	52	A 16
Rubh'an Dùnain	65	A 12
Rubha a' Mhail	52	B 16
Rubha Còigeach	72	D 9
Rubha Dubh	58	Z 14
Rubha Hunish	65	A 10
Rubha na h-Easgainne	65	B 12
Rubha Réidh	71	C 10
Rubha Suisnish	65	B 12
Rudbaxton	14	F 28
Ruddington	36	Q 25
Rudgeway	17	M 29
Rudgwick	11	S 30
Rudston	41	T 21
Rufford Old Hall	38	L 23
Rugby	28	Q 26

READING

Blagrave Street	Y 3	Chain Street	Z 7	Queen Victoria Street ... Y 28
Bridge Street	Z 4	Church Street	X 12	St. Mary's Butts ... Z 29
Broad Street	Y	Duke Street	Z 15	Station Hill ... Y 30
Broad Street Mall		Greyfriars Road	Y 17	Station Road ... Y 31
Shopping Centre	Z	Gun Street	Z 18	Tilehurst Road ... Z 33
Castle Street	Z 6	King Street	Z 20	Tudor Road ... Y 34
		Mill Lane	Z 21	Valpy Street ... Y 37
		Minster Street	Z 22	Watlington Street ... Z 40
		Mount Pleasant	Z 23	West Street ... Y 41

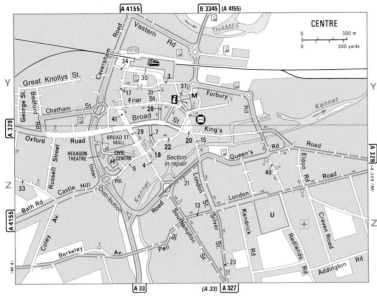

Sandy	29 T 27	Scarp	70 Y 9
Sandygate	42 G 20	Scavaig (Loch)	65 B 12
Sandyhills	43 I 19	Schiehallion	61 H 13
Sanquhar	49 I 17	Scilly (Isles of)	2 B 34
Santon Head	42 G 21	Scone Palace	56 J 14
Sarisbury	10 Q 31	Scopwick	37 S 24
Sark (Channel I.)	5	Scorton	46 P 20
Sarre	13 X 29	Scotch-Corner	46 P 20
Satterthwaite	44 K 21	Scothern	36 S 24
Saundersfoot	14 F 28	Scotlandwell	56 K 15
Saunderton	19 R 28	Scotney	12 V 30
Sawbridgeworth	20 U 28	Scotter	41 S 23
Sawrey	44 L 20	Scourie	72 E 8
Sawston	22 U 27	Scousburgh	75 Q 4
Sawtry	29 T 26	Scrabster	74 J 8
Saxilby	36 S 24	Scridain (Loch)	59 B 14
Saxlingham		Scunthorpe	41 S 23
Nethergate	31 X 26	Sea Palling	31 Y 25
Saxmundham	23 Y 27	Seaford	11 U 31
Saxtead Green	23 X 27	Seaforth (Loch)	70 Z 10
Scadavay (Loch)	64 Y 11	Seaham	46 P 19
Scaddle (Glen)	60 D 13	Seale	10 R 30
Scafell Pikes	44 K 20	Sealga (Loch na)	66 D 10
Scalasaig	52 B 15	Seasalter	13 X 29
Scalby	47 S 21	Seascale	44 J 20
Scalloway	75 Q 3	Seaton	7 K 31
Scalpay (Highland)	65 C 12	Seaton Carew	46 Q 20
Scalpay (Western		Seaton Delaval	51 P 18
Isles)	70 A 10	Seaton Delaval Hall	51 P 18
Scampton	36 S 24	Seaview	10 Q 31
Scapa Flow	74 K 7	Sebergham	44 L 19
Scarba	52 C 15	Sedbergh	45 M 21
Scarborough	47 S 21	Sedgebrook	36 R 25
Scarcliffe	36 Q 24	Sedgley	27 N 26
Scarisbrick	34 L 23	Sedlescombe	12 V 31
Scarista	70 Y 10	Seend	18 N 29
Seething	31 Y 26
Seil (Isle of)	54 D 15
Seilich (Loch an t-)	61 H 13
Selborne	10 R 30
Selby	40 Q 22
Selker Bay	44 J 21
Selkirk	50 L 17
Sellindge	13 W 30
Selmeston	11 U 31
Selsey	10 R 31
Selworthy	7 J 30
Semley	9 N 30
Senghenydd	16 K 29
Sennen	2 C 33
Sennybridge	16 J 28
Settle	39 N 21
Seven Sisters	
(Neath and Port	
Talbot)	15 I 28
Seven Sisters (East	
Sussex)	11 U 31
Sevenoaks	11 U 30
Severn (River)	17 M 28
Severn Bridge	17 M 29
Sgiabacleit (Loch)	70 A 9
Sgiwen	15 I 29
Sgurr Mór	66 E 10
Shaftesbury	8 N 30
Shalbourne	18 P 29
Shaldon	4 J 32
Shalford	10 S 30
Shandon	54 F 15
Shanklin	10 Q 32
Shap	45 L 20
Shapinsay	74 L 6
Sharnbrook	28 S 27

SHEFFIELD
CENTRE

Angel Street	DY 3	Commercial Street	DZ 16
Blonk Street	DY 6	Cumberland	
Castle Gate	DY 13	Street	CZ 17
Charter Row	CZ 14	Fargate	CZ
Church Street	CZ 15	Fitzwilliam Gate	CZ 19
		Flat Street	DZ 20
		Furnival Gate	CZ 21
		Furnival Street	CZ 22
		Haymarket	DY 25
		High Street	DZ
Leopold Street	CZ 31
Moorfields	CY 35
Pinstone Street	CZ 37
Queen Street	CY 38
St. Mary's Gate	CZ 40
Shalesmoor	CY 41
Snig Hill	DY 42
Waingate	DY 44
West Bar Green	CY 45
West Street	CZ

Rugeley	27 O 25	St. David's /		St. Peter Port	
Rumney	16 K 29	Tyddewi	14 E 28	(Channel I.)	5
Runcorn	34 L 23	St. Day	2 E 33	St. Peter's	13 Y 29
Runwell	21 V 29	St. Dennis	3 F 32	St. Stephen	3 F 32
Rushden	28 S 27	St. Dogmaels	14 F 27	St. Teath	3 F 32
Ruskington	37 S 24	St. Donats	16 J 29	St. Tudwal's Islands	32 G 25
Rusper	11 T 30	St. Ewe	3 F 33	St. Tudy	3 F 32
Rustington	10 S 31	St. Fagans	16 K 29	St. Vigeans	63 M 14
Ruswarp	47 S 20	St. Fergus	69 O 11	Salcombe	4 I 33
Rutherglen	55 H 16	St. Gennys	6 G 31	Sale	34 N 23
Ruthin / Rhuthun	33 K 24	St. Germans	3 H 32	Salen (Argyll and	
Ruthven	62 K 14	St. Govan's Head	14 F 29	Bute)	59 C 14
Ruthven (Loch)	67 H 12	St. Helens (I.O.W.)	10 Q 31	Salen (Highland)	59 C 13
Ruthwell	49 J 19	St. Helens		Salfleet	37 U 23
Rutland Water	28 S 26	(Merseyside)	34 L 23	Salford	34 N 23
Ruyton of the		St. Ishmael's	14 E 28	Salfords	11 T 30
Eleven Towns	34 L 25	St. Issey	3 F 32	Saline	56 J 15
Ryan (Loch)	42 E 19	St. Ive	3 G 32	Salisbury	9 O 30
Rycote	19 Q 28	St. Ives (Cambs.)	29 T 27	Salisbury Plain	9 O 30
Rydal	44 L 20	St. Ives (Cornwall)	2 D 33	Saltash	3 H 32
Ryde	10 Q 31	St. John's	42 G 21	Saltburn	67 H 10
Rye	12 W 31	St. John's Loch	74 J 8	Saltburn-by-the-	
Ryhall	28 S 25	St. John's Chapel	45 N 19	Sea	47 R 20
Ryhill	40 P 23	St. Just	2 C 33	Saltcoats	48 F 17
Ryhope	46 P 19	St. Just in Roseland	2 E 33	Saltford	17 M 29
Ryton	51 O 19	St. Keverne	2 E 33	Samala	64 X 11
		St. Kew	3 F 32	Samlesbury Old	
		St. Leonards		Hall	38 M 22
		(Dorset)	9 O 31	Sampford	
S		St. Leonards (East		Courtenay	4 I 31
Sadberge	46 P 20	Sussex)	12 V 31	Sampford Peverell	7 J 31
Saddell Bay	53 D 17	St. Mabyn	3 F 32	Sancreed	2 D 33
Saffron Walden	22 U 27	St. Magnus Bay	75 P 2	Sand Side	38 K 21
St. Abb's Head	57 N 16	St. Margaret's		Sanda Island	53 D 18
St. Agnes	2 E 33	at Cliffe	13 Y 30	Sanday (Highland)	65 A 12
St. Albans	20 T 28	St. Margaret's Bay	13 Y 30	Sanday (Orkney	
St. Aldhelm's Head	9 N 32	St. Margaret's		Islands)	74 M 6
St. Andrews	57 L 14	Hope	74 L 7	Sandbach	34 M 24
St. Ann's Head	14 E 28	St. Martin's	33 K 25	Sandbank	54 F 16
St. Arvans	17 L 29	St. Mary		Sandbanks	9 O 31
St. Asaph	33 J 24	in the Marsh	12 W 30	Sandend	68 L 10
St. Athan	16 J 29	St. Mary's	74 L 7	Sandford	7 J 31
St. Austell	3 F 32	St. Mary's Loch	50 K 17	Sandford Orcas	8 M 31
St. Bees	44 J 20	St. Mawes	2 E 33	Sandgate	13 X 30
St. Bees Head	44 J 20	St. Mawgan	3 F 32	Sandgreen	43 H 19
St. Blazey	3 F 32	St. Mellion	3 H 32	Sandhaven	69 N 10
St. Breock	3 F 32	St. Merryn	2 F 32	Sandhurst (Berks.)	19 R 29
St. Briavels	17 M 28	St. Michael's		Sandhurst (Kent)	12 V 30
St. Brides Major	16 J 29	Mount	2 D 33	Sandleigh	19 Q 28
St. Brides		St. Michaels-		Sandlins	23 Y 27
-Super-Ely	16 K 29	on-Wyre	38 L 22	Sandness	75 P 3
St. Buryan	2 D 33	St. Monans	57 L 15	Sandon	35 N 25
St. Catherine's		St. Neot	3 G 32	Sandown	10 Q 32
Point	10 Q 32	St. Neots	29 T 27	Sandray	58 X 13
St. Clears / Sanclêr	15 G 28	St. Nicholas-at-		Sandridge	20 T 28
St. Cleer	3 G 32	Wade	13 X 29	Sandringham	
St. Columb Major	2 F 32	St. Ninian's Isle	75 P 4	House	30 V 25
St. Combs	69 O 11	St. Osyth	21 X 28	Sandwell	27 O 26
St. Cyrus	63 M 13	St. Patrick's Isle	42 F 21	Sandwich	13 Y 30
St. David's Head	14 D 28	St. Paul's Walden	20 T 28	Sandwood Loch	72 E 8

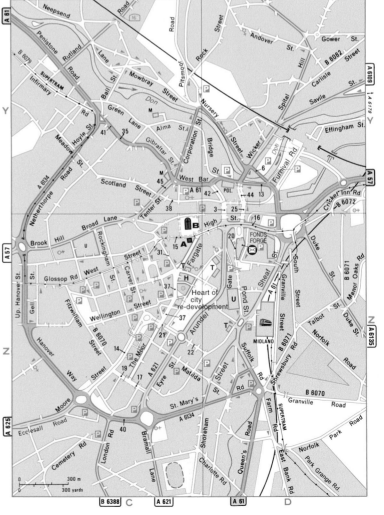

Sharpness 17 M 28
Shaw (Gtr. Mches.) 39 N 23
Shaw (Wilts.) 18 N 29
Shawbost 70 Z 9
Shawbury 34 M 25
Shawford 10 Q 30
Shebbear 6 H 31
Shebster 73 I 8
Sheepwash 6 H 31
Sheering 20 U 28
Sheerness 21 W 29
Sheffield 35 P 23
Sheffield Park 11 T 31
Shefford 29 S 27
Sheldon 18 N 29
Sheldon Manor 18 N 29
Sheldwich 12 W 30
Shell or Sealg (Loch) 70 A 9
Shelley 39 O 23
Shenstone 27 O 26
Shenval 68 K 11
Shepley 39 O 23
Sheppey (Isle of) 21 W 29
Shepreth 29 U 27
Shepshed 36 Q 25
Shepton Mallet 8 M 30
Sherborne 8 M 31
Sherborne St. John 19 Q 30
Sherburn 41 S 21
Sherburn-in-Elmet 40 Q 22
Shere 11 S 30
Sheriff Hutton 40 Q 21
Sheriffhales 26 M 25
Sheringham 31 X 25
Sherston 17 N 29
Sherwood Forest 36 Q 24
Shiant (Sound of) 71 A 10
Shiel (Glen) 66 D 12
Shiel (Loch) 60 D 13
Shieldaig 66 D 11
Shieldaig (Loch) 66 C 11
Shifnal 26 M 25
Shilbottle 51 O 17
Shildon 46 P 20
Shillingford 7 J 30
Shillington 20 S 28
Shimpling 31 X 26
Shin (Loch) 72 G 9
Shinfield 19 R 29
Shipdham 30 W 26
Shipley (Salop) 26 N 26
Shipley (West Yorks.) 39 O 22
Shipston-on-Stour 27 P 27
Shipton 26 M 26
Shipton-under-Wychwood 18 P 28
Shira (Lochan) 54 F 14
Shirebrook 36 Q 24
Shirley 27 O 26
Shobdon 26 L 27
Shoeburyness 21 W 29
Shoreham 11 T 31
Shorne 21 V 29
Shorwell 9 P 32
Shotley Bridge 46 O 19
Shotley Gate 23 X 28
Shottermill 10 R 30
Shotton Colliery Thornley 46 P 19
Shotts 55 I 16
Shrewsbury 26 L 25
Shrewton 9 O 30
Shrivenham 18 P 29
Shropshire (County) 26 M 26
Shuna Sound 54 D 15
Shurdington 18 N 28
Sible Hedingham 22 V 28
Sibsey 37 U 24
Sidbury 7 K 31
Siddington 34 N 24
Sidford 7 K 31
Sidlaw Hills 62 K 14
Sidlesham 10 R 31
Sidmouth 7 K 31
Sighthill 56 K 16
Sileby 28 Q 25
Silecroft 38 K 21
Silkstone 40 P 23
Silloth 44 J 19
Silsden 39 O 22
Silver End 22 V 28
Silverdale 38 L 21
Silverstone Circuit 28 Q 27
Silverton 7 J 31
Simonsbath 7 I 30
Sinclair's Bay 74 K 8
Sionascaig (Loch) 72 E 9
Sissinghurst 12 V 30
Sittingbourne 21 W 29
Skara Brae 74 J 6
Skares 48 H 17
Skeabost 65 B 11
Skegness 37 V 24
Skellingthorpe 36 S 24
Skelmanthorpe 39 P 23
Skelmersdale 38 L 23
Skelmorlie 54 F 16
Skelton (Cleveland) 47 R 20
Skelton (Cumbria) 45 L 19
Skelwith Bridge 44 K 20
Skenfrith 17 L 28
Skerray 73 H 8
Skervuile Lighthouse 52 C 16
Skiddaw 44 K 20
Skilgate 7 J 30
Skipness 53 D 16
Skipport (Loch) 64 Y 12
Skipsea 41 T 22
Skipton 39 N 22
Skirza 74 K 8
Skokholm Island 14 E 28
Skomer Island 14 E 28
Skye (Isle of) 65 B 12
Slaidburn 39 M 22
Slaithwaite 39 O 23
Slamannan 55 I 16
Slapin (Loch) 65 B 12
Slapton 4 J 33
Sleaford 37 S 25
Sleat (Sound of) 59 C 12
Sledmere 41 S 21
Sleekburn 51 P 18
Sleights 47 S 20
Sligachan 65 B 12
Sligachan (Loch) 65 B 12
Slimbridge 17 M 28
Slindon 10 S 31
Slockavullin 54 D 15
Slough 19 S 29
Sloy (Loch) 54 F 15
Small Hythe 12 W 30
Smallfield 11 T 30
Smarden 12 W 30
Smedmore 9 N 32
Snaefell 42 G 21
Snainton 47 S 21
Snaith 40 Q 22
Snape 23 Y 27
Snetterton Circuit 30 W 26
Snettisham 30 V 25
Snizort (Loch) 65 A 11
Snodland 12 V 30
Snowdon / Yr Wyddfa 32 H 24
Snowdonia National Park 33 I 24
Snowshill 18 O 27
Soa 58 Z 14
Soa Island 52 A 15
Soar (River) 36 Q 25
Soay 65 B 12
Soay Sound 65 B 12
Soham 30 V 26
Solent (The) 10 Q 31
Solihull 27 O 26
Sollas 64 X 11
Solva 14 E 28
Solway Firth 44 J 19
Somercotes 35 P 24
Somerset (County) 8 M 29
Somersham 29 U 26
Somerton (Norfolk) 31 Y 25
Somerton (Oxon.) 19 Q 28
Somerton (Somerset) 8 L 30
Sompting 11 S 31
Sonning Caversham 19 R 29
Sonning Common 19 R 29
Sopley 9 O 31
Sorbie 42 G 19
Sorn 48 H 17
Sound (The) 3 H 32
South Brent 4 I 32
South Cave 41 S 22
South Cerney 18 O 28
South Downs 10 R 31
South Elmsall 40 Q 23
South Esk (River) 63 L 13
South Foreland 13 Y 30
South Hanningfield 21 V 29
South Harris 70 Z 10
South Harris Forest 70 Z 10
South Hayling 10 R 31
South Kelsey 36 S 23
South Kirkby 40 Q 23
South Lancing 11 T 31
South Leverton 36 R 24
South Lopham 30 X 26
South Mimms 20 T 28
South Molton 7 I 30
South Morar 60 C 13
South Normanton 35 P 24
South Ockendon 20 U 29
South Oxhey 20 S 29
South Petherton 8 L 31
South Petherwin 3 G 32
South Queensferry 56 J 16
South Ronaldsay 74 L 7
South Shields 51 P 19
South Stack 32 F 24
South Tawton 4 I 31
South Uist 64 X 12
South Walls 74 K 7
South Warnborough 10 R 30
South Woodham Ferrers 21 V 29
South Zeal 4 I 31
Southam 27 P 27
Southampton 9 P 31
Southborough 11 U 30
Southbourne (Dorset) 9 O 31
Southbourne (West Sussex) 10 R 31
Southend 53 D 18
Southend-on-Sea 21 W 29
Southery 30 V 26
Southminster 21 W 29
Southport 38 K 23
Southsea 10 Q 31
Southwark (London Borough) 20 T 29
Southwater 11 S 30
Southwell 36 R 24
Southwick (West Sussex) 11 T 31
Southwick (Wilts.) 8 N 30
Southwick Widley 10 Q 31
Southwold 31 Z 27
Sowerby Bridge 39 O 22
Spalding 37 T 25
Spaldwick 29 S 26
Spanish Head 42 F 21
Sparkford 8 M 30
Spean (Glen) 61 F 13
Spean Bridge 60 F 13
Spelve (Loch) 59 C 14
Spennymoor 46 P 19
Spey (River) 61 G 12
Spey Bay 68 K 10
Speymouth Forest 68 K 11
Spilsby 37 U 24
Spinningdale 73 H 10
Spithead 10 Q 31
Spittal (Highland) 74 J 8
Spittal (Northumb.) 57 O 16
Spittal of Glenshee 62 J 13
Spofforth 40 P 22
Spondon 35 P 25
Spreyton 4 I 31
Springfield 56 K 15
Sprotbrough 40 Q 23
Spurn Head 41 U 23
St. Bride's Bay 14 E 28
St. Nicholas (Pembrokes) 14 E 28
St. Nicholas (Vale of Glamorgan) 16 K 29
Stack (Loch) 72 F 8
Stack Island 64 Y 12
Stack Rocks 14 E 29
Staffa 59 A 14
Staffin Bay 65 B 11
Stafford 35 N 25
Staffordshire (County) 35 N 25
Staindrop 46 O 20
Staines 19 S 29
Stainforth (North Yorks.) 39 N 21
Stainforth (South Yorks.) 40 Q 23
Staithes 47 R 20
Stalbridge 8 M 31
Stalham 31 Y 25
Stalmine 38 L 22
Stalybridge 35 N 23
Stamford 28 S 26
Stanbridge 19 S 28
Standing Stones 70 Z 9
Standlake 18 P 28
Standon 20 U 28
Standford-in-the-Vale 18 P 29
Stanford-le-Hope 21 V 29
Stanford-on-Avon 28 Q 26
Stanhope 46 N 19
Stanley (Perthshire and Kinross) 62 J 14
Stanley (Durham) 46 O 19
Stanley (Wakefield.) 40 P 22
Stanmer Park 11 T 31
Stanstead Abbotts 20 U 28
Stansted Mountfitched 20 U 28
Stanton 30 W 27
Stanton Harcourt 18 P 28
Stanwell 20 S 29
Stapleford (Notts.) 36 Q 25
Stapleford (Wilts.) 9 O 30
Staplehurst 12 V 30
Start Point 4 J 33
Startforth 46 O 20
Stathern 36 R 25
Staughton Highway 29 S 27
Staunton 17 N 28
Staveley (Cumbria) 45 L 20
Staveley (Derbs.) 35 P 24
Staxigoe 74 K 8
Staxton 41 S 21
Staylittle 25 J 26
Stedham 10 R 31
Steeple 22 W 28
Steeple Ashton 18 N 30
Steeple Aston 19 Q 28
Steeple Bumpstead 22 V 27
Steeple Claydon 19 R 28
Steeple Morden 29 T 27
Stenhousemuir 55 I 15
Stenness (Orkney Islands) 74 K 7
Stenness (Shetland Islands) 75 P 2
Stevenage 20 T 28
Stevenston 48 F 17
Steventon 19 Q 29
Stewartby 28 S 27
Stewarton 55 G 16
Stewkley 19 R 28
Steyning 11 T 31
Sticklepath 4 I 31
Stilligarry 64 X 12
Stillington 40 Q 21
Stilton 29 T 26
Stirling 55 I 15
Stithians 2 E 33
Stob Choire Claurigh 60 F 13
Stock 21 V 29
Stockbridge 9 P 30
Stockland 7 K 31
Stockport 35 N 23
Stocksbridge 35 P 23
Stockton Heath 34 M 23
Stockton-on-Tees 46 P 20
Stockton-on-Teme 26 M 27
Stoer 72 D 9
Stogumber 7 K 30
Stogursey 7 K 30
Stoke Albany 28 R 26
Stoke-by-Nayland 22 W 28
Stoke Climsland 3 H 32
Stoke Fleming 4 J 33
Stoke Gabriel 4 J 32
Stoke Lacy 26 M 27
Stoke Mandeville 19 R 28
Stoke-on-Trent 35 N 24
Stoke Poges 19 S 29
Stoke sub Hamdon 8 L 31
Stokenchurch 19 R 29
Stokenham 4 I 33
Stokesay 26 L 26
Stokesley 46 Q 20
Stone (Bucks.) 19 R 28
Stone (Staffs.) 35 N 25
Stonehaven 63 N 13
Stonehenge 9 O 30
Stonehouse (South Lanarkshire) 55 I 16
Stonehouse (Devon) 3 H 32
Stonehouse (Glos.) 17 N 28
Stonesfield 18 P 28
Stoneybridge 64 X 12
Stoneykirk 42 F 19
Stoneywood 69 N 12
Stony Stratford 28 R 27
Stornoway 71 A 9
Storr (The) 65 B 11
Storrington 11 S 31
Stort (River) 20 U 28
Stotfold 20 T 27
Stottesdon 26 M 26
Stour (River) (English Channel) 9 N 31
Stour (River) (North Sea) 22 V 27
Stour (River) (R. Severn) 26 N 26
Stourbridge 27 N 26
Stourhead House 8 N 30
Stourport-on-Severn 26 N 26
Stow 50 L 16
Stow-on-the-Wold 18 O 28
Stowe School 28 Q 27
Stowmarket 22 W 27
Strachan 63 M 12
Strachur 54 E 15
Stradbroke 31 X 27
Stradishall 22 V 27
Stradsett 30 V 26
Straiton 48 G 18
Straloch 62 J 13
Stranraer 42 E 19
Strata Florida Abbey 25 I 27
Stratfield Saye 19 Q 29
Stratford St. Mary 22 W 28
Stratford-upon-Avon 27 O 27
Strath Brora 73 H 9
Strath Dearn 67 I 11
Strath Halladale 73 I 8
Strath Isla 68 K 11
Strath More 66 E 10
Strath Mulzie 72 F 10
Strath of Kildonan 73 I 9
Strath Oykel 72 F 10
Strath Skinsdale 73 H 9
Strath Tay 62 J 14
Strathallan 55 I 15
Strathardle 62 J 13
Strathaven 49 H 16
Strathbeg (Loch of) 69 O 11
Strathblane 55 H 16
Strathbogie 68 L 11
Strathbraan 62 I 14
Strathcarron 66 D 11
Strathconon 66 F 11
Strathconon Forest 66 F 11
Strathearn 55 I 14
Stratherrick 67 G 12
Strathkinness 56 L 14
Strathmiglo 56 K 15
Strathmore 62 K 14
Strathnairn 67 H 11
Strathnaver 73 H 8
Strathpeffer 67 G 11
Strathspey 68 J 11
Strathvaich Lodge 66 F 10
Strathy 73 I 8
Strathy Point 73 H 8
Strathyre 55 H 15
Stratton (Cornwall) 6 G 31
Stratton (Glos.) 18 O 28
Stratton-on-the-Fosse 8 M 30
Stratton-St. Margaret 18 O 29
Streatley 19 Q 29
Street 8 L 30
Strensall 40 Q 21
Stretford 34 N 23
Stretham 29 U 26
Stretton (Cheshire) 34 M 23
Stretton (Staffs.) 27 N 25
Strichen 69 N 11
Striven (Loch) 54 E 16
Stroma (Island of) 74 K 7
Stromeferry 66 D 11
Stromemore 66 D 11
Stromness 74 K 7
Stronachlachar 55 G 15
Stronchreggan 60 E 13
Stronsay 74 M 6
Stronsay Firth 74 L 6
Strontian 60 D 13
Stroud 17 N 28
Strumble Head 14 E 27
Stuart Castel 67 H 11
Stuartfield 69 N 11

SOUTHAMPTON CENTRE

Above Bar Street
Avenue (The) 3
Bargate Street 4
Brunswick Place 6
Central Bridge 7
Central Station Bridge 8
Civic Centre Road 13
Cumberland Place 14
Hanover Buildings 17
High Street
Houndwell Place 20
Inner Avenue 22
Marlands Shopping Centre 25
Marsh Lane 26
Mountbatten Way 27
Orchard Place 32
Oxford Avenue 33
Portland Street 34
Pound Tree Road 35
Queen's Terrace 38
Queen's Way 39
Radcliffe Road 41
St. Andrew's Road 43
South Front 48
Terminus Terrace 52
Threefield Lane 56
Town Quay 57

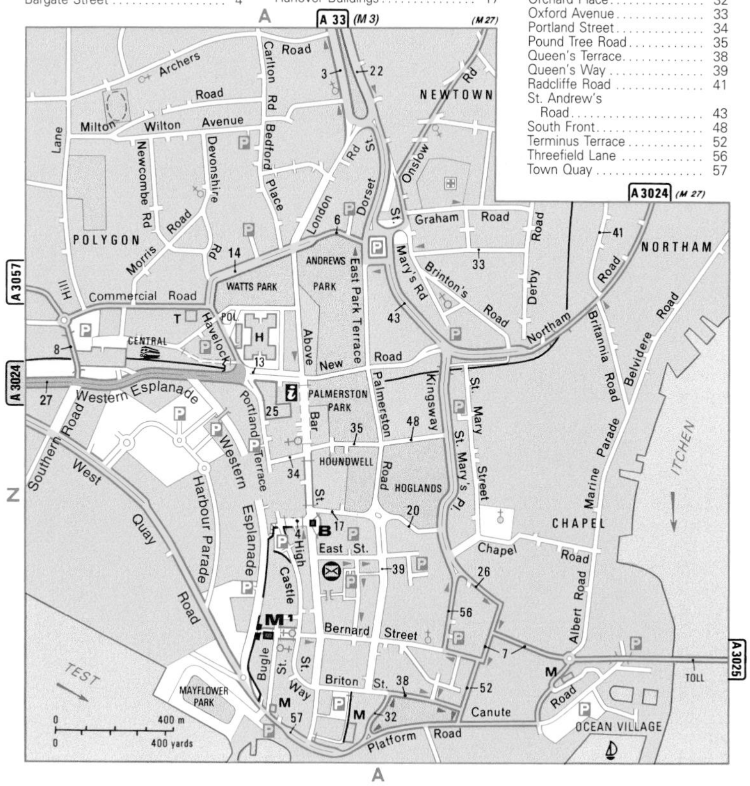

STIRLING CENTRE

Barnton Street	B	2
Causewayhead Road	B	4
Corn Exchange Road	B	5
Drummond Place	B	9
Dumbarton Road	B	10
Goosecroft Road	B	12
King Street	B	13
Leisure Centre		
Murray Place	B	15
Port Street		
Queen Street	B	20
St. John Street	B	23
St. Mary's Wynd	B	24
Seaforth Place	B	25
Spittal Street	B	27
Thistle Centre	B	28
Union Street	B	28
Upper Craigs	B	29

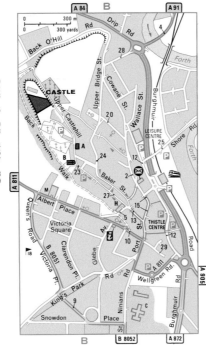

STOKE

Campbell Place	14
Church Street	
Elenora Street	26
Fleming Road	28
Hartshill Road	33
London Road	42
Shelton Old Road	62
Station Road	66
Vale Street	72

STOKE

Stubbington	10	Q 31
Studland	9	O 32
Studley (Warw.)	27	O 27
Studley (Wilts.)	18	N 29
Studley Royal Gardens	39	P 21
Stuley	64	Y 12
Sturminster Marshall	9	N 31
Sturminster Newton	8	N 31
Sturry	13	X 30
Sturton-le-Steeple	36	R 23
Suainaval (Loch)	70	Z 9
Sudbury (Derbs.)	35	O 25
Sudbury (Suffolk)	22	W 27
Sudbury Hall	35	O 25
Sudeley Castle	18	O 28
Suffolk (County)	23	X 27

Sùil Ghorm	59	A 13
Sulby	42	G 21
Sulgrave	28	Q 27
Sullom Voe	75	P 2
Sumburgh	75	Q 4
Sumburgh Roost	75	P 4
Summer Bridge	39	O 21
Summer Island	72	D 9
Summercourt	2	F 32
Sunart	60	D 13

Sunart (Loch)	59	C 13
Sunbury	20	S 29
Sunderland	46	P 19
Sunningdale	19	S 29
Sunninghill	19	S 29
Surfleet	37	T 25
Surrey (County)	10	S 30
Sutterton	37	T 25
Sutton (Cambs.)	29	U 26

STOKE-ON-TRENT NEWCASTLE-UNDER-LYME BUILT UP AREA

Alexandra Road	U	3
Bedford Road	U	4
Brownhills Road	U	12
Church Lane	U	19
Cobridge Road	U	21
Davenport Street	U	23
Elder Road	U	24
Etruria Vale Road	U	27
Grove Road	U	30
Hanley Road	U	31
Heron Street	V	34
High Street	U	35
Higherland	V	37
Manor Street	V	44
Mayne Street	V	45
Moorland Road	U	48
Porthill Road	U	59
Snow Hill	U	63
Stoke Road	U	68
Strand (The)	U	69
Victoria Park Road	U	75
Victoria Place Link	U	76
Watlands View	U	77
Williamson Street	U	78

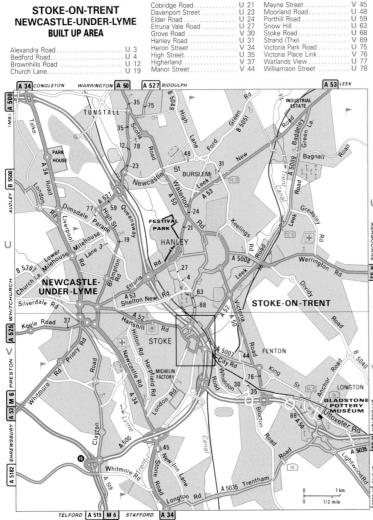

Sutton (London Borough)	20	T 29
Sutton-on-the-Forest	40	Q 21
Sutton (Salop)	34	M 25
Sutton Bank	46	Q 21
Sutton Benger	18	N 29
Sutton Bridge	37	U 25
Sutton Coldfield	27	O 26
Sutton Courtenay	19	Q 29
Sutton-in-Ashfield	36	Q 24
Sutton-on-Hull	41	T 22
Sutton-on-Sea	37	U 24
Sutton-on-Trent	36	R 24
Sutton Scotney	10	P 30
Sutton Valence	12	V 30
Swadlincote	35	P 25
Swaffham	30	W 26
Swaffham Bulbeck	22	U 27
Swale (River)	40	P 21
Swale (The)	21	W 29
Swale Dale	46	O 20
Swallow	41	T 23
Swallow Falls	33	I 24
Swanage	9	O 32
Swanland	41	S 22
Swanley	20	U 29
Swanscombe	20	U 29
Swansea / Abertawe	15	I 29
Swarbacks Minn	75	P 2
Sway	9	P 31
Swaythling	9	P 31
Swimbridge	6	I 30
Swinbrook	18	P 28
Swindon	18	O 29
Swineshead	37	T 25
Swinton (Scottish Borders)	57	N 16
Swinton (Rotherham.)	35	Q 23
Swynnerton	34	N 25
Symbister	75	Q 2
Symonds Yat	17	M 28
Symonds Yat Rock	17	M 28
Symondsbury	8	L 31
Syresham	28	Q 27
Syston	28	Q 25

T

Tadcaster	40	Q 22
Tadley	19	Q 29
Tadmarton	27	P 27
Tadworth	20	T 30
Taff (River)	16	K 29
Taibach	15	I 29
Tain	67	H 10
Takeley	20	U 28
Tal-y-bont (Dyfed)	24	I 26
Tal-y-Llyn Lake	25	I 25
Talgarth	16	K 28
Talke	34	N 24
Talladale	66	D 10
Talley	15	I 28

Talsarnau	32	H 25
Talybont-on-Usk (Powys)	16	K 28
Tamanavay (Loch)	70	Y 9
Tamar (River)	6	G 31
Tamworth	27	O 26
Tan Hill	45	N 20
Tanera Beg	72	D 9
Tanera Mór	72	D 9
Tannadice	62	L 13
Tantallon Castle	57	M 15
Taransay	70	Y 10
Taransay (Sound of)	70	Z 10
Tarbat Ness	67	I 10
Tarbert (Argyll and Bute)	53	D 16
Tarbert (Western Isles)	70	Z 10
Tarbert (Loch)	52	C 16
Tarbet	54	F 15
Tarbolton	48	G 17
Tardy Gate	38	L 22
Tarland	68	L 12
Tarleton	38	L 22
Tarn (The)	45	L 20
Tarporley	34	M 24
Tarrant Hinton	9	N 31
Tarrant Keyneston	9	N 31
Tarrington	26	M 27
Tarskavaig Point	65	B 12
Tarves	69	N 11
Tarvin	34	L 24
Tattershall	37	T 24
Tatton Hall	34	M 24
Taunton	7	K 30
Taunton Deane	7	K 30
Taverham	31	X 25
Tavistock	3	H 32
Taw (River)	6	I 31
Tay (Firth of)	56	K 14
Tay (Loch)	61	H 14
Tay Road Bridge	62	L 14
Taynuilt	60	E 14
Tayport	62	L 14
Tayvallich	54	D 15
Teacuis (Loch)	59	C 14
Tebay	45	M 20
Tedburn St. Mary	4	I 31
Tees (River)	46	P 20
Teesdale	45	N 20
Teifi (River)	24	G 27
Teignmouth	4	J 32
Telford	26	M 26
Teme (River)	26	M 27
Temple Ewell	13	X 30
Temple Sowerby	45	M 20
Templeton	14	F 28
Tempsford	29	T 27
Tenbury Wells	26	M 27
Tenby / Dinbych-y-pysgod	14	F 28
Tendring	21	X 28
Tenterden	12	W 30
Terling	22	V 28
Tern Hill	34	M 25

Terrington St. Clement	37	U 25
Tetbury	18	N 29
Tetford	37	T 24
Tetney	41	T 23
Tettenhall	26	N 26
Teviotdale	50	L 17
Tewin	20	T 28
Tewkesbury	18	N 28
Texa	52	B 17
Teynham	12	W 30
Thakeham	11	S 31
Thame	19	R 28
Thame (River)	19	R 28
Thames (River)	19	Q 29
Thanet (Isle of)	13	Y 29
Thatcham	19	Q 29
Thaxted	22	V 28
Theale (Berks.)	19	Q 29
Theale (Somerset)	8	L 30
Theddlethorpe St. Helen	37	U 23
Thetford	30	W 26
Theydon Bois	20	U 28
Thirsk	46	P 21
Thoralby	46	N 21
Thornaby-on-Tees	46	Q 20
Thornaganby	40	R 22
Thornbury (South Glos.)	17	M 29
Thornbury (Heref.)	26	M 27
Thornby	28	Q 26
Thorne	40	R 23
Thorner	40	P 22
Thorney	29	T 26
Thornham	30	V 25
Thornhill (Stirling)	55	H 15
Thornhill (Dumfries and Galloway)	49	I 18
Thornton (Fife)	56	K 15
Thornton (Lancs.)	38	K 22
Thornton Curtis	41	S 23
Thornton Dale	47	R 21
Thornton-in-Craven	39	N 22
Thornyhive Bay	63	N 13
Thorpe (Derbs.)	35	O 24
Thorpe (Essex)	21	W 29
Thorpe-le-Soken	21	X 28
Thorpe-on-the-Hill	36	S 24
Thorpeness	23	Y 27
Thorrington	21	X 28
Thorverton	7	J 31
Thrapston	28	S 26
Three Cocks	25	K 27
Threlkeld	44	K 20
Throckley	51	O 19
Throwleigh	4	I 31
Thruxton Circuit	9	P 30
Thundersley	21	V 29
Thurcroft	36	Q 23
Thurlby	29	S 25
Thurlestone	4	I 33
Thurlow	22	V 27
Thurmaston	28	Q 25
Thursby	44	K 19
Thurso	74	J 8
Thwaite	45	N 20
Tibberton (Glos.)	17	M 28
Tibberton (Salop)	34	M 25
Ticehurst	12	V 30
Tickhill	36	Q 23
Ticknall	35	P 25
Tideswell	35	O 24
Tigerton	63	L 13
Tigharry	64	X 11
Tighnabruaich	54	E 16
Tillicoultry	55	I 15
Tillington	10	S 31
Tilshead	9	O 30
Tilt (Glen)	63	I 13
Tilton-on-the-Hill	28	R 26
Timberscombe	7	J 30
Timsbury	17	M 30
Tingwall (Loch)	75	P 3
Tintagel	3	F 32
Tintern Abbey	17	L 28
Tintinhull	8	L 31
Tipton	27	N 26
Tiptree	22	W 28
Tiree	58	Z 14

STRATFORD-UPON-AVON

Banbury Road	B	2
Benson Road	B	3
Bridge Foot	B	6
Bridge Street	B	8
Chapel Lane	A	13
Chapel Street	A	14
Church Street	A	16
Clopton Bridge	B	18
College Lane	A	19
Ely Street	A	22
Evesham Place	A	24
Great William Street	A	25
Greenhill Street	A	27
Guild Street	A	28
Henley Street	A	29
High Street	A	31
Rother Street	A	32
Scholars Lane	A	33
Sheep Street	AB	35
Tiddington Road	B	38
Trinity Street	A	40
Warwick Road	B	42
Waterside	B	43
Windsor Street	A	45
Wood Street	A	47

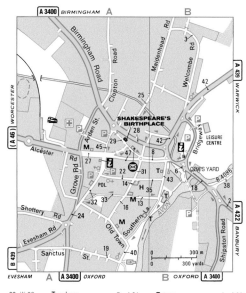

Trealaval (Loch)	70	A 9	Troon	48	G 17	Tynewydd	16	J 28
Trearddur Bay	32	G 24	Trossachs (The)	55	G 15	Tytherington	17	M 29
Trecastle	16	J 28	Trotternish	65	B 11	Tywardreath	3	F 32
Trefaldwyn			Troutbeck	44	L 20	Tywi (River)	25	I 27
/Montgomery	25	K 26	Trowbridge	8	N 30	Tywyn	24	H 26
Treffynnon /			Truim (Glen)	61	H 13			
Holywell	33	K 24	Trull	7	K 31	**U**		
Trefnant	33	J 24	Trumpington	29	U 27			
Trefyclawdd			Truro	2	E 33	Uckfield	11	U 31
/Knighton	26	K 26	Trwyn Cilan	32	G 25	Uddingston	55	H 16
Trefynwy			Tuath (Loch)	59	B 14	Uffculme	7	K 31
/Monmouth	17	L 28	Tuddenham	30	V 27	Ufford	23	Y 27
Tregaron	25	I 27	Tudweiliog	32	G 25	Ugadale Bay	53	D 17
Tregony	3	F 33	Tugford	26	M 26	Ugborough	4	I 32
Treharris	16	K 29	Tulla (Loch)	60	F 14	Uig (Highland)	65	A 11
Treherbert	16	J 28	Tullibody	55	I 15	Uig (Western Isles)	70	Y 9
Treig (Loch)	60	F 13	Tumble	15	H 28	Uisg (Loch)	59	C 14
Trelech	15	G 28	Tummel (Loch)	61	I 13	Uiskevagh (Loch)	64	Y 11
Trelissick Gardens	2	E 33	Tunstall (Staffs.)	35	N 24	Uley	17	N 28
Trelleck	17	L 28	Tunstall (Suffolk)	31	Y 25	Ullapool	72	E 10
Tremadog	32	H 25	Turnberry	48	F 18	Ulleskelf	40	Q 22
Tremadog Bay	32	H 25	Turnditch	35	P 24	Ullesthorpe	28	Q 26
Trengwainton			Turret (Loch and			Ullswater	45	L 20
Garden	2	D 33	Reservoir)	61	I 14	Ulpha	44	K 21
Trent (River)	35	N 25	Turriff	69	M 11	Ulsta	75	Q 2
Trentham	35	N 25	Turvey	28	S 27	Ulva	59	B 14
Treorchy	16	J 29	Tusker Rock	15	I 29	Ulverston	38	K 21
Trerice	2	E 32	Tutbury	35	O 25	Unapool	72	E 9
Treshnish Isles	59	A 14	Tuxford	36	R 24	Unst	75	R 1
Treshnish Point	59	A 14	Twatt	74	K 6	Upavon	9	O 30
Tretower	16	K 28	Tweed (River)	49	J 17	Uphall	56	J 16
Trevone	2	F 32	Tweeddale	49	J 17	Uphill	17	L 30
Trevor	32	G 25	Tweedmouth	57	N 16	Uplyme	8	L 31
Trevose Head	2	E 32	Tweedsmuir Hills	49	J 17	Upottery	7	K 31
Trewithen	3	F 33	Twickenham	20	S 29	Upper Badcall	72	E 9
Trimdon	46	P 19	Twyford (Berks.)	19	R 29	Upper Beeding	11	T 31
Trimley Heath	23	X 28	Twyford (Hants.)	10	Q 30	Upper Chapel	25	J 27
Trimsaran	15	H 28	Twyford (Leics.)	36	R 25	Upper Dicker	11	U 31
Tring	19	R 28	Twynholm	43	H 19	Upper Knockando	68	J 11
Trispen	2	E 33	Tyddewi			Upper Loch		
Trochry	62	J 14	/St. David's	14	E 28	Torridon	66	D 11
Troedyrhiw	16	J 28	Tyldesley	39	M 23	Upper Poppleton	40	Q 22
Trollamarig (Loch)	70	Z 10	Tyne (River)	46	P 19	Upper Tean	35	O 25
Tromie (Glen)	61	H 12	Tynemouth	51	P 18			

rga Mór	70	Z 10	Tolleshunt d'Arcy	22	W 28	Topsham	7	J 31
oran	59	B 14	Tolpuddle	8	N 31	Tor Ness	74	K 7
sbury	9	N 30	Tolsta	71	B 8	Torbay	4	J 32
tchfield	10	Q 31	Tolsta Chaolais	70	Z 9	Torcross	4	J 33
umpan Head	71	B 9	Tolsta Head	71	B 8	Torksey	36	R 24
verton	7	J 31	Tomatin	67	I 11	Torlundy	60	E 13
bermory	59	B 14	Tombreck	67	H 11	Torphichen	56	J 16
beronochy	54	D 15	Tomintoul	68	J 12	Torphins	69	M 12
bson	70	Z 9	Tonbridge	11	U 30	Torpoint	3	H 32
ddington	19	S 28	Tongland	43	H 19	Torquay	4	J 32
dmorden	39	N 22	Tongue	73	G 8	Torridon (Loch)	65	C 11
e Head	70	Y 10	Tonna	15	I 28	Torrisdale Bay	73	H 8
ll of Birness	69	O 11	Tonypandy	16	J 29	Torthorwald	49	J 18
llerton	40	Q 21	Tonyrefail	16	J 29	Torver	44	K 20
lesbury	22	W 28	Topcliffe	40	P 21	Totland	9	P 31
						Totnes	4	I 32
						Totton	9	P 31
						Tow Law	46	O 19
						Towcester	28	R 27
						Tower Hamlets		
						(London Borough)	20	T 29
						Town Yetholm	50	N 17
						Towneley Hall	39	N 22
						Traborton	48	G 17
						Trallwng /		
						Welshpool	25	K 26
						Tranent	56	L 16
						Traquair House	50	K 17
						Trawden	39	N 22
						Trawsfynydd	33	I 25

SUNDERLAND

Albion Place		2
Bedford Street		4
Borough Road		5
Bridge Street		6
Chester Road		10
Crowtree Road		11
Derwent Street		12
Fawcett Street		
High Street West		15
Holmeside		
John Street		16
Livingstone Road		18
New Durham		
Road		19
Park Lane		23
St. Mary's Way		27
Southwick Road		30
The Bridges		
Vine Place		36

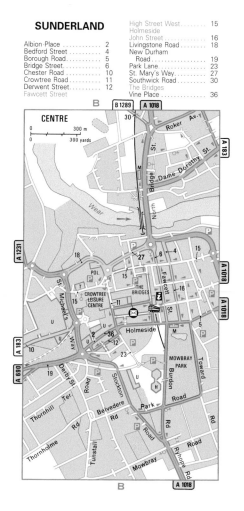

SWANSEA/ABERTAWE

Alexandra Road	B	2	Clarence Terrace	B	10
Belle Vue Way	B	4	College Street	B	13
Carmarthen Road	B	7	De la Beche Street	B	15
Castle Street	B	8	Dillwyn Street	B	17
Christina Street	B	9	East Bank Way	C	18
			Grove Place	B	22
			Kingsway (The)	B	
			Nearth Road	B	25
			Nelson Street	B	26
			New Cut Bridge	C	27
Oxford Street	B				
Parc Tawe Shopping Centre	B				
Princess Way	B				
Quadrant Centre	B				
St. David's Square	B				
St. Mary's Square	B	42			
Tawe Bridge	C	43			
Union Street	B	47			
Wellington Street	B	54			
West Way	B	55			

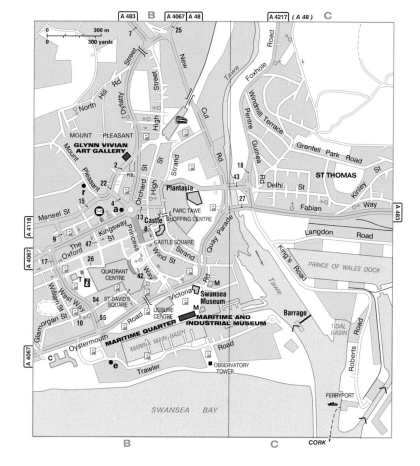

SWINDON

Beckhampton Street .... Y 3
Bridge Street .... Y 7
Brunel Shopping Centre ... YZ
Canal Walk .... Y 9
Cricklade Street .... Z 13
Cross Street .... Z 15
Deacon Street .... Z 16
Dryden Street .... Z 19
Edmund Street .... Z 21
Faringdon Road .... Y 22
Farnsby Street .... YZ 24
High Street .... Y 27
Islington Street .... Y 29
London Strand .... Y 31
Milton Road .... YZ 33
North Star Avenue .... Y 37
North Street .... Y 39
Ocotal Way .... Y 40
Prospect Hill .... Z 45
Regent Street .... YZ 46
Sheppard Street .... Y 49
South Street .... Z 52
Southampton
    Street .... Y 54
Spring Gardens .... Y 55
The Parade .... Y 58
Upham Road .... Y 60
Warwick Road .... Z 63
Wood Street .... Z 67

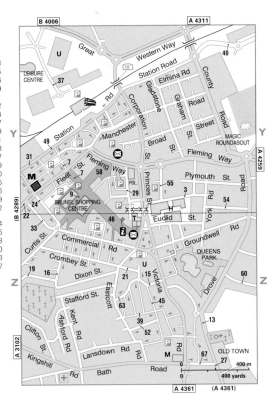

WINCHESTER

Andover Road 3
Bridge Street 6
Broadway (The) 7
Brooks Shopping
    Centre 8
City Road 10
Clifton Terrace 12
East Hill 15
Eastgate Street 16
Friarsgate 19
High Street
Magdalen Hill 23
Middle Brook Street ... 24
St. George's Street 32
St. Paul's Hill 33
St. Peter's Street 34
Southgate Street 35
Stockbridge Road 37
Sussex Street 38
Union Street 39
Upper High Street 40

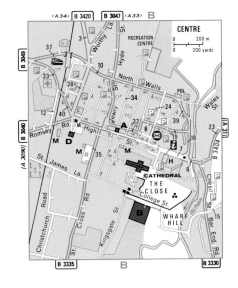

WARWICK

Bowling Green Street .... Y 9
Brook Street .... Y 12
Butts (The) .... Y 13
Castle Hill .... Y 15
Church Street .... Y 17
High Street .... Y 23
Jury Street .... Y
Lakin Road .... Y 25
Linen Street .... Y 26
Market Place .... Y 29
North Rock .... Y 32
Old Square .... Y 35
St. John's Road .... Y 42
St. Nicholas
    Church Street .... Y 43
Smith Street .... Y
Swan Street .... Y 46
Theatre Street .... Y 48
West Street .... Y 50

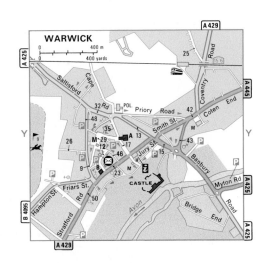

Uppertown	74	K 7	Ve Skerries	75	O 2	Wallace		
Uppingham	28	R 26	Venachar (Loch)	55	H 15	Monument	55	I 15
Upton (Dorset)	9	N 31	Ventnor	10	Q 32	Wallasey	33	K 23
Upton (Notts.)	36	R 24	Verwood	9	O 31	Wallingford	19	Q 29
Upton Grey	10	Q 30	Veryan	2	F 33	Wallington House	51	O 18
Upton House	27	P 27	Veyatie (Loch)	72	E 9	Walls	75	P 3
Upton Magna	26	M 25	Vindolanda	50	M 19	Wallsend	51	P 18
Upton-upon-			Voe	75	Q 2	Walney		
Severn	26	N 27	Voil (Loch)	55	G 14	(Isle of)	38	K 21
Upwell	29	U 26	Vowchurch	17	L 27	Walpole		
Urchfont	18	O 30	Vyrnwy (Lake)	33	J 25	St. Andrew	30	U 25
Ure (River)	40	Q 21				Walpole		
Urigill (Loch)	72	F 9				St. Peter	30	U 25
Urmston	34	M 23	**W**			Walsall	27	O 26
Urquhart Castle	67	G 12				Waltham (North		
Urquhart (Glen)	67	G 11	Waddesdon	19	R 28	East Lincs.)	41	T 23
Urrahag (Loch)	70	A 8	Waddington			Waltham (Kent)	13	X 30
Urswick	38	K 21	(Lancs.)	39	M 22	Waltham		
Usk (River)	16	J 28	Waddington			Abbey	20	U 28
Usk / Brynbuga	17	L 28	(Lincs.)	36	S 24	Waltham Forest		
Uttoxeter	35	O 25	Wadebridge	3	F 32	(London Borough)	20	T 29
Uyea	75	R 2	Wadhurst	11	U 30	Waltham-		
Uyeasound	75	R 1	Wainfleet			on-the-Wolds	36	R 25
			All Saints	37	U 24	Walton-		
			Wakefield	40	P 22	le-Dale	38	M 22
V			Wakes Colne	22	W 28	Walton-		
			Walberswick	31	Y 27	on-Thames	20	S 29
Vallay Strand	64	X 11	Walderslade	21	V 29	Walton-on-the-		
Valle Crucis	33	K 25	Walkden	39	M 23	Naze	23	X 28
Valley	32	G 24	Walkeringham	36	R 23	Wanborough	18	O 29
Valtos	70	Z 9	Walkern	20	T 28	Wandsworth		
Vatersay	58	X 13	Wall	27	O 26	(London Borough)	20	T 29

Wanlockhead	49	I 17						
Wansford	29	S 26						
Wanstrow	8	M 30						
Wantage	18	P 29						
Wappenham	28	Q 27						
Warboys	29	T 26						
Wardington	28	Q 27						
Wardour								
Castle	9	N 30						
Ware	20	T 28						
Wareham	9	N 31						
Wargrave	19	R 29						
Wark	50	N 17						
Wark Forest	50	M 18						
Warkworth	51	P 17						
Warley	27	O 26						
Warlingham	20	T 30						
Warmington	27	P 27						
Warminster	9	N 30						
Warmsworth	40	Q 23						
Warren (The)	13	X 30						
Warrington	34	M 23						
Warsash	10	Q 31						
Warsop	36	Q 24						
Warwickshire								
(County)	27	P 27						
Warwickshire								
(County)	27	P 27						

Wasbister	74	K 6	Wembley	20	T 29	West Walton	29	U 2
Wasdale Head	44	K 20	Wembury	4	H 33	West Wellow	9	P 3
Wash (The)	37	U 25	Wembworthy	6	I 31	West Wittering	10	R 3
Washington			Wemyss Bay	54	F 16	West Witton	46	O 2
(Tyne and Wear)	46	P 19	Wendens Ambo	20	U 27	West Wycombe	19	R 2
Washington (West			Wendover	19	R 28	Westbourne	10	R 3
Sussex)	11	S 31	Wendron	2	E 33	Westbury		
Wast Water	44	K 20	Wenlock Edge	26	L 26	(Cheshire)	26	L 2
Watchet	7	K 30	Wennington	38	M 21	Westbury (Wilts.)	9	N 3
Watchfield	18	P 29	Wensley	46	O 21	Westbury-on-		
Watchgate	45	L 20	Wensleydale	46	O 21	Severn	17	M 2
Water Orton	27	O 26	Wentbridge	40	Q 23	Westcliff	21	W 2
Waterbeach	22	U 27	Weobley (Hereford			Westcott	11	S 3
Watergate Bay	2	E 32	and Worcester)	26	L 27	Wester Ross	66	D 1
Waterhouses	35	O 24	Wereham	30	V 26	Westerham	11	U 3
Wateringbury	12	V 30	West Alvington	4	I 33	Western Cleddau	14	E 2
Waterlooville	10	Q 31	West Auckland	46	O 20	Westfield	12	V 3
Waternish Point	65	A 11	West Bay	5	M 32	Westgate-on-Sea	13	Y 2
Waters Upton	34	M 25	West Bergholt	22	W 28	Westham	11	U 3
Waterside	48	G 17	West Bridgford	36	Q 25	Westhoughton	38	M 2
Watford	20	S 29	West			Westleton	23	Y 2
Wath-			Bromwich	27	O 26	Westmill	20	T 2
upon-Dearne	35	P 23	West Calder	56	J 16	Westminster		
Watlington	19	Q 29	West Camel	8	M 30	(London Borough)	20	T 2
Watten	74	K 8	West Charleton	4	I 33	Westnewton	44	J 1
Watton	30	W 26	West Chiltington	11	S 31	Weston (Devon)	7	K 3
Watton at Stone	20	T 28	West Coker	8	L 31	Weston (Staffs.)	35	N 2
Waunfawr	32	H 24	West Dean	9	P 30	Westonbirt	17	N
Waveney (River)	31	Y 26	West Down	6	H 30	Weston-on-the-		
Wear (River)	46	O 20	West End	10	Q 31	Green	19	Q
Weardale	45	N 19	West Farleigh	12	V 30	Weston-on-Trent	35	P
Weaver (River)	34	M 24	West Geirinish	64	X 11	Weston-super-		
Weaverthorpe	41	S 21	West Harptree	17	M 30	Mare	17	L
Wedmore	8	L 30	West Hoathly	11	T 30	Weston Turville	19	R
Wednesbury	27	N 26	West Kilbride	54	F 16	Weston-under-		
Wednesfield	27	N 26	West			Lizard	26	N
Weedon-Bec	28	Q 27	Kingsdown	20	U 29	Weston-		
Week St. Mary	6	G 31	West Kirby	33	K 23	under-Penyard	17	M
Weeley	21	X 28	West Linton	56	J 16	Westonzoyland	8	L
Weem	61	I 14	West Loch Roag	70	Z 9	Westray	74	K
Welcombe	6	G 31	West Loch Tarbert			Westruther	57	M
Welham Green	20	T 28	(Argyll and Bute)	53	D 16	Westward Ho	6	H
Welland	26	N 27	West Loch Tarbert			Westwood	17	N
Welland (River)	37	T 25	(Western Isles)	70	Z 10	Wetheral	45	L
Wellesbourne	27	P 27	West Looe	3	G 32	Wetherby	40	P
Wellingborough	28	R 27	West Lulworth	8	N 32	Wethersfield	22	V
Wellington (Salop)	26	M 25	West Malling	12	V 30	Wetwang	41	S
Wellington			West Malvern	26	M 27	Wey (River)	10	R
(Somerset)	7	K 31	West Meon	10	Q 30	Weybourne	31	X
Wells	8	M 30	West Mersea	22	W 28	Weybridge	20	S
Wells-			West Midlands			Weyhill	9	P
next-the-Sea	30	W 25	(Metropolitan			Weymouth	8	M
Welshpool /			County			Whaley		
Trallwng	25	K 26	Birmingham)	27	O 26	Bridge	35	O
Welton	36	S 24	West Moors	9	O 31	Whalley	39	M
Welwyn	20	T 28	West Runton	31	X 25	Whalsay	75	R
Welwyn Garden			West Sussex			Whaplode	29	T
City	20	T 28	(County)	10	S 30	Wharfe (River)	40	Q
Wem	34	L 25	West Tanfield	39	P 21	Wharfedale	39	O
Wembdon	8	K 30	West Thorney	10	R 31	Whauphill	42	G

WINDSOR

Bexley Street .... Z 2
Castle Hill .... Z 4
Claremont Road .... Z 6
Clarence Crescent .... Z 7
Clewer Crescent Road ...... Z 8
Datchet Rd .... Z 9
Goswell Road .... Z 10
Grove Road .... Z 12
High Street .... Z 14
Keats Lane .... Z 17
King Edward Court Centre ... Z
Peascod Street .... Z 18
Peascod Street .... Z
River Street .... Z 22
Stovell Road .... Z 23
Thames Avenue .... Z 24
Thames Street .... Z 25
Trinity Place .... Z 27
Windsor Bridge .... Z 28

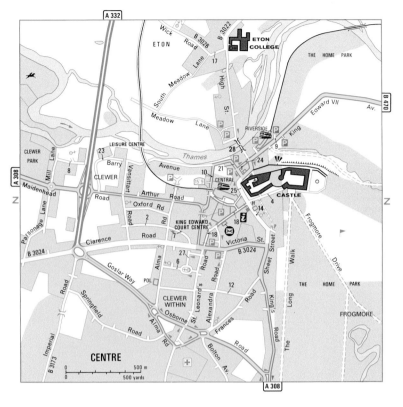

Whauphill	42	G 21	Whitehills	69	M 10	Whitwick	27 P 25
Wheathampstead	20	T 28	Whitehouse	53	D 16	Whitworth	39 N 23
Wheatley (Notts.)	36	R 23	Whiten Head	72	G 8	Wiay (Highland)	65 A 11
Wheatley (Oxon.)	19	Q 28	Whiteness Sands	67	I 10	Wiay	
Wheatley Hill	46	P 19	Whiteparish	9	P 30	(Western Isles)	64 Y 11
Wheaton Aston	26	N 25	Whiterashes	69	N 12	Wick (South Glos.)	17 M 29
Wheldrake	40	R 22	Whitesand Bay (Pembrokes)	14	E 28	Wick (Highland)	74 K 8
Whernside	39	M 21	Whitesand Bay (Cornwall)	2	C 33	Wicken (Cambs.)	28 R 27
Wherwell	9	P 30	Whitewell	38	M 22	Wicken (Northants.)	30 U 27
Whickham	46	O 19	Whitfield	13	X 30	Wickenby	37 S 24
Whimple	7	J 31	Whithorn	42	G 19	Wickford	21 V 29
Whipsnade	19	S 28	Whiting Bay	53	E 17	Wickham	10 Q 31
Whissendine	36	R 25	Whitland	14	G 28	Wickhambrook	22 V 27
Whitburn (West Lothian)	56	I 16	Whitley	19	R 29	Wickham Market	23 Y 27
Whitburn (South Tyneside)	46	P 19	Whitley Bay	51	P 18	Wickwar	17 M 29
Whitby	47	S 20	Whitsand Bay	3	H 32	Widecombe-in-the-Moor	4 I 32
Whitchurch (Bath and N.E. Somerset)	17	M 29	Whitstable	13	X 29	Wideford Hill Cairn	74 K 7
Whitchurch (Bucks.)	19	R 28	Whitstone	6	G 31	Widford	20 U 28
Whitchurch (Devon)	3	H 32	Whittingham	51	O 17	Widnes	34 L 23
Whitchurch (Heref. and Worc.)	17	M 28	Whittington (Derbs.)	35	P 24	Wigan	34 M 23
Whitchurch (Oxon.)	19	Q 29	Whittington (Lancs.)	38	L 21	Wiggenhall St. Mary Magdalen	30 V 25
Whitchurch (Salop)	34	L 25	Whittington (Salop)	34	L 25	Wight (Isle of) (County)	9 P 32
White Coomb	49	K 17	Whittle le Woods	38	M 22	Wigmore	21 V 29
White Horse Hill	18	P 29	Whittlebury	28	R 27	Wigston	28 Q 26
White Scarcaves	38	M 21	Whittlesey	29	T 26	Wigton	44 K 19
White Waltham	19	R 29	Whitton (Powys)	25	K 27	Wigtown	42 G 19
Whitebridge	67	G 12	Whitton (Suffolk)	23	X 27	Wigtown Bay	43 H 19
Whitefield	39	N 23	Whittonstall	46	O 19	Wilberfoss	40 R 22
Whitehaven	44	J 20	Whitwell (Derbs.)	36	Q 24	Wilcot	18 O 29
Whitehill	10	R 30	Whitwell (I.O.W.)	10	Q 31	Wild Animal Kingdom	19 S 28
			Whitwell-on-the-Hill	40	R 21	Willand	7 J 31

WOLVERHAMPTON

Cleveland Street 7
Darlington Street
Garrick Street 8
Lichfield Street 12
Mander Centre
Market Street 14
Princess Street 15
Queen Square 17
Railway Drive 20
Salop Street 22
Victoria Street 24
Wulfrun Centre

YORK CENTRE

Bishopgate Street .... CZ 3
Bishophill Senior .... CZ 4
Blake Street .... CY 5
Church Street .... DY 8
Clifford Street .... DY 10
Colliergate .... DY 12
Coney Street .... CY 13
Cromwell Road .... CZ 15
Davygate .... CY 16
Deangate .... DY 18
Duncombe Place .... CY 20
Fawcett Street .... DZ 21
Fetter Lane .... CY 22
Goodramgate .... DY 25
High Ousegate .... DY 26
High Petergate .... CY 28
Leeman Road .... CY 30
Lendal .... CY 32
Lord Mayor's Walk .... DX 33
Low Petergate .... DY 35
Museum Street .... CY 39
Parliament Street .... DY 42
Pavement .... DY 43
Peasholme Green .... DY 45
Penley's Grove Street ...... DX 46
Queen Street .... CZ 49
St. Leonard's Place .... CY 52
St. Maurice's Road .... DXY 53
Shambles (The) .... DY 54
Station Road .... CY 55
Stonebow (The) .... DY 56
Stonegate .... CY 58
Tower Street .... DZ 59

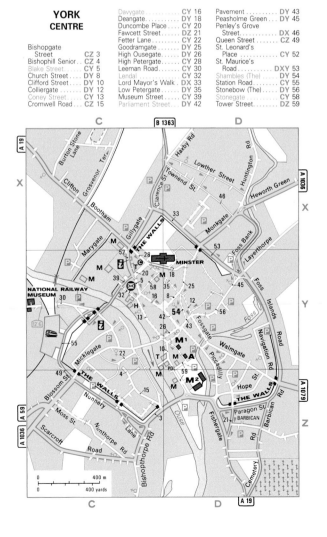

Willenhall	27 N 26	Windrush	18 O 28	Winterbourne Abbas	8 M 31
Willerby	41 S 22	Windrush (River)	18 O 28	Winterbourne Stoke	9 O 30
Willersey	27 O 27	Windsor	19 S 29	Winteringham	41 S 22
Willingdon	11 U 31	Windsor Great Park	19 S 29	Winterton	41 S 23
Willingham	29 U 27	Windygates	56 K 15	Winterton-on-Sea	31 Z 25
Willingham Forest	37 T 23	Winfarthing	31 X 26	Winton	45 N 20
Willington (Beds.)	29 S 27	Winforton	25 K 27	Winwick	29 S 26
Willington (Derbs.)	35 P 25	Winfrith Newburgh	8 N 32	Wirksworth	35 P 24
Willington (Durham)	46 O 19	Wing	19 R 28	Wirral	34 K 24
Williton	7 K 30	Wingate	46 P 19	Wisbech	29 U 25
Wilmcote	27 O 27	Wingfield	35 P 24	Wisborough Green	10 S 30
Wilmington (East Essex)	11 U 31	Wingham	13 X 30	Wishaw	55 I 16
Wilmington (Kent)	20 U 29	Wingrave	19 R 28	Wisley	20 S 30
Wilmslow	34 N 24	Winkfield	19 R 29	Wissey (River)	30 V 26
Wilton	9 O 30	Winkleigh	6 I 31	Witchford	29 U 26
Wiltshire (County)	9 O 30	Winnersh	19 R 29	Witham	22 V 28
Wimbledon	20 T 29	Winscombe	17 L 30	Witham (River)	37 T 24
Wimblington	29 U 26	Winsford (Cheshire)	34 M 24	Witheridge	7 I 31
Wimborne Minster	9 O 31	Winsford (Somerset)	7 J 30	Withernsea	41 U 22
Wimborne St. Giles	9 O 31	Winshill	35 P 25	Withington	18 O 28
Wincanton	8 M 30	Winslow	19 R 28	Withycombe	4 J 32
Winchcombe	18 O 28	Winster	35 P 24	Withypool	7 J 30
Winchelsea	12 W 31	Winterborne Kingston	8 N 31	Witley	10 S 30
Winchester	10 P 30	Winterborne Stickland	8 N 31	Witney	18 P 28
Windermere	45 L 20	Winterborne Whitechurch	8 N 31	Wittering	28 S 26
Windlesham	19 S 29	Winterbourne	17 M 29	Wittersham	12 W 30
				Wiveliscombe	7 K 30
				Wivenhoe	22 W 28
				Woburn	19 S 28
				Woburn Abbey	19 S 28
				Woburn Sands	19 S 27

Woking	19 S 30	Woolfardisworthy	6 G 31	Wrexham / Wrecsam	34 L 24
Wokingham	19 R 29	Woolpit	23 X 27	Wrington	17 L 29
Woldingham	20 T 30	Woolsthorpe	36 R 25	Writtle	22 V 28
Wollaston	28 S 27	Woore	34 M 25	Wrotham	20 U 30
Wollaton Hall	36 Q 25	Wootton Bassett	18 O 29	Wroughton	18 O 29
Wolsingham	46 O 19	Wootton Courtenay	7 J 30	Wroxham	31 Y 25
Wolvercote	19 Q 28	Wootton-Wawen	27 O 27	Wroxton	27 P 27
Wolverhampton	27 N 26	Worcester	26 N 27	Wyche	26 M 27
Wolverton	28 R 27	Worcester (County)	26 N 27	Wye	12 W 30
Wolviston	46 Q 20	Workington	44 J 20	Wye (River)	17 M 28
Wombourn	27 N 26	Worksop	36 Q 24	Wylam	51 O 19
Wombwell	40 P 23	Worle	17 L 29	Wylye	9 O 30
Womersley	40 Q 22	Wormit	56 L 14	Wymondham (Leics.)	36 R 25
Wonersh	10 S 30	Worms Head	15 H 29	Wymondham (Norfolk)	31 X 26
Wood Dalling	31 X 25	Worplesdon	10 S 30	Wyre	74 L 6
Woodbridge	23 X 27	Worsbrough	40 P 23		
Woodbury	7 J 31	Worsley	34 M 23		
Woodchurch	12 W 30	Worthen	26 L 26	**Y**	
Woodcote	19 Q 29	Worthing	11 S 31		
Woodford Halse	28 Q 27	Wortwell	31 Y 26	Y-Fenni / Abergavenny	17 L 28
Woodhall Spa	37 T 24	Wotton-under-Edge	17 M 29	Y Ffor	32 G 25
Woodham Ferrers	21 V 29	Wragby	37 T 24	Y Llethr	32 I 25
Woodingdean	11 T 31	Wrangle	37 U 24	Yafforth	46 P 20
Woodnesborough	13 X 30	Wrawby	41 S 23	Yalding	12 V 30
Woodseaves	34 N 25	Wray	38 M 21	Yapton	10 S 31
Woodstock	18 P 28	Wrea Green	38 L 22	Yardley Hastings	28 R 27
Woodton	31 Y 26	Wrecsam / Wrexham	34 L 24	Yare (River)	30 W 26
Woody Bay	6 I 30	Wremtham	31 Z 26	Yarm	46 P 20
Wookey Hole	8 L 30				
Wool	8 N 31				
Woolacombe	6 H 30				
Wooler	51 N 17				

Yarmouth	9 P 31
Yate	17 M 29
Yateley	19 R 29
Yatton	17 L 29
Yaxham	30 W 26
Yaxley	29 T 26
Yeadon	39 O 22
Yealmpton	4 I 32
Yedingham	41 S 21
Yell	75 Q 1
Yelverton	4 H 32
Yeolmbridge	3 G 32
Yeovil	8 M 31
Yesnaby	74 J 6
Yetminster	8 M 31
Yetts o' Muckhart	56 J 15
Ynys / Lochtyn	24 G 27
York	40 Q 22
Yorkletts	13 X 30
Yorkley	17 M 28
Yorkshire Dales National Park	45 N 21
Yorkshire Wolds	41 S 21
Youlgreave	35 O 24
Yoxall	35 O 25
Yoxford	23 Y 27
Yr Wyddgrug / Mold	33 K 24
Ysbyty Ifan	33 I 24
Ystalyfera	15 I 28
Ystrad-Aeron	24 H 27
Ystradgynlais	15 I 28
Ystwyth (River)	24 H 26

Ireland

A

Abbeydorney	83	C 10
Abbeyfeale	83	E 10
Abbeylara	92	J 6
Abbeyleix / Mainistir Laoise	85	J 9
Achill Head	94	B 6
Achill Island	94	B 6
Achill Sound / Gob an Choire	94	C 6
Achillbeg Island	94	C 6
Aclare	95	F 5
Acoose (Lough)	76	C 11
Adamstown	80	L 10
Adare	84	F 10
Adrigole	76	C 12
Aghaboe	85	J 9
Aghabullogue	78	F 12
Aghada	78	H 12
Aghalee	99	N 4
Aghavannagh	87	M 9
Aghaville	77	D 13
Aghla Mountain	100	H 3
Aglish	79	I 11
Ahakista	77	D 13
Ahalia (Loughs)	88	D 7
Ahascragh	90	G 7
Ahenny	85	J 10
Aherlow (Glen of)	84	H 10
Ahoghill	102	M 3
Aillwee Cave	89	E 8
Ailt an Chorráin / Burtonport	100	G 3
Aird Mhór / Ardmore	79	I 12
Allen (Bog of)	86	K 8
Allen (Lough)	96	H 5
Allenwood	86	L 8
Allihies	76	B 13
Allua (Lough)	77	E 12
Altan Lough	100	H 2
An Blascaod Mór / Blasket Islands	82	A 11
An Bun Beag / Bunbeg	100	H 2
An Cabhán / Cavan	97	J 6
An Caiseal / Cashel (Galway)	88	C 7
An Caisleán Nua / Newcastle West	83	E 10
An Caisleán Riabhach / Castlerea	96	G 6
An Charraig / Carrick	100	G 4
An Chathair / Caher	85	I 10
An Cheathrú Rua / Carraroe	88	D 8
An Chloich Mhóir / Cloghmore	94	C 6
An Clochán / Clifden	88	B 7
An Clochán / Cloghan (Donegal)	100	I 3
An Clochán Liath / Dunglow	100	G 3
An Cloigeann / Cleegan	88	B 7
An Cóbh / Cobh	78	H 12
An Coimín / Commeen	100	I 3
An Coireán / Waterville	76	B 12
An Corrán / Currane	94	C 6
An Creagán / Mount Bellew	90	G 7
An Daingean / Dingle	82	B 11
An Droichead Nua / Newbridge	86	L 8
An Dúchoraidh / Doocharry	100	H 3
An Fál Carrach / Falcarragh	100	H 2
An Fhairche / Clonbur	89	D 7
An Geata Mór	94	B 5
An Gleann Garbh / Glengarriff	77	D 12
An Gort / Gort	89	F 8

An Gort Mór / Gortmore	88	D 7
An Leacht / Lahinch	89	D 9
An Longfort / Longford	90	I 6
An Mám / Maam Cross	88	D 7
An Mhala Raithní / Mulrany	94	C 6
An Móta / Moate	90	I 7
An Muileann gCearr / Mullingar	92	J 7
An Nás / Naas	87	M 8
An Ráth / Charleville	84	F 10
An Ráth / Rath Luirc (Charleville)	84	F 10
An Ros / Rush	93	N 7
An Scairbh / Scarriff	84	G 9
An Sciobairín / Skibbereen	77	E 13
An Seanchaisleán / Oldcastle	92	K 6
An Spidéal / Spiddal	89	E 8
An tAonach / Nenagh	84	H 9
An Teampall Mór / Templemore	85	I 9
An Tearmann / Termon	101	I 2

An tInbhear Mór / Arklow	81	N 9
An tSraith / Srah	95	E 6
An Tulach / Tullow	80	L 9
An Uaimh / Navan	93	L 7
Anascaul	82	B 11
Annacarriga	84	G 9
Annacotty	84	G 9
Annagary	100	H 2
Annagassan	93	M 6
Annageeragh (River)	83	D 9
Annagh Head	94	B 5
Annaghdown	89	E 7
Annaghmore Lough	90	H 6
Annalee	97	J 5
Annalong	99	O 5
Annamoe	87	N 8
Annestown	80	K 11
Antrim	103	N 3
Antrim (County)	102	M 3
Antrim Coast	75	O 2
Antrim (Glens of)	103	N 2
Antrim Mountains	103	N 2
Anure (Lough)	100	H 3
Araglin	78	H 11
Árainn Mhór / Aran or Aranmore Island	100	G 2
Árainn (Oiléain) / Aran Islands	88	C 8
Aran Islands / Oiléain Árainn	88	C 8

Aran or Aranmore Island / Árainn Mhór	100	G 2
Archdale (Castle)	97	I 4
Ardagh	83	E 10
Ardara	100	G 3
Ardboe	98	M 4
Ardcath	93	M 7
Ardcrony	84	H 9
Ardea	76	C 12
Ardee / Baile Átha Fhirdhia	93	M 6
Ardfert	82	C 11
Ardfinnan	79	I 11
Ardglass	75	P 5
Ardgroom	76	C 12
Ardkeen	75	P 4
Ardmore / Aird Mhór	79	I 12
Ardrahan	89	F 8
Ardress House	98	M 4
Ards Forest Park	101	I 2
Ards Peninsula	75	P 4
Argideen	77	F 13
Argory (The)	98	M 4
Arigna	96	H 5
Arklow / An tInbhear Mór	81	N 9
Armagh	98	M 4
Armagh (County)	74	L 5
Armoy	103	N 2
Arney	97	I 5
Arrow (Lough)	96	H 5

Arthurstown	80	L 11
Arvagh	97	J 6
Ashbourne	93	M 7
Ashford	87	N 8
Ashford Castle	89	E 7
Askeaton	83	F 10
Astee	83	D 10
Áth Cinn / Headford	89	E 7
Athassel Abbey	85	I 10
Athboy	92	L 7
Athea	83	E 10
Athenry / Baile Átha an Rí	89	F 8
Athleague	90	H 7
Athlone / Baile Átha Luain	90	I 7
Athy / Baile Átha	86	L 9
Attymon	89	G 8
Audley's Castle	75	P 4
Augher	97	K 4
Aughils	82	C 11
Aughnacloy	98	M 4
Aughnanure Castle	89	E 7
Aughrim (Galway)	90	H 8
Aughrim (Wicklow)	87	N 9
Aughris Head	95	F 5
Avoca	87	N 9
Avoca (River)	81	N 9
Avoca (Valle of)	87	N 9
Avonbeg	87	M 9
Avondale Forest Park	87	N 9

B

Bagenalstown / Muine Bheag	80	L 9
Baile an Fheirtéaraigh / Ballyferriter	82	A 11
Baile an Mhóta / Ballymote	96	G 5
Baile an Róba / Ballinrobe	89	E 7
Baile an Sceilg / Ballinskelligs	76	B 12
Baile Átha an Rí / Athenry	89	F 8
Baile Átha Cliath / Dublin	87	N 8
Baile Átha Fhirdhia / Ardee	93	M 6
Baile Átha / Athy	86	L 9
Baile Átha Luain / Athlone	90	I 7
Baile Átha Troim / Trim	93	L 7
Baile Bhuirne / Ballyvourney	77	E 12
Baile Brigín / Balbriggan	93	N 7
Baile Chláir / Claregalway	89	F 7
Baile Locha Riach / Loughrea	90	G 8

Baile Mhic Andáin / Thomastown	80	K 10
Baile Mhic re / Ballymakeery	77	E 12
Baile Mhistéala / Mitchelstown	78	H 11
Baile na Finne / Fintown	100	H 3
Baile na Lorgan / Castleblayney	98	L 5
Baile Uí Fhiacháin / Newport	95	D 6
Baile Uí Mhatháin / Ballymahon	90	I 7
Bailieborough / Coill an Chollaigh	92	L 6
Balbriggan / Baile Brigín	93	N 7
Baldoyle	93	N 7
Balla	95	E 6
Ballagan Point	99	N 5
Ballaghaderreen / Bealach an Doirín	96	G 6
Ballaghbeama Gap	76	C 12
Ballaghisheen Pass	76	C 12
Ballina / Béal an Átha	95	E 5
Ballina (Tipperary)	84	G 9
Ballinaboy	88	B 7
Ballinadee	78	G 12
Ballinafad	96	G 5
Ballinagar	86	J 8

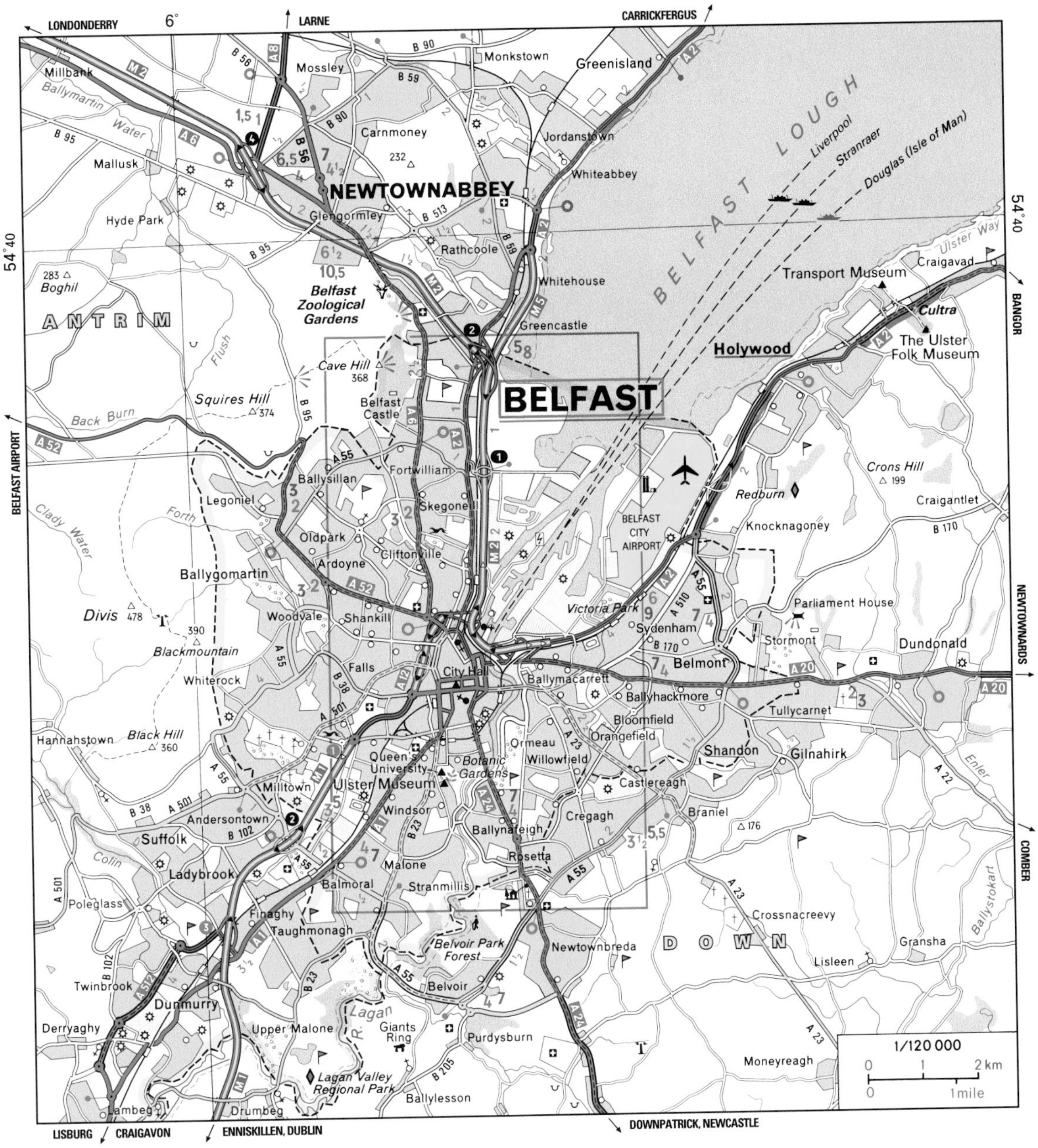

Map of Belfast area (scale 1/120 000). Place labels include: LONDONDERRY, LARNE, CARRICKFERGUS, Millbank, Ballymartin Water, Mossley, Monkstown, Greenisland, Carnmoney, Jordanstown, Whiteabbey, BELFAST LOUGH, Liverpool, Stranraer, Douglas (Isle of Man), Mallusk, NEWTOWNABBEY, Glengormley, Rathcoole, Whitehouse, Greencastle, Transport Museum, Craigavad, BANGOR, Hyde Park, Boghil, Belfast Zoological Gardens, Cultra, Holywood, The Ulster Folk Museum, ANTRIM, Cave Hill 368, Squires Hill 374, Belfast Castle, Whitehouse, BELFAST, Crons Hill 199, Redburn, Craigantlet, BELFAST AIRPORT, Clady Water, Back Burn, Flush, Ballysillan, Fortwilliam, Skegoneill, Legoniel, Knocknagoney, Oldpark, Ardoyne, Cliftonville, BELFAST CITY AIRPORT, NEWTOWNARDS, Ballygomartin, Victoria Park, Parliament House, Divis 478, Woodvale, Shankill, Sydenham, Stormont, Dundonald, Blackmountain 390, Falls, City Hall, Ballymacarrett, Belmont, A 20, Whiterock, Black Hill 360, Queen's University, Botanic Gardens, Ormeau, Willowfield, Bloomfield, Orangefield, Shandon, Gilnahirk, Hannahstown, Ulster Museum, Windsor, Ballynafeigh, Castlereagh, COMBER, Andersontown, Suffolk, Malone, Stranmillis, Rosetta, Cregagh, Braniel, Ladybrook, Balmoral, Colin, Poleglass, Finaghy, Taughmonagh, Belvoir Park Forest, Newtownbreda, DOWN, Crossnacreevy, Gransha, Lisleen, Twinbrook, Dunmurry, Upper Malone, Giants Ring, Purdysburn, Moneyreagh, Derryaghy, Lagan, Lambeg, Drumbeg, Lagan Valley Regional Park, Ballylesson, LISBURN / CRAIGAVON, ENNISKILLEN, DUBLIN, DOWNPATRICK, NEWCASTLE. Scale 1/120 000, 0 1 2 km, 0 1 mile.

BELFAST

Albert Square	BY 3	Clifton Street	BY 15	Lagan Bridge	BY 32
Ann Street	BZ 5	Corporation Square	BY 16	Queen Elizabeth Bridge	BZ 40
Bridge Street	BZ 12	Donegal Place	BZ	Queen's Bridge	BZ 41
Castlecourt Shopping Centre	BYZ	Donegall Quay	BYZ 19	Queen's Square	BY 42
Castle Place	BZ	Donegall Square	BZ 20	Rosemary Street	BZ 44
		Great Victoria Street	BZ 26	Royal Avenue	BYZ
		High Street	BYZ 28	Waring Street	BY 54
		Howard Street	BZ 29	Wellington Place	BZ 55

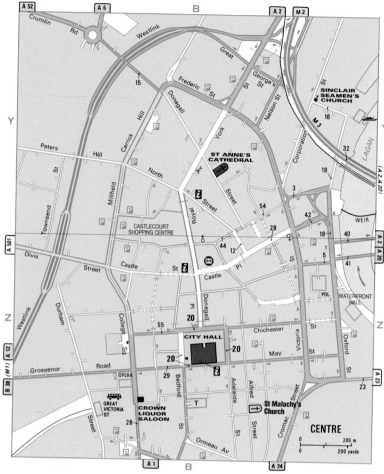

Ballinakill	86 K 9
Ballinalack	92 J 7
Ballinalea	87 N 8
Ballinalee	92 J 6
Ballinamallard	97 J 4
Ballinamore / Béal an Átha Mhóir	97 I 5
Ballinamore Bridge	90 G 7
Ballinascarty	77 F 12
Ballinasloe / Béal Átha na Sluaighe	90 H 8
Ballincollig	78 G 12
Ballincrea	80 K 11
Ballincurrig	78 H 12
Ballindarragh	74 J 5
Ballinderry	84 H 8
Ballindine	95 F 6
Ballineen	77 F 12
Ballingarry (Galway)	85 H 8
Ballingarry (Limerick)	84 F 10
Ballingarry (Tipperary)	85 J 10
Ballingeary / Béal Átha an Ghaorthaidh	77 E 12
Ballinhassig	78 G 12
Ballinlough	90 G 6
Ballinrobe / Baile an Róba	89 E 7
Ballinskelligs / Baile an Sceilg	76 B 12
Ballinskelligs Bay	76 B 12
Ballinspittle	78 G 12
Ballintober (Roscommon)	90 G 6
Ballintogher	96 G 5
Ballintoy	102 M 2
Ballintra	100 H 4
Ballinure	85 I 10
Ballitore	86 L 8
Ballivor	92 L 7
Ballon	80 L 9

Ballyagran	84 F 10
Ballybay	98 L 5
Ballybofey / Bealach Féich	101 I 3
Ballyboghil	93 N 7
Ballyboy	90 I 8
Ballybrittas	86 K 8
Ballybrophy	85 J 9
Ballybunnion	83 D 10
Ballycanew	81 N 10
Ballycarney	81 M 10
Ballycastle (Antrim)	103 N 2
Ballycastle (Mayo)	95 D 5
Ballycastle Bay	103 N 2
Ballyclare (Antrim)	103 N 3
Ballyclare (Roscommon)	90 I 6
Ballyclough	78 F 11
Ballycolla	85 J 9
Ballyconneely	88 B 7
Ballyconneely Bay	88 B 7
Ballyconnell	97 J 5
Ballycopeland	75 P 4
Ballycotton	78 H 12
Ballycotton Bay	78 H 12
Ballycroy	94 C 5
Ballydavid	82 A 11
Ballydavid Head	82 A 11
Ballydavis	86 K 8
Ballydehob	77 D 13
Ballydesmond	83 E 11
Ballydonegan	76 B 13
Ballyduff (Dingle)	82 B 11
Ballyduff (Kerry)	83 D 10
Ballyduff (Waterford)	78 H 11
Ballyeighter Loughs	89 F 9
Ballyfarnan	96 H 5
Ballyferriter / Baile an Fheirtéaraigh	82 A 11
Ballyforan	90 H 7
Ballygalley	75 O 3

Ballygalley Head	75 O 3
Ballygar	90 H 7
Ballygawley (Sligo)	96 G 5
Ballygawley (Tyrone)	97 K 4
Ballygorman	102 K 1
Ballygowan (near Belfast)	99 O 4
Ballyhack	80 L 11
Ballyhahill	83 E 10
Ballyhaise	97 K 5
Ballyhalbert	75 P 4
Ballyhale	80 K 10
Ballyhaunis / Béal Átha hAmhnais	95 F 6
Ballyhean	95 E 6
Ballyheige	82 C 10
Ballyheige Bay	82 C 10
Ballyhoe Lough	93 L 6
Ballyhooly	78 G 11
Ballyhoura Mountains	78 G 11
Ballyjamesduff	92 K 6
Ballykeeran	90 I 7
Ballykelly	102 K 2
Ballylanders	84 G 10
Ballylickey	77 D 12
Ballyliffin	101 J 2
Ballylongford	83 D 10
Ballylongford Bay	83 D 10
Ballylynan	86 K 9
Ballymacarbry	79 I 11
Ballymacoda	79 I 12
Ballymagorry	101 J 3
Ballymahon / Baile Uí Mhatháin	90 I 7
Ballymakeery / Baile Mhic re	77 E 12
Ballymartin	99 O 5
Ballymena	103 N 3
Ballymoe	90 G 6
Ballymoney (Antrim)	102 M 2

Ballymore	91 I 7
Ballymore Eustace	87 M 8
Ballymote / Baile an Mhóta	96 G 5
Ballymurphy	80 L 10
Ballynabola	80 L 10
Ballynacarrigy	92 J 7
Ballynacorra	78 H 12
Ballynagore	92 J 7
Ballynagree	77 F 12
Ballynahinch	99 O 4
Ballynahinch Lake	88 C 7
Ballynahown	88 D 8
Ballynakill Harbour	88 B 7
Ballyneety	84 G 10
Ballynoe	78 H 11
Ballynure	75 O 3
Ballyorgan	84 G 11
Ballypatrick	85 J 10
Ballyporeen	78 H 11
Ballyquintin Point	75 P 5
Ballyragget	85 J 9
Ballyroan	86 K 9
Ballyronan	102 M 3
Ballyroney	99 N 5
Ballysadare	96 G 5
Ballyshannon / Béal Átha Seanaidh	96 H 4
Ballysteen	83 F 10
Ballyteige Bay	80 L 11
Ballyvaughan	89 E 8
Ballyvaughan Bay	89 E 8
Ballyvourney / Baile Bhuirne	77 E 12
Ballywalter	75 P 4
Ballywilliam	80 L 10
Balrath	93 M 7
Baltimore	77 D 13
Baltinglass / Bealach Conglais	87 L 9
Baltray	93 N 6
Banagher	90 I 8
Banbridge	99 N 4

Bandon / Droichead na Bandan	78 F 12
Bandon River	77 F 12
Bangor (Down)	99 O 4
Bangor (Mayo)	94 C 5
Bann (River) (Lough Neagh)	99 N 5
Bann (River) (R. Slaney)	81 M 10
Banna Strand	82 C 11
Bannow	80 L 11
Bansha	84 H 10
Banteer	77 F 11
Bantry / Beanntraí	77 D 12
Bantry Bay	76 C 13
Barefield	84 F 9
Barley Cove	76 C 13
Barna / Bearna	89 E 8
Barnaderg	89 F 7
Barnatra / Barr na Trá	94 C 5
Barnesmore Gap	100 I 3
Baronscourt Forest	101 J 3
Barra (Lough)	100 H 3
Barraduff	77 D 11
Barr na Trá / Barnatra	94 C 5
Barrow (River)	86 J 8
Barrow Harbour	82 C 11
Barrow (River)	86 K 8
Beagh (Lough)	100 I 2
Béal an Átha / Ballina	95 E 5
Béal an Átha Mhóir / Ballinamore	97 I 5
Béal an Mhuirthead / Belmullet	94 C 5
Béal Átha an Ghaorthaidh / Ballingeary	77 E 12
Béal Átha hAmhnais / Ballyhaunis	95 F 6
Béal Átha na Muice / Swinford	95 F 6
Béal Átha na Sluaighe / Ballinasloe	90 H 8
Béal Átha Seanaidh / Ballyshannon	96 H 4
Béal Deirg / Belderrig	95 D 5
Béal Tairbirt / Belturbet	97 J 5
Bealach an Doirín / Ballaghaderreen	96 G 6
Bealach Conglais / Baltinglass	87 L 9
Bealach Féich / Ballybofey	101 I 3
Bealaclugga	89 E 8
Bealadangan	88 D 8
Bealaha	83 D 9
Beanntraí / Bantry	77 D 12
Beara	76 C 12
Bearna / Barna	89 E 8
Beaufort	77 D 11
Beehive Huts	82 A 11
Beenoskee	82 B 11
Beg (Lough)	102 M 3
Behy	76 C 11
Belcarra	95 E 6
Belclare	89 F 7
Belcoo	97 I 5
Belderrig / Béal Deirg	95 D 5
Belfast	99 O 4
Belfast Lough	75 O 3
Belgooly	78 G 12
Belhavel Lough	96 H 5
Bellacorick	95 D 5
Bellaghy	102 M 3
Bellanagare	96 G 6
Bellanaleck	74 J 5
Bellananagh	97 J 6
Bellavary	95 E 6
Belleek (Armagh)	74 M 5
Belleek (Fermanagh)	96 H 4
Belmullet / Béal an Mhuirthead	94 C 5
Beltra	95 D 6
Beltra Lough	95 D 6

Belturbet / Béal Tairbirt	97 J 5
Benbane Head	102 M 2
Benbrack	96 I 5
Benbulben	96 G 4
Benburb	98 L 4
Bencroy or Gubnaveagh	96 I 5
Benmore or Fair Head	103 N 2
Benettsbridge	80 K 10
Benwee Head	94 C 4
Beragh	97 K 4
Bere Island	76 C 13
Bernish Rock	74 M 5
Bertraghboy Bay	88 C 7
Bessbrook	74 M 5
Bettystown	93 N 6
Binevenagh	102 L 2
Binn Éadair / Howth	93 N 7
Biorra / Birr	90 I 8
Birdhill	84 G 9
Birr / Biorra	90 I 8
Black Head (Antrim)	75 O 3
Black Head (Clare)	89 E 8
Black Ball Head	76 B 13
Black Bull	93 M 7
Black Gap (The)	100 I 4
Blacklion	96 I 5
Blackrock	87 N 8
Blackrock (Louth)	93 M 6
Blacksod Bay	94 B 5
Blacksod Point	94 B 5
Blackstairs Mountains	80 L 10
Blackwater	81 M 10
Blackwater Bridge	76 C 12
Blackwater (River) (Cork)	77 F 11
Blackwater (River) (Lough Neagh)	98 L 4
Blackwater (River) (R. Boyne)	93 L 6
Blarney	78 G 12
Blasket Islands / An Blascaod Mór	82 A 11
Blennerville	83 C 11
Blessington	87 M 8
Bloody Foreland	100 H 2
Blue Ball	86 J 8
Blue Stack Mountains	100 H 3
Boderg (Lough)	96 I 6
Bodyke	84 G 9
Bofin (Lough) (Galway)	89 D 7
Bofin (Lough) (Roscommon)	96 I 6
Boggeragh Mountains	77 E 12
Boheraphuca	84 I 8
Boherbue	77 E 11
Bohermeen	93 L 7
Bola (Lough)	88 C 7
Boley	86 L 8
Boliska Lough	89 E 8
Bolus Head	76 A 12
Bonet	96 H 5
Boobyglass	80 K 10
Borris	80 L 10
Borris in Ossory	85 J 9
Borrisokane / Buiríos Uí Chéin	84 H 9
Borrisoleigh	85 I 9
Bouladuff	85 I 9
Boyle / Mainistir na Búille	96 H 6
Boyle (River)	96 H 6
Boyne (River)	92 K 7
Bracklin	92 K 7
Brandon / Cé Bhréanainn	82 B 11
Brandon Bay	82 B 11
Brandon Head	82 B 11
Brandon Hill	80 L 10
Bray / Bré	87 N 8
Bray Head (Kerry)	76 A 12
Bray Head (Wicklow)	87 N 8
Bré / Bray	87 N 8
Breenagh	101 I 3
Bride (River)	79 I 11
Bridebridge	78 H 11
Bridge End	101 J 2
Bridgeland	81 M 9

Bridget Lough	84 G 9
Bridgetown	81 M 11
Briensbridge	84 G 9
Brinlack / Bun na Leaca	100 H 2
Brittas	87 M 8
Brittas Bay	87 N 9
Broad Haven	94 C 5
Broad Meadow	93 N 7
Broadford (Clare)	84 G 9
Broadford (Limerick)	83 F 10
Broadway	81 M 11
Brookeborough	74 J 5
Brosna	83 E 11
Brosna (River)	90 I 8
Broughshane	103 N 3
Brow Head	76 C 13
Brown Flesk	83 D 11
Brownstown Head	80 K 11
Bruff	84 G 10
Bruree	84 G 10
Buckode	96 H 4
Buiríos Uí Chéin / Borrisokane	84 H 9
Bull Point	103 N 2
Bull's Head	82 B 11
Bullaun	90 G 8
Bun an Phobail / Moville	102 K 2
Bun Cranncha / Buncrana	101 J 2
Bun Dobhráin / Bundoran	96 H 4
Bun na hAbhna / Bunnahowen	94 C 5
Bun na Leaca / Brinlack	100 H 2
Bunacurry	94 C 6
Bunbeg / An Bun Beag	100 H 2
Bunclody	81 M 10
Buncrana / Bun Cranncha	101 J 2
Bundoran / Bun Dobhráin	96 H 4
Bunmahon	79 J 11
Bunnahowen / Bun na hAbhna	94 C 5
Bunnanaddan	96 G 5
Bunny (Lough)	89 F 8
Bunnyconnellan	95 E 5
Bunowen	94 C 6
Bunratty	84 F 9
Burncourt	78 H 11
Burnfort	78 G 11
Burren (The)	89 E 8
Burrishoole Abbey	95 D 6
Burtonport / Ailt an Chorráin	100 G 3
Bush	102 M 2
Bushfield	84 G 9
Bushmills	102 M 2
Butler's Bridge	97 J 5
Butlerstown	78 F 13
Buttevant	78 F 11
Bweeng	78 F 11

C

Caha Mountains	76 C 12
Caharagh	77 E 13
Caher / An Chathair	85 I 10
Caher Island	94 B 6
Caherbarnagh	77 E 11
Caherconlish	84 G 10
Caherdaniel	76 B 12
Cahersiveen / Cathair Saidhbhín	76 B 12
Cahore Point	81 N 10
Caiseal / Cashel (Tipperary)	85 I 10
Caisleán an Bharraigh / Castlebar	95 E 6
Caisleán an Chomair / Castlecomer	86 K 9
Calafort Ros Láir / Rosslare Harbour	81 M 11
Caledon	98 L 4
Callainn / Callan	85 J 10
Callan / Callainn	85 J 10

Caltra	90	G	7
Camlough	74	M	5
Camolin	81	M	10
Camp	82	C	11
Campile	80	L	11
Canglass Point	76	B	12
Canningstown	97	K	6
Cappagh White	84	H	10
Cappamore	84	G	10
Cappoquin / Ceapach Choinn	79	I	11
Car (Slieve)	94	D	5
Caragh (Lough)	76	C	11
Caragh (River)	76	C	12
Carbery's Hundred Isles	77	D	13
Carbury	92	L	7
Carhan House	76	B	12
Cark Mountain	101	I	3
Carlanstown	92	L	6
Carlingford	99	N	5
Carlingford Lough	99	N	5
Carlow / Ceatharlach	86	L	9
Carlow (County)	80	L	9
Carn Domhnach / Carndonagh	102	K	2
Carna	88	C	8
Carncastle	75	O	3
Carndonagh / Carn Domhnach	102	K	2
Carne	81	M	11
Carnew	81	M	9
Carney	96	G	4
Carnlough	75	O	3
Carnlough Bay	75	O	3
Carnsore Point	81	M	11
Carra (Lough)	95	E	6
Carraig Airt / Carrigart	101	I	2
Carraig Mhachaire Rois / Carrickmacross	98	L	6
Carraig na Siúire / Carrick-on-Suir	79	J	10
Carran	89	E	8
Carrantuohill	76	C	11
Carraroe / An Cheathrú Rua	88	D	8
Carrick-a-Rede Rope Bridge	102	M	2
Carrick / An Charraig (Donegal)	100	G	4
Carrick (Wexford)	80	L	11
Carrick-on-Shannon-Cora Droma Rúisc	96	H	6
Carrick-on-Suir / Carraig na Siúire	79	J	10
Carrickboy	91	I	7
Carrickfergus	75	O	3
Carrickmacross / Carraig Mhachaire Rois	98	L	6
Carrickmore	97	K	4
Carrigafoyle Castle	83	D	10
Carrigaholt	83	C	10
Carrigaline	78	G	12
Carrigallen	97	J	6
Carriganimmy	77	E	12
Carrigans	101	J	3
Carrigart / Carraig Airt	101	I	2
Carrigglass Manor	92	I	6
Carrigkerry	83	E	10
Carrigtohill	78	H	12
Carrowkeel	101	J	2
Carrowmore	96	G	5
Carrowmore Lake	94	C	5
Carrownisky	94	C	6
Carrowteige / Ceathrú Thaidhg	94	C	5
Carrybeg	79	J	10
Carryduff	99	O	4
Cashel / An Caiseal (Galway)	88	C	7
Cashel / Caiseal (Tipperary)	85	I	10
Cashel (Rock of)	85	I	10
Cashen River	83	D	10
Cashla Bay	88	D	8
Casla / Costelloe	88	D	8
Castle Coole	97	J	4
Castle Espie Centre	99	O	4
Castle Gardens	78	F	13
Castle Haven	77	E	13
Castle Point	83	C	10
Castlebaldwin	96	G	5
Castlebar / Caisleán an Bharraigh	95	E	6
Castlebellingham	93	M	6
Castleblakeney	90	G	7
Castleblayney / Baile na Lorgan	98	L	5
Castlebridge	81	M	10
Castlecaulfield	98	L	4
Castlecomer / Caisleán an Chomair	86	K	9
Castleconnell	84	G	9
Castlecove	76	B	12
Castledawson	102	M	3
Castlederg	101	J	3
Castledermot	86	L	9
Castlefinn	101	J	3
Castlefreke	77	F	13
Castlegal	96	G	4
Castlegregory	82	B	11
Castlehill	94	C	6
Castleisland / Oileán Ciarraí	83	D	11
Castlelyons	78	H	11
Castlemaine	83	C	11
Castlemaine Harbour	82	C	11
Castlemartyr	78	H	12
Castleplunket	90	G	6
Casltepollard	92	K	6
Castlerea / An Caisleán Riabhach	90	G	6
Castlerock	102	L	2
Castletown (Laois)	85	J	9
Castletown (Westmeath)	92	J	7
Castletown (Wexford)	81	N	9
Castletownbere	76	C	13
Castletownroche	78	G	11
Castletownshend	77	E	13
Castleward House	75	P	4
Castlewellan	99	O	5
Castlewellan Forest Park	99	O	5
Cathair na Mart / Westport	95	D	6
Cathair Saidhbhín / Cahersiveen	76	B	12
Causeway	83	C	10
Cavan / An Cabhán	97	J	6
Cavan (County)	92	J	6
Cé Bhréanainn / Brandon	82	B	11
Ceanannas / Ceanannus Mór (Kells)	92	L	6
Ceanannus Mór (Kells) / Ceanannas	92	L	6
Ceann Toirc / Kanturk	77	F	11
Ceapach Choinn / Cappoquin	79	I	11
Ceatharlach / Carlow	86	L	9
Ceathrú Thaidhg / Carrowteige	94	C	5
Cecilstown	78	F	11
Celbridge	93	M	7
Chapeltown	75	P	5
Charlestown (Armagh)	98	M	4
Charlestown (Mayo)	95	F	6
Charleville (Ráth Luirc) / An Ráth	84	F	10
Church Hill	101	I	3
Church Quarter	103	N	2
Churchtown	80	L	11
Cill Airne / Killarney	77	D	11
Cill Chainnigh / Kilkenny	80	K	10
Cill Chaoi / Kilkee	83	D	9
Cill Chiaráin / Kilkieran	88	C	8
Cill Dalua / Killaloe	84	G	9
Cill Dara / Kildare	86	L	8
Cill Mhantáin / Wicklow	87	N	9
Cill Mocheallóg / Kilmallock	84	G	10
Cill Orglan / Killorglin	76	C	11
Cill Rois / Kilrush	83	D	10
Cill Rónáin / Kilronan	88	C	8
Cionn tSáile / Kinsale	78	G	12
Clady	101	J	3
Clane	87	L	8
Clár Chlainne Mhuiris / Claremorris	95	F	6
Clara / Clóirtheach (Offaly)	92	J	7
Clara (Wicklow)	87	N	9
Clare (County)	83	F	9
Clare Island	94	B	6
Clare (River)	89	F	7
Clarecastle	83	F	9
Claregalway / Baile Chláir	89	F	7
Claremorris / Clár Chlainne Mhuiris	95	F	6
Clarinbridge	89	F	8
Clashmore	79	I	11
Claudy	102	K	3
Clear (Cape)	77	D	13
Clear Island / Cléire (Oileán)	77	D	13
Cleegan Bay	88	B	7
Cleggan / An Cloigeann	88	B	7
Cléire (Oilean) / Clear Island	77	D	13
Clew Bay	94	C	6
Clifden / An Clochán	88	B	7
Cliffony	96	G	4
Clogh (Antrim)	103	N	3
Clogh (Kilkenny)	86	K	9
Clogh (Wexford)	81	M	10
Clogh Mills	103	N	3
Cloghan / An Clochán (Donegal)	100	I	3
Cloghan (Offaly)	90	I	8
Cloghan (Westmeath)	92	K	7
Cloghane	82	B	11
Cloghaneely	100	H	2
Cloghbrack	89	D	7
Clogheen	79	I	11
Clogher	97	K	4
Clogher Head (Kerry)	82	A	11
Clogher Head	93	N	6
Clogherhead	93	N	6
Cloghjordan	85	H	9
Cloghmore / An Chloich Mhóir	94	C	6
Cloghy	75	P	4
Clohamon	81	M	10
Cloich na Coillte / Clonakilty	77	F	13
Clóirtheach / Clara	92	J	7
Clonakilty / Cloich na Coillte	77	F	13
Clonakilty Bay	77	F	13
Clonalis House	90	G	6
Clonaslee	86	J	8
Clonbern	89	G	7
Clonbulloge	86	K	8
Clonbur / An Fhairche	89	D	7
Clonco Bridge	90	G	8
Clondalkin	87	M	8
Clonea	79	J	11
Clonea Bay	79	J	11
Clonee	93	M	7
Cloneen	85	J	10
Clonegall	81	M	9
Clones / Cluain Eois	97	K	5
Clonfert	90	H	8
Clonmacnois	90	I	8
Clonmany	101	J	2
Clonmel / Cluain Meala	85	I	10
Clonmellon	92	K	7
Clonmore	81	M	9
Clonmult	78	H	12
Clonroche	80	L	10
Clontarf	93	N	7
Clontibret	98	L	5
Clonygowan	86	K	8
Cloon Lake	76	C	12
Cloonacleigha Lake	96	G	5
Cloonacool	95	F	5
Cloonaghmore	95	D	5
Cloondara	90	I	6
Cloone	97	I	6
Cloonee Loughs	76	C	12
Cloonfad	95	F	6
Cloonfree Lough	90	H	6
Cloonlara	84	G	9
Clough	99	O	5
Cloyne	78	H	12
Cluain Eois / Clones	97	K	5
Cluain Meala / Clonmel	85	I	10
Cluainín / Manorhamilton	96	H	5
Coachford	78	F	12
Coagh	98	M	4
Coalisland	98	L	4
Cobh / An Cóbh	78	H	12
Cod's Head	76	B	13
Coill an Chollaigh / Bailieborough	92	L	6
Coleraine	102	L	2
Colgah Lough	96	G	5
Colligan (River)	79	I	11
Collinstown	92	K	7
Collon	93	M	6
Collooney	96	G	5
Comber	99	O	4
Comeragh Mountains	79	J	11
Commeen / An Coimín	100	I	3
Cong / Conga	89	E	7
Conga / Cong	89	E	7
Conlig	99	O	4
Conn (Lough)	95	E	5
Conna	78	H	11
Connemara	88	C	7
Connemara National Park	88	C	7
Connor Pass	82	B	11
Convoy	101	I	3
Cookstown	98	L	4
Coola	96	G	5
Coolaney	96	G	5
Coole (Castle)	97	J	4
Coolea / Cúil Aodha	77	E	12
Coolgreany	81	N	9
Coolmore	100	H	4
Coolrain	85	J	9
Coomacarrea	76	B	12
Coomhola	77	D	12
Cooraclare	83	D	9
Cootehill / Muinchille	97	K	5
Copeland Island	75	P	3
Cora Droma Rúisc / Carrick-on-Shannon	96	H	6
Corbally	95	E	5
Corcaigh / Cork	78	G	12
Corcomroe Abbey	89	E	8
Cork / Corcaigh	78	G	12
Cork (County)	77	F	12
Cork Harbour	78	H	12
Corkscrew Hill	89	E	8
Cornamona	89	D	7
Corrandulla	89	F	7
Corraun Peninsula	94	C	6
Corrib (Lough)	89	E	7
Corrigeenroe	96	H	5
Corrofin	89	E	9
Costelloe / Casla	88	D	8
Cottoners	76	C	11
Coulagh Bay	76	B	12
Courtmacsherry	78	F	13
Courtmacsherry Bay	78	G	13
Courtown	81	N	10
Cousane Gap	77	E	12
Crag Cave	83	D	11
Craggaunowen Megalithic Centre	84	F	9
Craigavon	98	M	4
Crana	101	J	2
Cranfield Point	99	N	5
Cranford	101	I	2
Cratloe	84	F	9
Craughwell	89	F	8
Crawfordsburn	99	O	4
Creeslough	101	I	2
Creevykeel	96	G	4
Creggs	90	G	7
Croagh	84	F	10
Croagh Patrick	94	C	6
Croaghnageer	100	I	3
Croaghnakeela Island	88	C	8
Croangar (Lough)	100	H	3
Croghan	96	H	6
Crohy Head	100	G	3
Crois Mhaoilíona / Crossmolina	95	E	5
Croithlí / Crolly	100	H	2
Crolly / Croithlí	100	H	2
Cromane	76	C	11
Crookedwood	92	K	7
Crookhaven	76	C	13
Crookstown	77	F	12
Croom	84	F	10
Croos	90	H	7
Cross	89	E	7
Cross Barry	78	G	12
Cross (River)	95	D	7
Crossakeel	92	K	6
Crossdoney	97	J	6
Crossgar	99	O	4
Crosshaven	78	H	12
Crossmaglen	74	M	5
Crossmolina / Crois Mhaoilíona	95	E	5
Crow Head	76	B	13
Cruit Island	100	G	2
Crumlin	99	N	4
Crusheen	84	F	9
Cúil an tSúdaire / Portarlington	86	K	8
Cúil Aodha / Coolea	77	E	12
Cuilcagh	97	I	5
Culdaff	102	K	2
Culdaff Bay	102	K	2
Culleens	95	F	5
Cullenagh (River)	89	E	9
Cullin (Lough)	95	E	6
Cullybackey	102	M	3
Cummeragh	76	B	12
Curlew Mountains	96	G	6
Curracloe	81	M	10
Curragh (The)	86	L	8
Curraghmore Gardens	79	J	11
Curraghroe	90	H	6
Currahchase Forest Park	84	F	10
Currane / An Corran	94	C	6
Currane (Lough)	76	B	12
Currans	83	D	11
Curreel (Lough)	88	C	7
Cushendall	103	N	2
Cushendun	103	N	2
Cushina	86	K	8
Cutra (Lough)	89	F	8
Daingean	86	K	8
Dalkey	87	N	8
Dan (Lough)	87	N	8
Darragh	83	E	9
Dartry Mountains	96	G	4
Davagh Forest Park	102	L	3
Dawros Head	100	G	3
Deel	83	F	10
Deel (Mayo)	95	D	5
Delamont	99	O	4
Delgany	87	N	8
Delphi	94	C	7
Delvin	92	K	7
Delvin (River)	93	N	7
Derg	101	J	3
Derg (Lough)	84	H	9
Derg (Lough) (Donegal)	101	I	4
Dernagree	77	E	11
Derravaragh (Lough)	92	J	7
Derreeny Bridge	77	E	13
Derriana Lough	76	C	12
Derrybeg	100	H	2

CORK/CORCAICH

Camden Place	Y 5
Coburg Street	Y 10
Corn Market Street	Y 13
Dominick Street	Y 15
Eason's Hill	Y 17
Emmet Place	Y 18
Gerald Griffin St.	Y 21
Infirmary Road	Z 24
John Redmond Street	Z 26
Lancaster Quay	Z 28
Langford Row	Z 29
Lower Glanmire Road	Y 30
Merchant's Quay	Y 32
Merchant's Quay Shopping Centre	Y
Newsom's Quay	Y 34
North Mall	Y 35
O'Connell's Square	Y 36
Oliver Plunkett Street	Z
Parnell Place	Z 38
Pembroke Street	Z 39
Proby's Quay	Z 40
Roman Street	Y 42
St Patrick's Quay	Y 44
St Patrick's Street	
Southern Road	Z 45
South Link	Z 46
South Main Street	Z 47
Summer Hill	Y 48
Wolfe Tone Street	Y 56

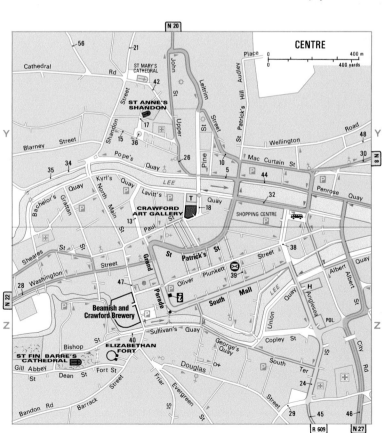

Derryclare Lough	88 C 7	Donegal	
Derrycraff	95 D 6	Airport	100 G 2
Derrygonnelly	97 I 4	Donegal Bay	96 G 5
Derrylin	74 J 5	Doneraile	78 G 11
Derrynane	76 B 12	Donoughmore	78 F 12
Derrynane		Doo Lough	94 C 7
House	76 B 12	Dooagh	94 B 6
Derrynasaggart		Doocharry /	
Mountains	77 E 11	An Dúchoraidh	100 H 3
Derryveagh		Dooega /	
Mountains	100 H 3	Dumha Éige	94 B 6
Dervock	102 M 2	Dooega Head	94 B 6
Devenish Island	97 J 4	Doogort	94 B 5
Devilsbit	85 I 9	Doohooma	94 C 5
Dingle /		Doon Lough	84 F 9
An Daingean	82 B 11	Doonaha	83 D 10
Dingle Bay	76 B 11	Doonbeg	83 D 9
Dingle Harbour	82 B 11	Doulus Head	76 A 12
Divis	99 N 4	Down (County)	99 N 4
Doagh	101 I 2	Downhill	102 L 2
Doagh Beg /		Downings /	
Dumhaigh Bhig	101 J 2	Na Dúnaibh	101 I 2
Doe Castle	101 I 2	Downpatrick	99 O 5
Dolla	84 H 9	Downpatrick	
Domhnach		Head	95 D 5
Phádraig /		Downs (The)	92 K 7
Donaghpatrick	93 L 6	Dowra	96 H 5
Donabate	93 N 7	Dowth	93 M 6
Donagh	74 J 5	Drangan	85 J 10
Donaghadee	75 P 4	Draperstown	102 L 3
Donaghmore	98 L 4	Drimoleague	77 E 13
Donaghpatrick /		Drinagh	77 E 13
Domhnach		Dripsey	78 F 12
Phádraig	93 L 6	Drishane Bridge	77 D 13
Donard	87 M 8	Drogheda /	
Donard (Slieve)	99 O 5	Droichead Átha	93 M 6
Donegal /		Droichead Átha /	
Dún na nGall	100 H 4	Drogheda	93 M 6
Donegal (County)	100 H 3		

Droichead na		Dumha Éige /	
Bandan /		Dooega	94 B 6
Bandon	78 F 12	Dumhaigh Bhig /	
Dromahair	96 H 5	Doagh Beg	101 J 2
Dromara	99 N 4	Dún A'Rí Forest	
Dromcolliher	83 F 10	Park	93 L 6
Dromin	93 M 6	Dún Aengus	88 C 8
Dromina	84 F 11	Dún Chaoin /	
Dromineer	84 H 9	Dunquin	82 A 11
Dromiskin	93 M 6	Dún Dealgan /	
Dromod	96 I 6	Dundalk	98 M 5
Dromore (Down)	99 N 4	Dún Garbhán /	
Dromore (Tyrone)	97 J 4	Dungarvan	79 J 11
Dromore West	95 F 5	Dun Laoghaire	87 N 8
Drum	97 K 5	Dún Mánmhaí /	
Drum Hills	79 I 11	Dunmanway	77 E 12
Drum Manor Forest		Dún Mór /	
Park	98 L 4	Dunmore	89 F 7
Drumbeg	99 O 4	Dún na nGall /	
Drumcliff	96 G 5	Donegal	100 H 4
Drumcondra	93 M 6	Dunaff Head	101 J 2
Drumena Cashel	99 O 5	Dunamase (Rock	
Drumfin	96 G 5	of)	86 K 8
Drumfree	101 J 2	Dunany Point	93 N 6
Drumgoft	87 M 9	Dunboyne	93 M 7
Drumkeeran	96 H 5	Dunbrody Abbey	80 L 11
Drumlaheen		Duncannon	80 L 11
Lough	96 I 5	Duncormick	80 M 11
Drumlish	92 I 6	Dundalk /	
Drumone	92 K 6	Dún Dealgan	98 M 5
Drumquin	97 J 4	Dundalk Bay	93 N 6
Drumshanbo	96 H 5	Dundonald	99 O 4
Drumsna	96 H 6	Dundrum (Down)	99 O 5
Dublin / Baile Átha		Dundrum (Dublin)	87 N 8
Cliath	87 N 8	Dundrum	
Dublin Bay	93 N 7	(Tipperary)	84 H 10
Dublin (County)	99 O 5	Dundrum Bay	99 O 5
Duff	96 H 4	Dunfanaghy	100 I 2
Duleek	93 M 7	Dungannon	98 L 4

Dunganstown	80 L 10		
Dungarvan /			
Dún Garbhán	79 J 11		
Dungarvan			
Harbour	79 J 11		
Dungiven	102 L 3		
Dunglow /			
An Clochán			
Liath	100 G 3		
Dungonnell Dam	103 N 3		
Dungourney	78 H 12		
Dunguaire Castle	89 F 8		
Dunkerrin	85 I 9		
Dunkineely	100 G 4		
Dunlavin	87 L 8		
Dunleer	93 M 6		
Dunlewy	100 H 2		
Dunloe (Gap of)	77 D 11		
Dunluce Castle	102 M 2		
Dunmanus Bay	76 C 13		
Dunmanway /			
Dún Mánmhaí	77 E 12		
Dunmore / Dún Mór	89 F 7		
Dunmore Cave	80 K 9		
Dunmore Head	82 A 11		
Dunmore East	80 L 11		
Dunmurry	99 N 4		
Dunnamanagh	102 K 3		
Dunowen Head	77 F 13		
Dunquin / Dún			
Chaoin	82 A 11		
Dunshaughlin	93 M 7		
Durlas / Thurles	85 I 9		
Durrow	85 J 9		
Durrus	77 D 13		
Dursey Head	76 B 13		
Dursey Island	76 B 13		
Duvillaun More	94 B 5		
Dysert O'Dea	83 E 9		

E		
Éadan Doire		
/ Édenderry	92 K 7	
Eany	100 H 3	
Eanymore	100 H 3	
Easky	95 F 5	
East Ferry	78 H 12	
Édenderry /		
Éadan Doire	92 K 7	
Ederny	97 J 4	
Edgeworthstown	92 J 6	
Egish (Lough)	98 L 5	
Eglinton	102 K 2	
Emly	84 G 10	
Emo	86 K 8	
Emyvale	98 L 4	
Ennel (Lough)	92 J 7	
Ennis / Inis	83 F 9	
Enniscorthy /		
Inis Córthaidh	81 M 10	
Enniskean	77 F 12	
Enniskerry	87 N 8	
Enniskillen	97 J 4	
Ennistimon /		
Inis Díomáin	89 E 9	
Eochaill / Youghal	79 I 12	
Erne		
(Lower Lough)	97 I 4	
Erne (River)	97 J 6	
Erne		
(Upper Lough)	74 J 5	
Errew Abbey	95 E 5	
Erriff (River)	94 D 7	
Errigal		
Mountain	100 H 2	
Erris Head	94 B 5	
Eske (Lough)	100 H 3	
Eyeries	76 C 12	

F		
Fahan	101 J 2	
Fairy Glen	99 N 5	
Fairymount	96 G 6	
Falcarragh /		
An Fál Carrach	100 H 2	
Fanad	101 I 2	
Fanad Head	101 J 2	
Fane River	98 M 5	
Fanore	89 E 9	
Farnanes Cross		
Roads	78 F 12	
Farran Forest Park	78 F 12	
Farranfore	83 D 11	
Fastnet Rock	77 D 13	
Feakle	84 G 9	
Feale (River)	83 D 10	
Fedamore	84 G 10	
Fee (Lough)	88 C 7	
Feeagh (Lough)	95 D 6	
Feeny	102 K 3	
Fenagh	96 I 5	
Fenit	82 C 11	
Feohanagh (River)	90 I 8	
Ferbane	90 I 8	
Fergus (River)	89 E 9	
Fermanagh		
(County)	97 I 4	
Fermoy / Mainistir		
Fhear Maí	78 H 11	
Ferns	81 M 10	
Ferrycarrig	81 M 10	
Ferta	76 B 12	
Fethard / Fiodh Ard		
(Tipperary)	85 I 10	
Fethard (Wexford)	80 L 11	
Fiddown	80 K 10	

DUBLIN/
BAILE ÁTHA CLIATH
CENTRE

Anne Street South .... JYZ 6
Brunswick Street North ..... HX 24
Buckingham Street........ KX 25
Bull Alley .... HZ 27
Chancery Street .... HY 33
Clanbrassil Street .... HZ 40
College Green .... JY 45
College Street .... JY 46
Cornmarket .... HY 49
Dawson Street .... JYZ
D'Olier Street .... JY 51
Duke Street .... JY 58
Earlsfort Terrace.......... JZ 60
Essex Quay .... HY 66
Fishamble Street .... HY 67
George's Quay .... KY 69
Golden Lane .... HZ 70
Grafton Street .... JYZ
Henrietta Street .... HX 75
Henry Street .... JX
High Street .... HY 78
Ilac Centre .... HJX
Irish Life Mall Centre ...... JKX
Kevin Street Upper .... HZ 85
Kildare Street............. JKZ 87
King Street South .... JZ 88
Marlborough Street .... JX 100
Merchants Quay .... HY 103
Montague Street .... JZ 106
Mount Street Upper ...... KZ 112
Nicholas Street .... HY 118
North Great Georges Street .. JX 119
O'Connell Street .... JX
Parnell Square East ...... JX 126
Parnell Squatre North....... JX 127
Parnell Square West ...... HJX 129
St Mary's Abbey Street .... HY 148
St Patrick Close.......... HZ 150
Stephen Street .... HJY 165
Tara Street .... KY 171
Wellington Quay.......... HJY 181
Werburgh Street........... HY 183
Westland Row .... KY 186
Westmoreland Street ...... JY 187
Wexford Street .... HZ 189
Winetavern Street .... HY 193
Wood Quay .... HY 196

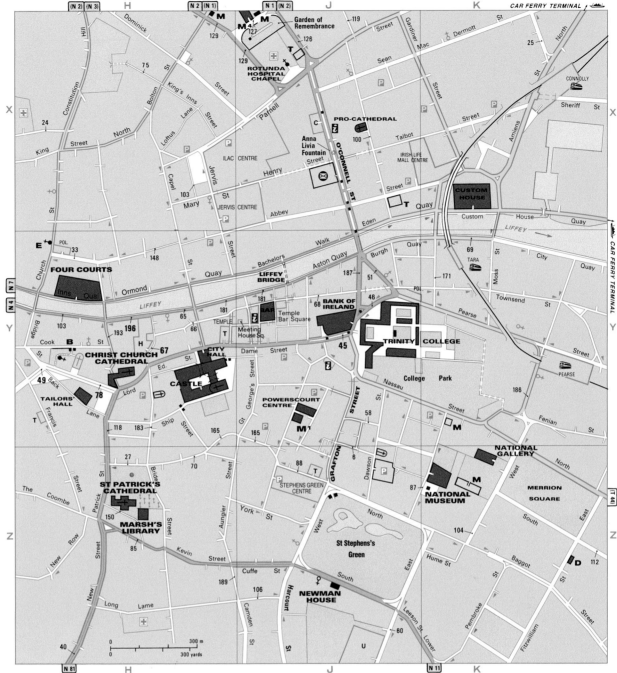

Finglas	93	N 7	Foxford	95	E 6	Gaoth Dobhair /			Glantane	78	F 11	Glenariff		
Finglass	76	C 11	Foxhall	89	E 7	Gweedore	100	H 2	Glanworth	78	G 11	or Waterfoot	103	N 2
Finn (Lough)	100	H 3	Foyle (Lough)	102	K 2	Gaoth Sáile /			Glasdrumman	99	O 5	Glenarm	75	O 3
Finn (River)	101	J 3	Foynes	83	E 10	Geesala	94	C 5	Glaslough	98	L 5	Glenavy	99	N 4
Finnea	92	J 6	Freemount	83	F 11	Gara (Lough)	96	G 6	Glassan	90	I 7	Glenbeigh	76	C 11
Finny / Fionnaithe	89	D 7	Frenchpark	96	G 6	Garadice Lough	97	I 5	Glasshouse Lake	97	J 5	Glenbrook	78	G 12
Fintona	97	K 4	Freshford	85	J 9	Garrane	77	E 12	Gleann Bhairr /			Glencar	76	C 12
Fintown /			Fuerty	90	H 7	Garrison	96	H 4	Glenvar	101	J 2	Glencar Lough	96	G 4
Baile na Finne	100	H 3	Furnace	88	D 7	Garristown	93	M 7	Gleann na Muaidhe			Glencolmcille Folk		
Fintragh Bay	100	G 4	Furnace Lough	95	D 6	Garron Point	75	O 2	/ Glenamoy	94	C 5	Village	100	F 3
Fiodh Ard / Fethard	85	I 10				Garryvoe	78	H 12	Gleann Cholm Cille /			Glenvar / Gleann		
Fionnaithe / Finny	89	D 7				Gartan Lough	101	I 3	Glencolumbkille	96	F 3	Bhairr	101	J 2
Fivealley	90	I 8	**G**			Garty Lough	97	J 6	Gleann Domhain /			Glencolumbkille /		
Fivemiletown	97	K 4	Gabhla / Gola			Garvagh	102	L 3	Glendowan	100	I 3	Gleann Cholm		
Flat Head	78	G 12	Island	100	G 2	Garvagh	96	L 6	Glen	101	I 2	Cille	100	F 3
Flesk	77	D 11	Gabriel (Mount)	77	D 13	Gearagh (The)	77	F 12	Glen Bay	100	F 3	Glencree	87	N 8
Florence Court	97	I 5	Gaddagh	77	C 11	Geashill	86	K 8	Glen Head	100	F 3	Glendalough	87	M 8
Florence Court			Gaillimh / Galway	89	E 8	Geesala / Gaoth			Glen Lough			Glendovan		
Forest Park	97	I 5	Galbally	84	H 10	Sáile	94	C 5	(Donegal)	101	I 2	Mountains	100	H 3
Foaty Island	78	H 12	Galey	83	D 10	Geevagh	96	H 5	Glen Lough			Glendowan /		
Fontstown	86	L 8	Gallarus Oratory	82	A 11	Gerahies	77	D 13	(Westmeath)	92	J 7	Gleann Domhain	100	I 3
Forbes (Lough)	90	I 6	Galley Head	77	F 13	Giant's Causeway	102	M 2	Glen (River)			Glenealy	87	N 9
Fore	92	K 6	Gallion (Slieve)	102	L 3	Giles Quay	99	N 6	(Donegal)	100	G 3	Glenealy	102	K 2
Forkill	74	M 5	Gallrus Mountains	84	H 10	Gilford	98	M 4	Glenade Lough	96	H 4	Glenelly Valley	102	K 3
Forlorn Point	81	M 11	Galty Mountains	84	H 10	Gill (Lough)	96	G 5	Glenamoy /			Glenfarne	96	I 5
Formoyle (Lough)	89	D 7	Galtymore			Glanaruddery			Gleann na			Glenflesk	77	D 11
Fota Island	78	H 12	Mountain	84	H 10	Mountains	83	D 11	Muaidhe	94	C 5	Glengad Head	102	K 1
Foul Sound	88	D 8	Galway / Gaillimh	89	E 8	Glandore	77	E 13	Glenamoy (River)	95	D 5	Glengarriff /		
Foulksmills	80	L 11	Galway (County)	89	F 7	Glandore Harbour	77	E 13	Glenariff	103	N 2	An Gleann Garbh	77	D 12
Four Mile House	90	H 6	Galway Bay	89	D 8	Glangevlin	96	I 5	Glenariff Forest			Glengarriff Harbour	77	D 12
Fourknocks	93	N 7	Galways Bridge	77	D 12	Glanmire	78	G 12	Park	103	N 2	Glengarriff (River)	77	D 12

Glenicmurrin			Gormanston	93	N 7
Lough	89	D 8	Gort / An Gort	89	F 8
Glenmalur	87	M 9	Gort an Choirce /		
Glenmore (Clare)	83	E 9	Gortahork	100	H 2
Glenmore (Kilkenny)	80	K 10	Gortahork /		
Glennamaddy	90	G 7	Gort an Choirce	100	H 2
Glenoe	75	O 3	Gorteen	96	G 6
Glenshane Pass	102	L 3	Gortin	102	K 3
Glenties	100	H 3	Gortin Glen		
Glenvar / Gleann			Forest Park	102	K 3
Bhairr	101	J 2	Gortmore /		
Glenveagh			An Gort Mór	88	D 7
National Park	100	I 2	Gorumna Island	88	C 8
Glenville	78	G 11	Gosford Forest Park	74	M 5
Glin	83	E 10	Gougane Barra		
Glin Castle	83	E 10	Forest Park	77	D 12
Glinsce / Glinsk	88	C 7	Gougane Barra		
Glinsk / Glinsce	88	C 7	Lake	77	E 12
Glyde (River)	93	M 6	Gowla	88	C 7
Glynn	75	O 3	Gowna (Lough)	97	J 6
Gob an Choire /			Gráig na Manach /		
Achill Sound	94	C 6	Graiguenamanagh	80	L 10
Gobbins (The)	75	O 3	Graiguenamanagh /		
Gola Island /			Graig na Manach	80	L 10
Gabhla	100	G 2	Gránárd /		
Golden	85	I 10	Granard	92	J 6
Golden Vale	84	H 10	Grand Canal	90	I 8
Goleen	76	C 13	Graney	86	L 9
Good's Cross	85	I 10	Grange (Kilkenny)	80	K 10
Goresbridge	80	K 10	Grange (Louth)	99	N 5
Gorey / Guaire	81	N 9	Grange (Sligo)	96	G 4

GALWAY/ GAILLIMH

Claddagh Bridge	AZ 2	
Corrib Shopping Centre	BY	
Dominick Street	AZ 3	
Father Griffin Avenue	AZ 5	
Forster Street	BY 6	
High Street	BY 7	
Main Guard St.	BY 8	
Market Street	BY 9	
Mary Street	BY 10	
New Dock Street	BZ 13	
Newton Smith	BY 14	
O'Brien Bridge	AY 15	
Presentation Street	AY 17	
Quay Street	BZ 18	
St. Francis Street	BY 20	
St. Vincent's Avenue	BY 21	
Shantalia Road	AY 22	
Shop Street	BY 24	
William Street	BY 25	

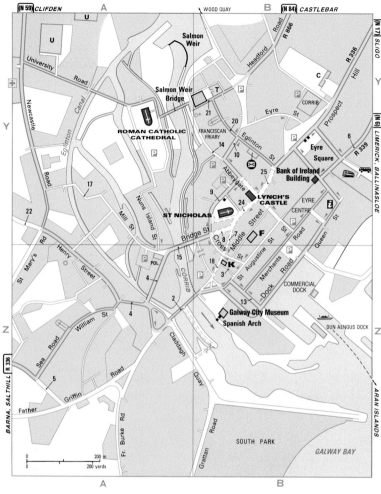

Irish Agricultural Museum	81	M 11	Kenmare River	76	B 12	
Irishtown	95	F 7	J. F. Kennedy Park	80	L 11	
Iron (Lough)	92	J 7	Kerry (County)	83	D 11	
Iron Mountains	96	I 5	Kerry Head	82	C 10	
Irvinestown	97	J 4	Kerry (Ring of)	76	B 12	
Iveragh	76	B 12	Kesh	97	I 4	
			Key (Lough)	96	H 5	
J			Key (Lough) Forest Park	96	H 5	
Jamestown	96	H 6	Kilbaha	82	C 10	
Japanese Gardens	86	L 8	Kilbeggan	92	J 7	
Jerpoint Abbey	80	K 10	Kilbeheny	78	H 11	
Johnstown	85	J 9	Kilberry	93	L 6	
Jonesborough	74	M 5	Kilbricken	85	J 9	
Joyce	88	D 7	Kilbride (near Blessington)	87	M 8	
Julianstown	93	N 6	Kilbrittain	78	F 12	
			Kilcar	100	G 4	
K			Kilchreest	89	G 8	
Kanturk / Ceann Toirc	77	F 11	Kilclief	75	P 5	
Katesbridge	99	N 5	Kilcock	93	L 7	
Keadew	96	H 5	Kilcolgan	89	F 8	
Keady	74	L 5	Kilconly (Galway)	89	F 7	
Kealduff	76	C 12	Kilcoo	99	N 5	
Kealkill	77	D 12	Kilcormac	90	I 8	
Kearney	75	P 4	Kilcrohane	76	C 13	
Keel	94	B 6	Kilcullen	87	L 8	
Keel Lough	94	B 6	Kilcummin (Kerry)	82	B 11	
Keem Strand	94	B 6	Kildare / Cill Dara	86	L 8	
Keimaneigh (The pass of)	77	E 12	Kildare (County)	86	L 8	
Kells (Antrim)	103	N 3	Kildorrery	78	G 11	
Kells (Kerry)	76	B 12	Kilfenora	89	E 9	
Kells (Ceanannus Mor) / Ceanannas (Meath)	92	L 6	Kilfinnane	84	G 10	
			Kilgarvan	77	D 12	
			Kilglass	95	E 5	
			Kilglass Lough	96	H 6	
			Kilgobnet	76	C 11	
			Kilgory Lough	84	F 9	
Kells Bay	76	B 11	Kilkee / Cill Chaoi	83	D 9	
Kenmare / Neidín	77	D 12	Kilkeel	99	N 5	
			Kilkeeran High Crosses	85	J 10	
Kilkenny / Cill Chainnigh	80	K 10				
Kilkenny (County)	85	J 10				
Kilkieran / Cill Chiaráin	88	C 8				
Kilkishen	84	F 9				
Kill	79	J 11				
Killadoon	94	C 6				
Killadysert	83	E 9				
Killala	95	E 5				
Killala Bay	95	E 5				
Killaloe / Cill Dalua	84	G 9				
Killamery	85	J 10				
Killann	80	L 10				
Killard Point	75	P 5				
Killarga	96	H 5				
Killarney / Cill Airne	77	D 11				
Killarney National Park	77	D 11				
Killary Harbour	94	C 7				
Killashandra	97	J 5				
Killavally	95	D 6				
Killavullen	78	G 11				
Killeagh	78	H 12				
Killeigh	86	J 8				
Killenagh	81	N 10				
Killenaule	85	I 10				
Killerrig	86	L 9				
Killeshin	86	K 9				
Killeter	101	I 3				
Killeter Forest	101	I 3				
Killevy Churches	74	M 5				
Killimer	83	D 10				
Killimor	90	H 8				
Killinaboy	89	E 9				
Killiney Bay	87	N 8				
Killiney (Dublin)	87	N 8				
Killinick	81	M 11				
Killinure Lough	90	I 7				
Killkelly	95	F 6				
Killmuckbridge	81	N 10				

KILLARNEY/ CILL AIRNE CENTRE

Bohereen Na Goun	CX 3	
Bohereencael	DX 4	
Brewery Lane	DX 6	
College Square	DX 7	
College Street	DX 9	
Green Lawn	CX 10	
Hillard's Lane	DX 12	
Mangerton	DX 13	
Marian Terrace	DX 15	
Muckross Drive	DXY 16	
O' Connell's Terrace	DX 18	
O' Sullivan's Place	DX 19	
Plunkett Street	DX 21	
St. Anthony's Place	DX 22	

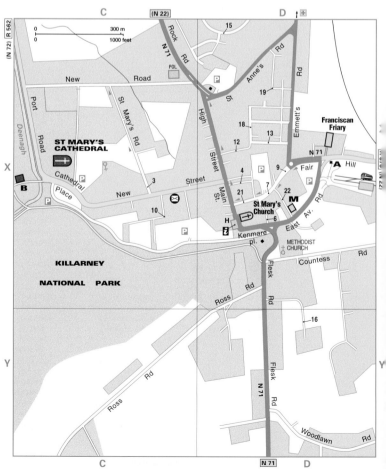

Gransha	75	O 3	Hillsborough	99	N 4	Inis Diomáin / Ennistimon	89	E 9
Great Island	78	H 12	Hilltown	99	N 5	Inis Meáin /		
Great Blasket Island	82	A 11	Hog's Head	76	B 12	Inishmaan	88	D 8
Great Newtown Head	80	K 11	Hollyford	84	H 10	Inis Mór /		
			Hollyfort	81	M 9	Inishmore	88	C 8
Great Skellig	76	A 12	Hollymount	95	E 7	Inis Oírr / Inisheer	88	D 8
Greenan	87	N 9	Hollywood	87	M 8	Inishannon	78	G 12
Greencastle (Donegal)	102	L 2	Holy Cross	85	I 10	Inishbofin / Inis Bó Finne (Donegal)	100	H 2
			Holy Island	84	G 9			
Greencastle (Down)	99	N 5	Holycross	84	G 10	Inishbofin (Galway)	94	B 7
Greencastle (Tyrone)	102	K 3	Holywood	99	O 4	Inishcarra	85	I 10
Greenfield	89	E 7	Hook Head	80	L 11	Inishcarra Reservoir	77	F 12
Greenisland	75	O 3	Hore Abbey	85	I 10	Inishcrone	95	E 5
Greenore	99	N 5	Horn Head	100	I 2	Inisheer / Inis Oírr	88	D 8
Greenore Point	81	N 11	Horseleap	92	J 7	Inishfree Bay	100	G 2
Grey Abbey	75	P 4	Hospital	84	G 10	Inishglora	94	B 5
Grey Point	75	O 3	Howth / Binn Éadair	93	N 7	Inishkea North	94	B 5
Greystones / Na Clocha Liatha	87	N 8	Hugginstown	80	K 10	Inishkea South	94	B 5
Grianan of Aileach	101	J 2	Hungry Hill	76	C 12	Inishmaan / Inis Meáin	88	D 8
Groomsport	75	P 3	Hurlers Cross	84	F 9	Inishmore / Inis Mór	88	C 8
Guaire / Gorey	81	N 9	Hyne (Lough)	77	E 13	Inishmurray	96	G 4
Gulladoo Lough	97	J 6				Inishnabro	82	A 11
Gullion (Slieve)	74	M 5	**I**			Inishowen	101	J 2
Gur (Lough)	84	G 10	Ilen	77	E 13	Inishowen Head	102	L 2
Gurteen	90	G 7	Inagh	83	E 9	Inishshark	94	B 7
Gweebarra Bridge	100	H 3	Inagh (Lough)	88	C 7	Inishtrahull	102	K 1
Gweebarra Bay	100	G 3	Inch	82	C 11	Inishtrahull Sound	102	K 1
Gweedore / Gaoth Dobhair	100	H 2	Inch Abbey	99	O 4	Inishturk	94	B 6
			Inch Island	101	J 2	Inistioge	80	K 10
Gweestin	77	D 11	Inchigeelagh	77	E 12	Infield	92	L 7
Gyleen	78	H 12	Inchiquin Lough (Kerry)	77	D 12	Inniskeen	98	M 5
			Inchydoney Island	77	F 13	Inny (River)	92	J 6
H			Indreabhán			Inver	100	H 4
Hacketstown	87	M 9	Inveran	89	D 8	Inver (Mayo)	94	C 5
Hags Head	88	D 9	Inis / Ennis	83	F 9	Inveran / Indreabhán	89	D 8
Headford / Áth Cinn	89	E 7	Inis Bó Finne / Inishbofin	100	H 2			
Healy Pass	76	C 12	Inis Córthaidh / Enniscorthy	81	M 10			
Helvick Head	79	J 11						
Herbertstown	84	G 10	Ireland's Eye	93	N 7			

Killorglin / Cill Orglan	76	C 11
Killough	75	P 5
Killucan	92	K 7
Killurin	81	M 10
Killybegs / Na Cealla Beaga	100	G 4
Killygordon	101	I 3
Killykeen Forest Park	97	J 5
Killylea	98	L 4
Killyleagh	75	P 4
Kilmacduagh Monastery	89	F 8
Kilmacow	80	K 11
Kilmacrenan	101	I 2
Kilmacthomas	79	J 11
Kilmaganny	80	K 10
Kilmaine	89	E 7
Kilmalkedar	82	B 11
Kilmallock / Cill Mocheallóg	84	G 10
Kilmanagh	85	J 10
Kilmeage	86	L 8
Kilmeedy	83	F 10
Kilmessan	93	M 7
Kilmichael	77	E 12
Kilmichael Point	81	N 9
Kilmihil	83	E 9
Kilmore	81	M 11
Kilmore Quay	81	M 11
Kilmurry (mear Kilkishen)	84	F 9
Kilmurvy	88	C 8
Kilnaleck	92	K 6
Kilrane	81	M 11
Kilrea	102	M 3
Kilreekill	90	G 8
Kilronan / Cill Rónáin	88	C 8
Kilrush / Cill Rois	83	D 10
Kilshanny	89	E 9
Kilsheelan	85	J 10
Kiltealy	80	L 10
Kiltegan	87	M 9
Kilternan	87	N 8
Kiltimagh	95	E 6
Kiltoom	90	H 7
Kiltormer	90	H 8
Kiltyclogher	96	H 4
Kilworth	78	H 11
Kilworth Mountains	78	H 11
Kinale (Lough)	92	J 6
Kincasslagh	100	G 2
Kings River	85	J 10
Kingscourt	93	L 6
Kinlough	96	H 4
Kinnegad	92	K 7

Kinnitty	90	I 8
Kinsale / Cionn tSáile	78	G 12
Kinsale (Old Head of)	78	G 13
Kinvarra	89	F 8
Kinvarra Bay	89	F 8
Kinvarra (near Screeb)	88	D 7
Kippure	87	N 8
Kircubbin	75	P 4
Kitconnell	90	G 8
Knappagh	95	D 6
Knappogue Castle	84	F 9
Knight's Town	76	B 12
Knock (Clare)	83	E 10
Knock (Mayo)	95	F 6
Knockadoon Head	79	I 12
Knockainy	84	G 10
Knockalongy	95	F 5
Knockcroghery	90	H 7
Knockferry	89	E 7
Knocklayd	103	N 2
Knocklong	84	G 10
Knockmealdown	79	I 11
Knockmealdown Mountains	78	H 11
Knockmoy Abbey	89	F 7
Knocknadobar	76	B 12
Knocknagree	77	E 11
Knockraha	78	G 12
Knocktopher	80	K 10
Knowth	93	M 6
Kylemore Abbey	88	C 7
Kylemore Lough	88	C 7

L

Labasheeda	83	E 10
Lack	97	J 4
Ladies View	77	D 12
Lady's Island Lake	81	M 11
Ladysbridge	78	H 12
Ladywell	80	K 10
Lagan (River)	99	N 4
Lagan Valley	99	O 4
Laghy	100	H 4
Lahinch / An Leacht	89	D 9
Lamb's Head	76	B 12
Lambay Island	93	N 7
Lanesborough	90	I 6
Laois (County)	85	J 9
Laragh	87	N 8
Larne	75	O 3
Larne Lough	75	O 3

Laune (River)	77	C 11
Lauragh	76	C 12
Laurencetown	90	H 8
Lavagh More	100	H 3
Lawrencetown	99	N 4
League (Slieve)	100	F 4
Leamaneh Castle	89	E 9
Leane (Lough)	77	D 11
Leannan (River)	101	I 2
Leap	77	E 13
Leap (The)	81	M 10
Lecarrow (Leitrim)	96	H 5
Lecarrow (Roscommon)	90	H 7
Leckanvy	94	C 6
Leckavrea Mountain	88	D 7
Lee	83	C 11
Lee (River)	78	G 12
Leenane	88	C 7
Legananny Dolmen	99	N 5
Leighlinbridge	80	L 9
Leinster (Mount)	80	L 10
Leitir Ceanainn / Letterkenny	101	I 3
Leitir Meallâin / Lettermullan	88	C 8
Leitir Mhic an Bhaird / Lettermacaward	100	H 3
Leitrim	96	H 6
Leitrim (County)	96	I 6
Leixlip	93	M 7
Lemybrien	79	J 11
Lene (Lough)	92	K 7
Letterfrack	88	C 7
Letterkenny / Leitir Ceanainn	101	I 3
Lettermacaward / Leitir Mhic an Bhaird	100	H 3
Lettermore	88	D 8
Lettermore Island	88	C 8
Lettermullan / Leitir Meallâin	88	C 8
Liffey (River)	87	M 8
Lifford	101	J 3
Limavady	102	L 2
Limerick / Luimneach	84	G 9
Limerick (County)	84	F 10
Limerick Junction	84	H 10
Lios Dúin Bhearna / Lisdoonvarna	89	E 8
Lios Mór / Lismore	79	I 11
Lios Póil / Lispole	82	B 11

LIMERICK/ LUIMNEACH

Arthur Quay	Y 2
Arthur Quay Shopping Centre	Y
Baal's Bridge	Y 4
Bank Place	Y 5
Barrington Street	Z 6
Bridge Street	Y 7
Broad Street	Y 8
Castle Street	Y 10
Cathedral Place	Z 12
Charlotte's Quay	Y 13
The Crescent	Z 14
Cruises Street	Z 15
Gerald Griffen St.	Z 16
Grattan Street	Y 17
High Street	Z 18
Honan's Quay	Y 19
John Square	Z 20
Lock Quay	Y 21
Lower Cecil Street	Z 22
Lower Mallow Street	Z 23
Mathew Bridge	Y 24
Mount Kenneth	Z 26
Newtown Mahon	Z 28
North Circular Rd	Z 29
O'Connell Street	Z
O'Dwyer Bridge	Y 30
Patrick Street	YZ 32
Penniwell Road	Z 33
Roches Street	Z
Rutland Street	Y 34
St Alphonsus St.	Z 35
St Gerard St.	Z 36
St Lelia Street	YZ 37
Sarfield Street	Y 40
Sexton Street North	Y 40
Shannon Street	Z 42
South Circular Rd.	Z 43
Thomond Bridge	Y 45
Wickham Street	Z 47
William Street	Z

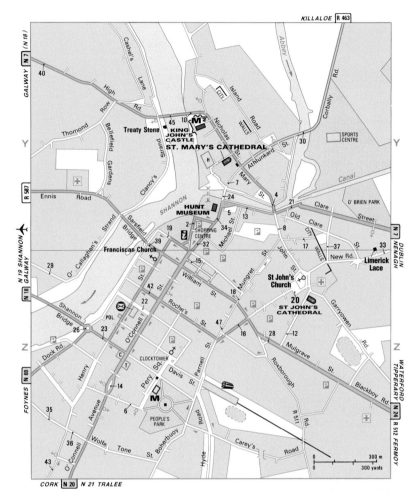

Lios Tuathail / Listowel	83	D 10
Lisbellaw	74	J 5
Lisburn	99	N 4
Liscannor	89	D 9
Liscannor Bay	89	D 9
Liscarroll	78	F 11
Lisdoonvarna / Lios Dúin Bhearna	89	E 8
Lismacaffry	92	J 6
Lismore / Lios Mór	79	I 11
Lisnacree	99	N 5
Lisnarrick	97	I 4
Lisnaskea	74	J 5
Lispole / Lios Póil	82	B 11
Lissadell House	96	G 4
Lissatinnig Bridge	76	C 12
Lisselton	83	D 10
Lissycasey	83	E 9
Listowel / Lios Tuathail	83	D 10
Little Island	78	G 12
Little Skellig	76	A 12
Littleton	85	I 10
Lixnaw	83	D 10
Loch Garman / Wexford	81	M 10
Loghill	83	E 10
Londonderry	102	K 3
Londonderry (County)	102	K 3
Long Island	77	D 13

Longford (County)	90	I 6
Longford / An Longfort		
Longford (Longford)	90	I 6
Longford (Offaly)	84	I 8
Loo Bridge	77	D 12
Loop Head	82	C 10
Lorrha	90	H 8
Lough Gowna	97	J 6
Loughgall	98	M 4
Loughbrickland	99	N 5
Loughglinn	96	G 6
Loughinisland	99	O 4
Loughrea / Baile Locha Riach	90	G 8
Loughros More Bay	100	G 3
Loughshinny	93	N 7
Louisburgh	94	C 6
Loup (The)	102	M 3
Louth	93	M 6
Louth (County)	93	M 6
Lower Lake	87	N 8
Lower Ballinderry	99	N 4
Lucan	93	M 7
Lugnaquillia Mountain	87	M 9
Luimneach / Limerick	84	G 10
Lullymore	86	L 8
Lurgan	99	N 4
Lusk	93	N 7
Lyracrumpane	83	D 10

M

Maam Cross / An Teach Dóite	88	D 7
Maas	100	G 3
Macgillycuddy's Reeks	76	C 12
Macnean Upper (Lough)	97	I 5
Macroom / Maigh Chromtha	77	F 12
Maganey	86	L 9
Magee (Island)	75	O 3
Maghera (Down)	99	O 5
Maghera (Donegal)	100	G 3
Maghera (Londonderry)	102	L 3
Magherafelt	102	M 3
Magheralin	99	N 4
Maghery	98	M 4
Magilligan	102	L 2
Magilligan Strand	102	L 2
Maguiresbridge	74	J 5
Mahee Island	75	P 4
Mahon	79	J 11
Mahoonagh	83	E 10
Maigh Chromtha / Macroom	77	F 12
Maigh Cuilinn / Moycullen	89	E 7
Maigh Nuad / Maynooth	93	M 7
Maigue (River)	84	F 10
Main	103	N 3
Maine (River)	83	C 11
Mainistir Fhear Maí / Fermoy	78	H 11

Mainistir Laoise / Abbey Leix	85	J 9
Mainistir na Búille / Boyle	96	H 6
Mainistir na Corann / Midleton	78	H 12
Máistir Gaoithe / Mastergeehy	76	B 12
Mal Bay	83	D 9
Mala / Mallow	78	G 11
Malahide / Mullach de	93	N 7
Málainn Bhig / Malin Beg	100	F 3
Malin	102	K 2
Malin Bay	100	F 3
Malin Beg / Málainn Bhig	100	F 3
Malin Head	102	J 1
Malin More	100	F 3
Mallow / Mala	78	G 11
Mamore (Gap of)	101	J 2
Mangerton Mountain	77	D 12
Mannin Bay	88	B 7
Mannin Lake	95	F 6
Manorcunningham	101	J 3
Manorhamilton / Cluainín	96	H 5
Mansfieldstown	93	M 6
Manulla	95	E 6
Maothail / Mohill	96	I 6
Marble Arch Caves	97	I 5
Marble Hill	101	I 2
Markethill	74	M 5
Mask (Lough)	89	D 7

LONDONDERRY

Barrack Street	X 2
Clooney Terrace	X 5
Creggan Street	X 6
Custom House Street	X 7
Dungiven Road	X 8
Duke Street	X 9
Foyle Road	X 10
Foyle Street	X 12
Francis Street	X 13
Glendermott Road	X 14
Harbour Square	X 15
Infirmary Road	X 17
John Street	X 18
Lecky Road	X 19
Limavady Road	X 20
Little James Street	X 22
Long Tower Street	X 23
Sackville Street	X 26
Simpsons Brae	X 29
Strand Road	X 30
Water Street	X 32
William Street	X 34

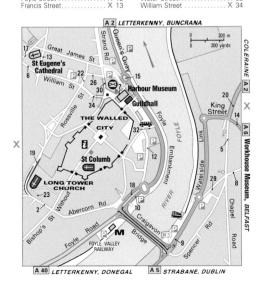

Mastergeehy / Máistir Gaoithe 76 B 12
Matrix (Castle) 83 F 10
Mattock (River) 93 M 6
Maum 88 D 7
Maumeen Lough 88 B 7
Maumtrasna 94 D 7
Maumturk Mountains 88 C 7
Maynooth / Maigh Nuad 93 M 7
Mayo 95 E 6
Mayo (County) 95 E 6
Mayo (Plains of) 95 E 6
Mealagh 77 D 12
Meath (County) 92 L 7
Meela (Lough) 100 G 3
Meenaneary / Mín na Aoire 100 G 3
Meenavean 100 F 3
Meeting of the Waters 87 N 9
Mellifont Abbey 93 M 6
Melmore Head 101 I 2
Melvin (Lough) 96 H 4
Menlough 90 G 7
Mew Island 75 P 3
Middletown (Armagh) 74 L 5
Middletown (Donegal) 100 H 2
Midleton / Mainistir na Corann 78 H 12
Milestone 84 H 9
Milford 84 F 10
Millford 101 I 2
Millisle 75 P 4
Millstreet 77 E 11
Milltown (Cavan) 97 J 5
Milltown (Galway) 89 F 7
Milltown (Kerry) 83 C 11
Milltown Malbay / Sráid na Cathrach 83 D 9
Mín na Aoire / Meenaneary 100 G 3
Minane Bridge 78 G 12
Minard Head 82 B 11
Mine Head 79 J 12
Mitchelstown / Baile Mhistéala 78 H 11
Mizen Head 76 C 13
Moate / An Móta 90 I 7
Moher (Cliffs of) 88 D 9
Moher Lough 95 D 6
Mohill / Maothail 96 I 6
Móinteach Mílic / Mountmellick 86 K 8
Moll's Gap 77 D 12
Monaghan / Muineachán 98 L 5
Monaghan (County) 97 K 5
Monasteraden 96 G 6
Monasteranenagh Abbey 84 G 10
Monasterboice 93 M 6
Monasterevin 86 K 8
Monavullagh Mountains 79 J 11
Mondello Park 87 L 8
Monea 97 I 4
Moneygall 85 I 9
Moneymore 102 L 3
Monivea 89 F 7
Monkstown (Antrim) 75 O 3
Monkstown (Cork) 78 G 12
Mooncoin 80 K 11
Moone 86 L 9
Moore Bay 82 C 9
Moorfields 103 N 3
Morley's Bridge 77 D 12
Mosney 93 N 7
Moss-Side 102 M 2
Mossley 75 O 3
Mostrim 92 J 6
Motte Stone 87 N 9
Mount Bellew / An Creagán 90 G 7
Mount Melleray Monastery 79 I 11
Mount Norris 74 M 5
Mount Nugent 92 K 6

Mount Stewart Gardens 75 P 4
Mount Usher Gardens 87 N 8
Mountcharles 100 H 4
Mountfield 97 K 4
Mountmellick / Móinteach Mílic 86 K 8
Mountrath 86 J 8
Mountshannon 84 G 9
Mourne (Lough) 75 O 3
Mourne Mountains 99 N 5
Mourne River 101 J 3
Moville / Bun an Phobail 102 K 2
Moy 98 L 4
Moy (River) 95 E 5
Moyard 88 B 7
Moyasta 83 D 9
Moycullen / Maigh Cuilinn 89 E 7
Moylough 90 G 7
Moynalty 92 L 6
Moyne Abbey 95 E 5
Moyvally 93 L 7
Moyvore 92 J 7
Muck (Isle of) 75 O 3
Muckamore 103 N 3
Muckanagh Lough 84 F 9
Muckish Mountain 100 H 2
Muckno Lake 98 L 5
Muckros Head 100 G 4
Muckross 77 D 11
Muff 102 K 2
Muggort's Bay 79 J 11
Muinchille / Cootehill 97 K 5
Muine Bheag / Bagenalstown 80 L 9
Muineachán / Monaghan 98 L 5
Muing 95 D 5
Muingnabo 94 C 5
Mulkear 84 G 10
Mullach de / Malahide 93 N 7
Mullagh (Cavan) 92 L 6
Mullagh (Meath) 93 M 7
Mullaghareirk Mountains 83 E 10
Mullaghcleevaun 87 M 8
Mullaghmore 96 G 4
Mullet Peninsula 94 B 5
Mullinahone 85 J 10
Mullinavat 80 K 10
Mullingar / An Muileann gCearr 92 J 7
Mulrany / An Mhala Raithní 94 C 6
Mulroy Bay 101 I 2
Multyfarnham 92 J 7
Mungret 84 F 10
Muntervary or Sheep's Head 76 C 13
Murlough Bay 103 N 2
Murntown 81 M 11
Murrisk 94 D 6
Murroe 84 G 10
Mussenden Temple 102 L 2
Mutton Island 83 D 9
Mweelrea Mountains 94 C 7
Myshall 80 L 9

N
Na Cealla Beaga / Killybegs 100 G 4
Na Clocha Liatha / Greystones 87 N 8
Na Dúnaibh / Downings 101 I 2
Na Sceirí / Skerries 93 N 7
Naas / An Nás 87 M 8
Nacung (Lough) 100 H 2
Nad 78 F 11
Nafooey (Lough) 88 D 7
Nagles Mountains 78 G 11
Naminn (Lough) 101 J 2
Namona (Lough) 76 B 12
Nanny 93 M 7
Naran 100 G 3
Narrow Water Castle 99 N 5

Naul 93 N 7
Navan / An Uaimh 93 L 7
Neagh (Lough) 98 M 4
Neale 89 E 7
Neidín / Kenmare 77 D 12
Nenagh / An tAonach 84 H 9
Nephin 95 D 5
Nephin (Glen) 95 D 6
Nephin Beg 94 D 5
Nephin Beg Range 94 C 5
New Inn (Cavan) 92 K 6
New Inn (Galway) 90 G 8
New Kildimo 84 F 10
New Ross / Ros Mhic Thriúin 80 L 10
Newbawn 80 L 10
New Birmingham 85 J 10
Newbliss 97 K 5
Newbridge / An Droichead Nua 86 L 8
Newbridge 93 N 7
Newcastle (Down) 99 O 5
Newcastle (Dublin) 87 M 8
Newcastle (Tipperary) 79 I 11
Newcastle (Wicklow) 87 N 8
Newcastle West / An Caisleán Nua 83 E 10
Newgrange 93 M 6
Newinn 85 I 10
Newmarket 83 F 11
Newmarket on Fergus 84 F 9
Newport / Baile Uí Fhiacháin (Mayo) 95 D 6
Newport (Tipperary) 84 G 9
Newport Bay 94 C 6
Newry 74 M 5
Newtown Cashel 90 I 7
Newtown-Crommelin 103 N 3
Newtown (Laois) 86 K 9
Newtown (Offaly) 90 H 8
Newtownabbey 99 O 4
Newtown Forbes 90 I 6
Newtown Gore 97 I 5
Newtown Mount Kennedy 87 N 8
Newtownards 99 O 4
Newtownbutler 74 J 5
Newtownhamilton 74 M 5
Newtownshandrum 84 F 10
Newtownstewart 101 J 3
Nier 79 J 11
Ninemilehouse 85 J 10
Nobber 93 L 6
Nohaval 78 G 12
Nore 85 J 9
Nore (River) 80 K 10
North Sound 88 C 8
North Ring 77 F 13
Nurney 86 L 8
Nurney (Carlow) 80 L 9

O
O'Brien's Tower 89 D 9
O'Grady (Lough) 84 G 9
Oileán Ciarraí / Castleisland 83 D 11
Oilgate 81 M 10
Oily 100 G 4
Old Court 77 E 13
Old Head 94 C 6
Old Kildimo 84 F 10
Oldcastle / An Seanchaisleán 92 K 6
Oldleighlin 80 K 9
Old Ross 80 L 10
Omagh 97 K 4
Omeath 99 N 5
Omey Island 88 B 7
Oola 84 H 10
Oorid Lough 88 D 7
Oranmore 89 F 8

Ossian's Grave 103 N 2
Oughterard / Uachtar Ard 89 E 7
Ougther (Lough) 97 J 6
Ovens 78 G 12
Owel (Lough) 92 J 7
Owenascaul 82 B 11
Owenavorragh 81 M 10
Owenbeg (River) 96 G 5
Owenboliska 89 E 8
Owencarrow 101 I 2
Owenea 100 G 3
Owengarve 94 D 6
Owenglin 88 C 7
Oweniny 95 D 5
Owenkillew 102 K 3
Owenkillew 101 J 2
Owenriff 89 D 7
Owentocker 100 H 3
Owey Island / Uaigh 100 G 2
Owvane 77 D 12
Oysterhaven 78 G 12

P
Pallas Green 84 G 10
Pallaskenry 84 F 10
Paps (The) 77 E 11
Parke's Castle 96 H 5
Parkmore Point 82 A 11
Parknasilla 76 C 12
Partry 95 E 6
Partry Mountains 95 D 7
Passage East 80 L 11
Passage West 78 G 12
Patrickswell 84 F 10
Peake 78 F 12
Peatlands 98 M 4
Pettigoe 97 I 4
Phoenix Park 93 M 7
Piltown 80 K 10
Pluck 101 J 3
Plumbridge 102 K 3
Pomeroy 98 L 4
Pontoon 95 E 6
Port Durlainne / Porturlin 94 C 5
Port Láirge / Waterford 80 K 11
Port Laoise / Portlaoise 86 K 8
Port Omna / Portumna 90 H 8
Portacloy 94 C 5
Portadown 98 M 4
Portaferry 75 P 4
Portarlington / Cúil an tSúdaire 86 K 8
Portavogie 75 P 4
Port Ballintrae 102 M 2
Portglenone 102 M 3
Portlaoise / Port Laoise 86 K 8
Portlaw 80 K 11
Portmagee 76 A 12
Portmagee Channel 76 A 12
Portmarnock 93 N 7
Portmuck 75 O 3
Portnablagh 101 I 2
Portnoo 100 G 3
Portrane 93 N 7
Portroe 84 G 9
Portrush 102 M 2
Portsalon 101 J 2
Portstewart 102 L 2
Portumna / Port Omna 90 H 8
Porturlin / Port Durlainne 94 C 5
Poulaphouca Reservoir 87 M 8
Poulnasherry Bay 83 D 10
Powerscourt Demesne 87 N 8
Poyntz Pass 74 M 5
Prosperous 87 L 8
Puckaun 84 H 9
Puffin Island 76 A 12

Q
Quigley's Point 102 K 2
Quilty 83 D 9
Quin 84 F 9

R
Rae na nDoirí / Reananeree 77 E 12
Raghly 96 G 5
Raharney 92 K 7
Ram Head 79 I 12
Ramor (Lough) 92 K 6
Randalstown 103 N 3
Raphoe 101 J 3
Rasharkin 102 M 3
Rath 90 I 8
Ráth Caola / Rathkeale 83 F 10
Ráth Droma / Rathdrum 87 N 9
Rath Luirc (Charleville) / An Ráth 84 F 10
Rathangan 86 L 8
Rathcool 77 F 11
Rathcoole 87 M 8
Rathcormack 78 H 11
Rathcroghan 96 H 6
Rathdangan 87 M 9
Rathdowney 85 J 9
Rathdrum / Ráth Droma 87 N 9
Rathfriland 99 N 5
Rathgormuck 79 J 11
Rathkeale / Ráth Caola 83 F 10
Rathlackan 95 E 5
Rathlin Island 103 N 2
Rathlin Sound 103 N 2
Rathmelton 101 J 2
Rathmolyon 92 L 7
Rathmore 77 E 11
Rathmullan 101 J 2
Rathnew 87 N 9
Rathowen 92 J 7
Rathvilla 86 K 8
Rathvilly 87 L 9
Ratoath 93 M 7
Raven Point (The) 81 M 10
Ray 100 H 2
Rea (Lough) 90 G 8
Reananeree / Rae na nDoirí 77 E 12
Rear Cross 84 H 9
Recess / Straith Salach 88 C 7
Red Bay 103 N 2
Redcastle 102 K 2
Redcross 87 N 9
Redhills 97 K 5
Ree (Lough) 90 I 7
Reelan 100 H 3
Relaghbeg 92 L 6
Rhode 92 K 7
Richhill 98 M 4
Ringabella Bay 78 H 12
Ringsend 102 L 2
Ringville / An Rinn 79 J 11
Rinn Lough 96 I 6
Rinvyle 94 C 7
Rinvyle Castle 94 B 7
Riverstown 96 G 5
Roadford 89 D 8
Roaringwater Bay 77 D 13
Robert's Head 78 H 12
Robertstown 86 L 8
Rochestown 80 K 11
Rochfortbridge 92 K 7
Rockabill 93 N 7
Rockchapel 83 E 10
Rockcorry 97 K 5
Rockhill 84 F 10
Rockmills 78 G 11
Roe 102 L 3
Roonah Quay 94 C 6
Roosky 96 I 6
Ros an Mhíl / Rossaveel 88 D 8
Ros Comáin / Roscommon 90 H 7
Ros Cré / Roscrea 85 I 9
Ros Láir / Rosslare 81 M 11

Ros Mhic Thriúin / New Ross 80 L 10
Rosapenna 101 I 2
Roscommon / Ros Comáin 90 H 7
Roscommon (County) 96 G 6
Roscrea / Ros Cré 85 I 9
Rosegreen 85 I 10
Rosenallis 86 J 8
Rosmuck 88 D 7
Rosnakill 101 I 2
Ross Abbey 89 E 7
Ross Port 94 C 5
Ross Lake 89 E 7
Rossaveel / Ros an Mhíl 88 D 8
Rossbeg 100 G 3
Rossbeigh Creek 76 C 11
Rosscarbery 77 E 13
Rosscarbery Bay 77 E 13
Rosserk Abbey 95 E 5
Rosses (The) 100 G 2
Rosses Point 96 G 5
Rossinver 96 H 4
Rosslare / Ros Láir 81 M 11
Rosslare Bay 81 M 11
Rosslare Harbour / Calafort Ros Láir 81 M 11
Rosslare Point 81 M 11
Rosslea 74 K 5
Rossmore Forest Park 98 L 5
Rossnowlagh 100 H 4
Rostrevor 99 N 5
Rough Point 82 B 11
Roughty 77 D 12
Roundstone 88 C 7
Roundwood 87 N 8
Rower (The) 80 L 10
Royal Canal 90 I 7
Royaloak 80 L 9
Rue Point 103 N 2
Runabay Head 103 N 2
Rush / An Ros 93 N 7
Russborough House 87 M 8
Rylane Cross 77 F 12

S
Saggart 87 M 8
St. Fachtnan's 83 E 9
St. Finan's Bay 76 A 12
St. John's Lough 96 I 5
St. John's Point (Donegal) 100 G 4
St. John's Point (Down) 75 P 5
St. Johnstown 101 J 3
St. Macdara's Island 88 C 8
St. Mochta's House 93 M 6
Saintfield 99 O 4
Sallins 87 M 8
Sally Gap 87 N 8
Sallybrook 78 G 12
Saltee Islands 81 M 11
Salthill 89 E 8
Santry 93 N 7
Saul 99 O 4
Sawel Mountain 101 K 3
Scairbh / An Scarriff 84 G 9
Scarriff Island 76 B 12
Scartaglin 83 D 11
Scarva 74 M 5
Schull / Skull 77 D 13
Scolban (Lough) 96 H 4
Scotshouse 97 K 5
Scotstown 97 K 5
Scrabo Hill 99 O 4
Scramoge 90 H 6
Screeb Cross 88 D 7
Screen 81 M 10
Scur (Lough) 96 I 5
Seaforde 99 O 5
Seven Heads 78 F 13
Seven Hogs or Magharee Islands (The) 82 B 11
Shanagarry 78 H 12
Shanagolden 83 E 10
Shanballymore 78 G 11

Shanes Castle 103 N 3
Shankill 87 N 8
Shannagh (Lough) 99 N 5
Shannon 84 F 9
Shannon Airport 84 F 9
Shannon (River) 90 H 8
Shannonbridge 90 H 8
Shannon Harbour 90 I 8
Shantonagh 98 L 5
Sheddings (The) 103 N 3
Sheeffry Hills 94 C 6
Sheelin (Lough) 92 K 6
Sheep Haven 101 I 2
Sheever (Lough) 92 K 7
Shehy Mountains 77 D 12
Shercock 98 L 6
Sherkin Island 77 D 13
Shillelagh 81 M 9
Shinrone 85 I 9
Shrule 89 E 7
Silent Valley 99 O 5
Sillan (Lough) 98 L 5
Silver Strand 94 C 6
Silvermine Mountains 84 H 9
Silvermines 84 H 9
Sion Mills 101 J 3
Six Towns (The) 102 L 3
Sixmilebridge 84 F 9
Sixmilecross 97 K 4
Skannive (Lough) 88 C 8
Skerries / Na Sceirí 93 N 7
Skibbereen / An Sciobairín 77 E 13
Skreen 96 F 5
Skull / Schull 77 D 13
Sky Road 88 B 7
Slade 80 L 11
Slane 93 M 6
Slane (Hill of) 93 M 6
Slaney (River) 81 M 10
Slea Head 82 A 11
Slemish Mountain 103 N 3
Slieve Anierin 96 I 5
Slieve Aught Mountains 89 G 8
Slieve Bernagh 84 G 9
Slieve Bloom Mountains 86 J 8
Slieve Gamph or the Ox Mountains 95 F 5
Slieve Mish Mountains 82 C 11
Slieve Miskish Mountains 76 C 13
Slieveanorra 103 N 2
Slievefelim Mountains 84 H 9
Slievenamon 85 J 10
Slievetooey 100 G 3
Sligeach / Sligo 96 G 5
Sligo / Sligeach 96 G 5
Sligo Bay 95 F 5
Sligo (County) 95 F 5
Sliveardagh Hills 85 J 10
Slyne Head 88 B 7
Smerwick 82 A 11
Smerwick Harbour 82 A 11
Smithborough 97 K 5
Snaght (Slieve) (Derryveagh Mts.) 100 H 3
Snaght (Slieve) (Inishowen) 101 J 2
Snave 77 D 12
Sneem 76 C 12
Sord / Swords 93 N 7
South Sound 88 D 8
Spa 82 C 11
Spanish Point 83 D 9
Spelga Dam 99 N 5
Sperrin Mountains 102 K 3
Spiddal / An Spidéal 89 E 8
Spink 86 K 9
Springhill 102 M 3
Srah / An tSraith 95 E 6
Srahmore 95 D 6
Sráid na Cathrach / Milltown Malbay 83 D 9
Stack's Mountains 83 D 11
Staigue Stone Fort 76 B 12
Stamullin 93 *N 7
Stewartstown 98 L 4
Stonyford 80 K 10

Strabane	101	J	3
Stracashel	100	H	3
Stradbally (Kerry)	82	B	11
Stradbally (Laois)	86	K	8
Stradbally (Waterford)	79	J	11
Strade	95	E	6
Stradone	97	K	6
Straffan	87	M	8
Straid (Antrim)	75	O	3
Straid (Donegal)	101	J	2
Straith Salach / Recess	88	C	7
Strandhill	96	G	5
Strangford	75	P	4
Strangford Lough	75	P	4
Stranorlar	101	I	3
Stratford	87	L	9
Strokestown	90	H	6
Stroove	102	L	2
Struell Wells	99	O	5
Suck	90	G	6
Suck (River)	90	G	6
Suir	85	I	9
Suir (River)	79	I	11
Summerhill	93	L	7
Sunderlin (Lough)	91	I	7
Swan	86	K	9
Swan's Cross Roads	97	K	5
Swanlinbar	97	I	5
Swatragh	102	L	3
Swilly (River)	101	I	3
Swilly (Lough)	101	J	2
Swilly (River)	101	J	2
Swinford / Béal Átha na Muice	95	F	6
Swords / Sord	93	N	7
Sybil Head	82	A	11

T

Table Mountain	87	M	8
Tacumshane	81	M	11
Tacumshin Lake	81	M	11
Taghmon	81	M	11
Tagoat	81	M	11
Tahilla	76	C	12
Tallaght	87	M	8
Tallanstown	93	M	6
Tallow	78	H	11
Tandragee	98	M	4
Tang	90	I	7
Tara (Hill of)	93	M	7
Tarbert	83	D	10
Tarker (Lough)	98	L	5
Tarsaghaunmore	94	C	5
Tay	79	J	11
Tay (Lough)	87	N	8
Teelin	100	G	4
Temple of the Winds	75	P	4
Temple (The)	99	O	4
Templeboy	95	F	5
Templeglentan	83	E	10
Templehouse Lake	96	G	5
Templemore / An Teampall Mór	85	I	9
Templenoe	76	C	12
Templepatrick	103	N	3
Templetouhy	85	I	9
Tempo	97	J	4
Terenure	87	N	8
Termon / An Tearmann	101	I	2
Termonbarry	90	I	6
Termonfeckin	93	N	6
Terryglass	84	H	8
Thomastown / Baile Mhic Andáin	80	K	10
Thoor Ballylee	89	F	8
Three Castle Head	76	C	13
Thurles / Durlas	85	I	9
Timahoe (Kildare)	86	L	8
Timoleague	78	F	13
Timolin	86	L	9
Tiobraid Árann / Tipperary	84	H	10
Tipperary / Tiobraid Árann	84	H	10
Tipperary (County)	85	H	10
Tobar an Choire / Tobercurry	95	F	5
Tobercurry / Tobar an Choire	95	F	5
Toberscanavan	96	G	5
Toe Head	77	E	13
Tollymore Forest Park	99	O	5
Tomhaggard	81	M	11
Toombeola	88	C	7
Toome	102	M	3
Toomyvara	85	H	9
Toormore	76	D	13
Toraigh / Tory Island	100	H	2
Torr Head	103	N	2
Tory Island / Toraigh	100	H	2
Tory Sound	100	H	2
Tourig (River)	78	I	11
Tourmakeady / Tuar Mhic Éadaigh	95	D	7
Tower	78	G	12
Trá Lí / Tralee	82	C	11
Trá Mhór / Tramore	80	K	11
Trabane Strand	100	F	4
Trafrask	76	D	12
Tragumna	77	E	13
Tralee / Trá Lí	82	C	11
Tralee Bay	82	C	11
Tramore / Trá Mhór	80	K	11
Tramore Bay	80	K	11
Tranarossan Bay	101	I	2
Trean	89	D	7
Trillick	97	J	4
Trim / Baile Átha Troim	93	L	7
Trostan	103	N	2
Tuaim / Tuam	89	F	7
Tuam / Tuaim	89	F	7
Tuamgraney	84	G	9
Tuar Mhic Éadaigh / Tourmakeady	95	D	7
Tulach Mhór / Tullamore	86	J	8
Tulla	84	F	9
Tullaghan	96	G	4
Tullaghobegly	100	H	2
Tullamore / Tulach Mhór	86	J	8
Tullaroan	85	J	10
Tullig Point	82	C	10
Tullow / An Tulach	80	L	9
Tully	97	I	4
Tully Cross	88	C	7
Tully National Stud	86	L	8
Tullyallen	93	M	6
Tullycanna	80	L	11
Tullyhogue	98	L	4
Tullynally Castle	92	J	6
Tulsk	90	H	6
Turlough (Mayo)	95	E	6
Turloughmore	89	F	7
Turner's Rock Tunnel	77	D	12
Tuskar Rock	81	N	11
Twelve Pins (The)	88	C	7
Tynagh	90	G	8
Tyrella	99	O	5
Tyrellspass	92	J	7
Tyrone (County)	97	J	4

U

Uachtar Ard / Oughterard	89	E	7
Uaigh / Owey Island	100	G	2
Ugga Beg (Lough)	89	D	8
Ulster American Folk Park	97	J	4
Union Hall	77	E	13
Unshin	96	G	5
Upper Ballinderry	99	N	4
Upperchurch	85	H	9
Urlingford	85	J	9

V

Valencia Island	76	A	12
Valley	94	C	5
Ventry	82	A	11
Ventry Harbour	82	A	11
Villierstown	79	I	11
Virginia	92	K	6

W

Ward	93	N	7
Waringstown	99	N	4
Warrenpoint	99	N	5
Waterfoot or Glenariff	103	N	2
Waterford / Port Láirge	80	K	11
Waterford (County)	79	J	11
Waterford Harbour	80	L	11
Watergrasshill	78	G	11
Waterville / An Coireán	76	B	12
Wellington Bridge	80	L	11
Wesport Bay	94	C	6
Westmeath (County)	92	J	7
Westport / Cathair na Mart	95	D	6
Westport House	95	D	6
Wexford / Loch Garman	81	M	10
Wexford Bay	81	N	10
Wexford (County)	80	L	10
Wexford Harbour	81	M	10
Wheathill	97	I	5
Whiddy Island	77	D	12
White Park Bay	102	M	2
Whitechurch	78	G	12
Whitegate	78	H	12
Whitehead	75	O	3
Wicklow (County)	87	M	9
Wicklow / Cill Mhantáin	87	N	9
Wicklow Gap	87	M	8
Wicklow Mountains	87	N	8
Wildfowl and Wetlands Trust	99	O	4
Wilkinstown	93	L	6
Williamstown	90	G	6
Windgap	85	J	10
Windy Gap	98	N	5
Woodenbridge	81	N	9
Woodford	74	J	5

Y

Youghal / Eochaill	79	I	12
Youghal Bay	79	I	12